You Cannot Surge Trust

You Cannot Surge Trust

Combined Naval Operations of the Royal Australian Navy, Canadian Navy, Royal Navy, and United States Navy, 1991–2003

Gary E. Weir, Principal Investigator
Sandra J. Doyle, Editor

NAVAL
HISTORY &
HERITAGE
★ COMMAND ★

DEPARTMENT OF THE NAVY
WASHINGTON, DC
2013

Published by

Naval History and Heritage Command
805 Kidder Breese Street SE
Washington Navy Yard, DC 20374-5060
www.history.navy.mil

Book design by Guy Tom

FRONT COVER: USS *Ronald Reagan* (CVN 76) leads a formation of ships from several allied navies in the Pacific Ocean during Rim of the Pacific (RIMPAC), the world's largest multinational maritime exercise, 24 July 2010. *MC1 Scott Taylor*

Library of Congress Cataloging-in-Publication Data

Weir, Gary E.
   You cannot surge trust : combined naval operations of the Royal
Australian Navy, Canadian Navy, Royal Navy, and United States Navy, 1991–
2003 / Gary E. Weir, principal investigator ; Sandra J. Doyle, editor.
      pages cm
   Includes bibliographical references and index.
   ISBN 978-0-945274-70-4 (paperback)—ISBN 978-0-945274-71-1 (PDF)
   1. Blockade—Case studies. 2. Navies—International cooperation—Case
studies. 3. Combined operations (Military science)—Case studies. 4.
Naval history, Modern—20th century. 5. Naval history, Modern—21st
century. I. Doyle, Sandra J. II. Title. III. Title: Combined naval
operations of the Royal Australian Navy, Canadian Navy, Royal Navy, and
United States Navy, 1991–2003.
   V180.W45 2013
   359.4'609049--dc23

                                                    2012048421

∞ The paper used in this publication meets the requirements for permanence established by the American National Standard for Information Sciences "Permanence of Paper for Printed Library Materials" (ANSI Z39.48-1984).

For sale by the Superintendent of Documents, U.S. Government Printing Office
Internet: Bookstore.gpo.gov; Phone: toll free 866-512-1800; DC area 202-512-1800; Fax: 202-512-2104
Mail: Stop SSOP, Washington, DC 20402-0001

ISBN 978-0-945274-70-4 (paperback)
ISBN 978-0-945274-71-1 (PDF)

CONTENTS

As our nation and our Navy shift their focus away from the land wars in Iraq and Afghanistan that have so dominated our internal conversations for more than a decade and pivot toward the Asia-Pacific region, it is most appropriate that this study, *You Cannot Surge Trust*, should make its appearance. The assembled authors, under the assured editorial hand of Sandra Doyle, bring forward a series of episodes that demonstrate the evolving and increasingly important nature of maritime coalition operations around the world. Beginning with a look at maritime interception operations in the Arabian Gulf during Operations Desert Shield and Desert Storm, this work moves forward through the post–Cold War era to include recent operations in the Middle East and central Asia. Written from a multinational point of view, the analysis suggests that nations, even superpowers, are increasingly dependent upon each other for support during major combat operations and that only by frequent consultation, exercises, cooperation in technology development, and understanding of force structure capabilities will future maritime coalitions be successful.

This study also advances a larger argument regarding the relevance of naval and maritime history in defense policy development. The challenges faced by coalition forces during the 1991 to 2005 period are not so different from what confronted those who sailed before. The crews of Continental Navy ships during the American Revolution had difficulty keeping up with French ships owing to differences in the size of the respective fleets and individual ship design. During World Wars I and II the U.S. and Royal navies consistently had to overcome problems inherent in differences in classification and communications. Lastly, in the increasingly geopolitical complexities of modern warfare, illustrated by our experiences operating alongside allies in Korea and Vietnam, history reveals that the different rules of engagement under which nations exercise their forces can cause conflicts within a partnership—even as the partners prosecute a conflict. Each of these issues has been raised before, each is examined within *You Cannot Surge Trust*, and each will raise its head again in some future hostility. To the extent that decision makers review history and anticipate the future they can anticipate success. Ignorance of the past necessarily results in a painful fate of rediscovering lessons hard learned.

It is through the efforts of such distinguished historians as Randy Papadopoulos, Jeffrey Barlow, Stephen Prince, Kate Brett, David Stevens, Robert Caldwell, and Edward Marolda under the research direction of Gary Weir that the lessons of the era encompassing my own operational career have been captured for those who follow to study. Given the steadily shrinking periods of peace between conflicts in the modern world, "those who follow" should begin reading now.

This work, as well as many others, would not have been possible without the concerted effort and the deep well of experience that Ms. Doyle brought to the task. This past January Ms. Doyle closed out a 31-year career in government service. During that time she had a hand in the publication of more than 70 printed works which were a key component of the Naval History and Heritage Command's (and its predecessor, the Naval Historical Center) mission of creating and delivering relevant historical knowledge to key decision makers. That Ms. Doyle did all this while operating quietly behind the scenes to help scholars and analysts present their work in a professional and polished manner is to her infinite credit, and to our collective benefit.

Henry J. Hendrix II
Captain, U.S. Navy (Ph.D.)
Director of Naval History

An International City at Sea

With the opening of Operation Iraqi Freedom (OIF) in 2003 and the subsequent debate in the United States about the *coalition of the willing,* a group of historians at the Naval Historical Center (now the Naval History and Heritage Command) joined the discussion by reflecting on the nature of effective coalitions. As head of the Contemporary History Branch during the opening phases of OIF, I asked the historians to consider recent coalitions engaging in *combined* naval operations. Under what circumstances did various national command authorities adopt a *combined* solution to an external threat rather than acting alone? What did these international coalitions look like? What assets and talents did the combined force need? Did efforts of this sort in the recent past work effectively given the mission? What critical factors contributed to the success or failure of the combined effort?

We soon realized that historical analysis, approaching problems as it does from the humanities perspective, could address these questions in an informative, unique, and stimulating way. Thus the growing public debate presented us with an unexpected opportunity to apply history directly to immediate naval needs in an age defined, in part, by 11 September 2001. In the end, the subject matter, the ongoing public debate, and the opportunity to apply historical methodology proved too compelling to remain as an informal discussion of combined operations.

Although initially conceived as an American project, it seemed counterproductive not to seek out other naval history programs officially pressed and intellectually stimulated by the same issues and possibilities. I asked a good friend, Michael Whitby of the Directorate of History and Heritage (DHH) in Ottawa, to reflect on the possible profit in informing the present by evaluating naval coalition experiences of the recent past. Together, we and other colleagues might examine a few select combined operations as case studies. Did he think my scheme worthwhile given the current interests of his navy and, perhaps more important, would the proposal interest his director, Dr. Serge Bernier?

I laid before him a plan to initiate a project involving four national navies, frequent allies, to examine historically the nature of naval combined operations. The project would endeavor to derive conclusions and lessons that serving naval officers might find immediately useful in their efforts to address their missions in the Near East. My plans called for participation by Canada, the United Kingdom, Australia, and the United States.

Dr. Bernier emerged from his discussion with Michael and DHH Senior Historian Dr. Steven Harris convinced that the proposal had merit. He assigned one of his more capable people, Robert Caldwell, as the Canadian member of the team. With the credibility provided by Dr. Bernier's generosity and willingness to take a measured risk, I recruited the balance of the team in 2003: Stephen Prince, who came to us courtesy of Captain Christopher Page, RN (Ret.), then the director of the Royal Navy's Naval Historical Branch in Portsmouth, United Kingdom; Dr. David Stevens of the Royal Australian Navy's Sea Power Centre in Canberra; and Drs. Jeffrey Barlow and Randy Papadopoulos from the Naval History and Heritage Command, Washington, D.C.

Dr. Bernier's faith also helped me achieve two important goals. I convinced then Director of Naval History Dr. William Dudley of the viability and value of the applied history project we proposed. With his help we made a successful application to the Naval Historical Foundation for a grant that sustained this effort and made the collaboration possible. Retired Vice Admiral Robert Dunn, president of the foundation, and his executive director, Captain Charles Todd Creekman, USN (Ret.), smoothed our way and contributed substantively to the positive outcome of the project.

An inaugural team meeting in 2004 hosted by DHH on a cold winter day in Ottawa determined the best and most evocative cases for study. Within the 1991–2003 timeframe, our historians would look at maritime interception operations in the 1990–1991 Gulf War and in Operation Enduring Freedom, 2001–2003; Operation Stabilise, the United Nations-mandated action to bring peace to East Timor in 1999; and Operation Sharp Guard in ethnically torn Yugoslavia through 1996.

We designed this study to remind policymakers, strategists, and operators living in a 21st-century coalition world of the very *human* nature of combined operations. While technology enables naval action, combined operations emerge from these pages as a human endeavor, based upon personal and professional relationships formed and reformed by sailors of all ranks across national and cultural boundaries.

In these pages communication and trust become paramount. Without the trust engendered by effective, well-trained liaison officers and frequent collaborative exercises at sea, combined operations become an exercise in futility. Deliberate and frequent contact allows people to broker the mutual understanding that served Admiral Lord Nelson so well within his own fleet two centuries ago and has become even more necessary given the potential contemporary barriers of language, culture, technology, and operational experience. The history of recent combined operations repeatedly speaks to these critical, but often overlooked, personal characteristics. *You Cannot Surge Trust* brings history to engaged naval forces as an essential professional tool that can help address current operational problems by more completely revealing the nature of coalition war.

National navies of the 21st century rarely look to history to provide this service. Thus historians recall with some envy the role played by historian and strategist Sir Julian Corbett in educating and advising the leadership of the Royal Navy at the turn of the 20th century. His applied history became critical to understanding the adversary and planning accordingly. Considering a formula in 1914 that might lure Kaiser Wilhelm's High Seas Fleet out of its secure bases and into a decisive defeat, Admiral Sir John Fisher repeatedly looked to Corbett for insights into German military behavior that extended as far back as England's participation in the Seven Years War (1756–1763), a conflict once described by Winston Churchill as the first true world war. Fisher concluded that only by actually or apparently threatening the German Baltic coast would Great Britain pose a threat sufficient to precipitate a decisive encounter at sea between the two major fleets. Drawing much of his preliminary planning from historical analysis, Fisher then asked his historical partner to prepare a paper on employing the fleet to gain control of the Baltic. With a nearly unrivaled knowledge of history across the entire Royal Navy experience and access to both Fisher and the sources emerging from the current war, Corbett complied. He provided the admiral with a conceptual foundation, resonating with past experience, which supported fleet expansion as well as the distribution and commitment of valuable assets.*

The relationship between Corbett and Fisher proved not only constructive but essential to the Royal Navy. The team composing this volume suggests that this relationship remains every bit as essential in this new century, in spite of a reluctance within modern navies to follow Fisher's lead in permitting past human behavior to inform the present. In our own time, advanced technology and its solutions represent the present and future in an immediate and dynamic way. For many, history pales by comparison. Indeed, to use history a la Corbett and Fisher implies that the participant has become an artifact rather than a modern player. In response the historian asks, can technology provide an understanding of our own professional behavior and that of our adversary, as well as insight into the very nature of a war currently claiming precious lives? Is our capable technology truly effective without such understanding? Naval ships and weapons systems can only serve as outward tools and choices. Only sailors and their support cast form the *substance* of any naval endeavor. Our team created this volume to demonstrate that through humanities analysis the historian can make common human experience speak in ways the contemporary sailor can immediately apply at sea. If those who waged the Seven Years War can inform and influence naval strategy nearly two centuries later in the Great War, who are we to ignore an invitation to have a historical conversation with those involved in combined operations over past last two decades?

The proposed 1,000-ship navy coalition, this *international city at sea* so essential to the vision of the maritime future first embraced by Chief of Naval Operations Admiral Michael Mullen, will not take shape without the aforementioned historical conversation. The level of international professional intimacy required to achieve or even approach Admiral Mullen's goal makes implementing the conclusions of the present volume necessary. If navies intend to keep the ocean open in an age of pervasive terrorism, combined operations regularly informed by official and professional historical perspective must become a permanent and essential part of naval practice.

Dr. Gary E. Weir
Chief Historian
National Geospatial-Intelligence Agency

*The discussion of Julian Corbett owes a great deal to email exchanges with Professor Andrew Lambert, Laughton Professor of Naval History at King's College London.

Dr. Jeffrey G. Barlow of the Naval History and Heritage Command (NHHC), Washington, D.C., graduated in history from Westminster College (Pennsylvania) and in international studies from the University of South Carolina. His 1981 Ph.D. dissertation analyzed the role of the U.S. Joint Chiefs of Staff during the Kennedy administration. Prior to coming to NHHC, he served as a defense analyst with the Heritage Foundation on Capitol Hill and as a military analyst for the National Institute for Public Policy/National Security Research. For the past 25 years he has been a historian at NHHC. The author of the award-winning book *Revolt of the Admirals: The Fight for Naval Aviation, 1945–1950* (1994), he has written more than a dozen chapters for books dealing with World War II and the Cold War. His book *From Hot War to Cold: The U.S. Navy and National Security Affairs, 1945–1955,* was published by Stanford University Press in January 2009.

Kate Brett is Historian and Curator at the Naval Historical Branch, Naval Staff, U.K. Ministry of Defence, based in Portsmouth. She graduated in English and German from the University of Exeter and completed a master's degree in museology from the University of East Anglia before joining the Naval Historical Branch as Curator in 1998. Working both with headquarters and the front line, she manages the Royal Navy's operational recordkeeping system, providing comment and analysis on the most recent phases of naval history and contributing evidence to support significant decisions on policy and procurement. She conducts research on the Royal Navy's contemporary role in offshore patrol, counterpiracy, and counternarcotics operations. She also has a leading role in unifying Royal Navy scientific and historical research.

Robert H. Caldwell of the Directorate of History and Heritage, National Defence Headquarters, Ottawa, Ontario, served in the Canadian Army for 35 years. He completed technical and general staff courses at the Royal Military College of Science at Shrivenham, the British Army Staff College at Camberley, and the Joint Warfare Establishment at Old Sarum. He passed the Master of Arts program in War Studies at the Royal Military College at Kingston in 1987, and thereafter was employed as a researcher and historian at the Operational Research and Analysis Establishment, followed by the Directorate of History and Heritage, in National Defence Headquarters. Mr. Caldwell has been a member of the Naval History Team for 17 years, and he is a contributing author for two books comprising the official history of the Royal Canadian Navy in the Second World War. He has completed several studies for the forthcoming postwar naval history. Since 2006, Mr. Caldwell has worked with the Canadian Forces in Afghanistan on the preparations for the official history.

Sandra J. Doyle, senior editor of the Naval History and Heritage Command (NHHC), graduated in history from Marymount College, Tarrytown, New York, and trained in professional editing at the George Washington University and EEI Communications. During her 30-year career, first as a naval historian compiling a history of U.S. naval operations in Vietnam and then as a writer-editor, she has guided through the publication process more than 70 works on 20th- and 21st-century U.S. naval operations, strategy, science, and policy. Authors of 12 of these works have received book awards from academic societies. She is coeditor of the NHHC series on the U.S. Navy and the Vietnam War. Ms. Doyle retired in January 2013.

Dr. Edward J. Marolda retired in September 2008 after 40 years of federal service with the Naval History and Heritage Command, Washington, D.C. Dr. Marolda served at one time or another as Acting Director of Naval History, Senior Historian, and Chief of Histories and Archives Division. He graduated from Pennsylvania Military College in 1967 with a bachelor of arts degree in history and served as a U.S. Army officer in the Republic of Vietnam from 1969 to 1970. He completed a master's degree at Georgetown University in 1971 and a doctorate at the George Washington University in 1990. He has authored, coauthored, or edited 12 books, including *By Sea, Air, and Land: An Illustrated History of the United States Navy and the War in Southeast Asia* (1994); *Shield and Sword: The United States Navy and the Persian Gulf War* (coauthor Robert J. Schneller Jr., 1998); *The U.S. Navy in the Korean War* (editor, 2007); and *The Approaching Storm: Conflict in Asia, 1945–1965* (2009), the first issue in a series on the U.S. Navy and the Vietnam War, which he coedits with Sandra Doyle. Marolda serves as an adjunct professor at Georgetown University, and as a consultant for the Cold War Gallery of the National

Museum of the U.S. Navy. His latest book *Ready Seapower: A History of the U.S. Seventh Fleet* was published in 2012.

Dr. Sarandis (Randy) Papadopoulos is the Secretariat Historian, Office of the Undersecretary of the Navy. Before assuming that position in April 2010, he spent ten years as a historian in the Contemporary History Branch of the former Naval Historical Center, now the Naval History and Heritage Command, Washington, D.C. He studied at the University of Toronto, the University of Alabama, and the George Washington University. His Ph.D. dissertation, "Feeding the Sharks: The Logistics of Undersea Warfare, 1935–1945," compares the German and U.S. submarine services. Between 1999 and 2010 he taught history at the George Washington University, Norwich University, and the University of Maryland University College. He is a principal coauthor of the book *Pentagon 9/11* published by the Historian, Office of the Secretary of Defense in 2007, and the author of several journal articles, book reviews, and contributions to reference works. He is the Region III Coordinator for the Society for Military History and chairs the Military Classics Seminar at Fort Myer, Virginia.

Stephen Prince heads the Naval Historical Branch, Naval Staff, U.K. Ministry of Defence, based in Portsmouth. He is a graduate of Warwick University and King's College London, where he received the Russell Prize for the best M.A. performance. He has been Sir Robert Menzies Scholar at the Australian War Memorial, lecturer at Britannia Royal Naval College, Dartmouth, senior lecturer at the U.K.'s Joint Services Command and Staff College, and a historian in the Naval Historical Branch. His publications include articles in the *Journal of Strategic Studies, Defense Analysis* and the *Royal United Services Institute Journal,* as well as his book *Raiding Zeebrugge* (2010). He has been Directing Staff for more than 50 British and International Defence training exercises from the Falkland Islands to Turkey. In 2006 he was deployed as the War Diarist for NATO's International Security Assistance Force in Afghanistan.

Dr. David Stevens is Director of Strategic and Historical Studies within the Sea Power Centre–Australia, Canberra. He has contributed articles and essays to many publications, and his work has been translated into several languages. His most recent publications include *A Critical Vulnerability: The Impact of the Submarine Threat on Australia's Maritime Defence, 1915–54* (2005); *The Royal Australian Navy: A History* (coauthor, 2006); *Australia's Navy in the Gulf* (coauthor, 2006); *The Royal Australian Navy in World War II* (editor, 2d ed., 2005); *The Face of Naval Battle: The Human Experience of Modern War at Sea* (coeditor, 2003); *The Navy and the Nation* (coeditor, 2005); and *Sea Power Ashore and In the Air* (coeditor, 2007).

Dr. Gary E. Weir of the National Geospatial-Intelligence Agency (NGA) served a year on the U.S. Naval Academy history faculty, in 1986–1987, before joining the Naval History and Heritage Command. He served 19 years as a historian and then head of the former Contemporary History Branch. He is the NGA chief historian, a professor of history with the University of Maryland University College, and a guest investigator with the Marine Policy Center of the Woods Hole Oceanographic Institution. His published works include *An Ocean in Common: American Naval Officers, Scientists, and the Ocean Environment* (2001), winner of the Organization of American Historians' Richard Leopold Prize; and *Rising Tide: The Untold Story of the Russian Submarines that Fought the Cold War* (coauthor, 2003). Dr. Weir created and led the Combined Operations Project from its inception in 2004.

A word about usage and editorial decisions

In general American English is used in the text except when it comes to formal names of Commonwealth institutions, titles of source materials, and Operation Stabilise named by the Royal Australian Navy. National definitions for the term MIO alternate between Maritime Interdiction Operations and Maritime Interception Operations. For purposes of clarity, note that these terms are used interchangeably throughout the work. U.S. sources often use the term Persian Gulf War to refer to the First Gulf War (or simply Gulf War) of 1990–1991, but in general the latter terms are used herein. For operational purposes, the U.S. Navy and its allies refer to the body of water geographically known as the Persian Gulf as the Arabian Gulf, the Northern Arabian Gulf, and the Southern Arabian Gulf to describe operations in those waters.

The Combined Framework: How Naval Powers Deal with Military Operations Other Than War

Sarandis Papadopoulos

In the aftermath of the Cold War political leaders and other analysts in the developed world suggested the rise of a period marked by a relative quiescence. The end of the East-West rivalry offered a diminution of military activity, resulting from the lowering of tensions, and a "peace dividend," with money saved from lower armed services' budgets. Despite such hopes, the decade of the 1990s and the first two years of the 21st century saw an intensification of activity for military forces, specifically the navies of Australia, Canada, the United Kingdom, and the United States. Operating "combined," that is as parts of multinational forces, three or four of these services enforced United Nations sanctions against Iraq for more than a decade, did the same against the former Yugoslav republics during their breakup between 1993 and 1996, landed and supported ground forces in East Timor in 1999, and in late 2001 launched a new worldwide campaign to combat terrorism. These navies worked continually alongside one another, sometimes operating within coalitions of more than a dozen allied nations. Their capability to do so reflected a longstanding commitment to developing the methods, technical needs, and exercises required to make complex naval operations work.

In studying the spectrum of armed conflict below major combat operations, analysts of naval operations contend with a significant constraint: their most common subject of study, the elements of sea power, loses autonomy. The focus on the primacy of the warship, or of sea battle, fades. This constraint applies to a greater degree when considering the post-Cold War period as established military forces witnessed their operations become even more political.[1] On the one hand, maritime commerce assumed greater importance with the end of superpower confrontation and the rise of international trade. Merchant shipping traveled throughout the oceans, carrying ever-increasing amounts of cargo.[2] Yet, following the close of the extended superpower rivalry, the four navies under discussion here proved busy despite facing no competitor for control of the sea. Instead, their ocean access provided them an opportunity to shape events on land, whether applying armed force from the sea or using the sea as a barrier.[3]

In contrast to the engagements historically characteristic of naval warfare, the four post-1991 cases took place with command of the sea assured. They discuss naval responses to trouble spots around the world—efforts to limit strife, prevent expansionism, halt ethnic and sectarian conflict, and cut off the roots of terrorist organizations.[4] Responding to such challenges is not unique in naval history.[5] Still, and unlike the British or American naval experiences prior to 1945, the four were not solely at-sea operations conducted relatively autonomously.[6] Starkly opposite to the first half of the 20th century, the period between 1991 and 2002 saw no Tsushimas, Jutlands, or Leyte Gulfs. In place of large engagements at sea, naval services have assumed a greater role since the end of the Cold War in confronting coastal or littoral challenges, sometimes halfway around the world from home, for extended periods of time, tests inextricably tied to events ashore.[7] That these cases in many respects represent slow-moving, even defensive activities should not be seen as a disadvantage or even atypical. Throughout history the dominant type of naval warfare has been attrition, rather than large-scale battle, which in the 21st century remains an entirely appropriate operational form when political circumstances demand it.[8]

Thus the case studies show the response of maritime forces to crises on land. Addressing the theme intrinsically makes sense, as any division between land and sea power is contrived.[9] Such a development should cause students to draw on the ideas of Sir Julian Corbett, written in 1909:

History shows that the actual functions of the Fleet (except in purely maritime wars) have been threefold:

1. The furtherance or hindrance of military operations ashore.

2. The protection or destruction of commerce.

3. The prevention or securing of alliances (i.e., deterring or persuading neutrals as to participating in the war).[10]

Allowing for the different levels of violence in the four case studies, the examples neatly fit into Corbett's description of the work of fleets.

Moreover, in the period studied the ability of maritime power to influence land events began to receive greater attention within naval circles. In 1992 the largest service discussed here, the U.S. Navy, consciously chose to emphasize its operations ". . . from the sea."[11] The doctrinal document noted naval operations should become increasingly "joint"; that is, working in conjunction with land and air forces, as well as combined, partnering with other navies. Such cooperation became more necessary as naval forces of all four nations confronted a dynamically evolving global political context and maintained high operating tempos in the face of declining budgets and fewer ships.[12] The U.S. Naval Doctrine Command, established in March 1993, reinforced the trend toward multinational operations.[13] That organization and its successor, Navy Warfare Development Command, arose explicitly to meet the joint and multinational requirements of the service. As well, during the last decade of the 20th century, U.S. military operations became increasingly combined in character.[14] Between 1991 and 2003, therefore, both the joint and combined attributes of United States naval planning assumed a greater role as the full spectrum of American national strength played its part in dealing with crises around the world.[15]

Finally, there is the nature of the conflicts represented here, only one of which involved a naval mission in the open war on terrorism. Between 1991 and 2001 the U.S. government increasingly focused on multinational peacekeeping operations.[16] As a result, the Iraqi and Yugoslav crises saw navies enforcing international sanctions, while East Timor challenged a naval intervention to enforce domestic plebiscite results. These three operations were designed to compel or deter behavior.[17] Naval forces carried out the operations under United Nations auspices, enforcing international will, but with limited aims. Without naval forces, the goals of the world community, as well as of the countries involved, would not have been achievable, or at the very least would have been much more expensive in human and material terms. At the level of conflicts below mass warfare studied here, when the subject of force is a minor military power, or if warships are asked to bring a selective, discrete measure of force, sea power offers an important means to influence events.

Their discretionary nature makes these operations more sensitive to political considerations. Naval autonomy is less than it would be in an all-out blue-water action.[18] Thus considerations such as restrictive rules of engagement (ROE) assume greater importance. Of equal weight these developments reflect the attainment of command of the sea, or at least an absolute level of access provided by the four navies to waters off the world's trouble spots. In that light the question posed in the case studies paraphrases Corbett, asking, "How do we employ our navies to influence the outcome of crises ashore?"

The Doctrinal Framework—Toward Interoperability[19]

Solutions to the problem of coordinating naval operations have their' roots in the 16th century when squadrons, divisions, and eventually fleets of ships began operating under sets of preplanned instructions.[20] Transmissions between the commanding admiral and ships' captains at first depended on signal pennants hoisted up the rigging, semaphore lamps, and in the 20th century, radio messages.[21] These signals allowed fleets to best distribute and maximize their combat power and leverage strength to maximum effect. To communicate securely and quickly the wishes of the senior officer, these messages depended upon encoded abbreviations, with both sender and recipient holding a copy of the codebook. For the historian, gaining an understanding of the particular tactical method employed proves difficult as doctrine tends to be classified as well as transitory.[22]

Unclear signaling and a lack of understanding between allied naval units risk causing disaster in battle. In February 1942 a force of five cruisers—one Australian, one British, one American, and two Dutch—

accompanied by a similar mix of destroyers, attempted to intercept the Japanese landings in Java. The resulting Battles of the Java Sea and Sunda Strait saw the loss of all five major warships and three destroyers at no loss to the Japanese.[23] Similarly, during the 1990–1991 Gulf War, differing British and American naval tactics led to contradictory responses to the Iraqi firing of a Silkworm missile, fortunately at no loss.[24] These actions amply demonstrated the need for comprehensible messages and assurances that subordinates knew how to carry out orders. Placed in a multinational context, the challenge of conducting naval operations becomes more difficult as different services address the same maneuvering and combat problems in varying ways.

Without a coherent set of responses, multilateral operations become more complex and oblige military forces to assume higher risks. In the words of one contemporary military analyst,

> . . . with several independent actors involved in multinational decision-making and implementation of strategies, command and control appears to be rather limited, while complexity and friction tend to be unlimited. Consequently, military alliances and coalitions face stronger problems of achieving consensus in strategy-making than purely national systems.[25]

For example, Western military personnel, including U.S. ground troops, participated in a UN-sponsored peacekeeping mission to Somalia, UNOSOMs (UN Operations in Somalia) I and II.[26] The commitment to the east African country arose in response to famine and civil war. The multinational military command, however, encountered difficulties operating in Somalia, confronting the influence of warlords in an anarchic "failed state." Crucial complexities constrained UN responsiveness, and the parallel U.S. command structure of Commander, U.S. Forces in Somalia, created an awkwardness that limited the peacekeepers' effectiveness.[27] The lesson is clear: for coalition operations to succeed, they must minimize extemporaneous actions.

Planning for multinational naval doctrine traces its roots to the 1950s when a series of agreements standardized the procedures for ships sailing together, especially merchant vessel convoys.[28] The former Allied navies of World War II initiated these agreements to ensure the ability of their services to cooperate in case of a conflict rooted in the Cold War rivalry.[29] At the conclusion of East-West rivalry, NATO and other allied navies had already formalized procedures for creating integrated groups of ships and their accompanying aircraft, and did so even by daily sharing of classified information with one another.[30]

The end of the Cold War generated further impetus to creating common operational methods. Both the Canadian and Royal Australian navies had instituted national naval officer training programs, pulling their procedures further away from British practice and adding to the need for international doctrine.[31] These separate training regimes punctuated the call for a multinational doctrine to ensure common responses when operating together. Royal Navy thought also coalesced in important ways in 1995 with the release of a new manual, BR 1806 "Fundamentals of British Maritime Doctrine."[32] Finally, when the U.S. Navy created the "Naval Doctrine Command" in the 1990s, the service added to its ambit the instruction "to develop common doctrine to support multinational maritime operations with non-NATO countries."[33] These measures demonstrated the full commitment and show the scope of the effort made by alliance and coalition naval planners to work together, especially after 1989.

By 2000 a full multilateral and multiservice hierarchy of military doctrine had been developed, under the auspices of the Multinational Interoperability Council. Its participants included Australia, Canada, the United Kingdom, and the United States, plus Germany and France.[34] By 2005 the organization included information sharing, doctrine, network, experimentation, and logistics working groups and continues as a forum for creating best practices in those fields. Beyond discussions at the highest level, these contacts have created a wide variety of agreed-upon NATO documents—Standardization Agreements, or STANAGs; Experimental Tactics, or EXTACs; Allied Tactical Publications, or ATPs; and national doctrinal publications. Many of these documents are classified, but some are available to the public,[35] such as NATO's Maritime Tactical Publication 1(D) Volume I, "Multinational Maritime Tactical Instructions and Procedures," the U.S. Navy's "Multinational Maritime Operations," and "The Commander's Handbook on the Law of Naval Operations," manuals serving as a framework for comprehending the underpinnings of these operations.[36] The last, a keystone publication providing the legal bases for at-sea operations, is employed by the U.S. Navy and by several foreign sea services.[37]

One should avoid overstating the value of doctrine, for its creation does not ensure the smooth operation of naval units with one another in all circumstances. A major reason for this general exception stems from national sovereignty: multinational plans cannot supersede any single country's reservations to operational choices, and multilateral arrangements will not violate national laws regarding, for example, the status of disputed territorial waters. Those reservations can be read in the opening pages of the most significant doctrinal manuals employed by NATO navies, Australia, and New Zealand and are announced to all participating nations.[38]

Nor can doctrine foresee every circumstance. Overburdened junior leaders, technical failures, misunderstood instructions, or headstrong subordinates can invalidate the best-prepared plans in an evolving situation with dispersed forces.[39] The addition of the multinational element to operations adds a further complication rooted in the political considerations noted above or in different procedures at sea. As one work bluntly suggested, "Ideal command arrangements or C^2 [Command and Control] have not been achieved in recent experience, particularly when coalition forces have been used for peace operations."[40] The inherent lack of familiarity of one force's procedures with those of even a close ally makes fulfilling objectives more challenging.[41] All the same, a framework of practice and its frequent exercise by operating forces at sea ease the path for naval cooperation. That Australian, Canadian, British, and United States navies, working with French and German partners, can coordinate the actions of half the world's surface warship strength makes their capabilities all the more impressive. Multinational groupings of ships can offer opportunities for action at lower cost to individual services and provide more abundant power than any single service could manage.[42]

One crucial element of the doctrine underlying the naval operations described here is the notion of rules of engagement.[43] They assign "when, where, against whom, and how much force can be used," and designate which officers have responsibility for ordering its use.[44] When conducting "operations other than war," the types of action discussed here, military forces require clear statements on the appropriate responses to unpredictable situations. These sorts of crises create a tension between military and political imperatives, and ROE can help bridge the gaps between them.[45] Typically the rules are presented in the form of a flowchart and are modified for each specific operation.

Rules of engagement in lower intensity campaigns, which can be accompanied by coalition differences over policy or a lack of distinction between friends and hostile parties, can confound operational commanders with their complexity. Unlike the Cold War, when more aggressive rules could be invoked, post-1991 opponents struck covertly and frequently mixed their forces with noncombatants.[46] The rules of this period require defined steps in, say, challenging by radio or signal lamp a third-country merchant ship suspected of carrying prohibited weapons before attempting to board it.[47] In some ways these national documents reduce the initiative of on-scene officers to the point they supplant the widely held notion of commander's intent by centralizing command in political hands. All the same they remain irreplaceable in conflicts of this sort.[48] Granting allies access to these frequently classified rules, an issue referred to as "releasability," also shapes multinational operations. In all four cases the authors have addressed the rules of engagement as they apply to a particular operation.

The Framework—Exercises

As operational armed forces, navies tend to eschew the use of planned concepts unless they have practiced them. Naval operators tend to master a particular skill in isolation and then hone their abilities and confidence by taking part in frequent exercises of increasing complexity. These drills cover a spectrum of activities. At the simplest end of the range, individual ships and aircraft conduct a Passage Exercise, or PASSEX, which allow two craft to acknowledge formally one another and familiarize their crews with one another.[49] Similar in nature to port visits, the exchanges of personnel between countries, called cross-decking, support the same purpose, giving sailors from other services the chance to understand one another as fellow ship handlers.[50]

More advanced exercises test the ability of navies to work together, using common doctrine, also called "tactics, techniques and procedures," to take on the tasks they perform in crises or wartime.[51] Some exercises tackle problems such as supply or radio procedures, and allow solutions to take place in the field.[52] These military practice sessions allow the participants to identify technical mismatches between component parts of multinational forces so they can work as cohesive units. Without making exercises so realistic, "combined, concurrent and/or collaborative planning" becomes degraded.[53] The range of these exercises encompasses amphibious movements to master the complex transportation of soldiers from ships to shore and the simulation of combat. Still other exercises test new communications systems required by fleets to work together.[54] At their most sophisticated, combined exercises become large-scale, week-long, multiservice, and international in nature, involving dozens of vessels and hundreds of aircraft.[55] Of these, the full-spectrum exercises are the most important. In addition to the particular confidence- and skills-development messages they provide, the largest events help sailors prepare for their most threatening challenge—combat. Such practice teaches personnel to respond to hostile forces, the units able to deny navies the opportunity to support humanitarian or peacekeeping missions, and in a lethal way.[56]

These exercises have evolved over time. For example, the first comprehensive NATO practice in the North Atlantic, Exercise Mainbrace, took place in September 1952. Involving more than 150 ships, including ten aircraft carriers from the British, Canadian, and United States navies, the exercise took place despite unresolved challenges posed by intelligence and signals interoperability.[57] The maneuvers proved such a success they set the stage for subsequent NATO operations throughout the Cold War and after. The practice of holding multilateral naval exercises in the Pacific Ocean area began with the formal cooperation of the Royal Navy and the U.S. Navy. Australia came under this so-called Combined Exercise Agreement in 1966, and Canada joined in 1978.[58] The agreement outlines common procedures for these services' unified training, and with these exercises naval vessels and aircraft cooperatively train. After 1989, navies in the English-speaking world had begun to steer away from exercises simulating a general war against the defunct Soviet Union, and by June 1996, instead practiced multinational peacekeeping operations.[59] At that time, for example, a Canadian-hosted war game uncovered many of the complexities in harmonizing differing national rules of engagement.[60]

The Royal Australian, Canadian, Royal, and United States navies (with occasional participation of the Royal New Zealand Navy) recognize the value of national and international drills and allow observation of and participation in each others' war games. Given their expense and complexity only some of these are annual events, such as Exercise Tandem Thrust conducted between Australian and U.S. forces.[61] Other rehearsals entail drills conducted in the midst of ongoing operations. Together, these exercises demonstrate the professional competence and, more important, the combat credibility of allied forces to one another.[62] Such experiences allow naval personnel to develop an otherwise intangible trust, the element essential to working together.[63] Members of navies see reliable friends as their best, in some cases sole, allies.

The experience gained in peacetime operations serves a final purpose. In the case of the American service, at least, the collection of "lessons learned" from exercises is highly developed, and in many cases (although not all) the answers are applied. These results can be impressionistic, for example, measuring the pace of a friendly navy's exercise, or determining the expectations of an ally in a type of operation, even combat.[64] The lesson derived from an exercise provides guidance to improve future operations service-wide, ensuring better performance of missions and greater protection for personnel.

The Framework—Technical Interoperability

World War II naval leaders in the English-speaking world began to look for better means to exchange combat information with one another. Their first efforts began with the creation of the Combined Communications Electronics Board and, after 1960, proceeded through the five-member AUSCANNZUKUS organization.[65] Alongside the Air

Standardization Coordinating Committee, AUSCANNZUKUS members work to create "interoperable" communications—compatible equipment and methods that allow the naval services to operate together.[66] The equipment and procedures enable friendly ships to radio one another, transfer fuel through common couplings, and provide ammunition or spare parts while at sea.

More specifically, the standardization of NATO navies' electronic information sharing began in the 1950s, with the convergence of separate efforts by the Commonwealth navies (Royal Australian, then-Royal Canadian, Royal New Zealand, and Royal) and the U.S. Navy.[67] In particular, warship crews portrayed evolving three-dimensional information in real time, using data derived from radar, and later from other sources, on two-dimensional displays. To match the high rate of data exchange from multiple sources cluttering the shared picture, each service sought to automate the transmission and display of radar and sonar returns in their combat information centers (or equivalents), rather than manually plot the information.[68] Complicating matters, all information sent and received by these ships is done so in a secure form to prevent interception by opposing naval forces. Setting much of the pace for these exchanges was the U.S. Navy's Naval Tactical Data System (NTDS).[69] Standardizing that system, the British, Canadian, and United States navies created in 1958 the Tactical Information Data Committee, which eventually set out the technical requirements for the ships of the three services to exchange an electronic picture with one another.

Shortly thereafter, in 1964, the Federal Republic of Germany purchased three *Charles F. Adams*-class guided missile destroyers designed and built in the United States. Hearing of the American NTDS system, German project managers purchased a smaller version of the same processing equipment fitted out with national software designed by the UNIVAC division of the Remington Rand Company.[70] Australian, French, Italian, Japanese, and Spanish orders for NTDS followed, allowing inclusion of British and Canadian information. By the 1970s the data exchange protocols had been formalized under a NATO STANAG. The agreed-upon version became the basis for the interoperable system created by the U.S. Navy and commonly referred to by all nations as Link 11.[71] More than any other method, that system allows multilateral naval operations to work successfully.

Link 11, however, has limits. By the 21st century, the information load that Link 11 could process—a transfer rate of one megabyte per second—was too low to keep up with demand. At the same time U.S. Navy ships had surpassed that rate of information transfer using other systems that rely on satellites, equipment not available to allied navies for reasons of releasability or cost.[72] The first of these concerns is central, for allied ships are not always given access to classified military systems administered by offices outside of the U.S. Navy, especially the Secret Internet Protocol Router Network (SIPRNET).[73] Sharing classified data consequently remains a tricky part of multinational collaboration. After 1998, that problem eased but was not resolved with the introduction of the Coalition Wide Area Network (COWAN), a classified website, email, and chat system. Sometimes called the Combined Enterprise Regional Information Exchange System (CENTRIXS), this information structure is used for command and control.[74] On at least one occasion after the operations described here, a lack of access to the American ROE and SIPRNET caused a Canadian ship commander to grumble.[75] In addition, domestic political constraints can prevent national governments from selling high-tech equipment abroad, even to longstanding allies.[76] Despite the comparatively great resources at their disposal and a longstanding commitment to sharing technology, by 2004 allied communications systems were still not completely interoperable with one another.[77] Not all nations can afford to make the trade offs needed to purchase electronics, weapons, and new hulls while keeping ships at sea for long periods. Thus some observers worry about creating an American "technology island," which means, in essence, the pricing of U.S. military capabilities beyond the reach of allied navies.[78] For the case studies discussed here, it remained up to the personnel in these operations to create the "human network" to bolster and fill in for the limits of releasability and communications.[79]

These constraints, however, were not so limiting in these four cases of multinational operations, for the allied ships used Link 11, the most widely held system for sharing information. It retained its usefulness as the method for exchanging data between vessels on the same mission.[80] Consequently, and alongside the COWAN/CENTRIXS system, Link 11 remained the common mode for information exchange among units of the Australian, British, Canadian, and United States navies during the period covered by these essays.[81]

Shape of the Study

In some ways the four cases presented are dissimilar. Two operations (Iraq and Yugoslavia) represented the long-term commitment of naval units, one (East Timor) indicated the role of navies in an armed intervention ashore, and the fourth (after September 2001) showed allies responding to an Afghanistan-based terrorist threat to all of them. One operation (Yugoslavia) was conducted under the established NATO alliance structure, while three took place under more ad hoc coalitions, creating initially less well-defined command relationships.[82] These dissimilarities demanded reconciliation by the authors, which they have addressed.

Two points reduce the challenge posed by a lack of command relationships. First, sailors consider themselves "operators," that is, people performing interchangeable work in peace and war. Their operational practices did not considerably diverge over the time covered by the studies and demonstrate the persistence characteristic of naval forces. Second, sailors in these allied navies share the same challenges and goals and, equally important, recognize the value their services bring to national governments as well as the international community.[83] They know and trust one another.

Moreover, between the fall of the Berlin Wall and the end of the Taliban regime in Afghanistan, these English-speaking navies operated in a consistently effective manner. They did so with an effectiveness that their sibling services, armies and air forces, wish to do, as multinational operations have become increasingly commonplace since the end of the

Cold War. All four operations fulfilled the expectations of both the United Nations and the countries involved, regardless of the command structures employed, demonstrating the state of naval evolution at the cusp of the 21st century. Members of these navies came to rely upon one another for support. Coalitions always have seams, especially in politically complex situations, but the trust built on common doctrine, shared training, and technically interoperable systems minimized any fraying of relations. The resulting product of compatibility and cooperation by the four sea services and their partners was, as described by two senior U.S. Navy leaders, a "self-synchronizing and self-organizing" network of a thousand ships, coordinated by a community of naval practice. In light of the need to address the similarities and differences between cases, the common interpretive lens of *combined* navies—working together—reduced the impact of disparate circumstance and command considerations.

The opinions expressed herein reflect those of the author, and do not necessarily reflect those of the United States Navy and the Department of Defense.

Notes

1. H. H. Gaffney et al., *The American Way of War and Its Transformation in the Post-Cold War Period, 1989–2003* (Alexandria, VA: CNA, February 2004), 3.

2. The weight of U.S.-foreign waterborne trade increased more than 41% between 1980 and 1999. See Donna J. Nincic, "Sea Lane Security and U.S. Maritime Trade: Chokepoints as Scarce Resources," in *Globalization and Maritime Power,* ed. Sam Tangredi (Washington, DC: National Defense University, 2002), 148.

3. On these dual natures of maritime warfare, see Norman Friedman, *Seapower as Strategy: Navies and National Interests* (Annapolis, MD: Naval Institute Press, 2001), 163.

4. On the diplomatic roles of navies, see Geoffrey Till, *Seapower: A Guide for the Twenty-First Century* (London and Portland: Frank Cass, 2004), chap. 9, especially 285–304.

5. On the historic utility of sea power in low-level crises, see James Cable, *The Political Influence of Naval Force in History* (Houndmills, UK: MacMillan, 1998), 160–61.

6. For the idea of lower autonomy, see Colin S. Gray, "History for Strategists: British Seapower as a Relevant Past," in *Seapower: Theory and Practice,* ed. Geoffrey Till (Ilford, UK: Frank Cass, 1994), 25.

7. U.S. Navy (USN) planners recognized these changes at the time; see Chief of Naval Operations, "OPNAV Instruction 3450.18: U.S. Naval Control of Shipping Organization," 15 December 1995, 1, at http://neds.daps.dla.mil/directives/3450_18.pdf, accessed 24 October 2005.

8. Derived in large measure from N. A. M. Rodger, "Image and Reality in Eighteenth-Century Naval Tactics," *The Mariner's Mirror* 89 (August 2003): 281.

9. Colin S. Gray, "Seapower and Landpower," in *Seapower and Strategy,* eds. Gray and Roger W. Barnett (Annapolis, MD: Naval Institute Press, 1989), 4.

10. Julian S. Corbett, *Some Principles of Maritime Strategy* (Annapolis, MD: Naval Institute Press, 1988), Appendix: "The Green Pamphlet," 336. An earlier version, which reverses the order, appears on 317. For similar views, see Gray, "Seapower and Landpower," 12, and Stephen Prince, "Maritime Warfare: An Historical Perspective," in *Effects Based Warfare,* ed. Christopher Finn (London: The Stationery Office, n.d.), 4.

11. Chief of Naval Operations, . . . *From the Sea: Preparing the Naval Service for the 21st Century* (Washington, DC: September 1992). Subsequent doctrinal statements refined the theme. See Chief of Naval Operations, *Forward . . . From the Sea* (Washington, DC: March 1994). See also Joel Sokolsky, "Colbert's Heirs: The United States, NATO and Multilateral Naval Cooperation in the Post Cold War Era," in *Multinational Naval Cooperation and Foreign Policy into the 21st Century,* eds. Fred Crickard et al. (Aldershot, UK: Ashgate, 1998), 79–81.

12. On USN budgets, see Dennis S. Ippolito, *Budget Policy Deficits and Defense: A Fiscal Framework for Defense Planning* (Carlisle Barracks, PA: U.S. Army War College, June 1995), 22–26, and H. H. Gaffney, "The Navy before and after September 11," in *Globalization and Maritime Power,* 536–37. On the broader context, see John B. Hattendorf, ed. *U.S. Naval Strategy in the 1990s: Selected Documents* (Newport, RI: Naval War College Press, September 2006), "Introduction," especially 3–5.

13. James J. Tritten, "Developing Naval Doctrine . . . From the Sea," *Joint Forces Quarterly* (Autumn 1995): 110–13. See James Tritten, "Implications for Multinational Naval Doctrine," in *Globalization and Maritime Power,* 259–79.

14. Such considerations are also applicable in joint (i.e. multiservice) operations. See Gaffney et al., *The American Way of War,* 4. Similarly, Australian discussions at the time noted "almost all modern navies operate from a very large base of shared international doctrine." See RAN Doctrine 1, *Australian Maritime Doctrine* (Canberra: Defence Publishing Service, 2000), 6.

15. Another regional arrangement reflecting the trend toward multinational operations is the Western Pacific Naval Symposium, established in 1988. See "The Western Pacific Naval Symposium," *Semaphore* 5 (March 2006), at http://www.navy.gov.au/spc/, accessed 31 March 2006.

16. For the political framework of the peacekeeping operations, see Presidential Review Directive (PRD) 13 "Peacekeeping Operations," at http://www.fas.org/irp/offdocs/pdd13.htm; and Presidential Decision Directive (PDD) 25, "U.S. Policy on Reforming Multilateral Peace Operations," 6 May 1994, at http://fas.org/irp/offdocs/pdd25.htm, both accessed 5 October 2005.

17. Till, *Seapower: A Guide,* 288–90. See also Gary C. Hufbauer et al., *Economic Sanctions Reconsidered: History and Current Policy,* 2nd ed. (Washington, DC: Institute for International Economics, 1990), 1:10–13. For a varying take on the compelling of states, see Adam Siegel, *To Deter, Compel, and Reassure in International Crises: The Role of U.S. Naval Forces* (Alexandria, VA: CNA, February 1995), 1–5.

18. In many ways, the themes arising in this essay were presaged in Ken E. Gause, *U.S. Navy Interoperability with Its High-End Allies* (Alexandria, VA: CNA, November 2001), especially 14–34; the author is indebted to Peter Swartz of CNA for pointing out this essay. On the political nature of warfare and American military reservations to that notion, see Antulio J. Echevarria, *Toward an American Way of War* (Carlisle, PA: U.S. Army War College, March 2004).

19. The term interoperability connotes more than compatible equipment, implying reliable methods for allowing people and commands to work together. See Keith G. Stewart et al., "Non-technical interoperability: the challenge of command leadership in multinational operations," unpublished paper (Farnborough: QinetiQ, 2004), 2, at http://www.dodccrp.org/events/2005/10th/CD/papers/298.pdf, accessed 22 August 2005. A scale of interoperability can be found in Andreas Tolk, "Beyond Technical Interoperability—Introducing a Reference Model for Measures of Merit for Coalition Interoperability," paper presented at the 8th International Command and Control Research and Technology Symposium (Washington, DC: National Defense University, June 2003), 3, at http://www.odu.edu/engr/vmasc/Publications/Tolk-BeTechInt.pdf, accessed 23 August 2005.

20. See Julian S. Corbett, ed., *Fighting Instructions, 1530–1816* (London: Naval Records Society, 1905); Andrew Gordon, *The Rules of the Game: Jutland and British Naval Command* (Annapolis, MD: Naval Institute Press, 1996), 195; and Michael A. Palmer, *Command at Sea: Naval Command and Control Since the Sixteenth Century* (Cambridge, MA: Harvard University Press, 2005), 223–24. The first naval officer to employ the term doctrine was an American. See Dudley W. Knox, "The Role of Doctrine in Naval Warfare," *U.S. Naval Institute Proceedings* 41 (March–April 1915): 325-54. Conversely, in the words of one analyst, the current USN is "wary of doctrine," concerned it robs commanders of initiative. See Peter M. Swartz, *U.S. Navy Capstone Strategies and Concepts (1970–2006): Insights of the U.S. Navy of 2006* (Alexandria, VA: CNA, June 2006), 35.

21. See "Visual Signalling in the Royal Australian Navy," *Semaphore* 8 (April 2006), at http://www.navy.gov.au/spc/semaphore/index.html, accessed 1 May 2006.

22. James Goldrick, "The Problems of Modern Naval History," in *Doing Naval History: Essays Toward Improvement,* ed. John B. Hattendorf (Newport, RI: Naval War College Press, 1995), 14.

23. Robert J. Cressman, *The Official Chronology of the U.S. Navy in World War II* (Annapolis, MD: Naval Institute Press, 2000), 79–80.

24. Till, *Seapower: A Guide,* 109–110. For a description of the Silkworm interception see also Edward J. Marolda and Robert J. Schneller Jr., *Shield and Sword: The United States Navy and the Persian Gulf War* (Annapolis, MD: Naval Institute Press, 2001), 293–94.

25. Uwe Hartmann, *Carl von Clausewitz and the Making of Modern Strategy* (Potsdam: miles-Verlag, 2002), 99. Hartmann draws upon Book I, Chapter 1 of Clausewitz's *On War* for this assessment.

26. A. Vernon, *Defining the Decade: Military Operations and Political Constraints in the 1990s* (Alexandria, VA: CNA, August 2004), 39–40.

27. U.S. Army Center of Military History, *United States Forces, Somalia After Action Report and Historical Overview: The United States Army in Somalia, 1992–1994* (Washington, DC: U.S. Army Center of Military History, 2003), 10, 120–24. UN and some American forces remained under divided operational control, with the U.S. logistics unit under the UN

commander (a U.S. Army officer), while the U.S. Quick Reaction Force reported directly to Commander, U.S. Central Command (see page 124).

28. Thomas R. Frame, *Pacific Partners: A History of Australian-American Naval Relations* (Sydney, NSW: Hodder & Stoughton, 1992), 87.

29. On American receptiveness to combined operations, as reflected in doctrine, see James Tritten, "Development Issues for Multinational Navy Doctrine" (Paper presented at the 13–15 July 1995 workshop "Multinational Naval Cooperation: Moving from Theory to Practice," Dalhousie University, Halifax, Nova Scotia), 3, 7, at http://www.dtic.mil/doctrine/jel/research_pubs/devissue.pdf, accessed 13 September 2005.

30. Thomas-Durell Young, "Cooperative Diffusion through Cultural Similarity: The Post-War Anglo-Saxon Countries' Experience" (Monterey, CA: Center for Civil-Military Relations, n.d), 13. Copy in author's possession.

31. Commodore James Stapleton, oral history, 14 December 2004, 6. The Canadian service began training naval officers in Canada in the 1950s, while "patriation" of the Principal Warfare Officer course took place in the 1980s in Australia. My thanks go to Robert H. Caldwell of the Directorate of History and Heritage, NDHQ, Ottawa, for clarifying the Canadian date in an email, 10 January 2006.

32. Eric Grove, "The discovery of doctrine. British naval thinking at the close of the twentieth century," in *The Development of British Naval Thinking: Essays in Memory of Bryan Ranft*, ed. Geoffrey Till (London and New York: Taylor and Francis, 2006), 182.

33. Michael T. Johnson, *Multinational Maritime Operations (MMOPS) for Naval Doctrine Command* (Alexandria, VA: CNA, September 1995), 3.

34. MIC, "Charter of the Multinational Interoperability Council," 2nd ed., Arlington, VA, 17 April 2002, at http://www.dtic.mil/jcs/mic/j3inn/mic.html, accessed 3 June 2005. A more comprehensive and different description of the doctrine writing process is in Directorate for Operational Plans and Joint Force Development, "Staffing Guide for Operational Plans and Joint Force Development (J-7)," Washington, DC, 15 August 2002, especially pages 17–22, at http://www.dtic.mil/doctrine/jel/other_pubs/ajpsg02.pdf, accessed 13 September 2005.

35. Joint Doctrine & Concepts Centre, "Joint Warfare Publication 3-00: Joint Operations Execution" (Shrivenham, UK: Ministry of Defence, March 2004), 1A4. See Navy Tactical Support Activity, "Draft EXTAC 1013 Regional Naval Control of Shipping" (Washington, DC: December 1995).

36. NATO Standardization Authority, MTP 1(D) Volume I, "Multinational Maritime Tactical Instructions and Procedures," December 2001; U.S. Naval Doctrine Command, "Multinational Maritime Operations," Norfolk, VA, 1 September 1996; and NWP 1-14M, "The Commander's Handbook on the Law of Naval Operations," Washington, DC, 1 October 1995.

37. On translation into foreign languages, see Michael Johnson, Peter Swartz, and Patrick Roth, *Doctrine for Partnership: A Framework for U.S. Multinational Naval Doctrine* (Alexandria, VA: CNA, March 1996), 21, fn18.

38. "Multinational Maritime Tactical Instructions and Procedures," v–vi.

39. One slightly different perspective of these constraints is Martha E. Maurer, *Coalition Command and Control: Key Considerations* (Washington, DC: National Defense University, May 1996), chap. 5, "People."

40. David S. Alberts and Richard E. Hayes, *Command Arrangements for Peace Operations* (Washington, DC: National Defense University, 1996), 41. On the complex politics of UN peacekeeping missions, including the inability of commanding officers to fire subordinates, see Romeo A. Dallaire, *Shake Hands With the Devil: The Failure of Humanity in Rwanda* (Toronto: Random House Canada, 2003), 273.

41. "Joint Warfare Publication 3-00: Joint Operations Execution," 2–4.

42. For a parallel version of this idea see Gray, "History for Strategists," 21; and "Joint Warfare Publication 3-00: Joint Operations Execution," 1A2.

43. For an opening study of ROE, see Guy R. Phillips, "Rules of Engagement: A Primer," *The Army Lawyer* (July 1993): 4–27. The author, a Canadian Navy lieutenant commander, published in a U.S. Army journal.

44. Eric S. Miller, *Interoperability of Rules of Engagement in Multinational Maritime Operations* (Alexandria, VA: CNA, October 1995), 1; and Till, *Seapower: A Guide*, 290–92. A differing perspective on ROE arises in Joshua Sinai et al., "United Nations Peacekeeping: Lessons Learned, a Report Prepared by an Interagency Agreement by the Federal Research Division, Library of Congress" (Washington, DC: Library of Congress, September 1995), 12: ROE "define how a peace operation force should act or react to an adversary's action in peaceful or crisis situation in the course of discharging its duties under the Security Council's mandate . . . [and] to prevent overreaction by members of the force that might endanger the U.N.'s crisis management activities." This wording reflects the aim of the UN to avoid employing force, or at least to minimize its use absolutely.

45. Bradd C. Hayes, *Naval Rules of Engagement: Management Tools for Crisis* (Santa Monica, CA: Rand Corp., July 1989), 2. The author is indebted to intern James Schwemlein for pointing out this publication.

46. For an example of less restrictive ROE, see Joseph T. Stanik, *El Dorado Canyon: Reagan's Undeclared War with Qaddafi* (Annapolis, MD: Naval Institute Press, 2003), 46–48, 123, 127–28.

47. Johnson, *Multinational Maritime Operations,* 38–39; Miller, especially "Problems with ROE in Multinational Operations," 13–19; Stacy A. Poe, "Rules of Engagement: Complexities of Coalition Interaction in Military Operations Other than War," unpublished paper, U.S. Naval War College, 13 February 1995; and "Joint Warfare Publication 3-00: Joint Operations Execution," 1A3.

48. On command independence, see Ulrike Kleemeier, "Clausewitz: Soldier and Thinker— Reflections on the Topicality of Clausewitz' Work," 37th Security Policy Information Conference, Clausewitz-Gesellschaft, 15 August 2003, at http://www.clausewitz-gesellschaft.de/Documents_in_English/Klee.pdf, accessed 22 June 2005.

49. For a Greek Navy and USN PASSEX with Russian Fleet ships, see "NATO and Russian Ships Conduct Joint Training," 25 November 2004, at http://www.afsouth.nato.int/releases/2004releases/PR_37_04.htm, accessed 6 June 2005.

50. Johnson et al., *Doctrine for Partnership,* 19. On the development of common armed forces culture between Australia, Canada, New Zealand, the United Kingdom, and the United States, see Young, "Cooperative Diffusion." See also Jack McCaffrie, "Australia's Maritime Interests and Policy," in *Issues in Maritime Strategy: Presentations of the Royal Australian Navy Maritime Studies Program,* ed. G. A. Cox (Canberra: Directorate of Publishing, 1994), 17. For an iconoclastic view of multinational exercises, see Cynthia

Enloe, "Beyond Steve Canyon and Rambo: Feminist Histories of Militarized Masculinity," in *The Militarization of the Western World*, ed. John R. Gillis (New Brunswick, NJ: Rutgers, 1989), 129–32.

51. Tritten, "Development Issues," 22.

52. Johnson et al., *Doctrine for Partnership*, 125–26.

53. Commander in Chief Pacific Fleet, "Common Operating System," Navy Lessons Learned Database, 14 December 2000.

54. As an aside—one 2002 USN Fleet Battle Experiment connected a ship and shore installations, to allow Australian, British, Canadian and American planners to reconcile systems. See Todd Michael Mansell, Andrew Tynan, and David Kershaw, "Investigating the Network Enabled Conventional Submarine: An Australian Perspective" (Paper presented at the Command and Control Research and Technology Symposium [CCRTS] Workshop, Monterey, CA), 10–12, at http://www.dodccrp.org/events/2002/CCRTS_Monterey/Tracks/Track_1.htm, accessed 7 September 2005.

55. See Eric Grove, with Graham Thompson, *Battle for the Fiørds: NATO's Forward Maritime Strategy in Action* (Annapolis, MD: Naval Institute Press, 1991). I am indebted to Dr. Thomas-Durell Young for commenting on an earlier draft of this paper and noting the joint nature of the largest exercises, especially as three participants in this study, Australia, Canada, and the United Kingdom, plus New Zealand, have naval aviation branches "owned" by their respective air forces.

56. An idea derived from Owen R. Cote Jr., "Buying '. . . From the Sea': A Defense Budget for a Maritime Strategy," in *Holding the Line: U.S. Defense Alternatives for the Early 21st Century*, ed. Cindy Williams (Cambridge, MA: MIT Press, 2001), 166.

57. Sean M. Maloney, *Securing Command of the Sea: NATO Naval Planning, 1948–1954* (Annapolis, MD: Naval Institute Press, 1995), 153 and footnotes, 236–37. Ships from Belgium, Denmark, France, the Netherlands, and Norway also participated.

58. Young, "Cooperative Diffusion," 13–14. New Zealand also employs the Combined Exercise Agreement (COMBEXAG). On the NATO Planning Board for Ocean Shipping, a merchant shipping control authority in case of escalation in the Cold War, and predecessor to the COMBEXAG, see Maloney, 236, fn30. Thomas-Durell Young refers to the World Wide Naval Control and Protection of Shipping in Young, *Australian, New Zealand, and United States Security Relations, 1951–1986* (Boulder, CO: Westview, 1992), 135. See also McCaffrie, "Australia's Maritime Interests," 17.

59. C. McKeown, "Joint and Combined Operational Training: MARCOT '96," in *Canadian Defence Quarterly* 25 (September 1996): 14.

60. Ibid., 17.

61. G. Fuentes, "U.S., Australia Ponder Future Tandem Training," *Navy Times*, 14 April 1997, 21. On the rarity of high-intensity exercises, see Tritten, "Development Issues," 21, 22.

62. Derived from Peter T. Haydon, "Evolution of the Canadian Naval Task Group," in *Canadian Gunboat Diplomacy: The Canadian Navy and Foreign Policy*, ed. Ann Griffiths et al. (Halifax: Centre for Foreign Policy Studies, 2000).

63. The author is indebted to Dr. Steve Harris, Directorate of History and Heritage, in arriving at the centrality of building trust to avoid fraying or opening the seams between allies, during a team discussion at HMAS *Watson*, 18 July 2005.

64. For the lessons derived from U.S. participation in a British antisubmarine exercise, see Commander Destroyer Squadron Fourteen, "ASWAC Battle Rhythm," Navy Lessons Learned Database, 22 January 1999.

65. Australia, Canada, New Zealand, United Kingdom, United States. For a historical overview, see http://auscannzukus-navalc3.hq.navy.mil/index.htm, accessed 2 June 2005; and R. Buck, "Canadian Perspectives on C4I Issues," in *Maritime War in the 21st Century: The Medium and Small Navy Perspective,* ed. David Wilson (Canberra: RAN Sea Power Centre, 2001), 132.

66. "Joint Warfare Publication 3-00: Joint Operations Execution," 1A4–1A5. U.S. Naval Doctrine Command, "Multinational Maritime Operations," page xi, defines interoperability as the "ability of systems, units or forces to provide services to and accept services from other systems, units or forces and the use of services so exchanged to enable them to operate effectively together." The same publication notes on page xii standardization refers to "compatibility, interoperability, interchangeability, and commonality in the fields of operations, administration and materiel."

67. Young, *Australian, New Zealand,* 121.

68. McCaffrie, "New Technologies," 68.

69. Daniel L. Boslaugh, *When Computers Went to Sea: The Digitization of the United States Navy* (Los Alamitos, CA: IEEE/ASNE, 1999), 284–91. The Royal Navy system was first called Action Data Automation (ADA), later ADAWS, with the Canadian Forces version called Digital Automated Tracking and Resolving System (DATAR), subsequently CCS-280. Some Canadian ships instead carried an interim "Automated Data-Link Plotting System," ADLIPS; see Richard H. Gimblett, "Command in the Canadian Navy: An Historical Survey," *The Northern Mariner* 14 (October 2004): 54–57. The Australian Naval Combat Data System (NCDC) came from a similar and slightly later effort. See G. Cannon, "Technology Transfer, Knowledge Partnerships, and the Advance of Australian Naval Combat Systems," in *The Navy and the Nation: The Influence of the Navy on Modern Australia,* eds. David Stevens and John Reeve (Sydney, NSW: Allen & Unwin, 2004), 249–52. The best guide to Link 11 is Logicon Inc., *Understanding Link-11: A Guidebook for Operators, Technicians, and Net Managers* (San Diego, CA: Logicon, Tactical Systems Division, September 1996). For an example of NTDS information inputs, see A. Gallotta, "Navy EW and C3CM," in *Naval Tactical Command and Control,* ed. G. Nagler (Washington, DC: AFCEA, 1985), 213–19. For sample NTDS symbols, see Rudolph P. Darken et al., "A Hybrid Virtual Environment Interface to Electronic Warfare Information" (Washington, DC: Naval Research Laboratory, 1996), 14.

70. Boslaugh, *When Computers Went to Sea,* 292–93. The Germans adopted the acronym SATIR for their system.

71. Boslaugh, *When Computers Went to Sea,* 294. For communication with most NATO aircraft, the standard is Link 4. On the datalinks' importance, see Norman Friedman, "Future C4I for Smaller Navies," in *Maritime War in the 21st Century,* ed. Wilson, 147–50, and Cannon, "Technology Transfer," 262.

72. The USN began deploying Link 16 in 1994. See Logicon Inc., *Understanding Link-16: A Guidebook for New Users* (San Diego, CA: Logicon, Tactical Systems Division, December 1998), 1-1. For a recent study on these developments, see Walter L. Perry et al., *Measures of Effectiveness for the Information-Age Navy: The Effects of Network-Centric Operations on*

Combat Outcomes (Santa Monica, CA: Rand Corp., 2002). The USN lead in networking ships can stress relations with close allies. One report notes the prospective 1990s switch from Link 11 to Link 16 in U.S. ships prompted concern in the Federal German Navy, which lacked resources and shipboard space to incorporate new equipment. See Gary Geipel, *Multinational Naval Cooperation Options With the North Atlantic Countries* (Alexandria, VA: CNA, December 1992), 77. As late as 2006 German ships employed Link 11 to share data with one another, while accepting information transmitted from allied Link 16-capable systems. See diagram in J. Mannhardt, "Die Deutsche Marine in der Transformation. Maritimes Aufgabenspektrum and Fähigkeitsprofil," *Wehrtechnischer Report,* February 2006, 8.

73. CG 2D MAW, G-2, "Network and Systems Interoperability With Allied Forces," Navy Lessons Learned Database, 20 May 1996. This report notes United Kingdom, Canadian, Australian, and New Zealand forces are ineligible to access SIPRNET under Defense Information System Agency policy. See also 2DMAW, "Access to Secure WAN by British Forces," Navy Lessons Learned Database, 23 May 1996. Both of these result from CJTF Exercise Purple Star 96.

74. Commander Cruiser Destroyer Group Three, "RIMPAC 00: RIMPAC Websites," Navy Lessons Learned Database, 27 June 2000. See "Common Operating System," cited above, on the observed need for an unclassified Local Area Network. I am indebted to Captain Sam Tangredi, USN, for making the distinction between Link 11, a tactical information exchange system, and CENTRIXS, a command and control network, during a presentation at CNA, 20 July 2006.

75. C. Lambie, "Communications Snafus Dogged Ship on Mission," *Halifax Daily News,* 15 November 2004. The ship was HMCS *Toronto,* deployed as part of the USS *George Washington* carrier strike group, but not a participant in Operation Iraqi Freedom.

76. On American reluctance to sell to both Australia and the United Kingdom, see the articles by Spiegel, "UK Denied Waiver for American Weapons Technology," "Congressman an Immovable Force on U.S. Arms Exports," and "No Way for America to Treat its Close Allies," in the *Financial Times,* U.S. ed., 23 November 2005, 1, 6, 12.

77. Secretary of the Navy, SECNAV Instruction 5000.36, "Department of the Navy Data Management and Interoperability," 1 November 2001, 4, at http://neds.daps.dla.mil/ directives/5000_36.pdf, accessed 24 October 2005.

78. Dean S. Mills, "Coalition Interoperability: An International Adventure," *Air and Space Power Chronicles,* n.d., 8, at http://www.airpower.maxwell.af.mil/airchronicles/cc/mills. html, accessed 27 April 2005.

79. Once more the author and team are indebted to Dr. Steve Harris, who arrived at the term human network during 2005 meetings in Australia.

80. T. Keithly, "Making Maritime Coalitions Work: The future C4I perspective," 165; and J. McHale, "VisiCom Retargeting Process and NTDS Help Navy Battle Obsolescence" *Military and Aerospace Electronics* (May 2000): 4.

81. CENTRIXS is sometimes proprietary, requiring Americans embarked on allied ships to encrypt messages. "U.S., Singapore Navies Take Combined Operations to New Level," *Navy News Stand,* 10 June 2004, at http://www.news.navy.mil/search/display.asp?story_ id=13715, accessed 15 November 2005. Initially only USN Pacific Fleet and Central Command ships employed CENTRIXS, although all were slated receive it. See Maryann

Lawlor, "Navy Embarks on Operational Sea Change" *AFCEA Signal* (May 2003), at http://www.afcea.org/signal/articles/anmviewer.asp?a=229&z=15, accessed 15 November 2005, and Jill L. Boardman and Donald W. Shuey, "Combined Enterprise Regional Information Exchange System (CENTRIXS): Supporting Coalition Warfare World-Wide," U.S. CENTCOM paper, April 2004, at http://www.au.af.mil/au/awc/awcgate/ccrp/centrixs.pdf, accessed 31 March 2006. Again, I am indebted to Dr. Thomas-Durell Young for highlighting CENTRIXS.

82. Exceptions are the NATO Standing Naval Forces, which rotate overall command through the participating ship commanders. Most important, however, in coalition operations the largest contributing nation generally commands, while in alliance operations all participants are eligible to play command roles, at least below the level of theater commander. See Maloney, 201–2. On the distinction between alliance relations and coalitions, see Johnson et al., *Doctrine for Partnership,* 23, 57–70; and Guy Killaby, "The Influence of Law Upon Canadian Naval Strategy: *Leadmark* and the Evolving Legal Regime" in *Intervention and Engagement: A Maritime Perspective,* eds. Robert H. Edwards and Ann L. Griffiths (Halifax: Centre for Foreign Policy Studies, 2003), 108–9.

83. Derived from James Goldrick, "Strangers in Their Own Seas: A Comparison of Australian and Canadian Naval Experience, 1910–1982," in *A Nation's Navy: In Quest of a Canadian Naval Identity,* eds. Michael Hadley et al. (Montreal, PQ, and Kingston, ONT: McGill-Queen's, 1996), 326. On developing and reinforcing friendships, see Siegel, *To Deter,* 21.

CHAPTER 1

The U.S. Navy's Role in Coalition Maritime Interception Operations in the Arabian Gulf Region, 1991–2001

Jeffrey G. Barlow

Introduction

While not new, naval blockade came into its own as an operational form following the Cold War. The U.S. Navy defines maritime interception operations (MIO) as "peacetime measure[s] designed to enforce embargoes sanctioned by the UNSC [United Nations Security Council], national authority, or other regional organization."[1] These actions fit into Operations Other Than War. The principal characteristics for a maritime interception operation that enforces an embargo are:

1. The interception terms—including the starting date of the operation, its location, and the prohibited items—are publicly announced.

2. Use of minimum force is required for carrying out the embargo.

3. Although an embargo is usually directed against the transportation of specific prohibited items, it may encompass virtually all imported and exported goods.

4. Ships and aircraft that are not carrying prohibited goods are permitted to pass through the embargo line.

5. Ships carrying prohibited items are turned back, diverted to a neutral port requested by the vessel being detained, or diverted to a port selected by the cognizant commander. The affected ships normally are not seized as prizes.[2]

Although the U.S. Navy possesses the ships and capability that enable it to carry out individual maritime interception operations unaided, in the post–Cold War era it has sought to take part in such operations as a member of a coalition. There are both political and military reasons for this choice. Sharing the operational risks with other nations produces political benefits for the United States. By participating in operations under the auspices of the United Nations, a particular alliance, or a coalition, the Navy helps build support for and maintain legitimacy of its operations.[3] As part of a coalition, the Navy accrues important military benefits of working with additional ships and aircraft that supplement or complement (e.g., by furnishing different force competencies) the offensive and defensive combat capabilities of the maritime forces and receiving access to ports, airfields, or training areas in the region that otherwise would be unavailable for its use.[4]

MIO during the First Gulf War, 1990–1991

On the morning of 2 August 1990, Iraqi armored and mechanized divisions invaded Kuwait. During the next two days, Iraq managed to seize control of the entire country. Within hours of the aggression against Kuwait, the United Nations Security Council (UNSC) passed Resolution 660 denouncing the Iraqi invasion and demanding the complete and unconditional withdrawal of its troops from that small country.[5] On 6 August the Security Council strengthened that stand against Saddam Hussein's Iraqi regime by passing Resolution 661, which forbade the export of cargo originating from Iraq or Kuwait and barred the importation of material into these countries, except for medical supplies and (in instances specifically authorized by a UN committee) food stuffs.[6]

On 16 August U.S. President George H. W. Bush directed Commander in Chief, U.S. Central Command (USCINCCENT) to execute maritime interdiction operations, effective the following day.[7] Multinational maritime participation in the embargo was facilitated nine days later when Resolution 665 passed on 25 August. It authorized maritime forces being deployed to the area "to use such measures commensurate to the specific circumstance as may be necessary . . . to halt all inward and outward maritime shipping

Kuwait

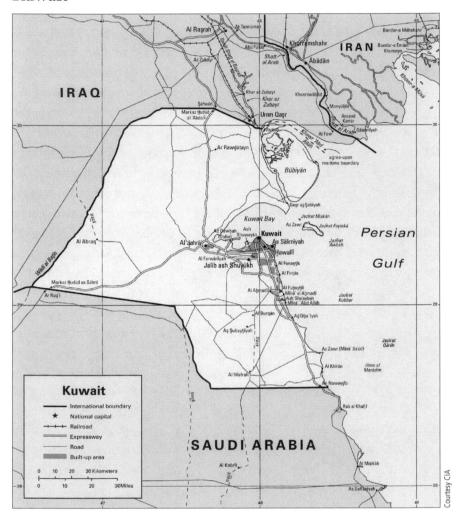

in order to inspect and verify their cargoes and destinations" and to ensure strict compliance with the provisions set forth in Resolution 661.[8]

By 1 September five countries in addition to the United States— Australia, Canada, France, the Netherlands, and the United Kingdom— had dispatched a total of 20 ships to Middle East waters but had not yet committed them to maritime interception operations.[9] USCINCCENT assigned overall coordination of MIO to U.S. Naval Forces Central Command (NAVCENT). Vice Admiral Henry H. Mauz Jr., the NAVCENT commander, convened the first of a monthly series of coordination conferences in Bahrain with the naval representatives of the countries readying ships for embargo enforcement on 9 and 10 September.[10]

During this first coordination meeting, the national representatives shared basic information on the rules of engagement (ROE) for each navy. This promulgation was only for informational purposes, however, since the committee possessed no power to align national ROE.[11]

It was also at this first coordination conference that national representatives discussed the need for some form of a central direction of the embargo. Although most attendees thought the U.S. Navy should assume the coordinating role because it possessed the largest combatant force in theater, this did not occur. When Vice Admiral Mauz put forth a plan for operational coordination along this line, a French representative objected and called for creating a separate role for the naval forces of the Western European Union (WEU) countries that were present.[12] As a result of the impasse, the conferees agreed that the national naval contingents would work in "loose association," wherein the ships remained under national control, while the on-scene task group commanders retained tactical and operational control.[13]

Following the initial coordination meeting, Mauz laid out the operating areas for the coalition navies. Eventually the ships of the 13 coalition navies making up the Maritime Interception Force (MIF)—Argentina, Australia, Belgium, Canada, Denmark, France, Greece, Italy, the Netherlands, Norway, Spain, the United Kingdom, and the United States—operated in one or more of these zones.[14] U.S. Navy and Royal Navy combatants were assigned the C (Charlie) sectors deep within the Arabian Gulf.[15] Canadian warships were located just slightly farther back in the central Gulf in areas designated C1 and C4.[16] The warships of Denmark, Italy, Norway, and the Netherlands were assigned the B (Bravo) sectors in the central and eastern Gulf. The ships of Australia, Argentina, Belgium, and Spain manned the A (Alpha) areas in the Gulf of Oman covering the approaches to the Strait of Hormuz. The French and Belgian ships were positioned much farther back, in the Bab al-Mandeb Strait separating the Gulf of Aden from the Red Sea. In the northern Red Sea, meanwhile, American, German, French, and Spanish warships monitored the Strait of Tiran leading into the Gulf of Aqaba, with Jordan's port of Aqaba at its head.[17] Finally, the navies of the Gulf Cooperation Council states—Saudi Arabia, Bahrain, Qatar, the United Arab Emirates (UAE), and Oman—supported the MIF by preventing merchantmen from using their coastal waters in an effort to skirt the embargo.[18]

The assignment of sectors well to the rear for the WEU naval contingents resolved the issue of a separate role for the Western European Union naval forces. As Mauz later recalled, "[W]e simply assigned the

Arabian Gulf Region

Courtesy CIA

[WEU] countries a separate operating area, off the UAE [United Arab Emirates] where there was almost no intercept action. [T]hey were happy and the rest of us got on with the program."[19] This division of labor proved fortuitous because as late as early November 1990 the French-controlled WEU forces still hadn't worked out a viable command structure. Analyst Thomas-Durell Young noted that according to a 7 November report of the Assembly of the Western European Union, its

> forces did not possess an accepted tactical command structure and were therefore unable to effect coordinated and directed responses, and that coordination of national ROE and logistic support had still not been achieved. The report also made a startling claim that it had only been during actual operations that U.S. forces in the area were discovered (much to the surprise of W.E.U. forces) to be using unique Identification Friend or Foe (IFF) procedures.[20]

During the force buildup of the Desert Shield period, the coalition navies handled maritime interception operations smoothly. In particular, the U.S. Navy and its major allies—the Royal Navy, the Canadian Navy, and the Royal Australian Navy—were experienced at working together through participation in regular bilateral and combined exercises. Moreover, they possessed upgraded communications equipment that enabled them to exchange secure track and identification data via Link 11 (the U.S.-operated tactical datalink).[21] This command and control interoperability allowed individual ships engaged in MIO to handle large numbers of air and surface contacts on a continuing basis. As the commanding officer of HMAS *Darwin* noted, "It was not uncommon for the 2–3 members of an FFG Air Picture Compilation Team to be confidently keeping tabs on up to 100 tracks. . . . The surface picture was no less complex. At any one time, within a surveillance range of 100 miles, the ships were tracking up to 200 contacts."[22]

The fluidity with which the coalition forces handled intercept operations was somewhat deceptive, however. The interception evolutions worked well in part because the Iraqi Air Force and Navy failed to strike at the coalition warships enforcing the embargo. The robustness of MIO conducted by ships operating under a command and control regime characterized by "loose association" thus was never seriously tested.[23]

The interoperability of the coalition navies in the Gulf region during the fall of 1990 did confront serious limitations on the ROE, intelligence, and war planning information that could be exchanged between the national naval contingents.[24] This issue of "releasability" was a particular problem for the U.S. Navy. The United States, Australia, and France, for example, did not share their ROE with the United Kingdom during most of Desert Shield.[25] Similarly, the British force commander, despite the presence of Royal Navy liaison officers on board U.S. command ships, found senior American naval officers unwilling to reveal the details of their plans for war against Iraq. This, in turn, created a negative effect on the forward positioning of the naval forces in the Arabian Gulf. As one analyst stated,

> The UK, for example, was eager to push farther up into the Gulf, but forces were not permitted north of a line from the Dhorra oilfield. Therefore, the allies were not allowed to deploy maritime patrol aircraft in the threatened area to track and counter the enemy mining effort or to allocate forces to establish a hold in the fighting area. In all likelihood, this led to a significant mining threat because the area was not covered.[26]

Rules of engagement mismatches could restrict operational flexibility as well. One problem posed by having coalition naval units with different ROE operating in loose association was demonstrated by the 8 October 1990 attempt to stop the Iraqi merchantman *Al Wasitti*. The ship was intercepted in the Gulf of Oman by three coalition frigates: HMS *Battleaxe*, HMAS *Adelaide*, and USS *Reasoner*. *Al Wasitti* refused to stop or acknowledge communications from the warships, even after all three had fired warning shots ahead of her.[27] At this point the on-scene commander decided to take control of the ship. Royal Marines flown by helicopter from *Battleaxe* fast-roped to the deck of the merchantman. However, because the British on-scene commander lacked the authority under his ROE to stop the ship without referring the matter to London, it took some time before he received permission from British authorities to allow the Royal Marines to take control and actually stop the ship. Yet, while all of this was going on, a U.S. boarding team was chasing along behind the merchantman in a motor whaleboat in an attempt to catch up.[28] The *Al Wasitti* incident highlighted the hazard to personnel when the naval forces lacked adequate operational cohesion.

By late November 1990, it was becoming evident to the United Nations that the effects of the embargo were insufficient to prod Saddam into withdrawing occupation forces from Kuwait. Accordingly, on 29 November the Security Council passed Resolution 678, authorizing coalition forces to employ "all means necessary" after 15 January 1991 to remove the Iraqi army from Kuwait.[29] With this indication that war with Iraq was fast approaching, and in response to national concerns about the haphazard MIO command and control arrangements, several of the more important coalition naval contingents—only a few weeks or, in some cases, days prior to the start of Desert Storm—were authorized by their governments to place themselves under U.S. Navy operational control, if it became necessary.

At the beginning of December, the commander of British forces in the Middle East directed his seagoing task group in the Gulf operating area to draft operational plans "for an offensive campaign by the Navy high up in the Gulf."[30] Subsequently, the task group's Type 42 destroyers were placed under U.S. tactical control.[31] Similarly, when the Australian ships HMAS *Brisbane* and HMAS *Sydney* rotated into the area of responsibility on 3 December to replace *Darwin* and *Adelaide* on station, their operating limit had been extended to include the Arabian Gulf, and they had been authorized, if necessary, to come under USN operational control. Two days later, the Australian Prime Minister publicly announced that Australian forces would carry out Resolution 678.[32]

Canada's theater representative, Commodore K. J. "Ken" Summers, CN, met with Rear Admiral Daniel P. March, USN, the new commander of the U.S. battle force in the Arabian Gulf, on 1 January 1991 to discuss a heightened role for the Canadian task group in the event of war. Because the destroyers HMCS *Athabaskan* and HMCS *Terra Nova* lacked area defenses for antiair warfare (AAW), the two commanders decided that the Canadian warships would serve as escorts for the Combat Logistics Force operating in the lower-threat area of the southern Gulf. A week later, on 9 January, the U.S. and coalition representatives attending the monthly MIO coordination meeting agreed that a Canadian officer would coordinate the renamed Combined Logistics Force operating in the Southern Arabian Gulf. Captain Duncan E. "Dusty" Miller, CN, was quickly designated the subordinate antisurface warfare commander for UNREP (underway replenishment) area Sierra.[33] It proved a fortuitous role, both for the Canadian task group and for the American battle force in the Gulf. As Canadian official historians Jean Morin and Richard Gimblett emphasized,

> Participation in, and command of, the CLF [Combined Logistics Force] was a task tailor-made for the Canadian naval task group. They had expressed a desire for an identifiable role, and there was a need for a separate logistical force. But nothing was preordained. Despite the extensive [command, control, and communications and Phalanx close-in weapons system] upgrades prior to deployment, neither Canadian destroyer could rightfully claim a spot in the defensive lines to the north, though they did credible service as escorts in the reduced threat area of the southern waters. To the credit of the Canadian navy must go the fact that each of its three ships in the Gulf had something specific to offer the Coalition. *Athabaskan* was fitted out as a command flagship for a task group, with a staff well-versed in coordinating NATO alliance operations. In *Terra Nova* Captain Miller had under his direct control a hardworking escort with which to encourage greater participation from the other partners. And *Protecteur*'s pre-war experience as the central Gulf MIF supply ship made her a natural model for the logistical force.[34]

The last of the major coalition partners to put their task groups under U.S. control were the Netherlands and Italy. In part because of the ongoing failure of the WEU forces in the region to create an effective naval command and control structure, on 9 January the Dutch government announced that it was placing its deployed warships under USN operational control to serve as escorts for the American aircraft carriers in the event of war. Italian warships were put under American operational control shortly thereafter.[35]

Coalition Maritime Interception Operations in the Gulf Region, 1991–2001

The conclusion of the fighting in Iraq at the end of February 1991 did not end the requirement for MIO in the Gulf region. On 2 March the UN Security Council passed Resolution 686 affirming that all 12 conditions relating to Iraq continued to have "full force and effect" and demanded that Iraq implement its acceptance of these measures. It also "recognized" that during the period required for Iraq to comply with these resolutions, its member states—in the furtherance of Resolution 678—should continue to use all necessary means to uphold and implement the United Nations' measures and to restore international peace and security in the area.[36] The Security Council was convinced that continuing enforcement of the maritime embargo against Iraq would be vital in helping to induce Saddam Hussein's regime to comply. The major problem with the plan, however, was that most of the national naval contingents involved during Desert Shield/Desert Storm were already on the verge of overstretching their available resources.

USN photo, PH3 Brad Dillon

The cruiser USS *Bunker Hill* launches a Tomahawk missile during Operation Desert Storm, the allied offensive against Iraq in January 1991.

General H. Norman Schwartzkopf Jr., USA, Commander in Chief, U.S. Central Command announced his intention on 16 April to keep the Middle East Force of five combatants, a carrier battle group, and a Special Operations Capable (SOC) Marine Expeditionary Unit (MEU) in the Gulf as the enhanced naval presence.[37] Nonetheless, even for the U.S. Navy, maintaining this level of presence in the region would be difficult as the United States scaled down its forces overall. In July 1991 Schwartzkopf's opposite number, Admiral Charles R. Larson, USN, Commander in Chief, U.S. Pacific Command called for providing additional flexibility by employing innovative scheduling and task organized forces, including components such as land-based Air Force and Army forces, to support exercises or contingencies in Central Command. As Larson stressed, "Any increases in forward deployed strength or additional commitments exacerbate already tight and frequently exceeded PERSTEMPO/OPTEMPO constraints. Naval force requirements . . . should not be viewed as the only presence option."[38]

Problems maintaining the maritime interdiction operations against Iraq were exacerbated because the end of the fighting offered a suitable excuse for many coalition partners to have their heavily burdened warships gradually return home. At the Second Post-Hostilities Maritime Commanders (MACOM) Conference on 7 June, Rear Admiral Raynor A. K. Taylor, USN, the dual-hatted head of U.S. Naval Forces in CENTCOM and Commander Middle East Force, who also served as Commander Task Force (CTF) 152 (Maritime Interception Force), stressed to his coalition colleagues present that because of the "expensive and resource-intensive" nature of MIO, they should advise their governments to replace sea-based operations with "simplified ashore methods."[39] The Royal Navy representative, Captain Peter J. Cowling, who was serving as Commodore Task Group 321.1, agreed completely with Taylor. He told the assembled officers, "The Western Europe . . . meeting in Paris had agreed that embargo operations could cease forthwith . . . it remains up to the individual governments . . . to support this position and to decide how to reallocate resources . . . a number of nations see their objectives in the Gulf as not being totally reliant on embargo operations."[40] Yet despite the plea made at this second postwar MACOM Conference for moving the embargo enforcement operation ashore, MIO evolutions continued as before, even as the number of coalition navies available to carry them out dwindled.

By mid-July 1991 the count of merchant vessels intercepted since August 1990 (the beginning of Desert Shield) numbered 10,929. Of these, 102 ships had been diverted after boarding.[41] Six weeks later, in a proposed press release on the anniversary of multinational maritime interception operations, Rear Admiral Taylor announced that in the Red Sea three U.S. Navy warships, an American support ship, and one French warship were enforcing the maritime embargo.[42] At the Sixth Post-Hostilities MACOM Conference on 24 October 1991, Taylor commented that while there had been 22 countries represented at the first conference, just nine remained. He noted that at the June and August conferences the attendees had agreed "it would be prudent" to move the embargo inspection teams ashore, but such a consideration remained within the purview of the foreign ministries of the participating countries, rather than their navies. Taylor remarked that the "current issue is the need for more multinational force participation, not only to provide some relief for the busy teams but also to send a signal to the international community that this is a multinational effort."[43]

In response to Taylor's October comments, the Australian representative replied that the Australian Navy would be represented in the embargo force until the end of January 1992 but that future participation by Australia's Commander Task Group (CTG) 627.4 beyond that time had not been decided.[44] In another pessimistic vein, the British representative, CTG 321.1, commented that the "UK understands the urgency of the request for Navy assistance, but awaits [a] Foreign Office formal request before they can participate in North Red Sea maritime interception ops."[45]

Less than ten days later, Secretary of State James A. Baker III sent a message to the American ambassadors in the coalition countries that had participated in the war with Iraq, asking them to encourage the host governments to continue participating in the multinational maritime interception force or to "re-engage" their naval forces in it. The message noted:

Since the end of Desert Storm, the number of ships and countries participating in maritime intercept operations has been steadily declining. In the Northern Red Sea, the number of intercepting ships has decreased by more than half, and the number of nations to just three (the U.S., France, and Australia).

We are concerned that support for maritime interception operations has eroded. If the withdrawal of ships continues, the multinational character of the force will be lost and less stringent enforcement of the UN sanctions regime against Iraq will have to be accepted.[46]

This need for adequate multinational naval presence in MIO remained a U.S. concern throughout much of the 1990s.[47] The overall burden of the maritime embargo was decreased somewhat beginning in late August 1994, however, when at-sea maritime interdiction operations in the North Red Sea were replaced by ship inspections ashore at Aqaba, Jordan. There, the United Nations contracted with Lloyd's Register of London to conduct the inspection regime.[48]

Despite the significantly smaller number of coalition vessels involved in day-to-day MIO during the latter half of the 1990s—Canada, for example, had no warships deployed in the Gulf region from April 1992 through the spring of 1995 and, beginning in 1997, deployed only a single patrol frigate to the region each year—the ships involved in the ongoing effort kept to a busy pace.[49] By the end of 1993, it was estimated that the total number of boardings since the start of Desert Shield had reached 8,500, and nearly 1,000 cargo ships carrying goods for Iraq had been diverted.[50] And by the end of 1995, U.S. Navy warships alone had conducted more than 23,000 maritime interceptions of merchantmen bound for or returning from Iraq.[51]

The U.S. Navy's role in Gulf region maritime interception continued to be the predominant one throughout the 1990s. In addition to being the coalition navy that maintained its presence in interception operations throughout the entire period, it maintained a larger number of ships in the area of responsibility than any of the other countries involved.

In addition to its specific interception responsibilities, the USN carried out two vital tasks that enabled maritime interception to be safely

Front to back, cruisers USS *Lake Erie* and USS *Chosin*, ammunition ship USS *Mount Hood*, and oiler USS *Cimarron* steam toward the area of responsibility assigned to Naval Forces Central Command, April 1997.

and effectively carried out. First, American warships—either *Ticonderoga*-class cruisers or *Arleigh Burke*-class destroyers equipped with Aegis radar and advanced C3I (command, control, communications, and intelligence) systems—took responsibility for providing defensive counter-air support (area AAW) to coalition warships engaged in intercept operations in the Arabian Gulf.[52] Although most of the combatants of the other coalition navies were equipped to furnish point defense against discrete incoming air attacks, area air defense was a role that only the USN Red Crown ships could provide for the surface forces engaged in the maritime interception effort.

Second, the U.S. Navy (and other service or national assets) provided the coalition with the strategic- and operational-level intelligence. Such information allowed the coalition navies to carry out maritime interception operations successfully against the wide variety of Gulf-region shipping with the small number of warships available for the effort. For example, USN P-3 Orion aircraft equipped with inverse-synthetic-aperture radar carried out extensive over-water surveillance in the region during the Gulf War and thereafter. As several members of VP-19 noted in an August 1991 article:

Within hours of the initiation of Operation Desert Shield, patrol aircraft commenced surveillance support of interdiction efforts on all sides of the Arabian Peninsula from detachments on the Red and North Arabian seas. These detachments provided four to five missions per day that queried all merchant ships plying routes to Iraqi or Jordanian ports as well as activity in the vicinity of the Gulf of Oman. This surveillance effort effectively blanketed all traffic in the region with unlimited support to boarding operations by providing initial location and query, tracking, and communications relay.[53]

Reinforcing this point about the value of U.S. Navy aerial surveillance during the conflict, in 1992 Rear Admiral Anthony Maness, Commander, Patrol Wings Pacific stated that in MIF operations during Desert Shield, P-3 patrol planes "identified and evaluated more than 6,300 ships and all critical contacts of interest entering the area."[54] That effort saved wear and tear on ships and their crews.

Moreover, the addition of new weapon systems and sensors to the U.S. Navy's inventory during the later half of the 1990s increased USN capability for maritime surveillance in the Gulf region and elsewhere. For example, the introduction of the new F-14D "Super" Tomcat fighter into the fleet in 1996 allowed the Navy to operationally deploy two advanced

USN photo, PH2 Rebecca Kerns

A rigid hull inflatable boat, or RHIB, used in approaching vessels suspected of carrying contraband, passes by USS *Benfold*. The *Arleigh Burke*-class guided missile destroyer is participating in multinational maritime interception operations in the Northern Arabian Gulf, enforcing UN sanctions against Iraq, 1997.

passive sensors—the Infrared Search and Track (IRST) system and night vision goggles (NVGs)—for use in the nighttime maritime interception role. As one officer noted, "For maritime TARPS [Tactical Air Reconnaissance Pod System], the IRST and NVGs provide battle group commanders a night visual-identification capability for naval and merchant ships. Ships steaming without running lights can still be identified on NVGs and the IRST and filmed using [the aircraft's] TARPS infrared line-scanner."[55] And a year later, the emergence of the TARPS (DI [digital imagery])-equipped F-14 aircraft added a near real-time imagery capability to the Navy's arsenal.[56] These systems proved of immediate value in helping to identify quickly merchant vessels entering the interception zone that were likely candidates for boarding.

Ultimately, the success of coalition MIO in the Gulf region during the 1990s was directly attributable to the ongoing efforts of the navies

An F-14A Tomcat from Fighter Squadron 32 took this photograph of bomb damage at an Iraqi fertilizer plant, using the tactical air reconnaissance pod system, or TARPS.

involved—particularly the USN and the allied navies of the United Kingdom, Canada, and Australia—to exercise together regularly and to maintain adequate operational and communications interoperability. Although the issues of differing national ROE and restrictions on the releasability of information continued to concern them, the coalition navies carried out their embargo enforcement operations with considerable skill and effectiveness throughout the turbulent decade of the 1990s.

The author made full use of both classified and unclassified material from the U.S. Navy, the U.S. Department of Defense, and other U.S. government agencies and activities. Although the classified information cited or quoted in this chapter was reviewed, subsequently declassified, and cleared for open publication by the Department of Defense's Office of Security Review, the classified documents used in drafting the chapter retain their original classifications.

Notes

1. *Maritime Interception Operations NTTP 3-07.11*, U.S. Navy NTTP 3-07.11/U.S. Coast Guard CGP 3-07.11, Edition Nov 2003 (Washington, DC: Office of the Chief of Naval Operations, Department of the Navy and Headquarters, U.S. Coast Guard, 2003), 2-1. Although many U.S. allies, including the Royal Navy and the Canadian Navy, use the term "maritime interdiction operations" rather than the U.S.-employed term "maritime interception operations," both terms are similarly defined in normal usage. Ibid., 8-1.

2. *Maritime Interception Operations NTTP 3-07*, 2-1–2-2.

3. Michael Johnson, Peter Swartz, and Patrick Roth, *Doctrine for Partnership: A Framework for U.S. Multinational Naval Doctrine* (Alexandria, VA: CNA, March 1996), 16d.

4. Johnson et al., *Doctrine for Partnership*, 17.

5. Edward J. Marolda and Robert J. Schneller Jr., *Shield and Sword: The United States Navy and the Persian Gulf War* (Washington, DC: Naval Historical Center, 1998), 52–53.

6. *Final Report to Congress: Conduct of the Persian Gulf War* (Washington, DC: Department of Defense, April 1992), 49; and Commander Tom Delery, USN, "Away, the Boarding Party!" U.S. Naval Institute (USNI) *Proceedings* 117 (May 1991): 66. Commander Delery was the Maritime Interception Force Officer on the staff of Commander Middle East Force at the time Desert Shield began.

7. *Final Report to Congress: Conduct of the Persian Gulf War*, 49.

8. United Nations Security Council Resolution 665, 25 August 1990, quoted in *Final Report to Congress: Conduct of the Persian Gulf War*, 49.

9. *Final Report to Congress: Conduct of the Persian Gulf War*, 51–52.

10. Marolda and Schneller, *Shield and Sword*, 87; and Lieutenant Commander Richard H. Gimblett, "Canadian Coordination of the Persian Gulf Combat Logistics Force," in

Multinational Naval Forces: Proceedings of a Workshop Held by the Centre for Foreign Policy Studies, Dalhousie University, 13–15 July 1995, eds. Peter T. Haydon and Ann L. Griffiths (Halifax: Centre for Foreign Policy Studies, Dalhousie University, 1996), 232.

11. Declassified information from Timothy J. Carroll, Eric S. Miller, and Commander James M. Warren, USN, *Case Studies of Rules of Engagement in Maritime Coalitions: Earnest Will, Desert Shield/Storm, and Bosnia-Herzegovina* (Alexandria, VA: CNA, July 1994), 40. It should be emphasized that the specific details of the national ROE were not provided during this coordination meeting.

12. Marolda and Schneller, *Shield and Sword*, 87; and Gimblett, "Canadian Coordination of the Persian Gulf Combat Logistics Force," 232–33.

13. Captain R. E. Shalders, RAN, "The Enforcement of Sanctions by the Multi-National Naval Force—An RAN Perspective," *Journal of the Australian Naval Institute* 18 (May 1991): 16. Captain Shalders commanded the Australian frigate *Darwin* that served in the Arabian Gulf from 3 September to 3 December 1990 as part of the initial RAN deployment to the region.

14. *Final Report to Congress: Conduct of the Persian Gulf War*, 52.

15. Declassified information from Timothy J. Carroll, *Multinational Naval Cooperation during Desert Shield and Desert Storm* (Alexandria, VA: CNA, November 1992), 22.

16. Major Jean Morin and Lieutenant Commander Richard H. Gimblett, *Operation Friction 1990–1991: The Canadian Forces in the Persian Gulf* (Toronto: Dundurn Press, 1997), 61–62, 76. See also the back endpapers displaying a map of the Gulf region, entitled "Multinational Interception Force Operations August–December 1990," which shows overlays of the designated Charlie, Bravo, and Alpha sector boxes in the waters of the Arabian Gulf and the Gulf of Oman. The Morin-Gimblett volume is the official Canadian military history of the Gulf War, published for the Directorate of History of the Department of National Defence. It should be noted that Timothy Carroll mistakenly had the Canadian ships operating in the Alpha sectors in the approaches to the Strait of Hormuz. Declassified information from Carroll, *Multinational Naval Cooperation*, 22.

17. Declassified information from Carroll, *Multinational Naval Cooperation*, 22. Aqaba was considered a port of coalition interest because Jordan's government allowed its use for the overland shipment of cargo to Iraq. Marolda and Schneller, *Shield and Sword*, 87.

18. *Final Report to Congress: Conduct of the Persian Gulf War*, 52. The final GCC member— Kuwait—was under Iraqi occupation at the time.

19. Letter, Mauz to Edward J. Marolda, 12 June 1996, quoted in Marolda and Schneller, *Shield and Sword*, 87.

20. Thomas-Durell Young, "Preparing the Western Alliance for the Next Out-of-Area Campaign," *Naval War College Review* 45 (Summer 1992): 35. Young was citing Assembly of the Western European Union, *Consequences of the Invasion of Kuwait: Continuing Operations in the Gulf Region*, Report, Document 1248 (Paris: 7 November 1990), 14.

21. Shalders, "The Enforcement of Sanctions by the Multi-National Naval Force," 16; and Gimblett, "Canadian Coordination of the Persian Gulf Combat Logistics Force," 237, 239. Indeed, Gimblett stated, "Even before the present crisis arose, interoperability with the USN was at a high level. . . . Those facilities were upgraded for the Gulf deployment, such that the Canadian 'connectivity' with the USN was arguably the best in the Coalition." Gimblett, 242 fn11.

22. Shalders, "The Enforcement of Sanctions by the Multi-National Naval Force," 17.

23. See [Rear Admiral] Ken Doolan [AO RANR], "The Gulf Challenge," in *Maritime Power in the Twentieth Century: The Australian Experience*, ed. David Stevens (St. Leonards, NSW: Allen & Unwin, 1998), 204. As Maritime Commander Australia during 1990–1991, Rear Admiral Doolan was in overall charge of the ships of the combatant force deployed to the Gulf for Desert Shield/Desert Storm. He remained in Sydney, however. Commodore Don Chambers initially served as the deployed task group commander of the three Australian warships. Commodore Chris Oxenbould reported as his relief in early December 1990.

24. Operational interoperability is "the ability of maritime forces to operate together as a team, to account for each other's abilities and constraints, and to press forward together to accomplish the mission." Michael Johnson, with Richard Kohout and Peter Swartz, *Guidelines for the World's Maritime Forces in Conducting Multinational Operations: An Analytic Framework* (Alexandria, VA: CNA, March 1996), 75.

25. Captain G. A. S. C. Wilson, Royal Navy (Retired), *Maritime Rules of Engagement: The European Perspective* (Alexandria, VA: CNA, July 1994), 42.

26. Wilson, *Maritime Rules of Engagement: The European Perspective*, 44. Echoing this concern about the lack of information on U.S. Navy war planning available to even allied navies at the time, Australian Rear Admiral Mark Bonser stressed, "[W]e saw very little detail until well after our ships had deployed and integrated into the relevant task force in the US naval component." Rear Admiral Mark Bonser, AO CSC RAN, "RAN Persian Gulf Operations in Perspective," *Journal of the Australian Naval Institute* 115 (Summer 2005): 7.

27. *Final Report to Congress: Conduct of the Persian Gulf War*, 58.

28. Declassified information from Carroll, *Multinational Naval Cooperation*, 15. The unfortunate delays caused by unacknowledged differences in delegated authority were specifically noted by Rear Admiral Doolan in "The Gulf Challenge," 203. Similarly, another senior Australian participant noted, "In one early operation where the scene of action coordinator had less flexible ROE than the assisting forces it took 37 hours to gain effective control of the Iraqi vessel—this despite the fact that we had a combined USN/RAN boarding party embarked for over 24 hours." Shalders, "The Enforcement of Sanctions by the Multi-National Naval Force," 19.

29. Gimblett, "Canadian Coordination of the Persian Gulf Combat Logistics Force," 233. For the complete text of UNSCR 678 see *Final Report to Congress: Conduct of the Persian Gulf War*, 329–330.

30. Gimblett, "Canadian Coordination of the Persian Gulf Combat Logistics Force," 233, quoting General Peter de la Billière, *Storm Command: A Personal Account of the Gulf War* (London: Harper Collins, 1992), 137.

31. Wilson, *Maritime Rules of Engagement: The European Perspective*, 44.

32. Commodore C. J. Oxenbould, RAN, "Maritime Operations in the Gulf War," *Journal of the Australian Naval Institute* 18 (May 1991): 33; and Gimblett, "Canadian Coordination of the Persian Gulf Combat Logistics Force," 233. Commodore Oxenbould was the Australian task group commander during Desert Storm.

33. Morin and Gimblett, *Operation Friction*, 180, 182–83. See also Gimblett, "Canadian Coordination of the Persian Gulf Combat Logistics Force," 234–37; and Marolda and Schneller, *Shield and Sword*, 128–29.

34. Morin and Gimblett, *Operation Friction*, 193. For a detailed listing of the upgrades made to the Canadian ships sent to the Gulf, see ibid., Appendix C, "Ship Equipment Upgrades for Operation Friction," 268–69.

35. Young, "Preparing the Western Alliance for the Next Out-of-Area Campaign," citing (respectively) *Hilversum International Service*, 9 January 1991 in *Foreign Broadcast Information Service—Western European Union*, No. 91-007, 10 January 1991, 12 and *ANSA (Roma)*, 18 January 1991 in *Foreign Broadcast Information Service—Western European Union*, No. 91-013, 18 January 1991, 45.

36. Text of UNSCR 686, 2 March 1991, in *Final Report to Congress: Conduct of the Persian Gulf War*, 330–31.

37. Declassified information from memorandum from Rear Admiral J. D. Cossey, Assistant Deputy Chief of Naval Operations (Plans, Policy, and Operations) to Chief of Naval Operations, Subj: "Desert Storm SITREP # 85 . . . " 19 April 1991, 1.

38. Declassified extract from a message from USCINCPAC to CJCS, Subj: "Post Desert Storm Force Presence Policy," 072300Z Jul 91, 1–2.

39. Minutes of Second MACOM Conference, 7 June 1991, 2, quoted in Robert H. Caldwell, "The Canadian Navy, Interoperability, and USN-Led Operations in the Gulf Region from the First Gulf War to 2003," chap. 7 herein, 195. On Taylor's elevation to the position of COMUSNAVCENT, see Marolda and Schneller, *Shield and Sword*, 336.

40. Minutes of Second MACOM Conference, 7 June 1991, 2–3, quoted in Caldwell, chap. 7 herein, 196.

41. Declassified information from message, COMUSNAVCENT to AIG One Six, Subj: "SITREP COMUSNAVCENT 014 Jul," 150843Z Jul 91 (Part Two of Two), 2.

42. Message, COMUSNAVCENT to USCINCCENT, Subj: "Proposed Press Release ICW [in connection with] the Anniversary of Multinational Maritime Intercept Operations," 280751Z Aug 91.

43. Declassified extract from message, USCINCCENT to CTG Six Two Three et al., Subj: "Maritime Commanders Conference Draft Minutes," 041829Z Nov 91, 2–3.

44. Declassified information from message, USCINCCENT to CTG Six Two Three et al., Subj: "Maritime Commanders Conference Draft Minutes," 041829Z Nov 91, 3.

45. Declassified extract from message, USCINCCENT to CTG Six Two Three et al., Subj: "Maritime Commanders Conference Draft Minutes," 041829Z Nov 91, 4.

46. Declassified extract from message, Secretary of State to AMEMBASSY Canberra et al., Subj: "Maintaining Maritime Interception Operations," 1.

47. Declassified information from, for example, message, COMUSNAVCENT to USCINCCENT, Subj: "Multinational Support for Maritime Intercept Operations," 110550Z Jun 92.

48. Declassified information from *U.S. Naval Forces Central Command /Middle East Force 1994 Command History*, enclosure to memorandum, Commander, U.S. Naval Forces Central Command to Director of Naval History, no serial, 15 April 1995, "Operations & Maritime Intercept Force" Section, 7-23. See also Scott C. Truver, "The U.S. Navy in Review," USNI *Proceedings* 121 (May 1995): 121.

49. See the chart in Richard Gimblett, *Operation Apollo: The Golden Age of the Canadian Navy in the War Against Terrorism* (Ottawa: Magic Light Publishing, 2004), 33. For a detailed examination of the Canadian deployments during this period, see Caldwell, chap. 7 herein, 199-212.

50. Scott C. Truver, "The U.S. Navy in Review," USNI *Proceedings* 120 (May 1994): 116.

51. Truver, "The U.S. Navy in Review," USNI *Proceedings* 122 (May 1996): 85.

52. For comments on the AAW role of the American Aegis-equipped warships, see, for example, Oxenbould, "Maritime Operations in the Gulf War," 34.

53. Commander Richard Brooks, USN, Lieutenant Commander Skip Hiser, USN, and Lieutenant Commander T. K. Kohl, USN, "If It Was There, P-3s Found It," USNI *Proceedings* 117 (August 1991): 41.

54. Rear Admiral Anthony R. Maness, USN, "Maritime Patrol: Gotcha Covered," USNI *Proceedings* 118 (August 1992): 87.

55. Lieutenant Commander John Wood, USN, "F-14D Exploits Passive Sensors," USNI *Proceedings* 122 (September 1996): 49.

56. Commander Mark L. Bathrick, USN, "Digital F-14s Get the Picture—Fast," USNI *Proceedings* 123 (October 1997): 74.

CHAPTER 2

Royal Navy Operations off the Former Yugoslavia: Operation Sharp Guard, 1991–1996

Stephen Prince and Kate Brett

The role and significance of the Royal Navy's involvement in the former Yugoslavia between 1991 and 1996 are not well known. This judgment could equally be applied to almost all the maritime forces that were connected with this conflict, which ultimately resulted in no allied combat at sea.[1] As the more visible activities of international land and air forces are generally seen only as secondary aspects of the complex Yugoslav conflict, this marginalization is not surprising. The deciding factors in this war were the capability and will of the internal participants on the ground. Yet, for nearly five years of operations, the Royal Navy committed significant resources to a series of international maritime tasks, including Operation Sharp Guard, and provided a national carrier task group to form the maritime element of Operation Hamden.[2] This account examines the Royal Navy's role in the conflict and demonstrates that the combined operations conducted with the armed forces of allies, as well as the joint operations with the other British services, were generally successful. These operations were also essential to fulfill the British government's policy requirements and illustrated many of the tasks that maritime forces have historically undertaken in times of complex emergencies. While many of the effects generated by the Royal Navy were not obvious, they still had significance for both the course of the conflict and the coherence of the western alliance.[3]

The Context of the Conflict

A summary of the conflict's major events is relatively straightforward. Post-1945 Yugoslavia was a complex balance of semi-autonomous elements presided over by its creator, Marshal Tito. After Tito's death on 4 May 1980, the subsequent decade saw local power bases increasingly bolstered by nationalist credentials, and in the first democratic elections in 1990, nationalist parties and politicians emerged as dominant. On 25 June 1991 Slovenia declared its independence, virtually unopposed. Croatia's simultaneous declaration prompted much greater Serb opposition and fighting that lasted into early 1992. Following these secessions, Bosnia-Herzegovina was in a difficult situation, given increasing Serbian domination in a reduced Yugoslavia. Bosnia-Herzegovina had not only a predominantly Muslim population but also large Serbian and Croat communities. Following a referendum, Bosnia-Herzegovina declared independence on 3 March, and later that month ethnic violence erupted, spreading to Sarajevo by 4–5 April. On 6 April the U.S. and European Union governments recognized Bosnia-Herzegovina as an independent state. Ethnic violence continued throughout the year, with the fighting between Muslims and Serbs escalating from March 1993. On 16 April the United Nations Security Council declared Srebrenica a "safe area," adding another five such areas, which became known as "safe havens," on 6 May 1993.[4]

On 5 February 1994 a mortar attack on a Sarajevo market killed 68 people, leading to international outrage and limited NATO air action. Intermittent ground fighting continued throughout 1994, with some limitations placed on heavy weapons' use and infrequent NATO close air support (CAS) to protect the "safe havens." The Muslim-Croat Federation was created in March 1994. After this point, the conflict increasingly focused on fighting between the Federation and the Serbs. Jimmy Carter, the former U.S. president, brokered a cease-fire, which endured throughout the winter of 1994–1995 but was breaking down by March 1995. By May a pattern of Serb attacks on the safe havens led to limited NATO air strikes and the Serbs taking lightly armed UN Protection Force (UNPROFOR) soldiers hostage. NATO authorized a Rapid Reaction Force (RRF) in June to assist UNPROFOR, but the safe havens began to fall, notably Srebrenica on 11 July, with horrific humanitarian consequences and UNPROFOR powerless to intervene. The beginning of August saw a major Croat ground offensive against the Serbs in the region of Krajina. Involving more than 200,000 troops, Operation Storm was the largest military operation in Europe since the Second World War and put the Serbs very much on the defensive for the first time.[5] The net effect of these events was that individual communities allied themselves more firmly with those from similar ethnic backgrounds and believed themselves to be more separate from other ethnic groups than ever before.

A second marketplace mortar attack on Sarajevo on 28 August further enraged world opinion against the Serbs and triggered NATO's Operation Deliberate Force, a selective bombardment, first of Serb

The Balkans

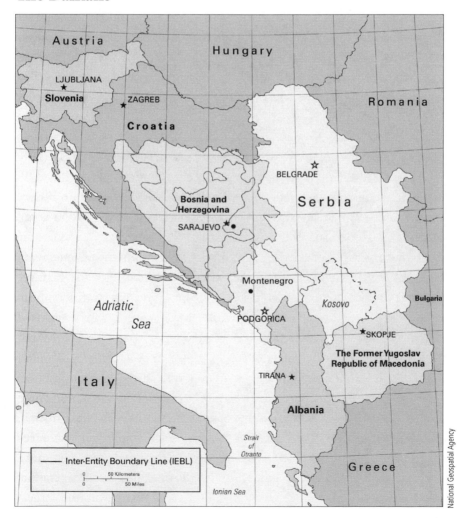

positions, and then of essential infrastructure, delivered by RRF artillery and air power. On 16 September the Serbs accepted all the international community's demands and withdrew from Sarajevo. The Bosnian Croats also agreed to a cease-fire. Following negotiations in Dayton, Ohio, beginning on 1 November, U.S. President Bill Clinton announced a peace agreement on 21 November. Signed in Paris on 14 December, the agreement divided Bosnia-Herzegovina into the Bosniak-Croat Federation of Bosnia and Herzegovina (51% of territory) and the Bosnian-Serb Republika Srpska (49% of territory). On 16 December the North Atlantic Council (NAC) approved Operation Joint Endeavor to implement the Dayton Peace Accords, and on 20 December, NATO's Implementation Force (IFOR) was charged with implementing the peace agreement, incorporating the UN Protection Force.

The international community's interaction with the conflict had gradually increased from 25 September 1991 when United Nations Security Council Resolution (UNSCR) 713 declared an arms embargo against the former Yugoslavia. UNSCR 724 established a Sanctions Committee to oversee the implementation of 713 but without an enforcement provision. UNSCR 743 created the UN Protection Force, initially for deployment in Croatia, although the mandate for this force was extended into Bosnia by June 1992.[6] UNSCR 757 of 30 May 1992 widened trade prohibitions against the former Yugoslavia to include all items except medicine and food, and the UN appealed to regional organizations for enforcement. NATO's North Atlantic Council authorized surveillance in the Adriatic in July 1992 with Operation Maritime Monitor. The Western European Union (WEU) responded with a similar monitoring remit, Operation Sharp Vigilance. On 9 October 1992 UNSCR 781 designated a "no-fly zone" over Bosnia, and under its protection, a UN "airbridge" for humanitarian supplies operated into Sarajevo.[7] On 17 November 1992 UNSCR 787 authorized the maritime monitoring forces to use minimum force to prevent ships from breaking sanctions.

On 17 April 1993 UNSCR 820 provided a much more detailed sanctions regime, which now permitted the international maritime forces, "to halt or otherwise control all shipping in order to inspect and verify their cargoes and destinations."[8] This resolution was part of a package of measures to increase activity at the margins of the conflict while avoiding a full-scale intervention. Between April and August 1993, Operation Deny Flight was established to enforce the no-fly zone, at the same time that the safe areas were designated, protected by NATO-authorized close air support. As part of this process the NATO and WEU maritime operations were combined as Operation Sharp Guard in June 1993. Simultaneously, police forces from the WEU began sanctions enforcement on the Danube in cooperation with Bulgaria, Hungary, and Romania.[9] As with Sharp Guard, this operation would continue until after the Dayton Peace Accords.

Although there was intermittent application of CAS for the UN Protection Force, and extensive enforcement of the no-fly zone from 1994, with NATO shooting down four Serbian fighters on 28 February 1994, international involvement would remain broadly similar from mid-1993 to mid-1995. With the endorsement of the Rapid Reaction Force in June 1995, a more forceful intervention, which included a significant introduction of heavy weapons to UNPROFOR, began.[10] Intervention escalated dramatically with Operation Deliberate Force and was sustained by the deployment of the Implementation Force and its follow-up Stabilization Force (SFOR). In contrast to UNPROFOR, IFOR included U.S. ground forces, a full range of combat equipment, and robust rules of engagement (ROE).[11]

The international community received severe criticism for its limited and gradual introduction of international military forces; some critics have implied that an earlier and more resolute intervention would have secured a swifter and less bloody end to hostilities.[12] However, it must be remembered that the level of intervention was, in large part, determined by perceptions of risk, likely success, and acceptability to domestic opinions. There were also considerable doubts among NATO and WEU political and military leaders that a solution could be imposed while the majority of the domestic participants were still prepared to carry on fighting to gain political advantage. In Bosnia, from 1992 to 1995, there were close to 400,000 personnel under arms, belonging to a wide range of armed forces and militias.[13] NATO judged that any decisive military intervention would have to be on a large scale, with a consequent risk of large-scale casualties as long as these forces and their leaders were still committed to and capable of fighting. As the final UNPROFOR commander in Bosnia put it, "in Bosnia the combatants did not want a collective peace so much as their three distinctive ideas of peace, and were bent on fighting for them."[14] Intervention in such a situation was unacceptable to public opinion in most allied countries, even when they were appalled by the atrocities that occurred during the conflict.[15]

There remained a serious division between the United States and the majority of its NATO allies concerning the best methods and likely consequences of intervention. American policymakers were attracted, certainly from early 1993 onwards, to intervention that would explicitly support the Bosnian Muslims and, later, the Muslim-Croat Federation. They believed that this intervention would enable the lifting of the arms embargo on Bosnia, while U.S. air power would support Bosnian military action against the Bosnian Serbs and Serbia itself. This was summarized as the "lift and strike" policy.[16] Most European states were unconvinced by this analysis, believing that such intervention would prove escalatory and ineffective; that it would endanger newly improved relations with Russia, given that country's close relationship with the Serbs; and that air power would be ineffective in compelling an end to hostilities without introducing ground forces, a measure America refused to contemplate, particularly after the casualties suffered by U.S. forces in Somalia in October 1993.[17] If the United States were to use air power, or if support for UN forces were to decline for any reason, the forces most vulnerable to retaliation would be the scattered units of UNPROFOR in Bosnia—fewer than 20,000 troops, predominantly provided by America's NATO allies, but without heavy weapons or U.S. participation.[18] James Gow, a leading academic from King's College London, has summarized the situation: "The paradox was that UNPROFOR in Bosnia could use force and could call on NATO for aerial support but that this would present risks for UNPROFOR in Bosnia as well as for other elements of UNPROFOR, for the UN in general and possibly for relations between Russia and its Western partners."[19]

This fundamental disagreement over what became the dominant security issue of the mid-1990s meant that "the Alliance itself had been threatened by the war in Bosnia."[20] Only in the early summer of 1995 did a transatlantic consensus for highly active military intervention grow, and even then this was implicit and limited, with much of its ultimate success arising from the previous evolution of events within Bosnia.[21] NATO needed another option for limiting the conflict.

Prior to the transatlantic agreement, the UN Protection Force represented a marginally more viable alternative that sought to manage and contain the worst effects of the conflict with limited liability, but with real and increasing risk.[22] Given its dispersed nature, limited armaments, and restrictive rules of engagement, UNPROFOR was really only effective as a largely symbolic barrier.[23] It relied upon the reluctance of factions to confront it directly and risk international condemnation and retaliation. Its credibility was increased by the threat and occasional employment of close air support in 1994–1995, but the limits of this policy were demonstrated during the widespread hostage-taking of 1995. The U.K. Chief of the Defence Staff, Field Marshal Peter Inge, stated, "It was clear the UN mission was collapsing."[24] UNPROFOR eventually had to evacuate most of its exposed positions and abandon its symbolic protection for Muslim communities before NATO could bombard Serbian positions.

Until that point, however, UNPROFOR had an important role both in mitigating the effects of the conflict and maintaining a minimum strategic consensus within the transatlantic alliance.[25] A similar logic sustained the enforcement of the no-fly zone, the delivery of humanitarian aid, and the maritime interdiction of former Yugoslavia. These measures were limited, developed only gradually, and could not resolve the conflict without more intervention from the international community. However, they provided the type of interventions that allies could manage and keep at acceptable risks, ones that brought genuine physical and psychological benefits, both internationally and in theater. These operations maintained a domestic and an international consensus that helped establish conditions for decisive intervention once the fighting escalated.

The Royal Navy and Maritime Interception Operations

The Adriatic Sea has historically been an area of intermittent Royal Navy deployments. Notably, during the Second World War, there was considerable RN activity, often, after October 1943, in association with the revived Royal Italian Navy. Much of this activity was intended to interdict Axis maritime supply routes to the Balkans and to support Allied forces ashore, including Britain's brigade-size Land Forces Adriatic (LFA) in 1944–1945. These forces operated in support of Tito's Partisans, providing them with supplies, artillery, and forward air controllers. In 1944, following a German air assault on his headquarters, Tito was evacuated to the RN-secured island of Vis. In early 1945, as political relations with Tito cooled, the Royal Navy evacuated the LFA.[26] The Royal Navy remained in the Mediterranean postwar and mounted a major freedom of the seas operation in 1946 in the Corfu Channel following the mining of RN ships. However, by the 1970s the RN permanent presence in the Mediterranean was withdrawn. When HMS *Ark Royal* entered Malta's Grand Harbor during her 1993 Adriatic deployment, she was the first RN carrier to visit the island in 15 years.

The first RN deployment to the Adriatic in response to the modern conflict was the frigate HMS *Minerva* from 1 December 1991. Following Slovenia's and Croatia's succession, John Major's government decided Britain should indicate its interest in the area and concern for the conflict, but without making any form of commitment. A maritime deployment was the most flexible way to achieve this goal and also allowed for contingency planning to evacuate entitled persons if the course of the fighting forced them to leave. In July 1992, following the North Atlantic Council's decision in Helsinki to implement monitoring in support of UN Security Council resolutions, Britain committed a ship to the new NATO operation, Maritime Monitor. The initial NATO force was based on the Standing Naval Force Mediterranean (SNFM, or STANAVFORMED), an international group of surface ships, predominantly destroyers and frigates. It was joined in its task by the WEU Contingency Maritime Force (CONMARFOR), which undertook Operation Sharp Vigilance. In November 1992, in response to UNSCR 787, the missions became enforcement with minimal force and the operations were renamed Maritime Guard and Sharp Fence. On 26 November the Type 42 destroyer HMS *Gloucester* undertook the first boarding operation, the first physical enforcement by a NATO asset, against the MV *Bore C.*

However, the rules of engagement did not permit entry into Montenegrin territorial waters, or the use of force to compel a vessel to submit to boarding. The force structure and posture were therefore inadequate for the task. In June 1993 the operations evolved again; the forces received more robust enforcement powers by the UN and became a single, combined NATO/WEU operation, Sharp Guard.

There was extensive overlap in the nationalities of the NATO and WEU contingents, the main difference being the presence of French ships and the absence of U.S. and Canadian vessels in the latter force. This overlap, as well as a common purpose, ensured close cooperation between the two forces, and the Adriatic was divided into two operational areas, or "opareas." The pair focused on the chokepoint of the Strait of Otranto and the coast of Montenegro, which between them covered 9,000 square miles of sea. The captain of a participating Royal Navy ship summarized the conditions and activities in these opareas:

> The first off the coast of Montenegro, characterized by high threat but low boarding rate and the second in the Otranto Strait, where the boarding rate was high but no threat existed.

> During all operations off the Montenegrin coast the ship patrolled in Defence Watches, remaining inside the envelope of shore based anti-ship missiles throughout her time in the area.

> Operations in Otranto involved monitoring the heavy volume of shipping flowing through the Strait, and conducting boarding and diversion operations as directed by CSNFM [Commander Standing Naval Force Mediterranean]. All boardings were conducted in this area. The threat was nil, and the patrols an extravaganza of boardings, seamanship and helicopter operations.

The Royal Navy was in no doubt that success in this environment required close interoperability, often created between ships which had not previously worked together. Another commanding officer characterized much of the underlying ability to achieve this goal as a remarkable testament to the effectiveness of NATO training and procedures over the years, noting only that the Adriatic does not look much like the RN's training area off Portland.

The Adriatic operations quickly illustrated the need for interoperability. The WEU Contingency Maritime Force was initially a designation of assets rather than a practiced formation. Standing Naval Force Mediterranean had also only been established for two months when Operation Maritime Monitor began. SNFM was the successor to the NATO On-Call Force Mediterranean, which dated back to 1969 but had come together only periodically for exercises. Initially, WEUCONMARFOR deployed to the Strait of Otranto and SNFM to the coast of Montenegro. However, the relative inexperience of these forces, certainly at sustained operations, meant that, despite the modest initial requirements of Maritime Monitor, SNFM was replaced by the more capable Standing Naval Force Atlantic (SNFL, or STANAVFORLANT) from September to December 1992.[27]

Formed in 1968, SNFL had been in permanent existence, regularly exercising, since that date. It was, and is, a combined force of unparalleled endurance and flexibility.[28] Built around a core of five permanent contributing nations, it was formed as a symbolic force that NATO could deploy during a crisis.[29] During the Cold War the force had developed many of NATO's antisubmarine warfare (ASW) concepts and had served as an ideal laboratory for experimentation, leading to the development of many of NATO's Allied Tactical Publications. It had also acted as a means of disseminating practical experience of international cooperation to the contributing navies. This valuable experience led to something of a virtuous circle, with many officers returning to the force throughout their careers. Indeed, at least one SNFL commander during Sharp Guard had served in the force at every rank from sub lieutenant to commodore.[30] This pattern was also linked to the opportunity SNFL gave to members of all participating navies to gain staff and command experience in both the management of a formation and the dynamics of an international force. For some smaller participating nations, service in naval force was the only route to such experience. In the early period of Adriatic operations, the

SNFL provided an excellent opportunity for the broader embargo forces to develop and hone their skills. In December 1992 SNFM relieved SNFL once more, and from this point onwards there was rotation of WEU and NATO ships through the different patrol areas.

The NATO and UN operations achieved full maturity in June 1993 when they were combined as Operation Sharp Guard, with enhanced UN authority to enforce the embargo. The operation faced two daily challenges. The first was achieving constant situational awareness of shipping movements in the busy Adriatic waters and then choreographing the tracking, challenging, inspection, and diversion of suspect vessels as required. The second and more dangerous challenge related to the potential threat posed by the Federal Republic of Yugoslavia (FRY) armed forces against the embargo forces, either in their support to blockade runners or as part of a general escalation of hostilities against the UN and NATO. The Montenegrin coast hosted the FRY's sole naval base in Kotor Bay where the fleet had considerable sea-denial potential. The fleet included four frigates, two corvettes, and a flotilla of about 20 fast attack craft (FAC), torpedo boats, and mine vessels. Five diesel submarines (SSKs), along with a small force of midget submarines and swimmer delivery vehicles, represented a subsurface threat. The frigates and 12 FAC were equipped with Styx antiship missiles, and three more Styx batteries were in place along the coast. The FRY operated a number of versions of the missile, but the most sophisticated types had a range of 50 miles and were sea-skimmers in their terminal stage of attack. In addition, 130mm, radar-directed artillery protected the coastline. The available number of platforms and systems declined during the conflict, in part from the impact of interdiction operations. However, NATO observations of the limited number of exercises undertaken by Yugoslavian forces confirmed that this decline was offset by their growing professional competence.[31]

The Styx missiles had the potential to reach halfway across the Adriatic. Given that the patrol sectors of the Montenegrin coast (oparea of Sharp Guard) lay just outside the 12-mile territorial sea limit, the weapons could strike at picket ships with only a 60–70-second warning.[32] Though an unrealized threat, these missiles remained potent challenges to the embargo forces. Naval forces might also have come under attack from the FRY air forces. Most of these aircraft could operate only during the day, but the FRY could deploy MiG-21 (and possibly MiG-29) jets with rockets, gravity bombs, and some American-made Maverick television-guided missiles. While this threat progressively fell within the enforcement of the no-fly zone, the improvement in conditions has to be set in context. The air picture over the Adriatic remained complex, with not only NATO flights supporting the no-fly zone but also logistical support activity as well as normal civil, commercial, and leisure flights. In these circumstances commanding officers faced the real and sustained prospect of a rapidly developing catastrophic event. The failure to react to a possible air threat could lead to ship loss or damage as in the case of the 1987 USS *Stark* incident when an Iraqi Exocet missile struck and badly damaged the guided missile frigate in the Arabian Gulf. Or, an incident could result from misinterpreting the intentions of a civilian flight as when the Aegis guided missile cruiser USS *Vincennes* accidentally destroyed Iranian Air Flight 655 in 1988. Commanding officers and crews had to prepare for the possibility of both scenarios, and the antiair warfare situation was described as testing.[33]

While no attack ever occurred, the prospect was plausible and enhanced by Yugoslav behavior. FRY ships, shore batteries, and aircraft confronted the blockading ships and their supporting maritime patrol aircraft (MPA); and Yugoslav units occasionally managed to get a missile lock on an allied platform.[34] One senior RN commander was particularly impressed by the restraint shown by a U.S. ship after a FRY frigate attempted to intimidate her with a missile lock. Overall, the four-star assessment of the threat off Montenegro was medium-to-high.

NATO's Commander in Chief, South (CINCSOUTH), a four-star U.S. admiral who made the assessment, was a subordinate of the Supreme Allied Commander Europe. CINCSOUTH in turn delegated control of Operation Sharp Guard to NATO's Commander, Naval Forces South (COMNAVSOUTH), an Italian vice admiral, whose command also dated from the NATO reforms of 1967. COMNAVSOUTH headed Combined Task Force (CTF) 440, whose staff was complemented by a WEU element. Three surface combined task groups operated under this command: CTG 440.1 for the Montenegro coast, CTG 440.2 for the Strait of Otranto, and CTG 440.3 for training and port visits. Each task group was led, in rotation, by the commanders of SNFL, SNFM, and WEUCONMARFOR. This pragmatic combination of established NATO structures and WEU commanders and staff facilitated a unified command with full French participation, while avoiding domestic criticism that France was subordinating itself to NATO.

NATO maritime patrol aircraft also operated in support of Sharp Guard.[35] The increased role of these planes in Sharp Guard from spring 1993, in terms of both data integration and volume of coverage, was a significant innovation to address the requirement to build an improved Recognized Air and Surface Picture (RASP) in the Adriatic as a tool for effective interdiction operations. Situational awareness, in the vicinity of and between the patrolling ships of each group, had been good from an early stage. This capacity was largely due to the almost universal distribution of the Link-11 data-sharing system as a minimum standard for NATO surface ships participating in Sharp Guard.[36] Utilizing their capabilities, Royal Navy ships acted frequently as the local commander for antiair and electronic warfare, but, as with the rest of the ships in the patrol areas, they were unable to cover the gaps between the patrol areas or effectively transmit data to COMNAVSOUTH in Naples, who also lacked the facilities to receive the data. As COMNAVSOUTH put it in late 1992, "A time-late synopsis of the surface picture at regular intervals may be satisfactory for those not directly involved in operations but it is not acceptable for decision making at the level of command responsible for task group planning."[37]

The shortfalls undercut the roles of Sharp Guard ships. An investigation by NATO's Permanent Assessment Team reported in February 1993 that coverage of the Adriatic surface picture extended out to each ship's sensor horizon and no farther, that coverage in the Strait of Otranto was less than 100 percent, and that COMNAVSOUTH's RASP was usually 12–18 hours out of date. It was a situation that blockade runners managed to exploit. The establishment of a U.S. Red Crown ship—usually an Aegis ship or equivalent—which developed a theater-wide Link-11 picture, unified the information from both operational task groups.

When combined with the information from the dramatically increased coverage of NATO/WEU maritime patrol aircraft—which filled the gaps in surface surveillance—a genuine theater picture was achieved. The Red Crown ship, using the U.S. officer in the Tactical Command Information Exchange Subsystem (a data satellite system), then transmitted this picture to COMNAVSOUTH in Naples, where the United States had donated the necessary receiving equipment. The data was also transmitted to the USN Fleet Ocean Surveillance Information Facility (FOSIF) in Rota, Spain, which added value by including broader U.S. information and data from any non-Link–11 NATO ships. FOSIF then retransmitted the enhanced data to all ships participating in Sharp Guard. The Royal Navy greatly admired the U.S. Navy's unique capacity to provide this enhancement for all coalition forces.

Operation Sharp Guard was thus significantly enhanced in spring 1993 by a command system and technical improvements, as well as the commitment of MPA resources, reflecting a general rise in NATO air activity. The operating forces were also physically reinforced when SNFL deployed to the Adriatic on a long-term basis in June 1993. However, the realities of intercepting and inspecting ships, and actually operating in the shadow of an imminent FRY threat, required the development of less-tangible assets. These were determined by the human interaction of the Sharp Guard personnel.

Cooperation at the command level over the application of NATO rules of engagement set the tone for this interaction. The ROE were laid out in the Military Committee's document MC192, guidance designed for actions prior to a general war, and NATO's main concern up to the early 1990s. One frontline RN commander described MC192 as rather inflexible and bald ROE. However, it was put into operation by a CINCSOUTH Implementation Signal, and then importantly expanded by task group commanders in a message known as ENFORCECOMS (Enforcement Coercive Measures). The procedure gave useful insight into the way in which NATO might operate in the future. Such inclusive and proactive consultation was a characteristic of Sharp Guard, with an emphasis on communication and the understanding of the intent of higher commanders. Much of the strength of the Sharp Guard ROE also came from the automatic assumption that an attack on any element of the operation would be considered an attack on all participants. This confidence reflected Article 5 of the NATO Treaty, upheld by all the nations involved since 1949, meaning that the most important element of ROE was established from the outset.

Working from this firm basis, commanders found it much easier to discuss and to accommodate national variations and caveats from the NATO ROE. These derived from national political stances or legal interpretations as well as technical limits. National ROE generally remained classified as national property. However, within the established context of NATO and an atmosphere of cooperation, it was possible to clarify many specific cases and informally acknowledge others. Informal reference sheets of this information were assembled by key staff officers. Ship operations officers also developed informal networks based on early mobile phones, which allowed discreet consultations with colleagues.[38] This situation permitted realistic planning for deployments and tasks, avoiding abrupt or disruptive surprises that had the potential to degrade operations. As the captain of one RN ship put it, "Ships are allocated to an area according to capability, and also as their national ROE and sensitivities permit—so for example neither Greek nor German ships take station in Area MONTENEGRO."[39]

This was no slight intended on Greek or German capabilities, but was a practical recognition that their national authorities would not permit them to board or fire upon sanction breakers. Both nations' ships were able to participate fully in the surveillance and challenge roles in the Strait of Otranto. Similarly, only Canadian, British, Dutch, and American maritime patrol aircraft had both the national permission and the capabilities required to operate over the Montenegrin oparea.[40] The cooperative methodology also facilitated minimal disruption when U.S. policy changed in November 1994, preventing U.S. forces from enforcing the arms embargo against Bosnia-Herzegovina.[41] The deployment of assets was simply adjusted to account for the new limits.

This successful coordination was achieved by a command team much admired by the RN, which found that the officers of the Spanish, Dutch, and Italian navies lost nothing in comparison to any RN officer of their rank, and it became clear that these important NATO seagoing appointments were reserved for men of the highest caliber. One captain thought the secret of success was that the three task group commanders worked together as a team, using the same Operational General Orders, and were consistent in the way they operated. A further comment suggested overall command and control arrangements worked well because coordination was effected by frequent meetings between task group commanders, who enjoyed enviably harmonious working and personal relationships among their staffs.

Effective cooperation also allowed the international forces to conduct extensive exercises during their deployments. When Standing Naval Force Atlantic deployed to Sharp Guard in 1993, it was able to remodel its NATO training package with assistance from France, Spain, and Portugal. This permitted SNFL to practice the embargo, boarding, antiair, and ASW roles that were most relevant to its new deployment. In 1994 realistic air defense exercises were conducted with German Tornados flying actual missile profiles against Royal Navy ships, ensuring that ROE reactions were fully tested. CTG 440.3 provided an opportunity for Sharp Guard ships to practice core skills such as boarding, using allied auxiliaries as targets, and contingency reactions to FRY attacks. Practicing reaction to attacks took place well away from the operational areas so as not to risk misinterpretation by Yugoslav forces or trigger a response. The Italian coast provided a safe "mirror" that all Sharp Guard forces exploited. Generally, Commander, Combined Task Force 440 required a period of training for all new Sharp Guard ships with CTG 440.3 before active deployment.

Royal Navy commanders believed the exercise program was particularly significant for several reasons. In addition to improving ship skills, the program enhanced ship-to-ship understanding and gauged likely international reaction so that these variations could be recognized and, if necessary, addressed or accommodated by the command system before a real incident occurred. It also provided a variety of scenarios for crews rotating through operating areas and reminded them of the potential threat to their operations. This was particularly important to prevent staleness or complacency in a high-threat environment, where crews spent days at defense watches undertaking largely mundane activity without incident. One commanding officer observed that a variety of exercises maintained motivation and served to remind crews of the operational nature of their deployment.

The Royal Navy generally found the activity in the Oparea Otranto the most stimulating. There was usually one RN destroyer or frigate among the five to seven Sharp Guard ships constantly on patrol. These ships surveyed and challenged maritime traffic, often 60 to 90 ships daily, heading through the chokepoint. These volumes were only manageable because of RASP and usually led to 6 to 12 boardings a day.[42] However, these numbers were only averages; in one 48-hour period, HMS *Nottingham* achieved nine boardings, each involving a three-hour search. If the circumstances were suspicious, or the configuration of the target prevented an adequate inspection at sea, the RN would divert the intercepted ship to Italy for a fuller examination.[43] Boardings were undertaken from both sea boats and helicopters. If necessary, some would be undertaken at night, or two boardings would be made simultaneously. This tempo was a severe test of professionalism and seamanship, particularly through the winter. The Royal Navy was justifiably proud of its capacity and record in these operations, which it credited to the RN experience in the somewhat harsher sea conditions around the United Kingdom. Most early boardings were provided by parties drawn from across a ship's departments, and only later were Royal Marine Protection Parties provided to enhance boarding capabilities. This change, together with a greater stress on ships' boats, was symbolic of a shift from the Cold War toward the more complex operations represented by Sharp Guard.[44]

However, the Royal Navy was equally admiring of the work of its allies. In particular, it noticed that the Dutch ships were just as unlikely as the RN to avoid operations during bad weather, and that the Dutch and French were robust and aggressive in their approach to boardings. An RN officer on the spot commented that none of the ships failed to pull its weight, and it was generally noted that Britain's allies worked well in the Sharp Guard environment, with punctilious attention to procedures.

Oparea Montenegro, again with five to seven ships, one of which was usually RN, contrasted sharply with the Strait of Otranto. The focus here was on surveillance just outside the 12-mile limit of FRY territorial waters, rather than a high level of activity. NATO managed to further tighten its blockade by gaining access to Croatian and Albanian territorial waters, thus preventing blockade runners from "hugging" the coast. The Royal Navy assisted with this process by cultivating improved relations with Albania. From 23 to 25 November 1992, HMS *Gloucester*, which had participated in Sharp Vigilance, transferred to Maritime Monitor and then to Maritime Guard, visited Durres in Albania. This Royal Navy visit, the first in 54 years, helped cement the recent restoration of diplomatic relations. Both RN and NATO vessels later benefited from improved relations with Albania. One ship reported in 1994 that the areas around Durres had become familiar territory and noted the surprisingly good cooperation by radio with the Albanian shore authorities who appeared keen to help the NATO forces in their task.

However, Oparea Montenegro was not entirely a zone of inactive tension. On several occasions FRY vessels fired on Italian fishing boats on the edge of their territorial waters. During one of these events, the Sharp Guard ship HMCS *Iroquois* physically interposed herself, causing the FRY vessel to retreat. There were also several attempts to run the blockade. On Christmas Eve 1993, the 90,000-ton fuel carrier MV *Gloria*, having declared a false port, attempted to run for the Montenegro coast under cover of heavy weather. A Dutch destroyer intercepted her, inserted a boarding team by helicopter despite the weather, and took control of the ship only 500 meters from FRY territorial waters.[45] On 1 May 1994 MV *Lido II* also attempted to run the embargo with 45,000–50,000 tons of fuel oils by first declaring a false destination, and then claiming an emergency in order to explain her approach to FRY territorial waters. CTG 440.1 responded by deploying HMS *Chatham*, HMNLS *Van Heemskerk* with a specialist boarding team, and a CP-140 Aurora. The cruiser USS *Philippine Sea* coordinated air demonstration support in the Red Crown role as a FRY corvette and three FAC came out to meet the *Lido II* and opened their missile silos, demonstrating a potentially hostile intent. While the Aurora provided cover, *Van Heemskerk* deployed her boarders to take control of *Lido II*. *Chatham* confronted the FRY force by maneuvering until she was much closer than the minimum range of the FRY missile systems.[46] Faced by this resolute and overwhelming force, the FRY vessels retreated. An RN damage control party determined *Lido II*'s flooding emergency was a fraud and diverted the ship to Italy.[47]

The *Lido II* incident was the most dramatic of Operation Sharp Guard and endorsed the forces involved, their application of ROE, and their enduring cooperation. The overall record of activity and achievement was less dramatic but is still impressive. From 22 November 1992 (the commencement of Maritime Guard and Sharp Vigilance) to 18 June 1996, NATO and WEU forces deployed 19,699 ship days and 13,325 sorties. They challenged 74,192 ships, boarded and inspected 5,951, and diverted 1,480 for further inspection in Italy. Six were found to be trying to break UN sanctions, and there is no record or indication of any successful blockade running after the commencement of Operation Sharp Guard, as opposed to the five ships that evaded the embargo before it commenced.[48]

On 15 May 1996 SNFL was released from Sharp Guard, left the Adriatic and the Mediterranean, and, in a significant moment, passed the Rock of Gibraltar into the Atlantic for the first time in more than three years. The verdict of the Royal Navy's commanding officers on the experience was positive but included an appreciation of the issues it highlighted. One recorded that, inevitably, not all was perfect and drew attention to the incompatibilities of equipment and communications, but also commented that, despite the problems, the overall impression was one of great cohesion.

Another officer summarized his experience as immensely satisfying and educational. He commented that operating alongside so many different ships, drawn from most of the NATO nations, had taught something to everyone on board, not least that each ship, of whatever nationality, was generally well able to operate very effectively at that intensity of maritime operations. There were impressive performances from ships who initially seemed either poorly equipped or trained, but who quickly became proficient at the task in hand.

Overall, Royal Navy reports repeatedly stress the importance of interaction, formal and informal, to appreciate the positions and potential of the other ship-contributing nations and an underlying admiration for the competence displayed. The development of this human network was central to Sharp Guard's success. However, a major part of this interaction was beyond Sharp Guard, with the wider network of maritime forces operating in the Adriatic.

The Royal Navy's National Task Group

From 26 January 1993 the Royal Navy maintained a national task group (UKTG 612) in the Adriatic, led by an *Invincible*-class aircraft carrier, initially HMS *Ark Royal*.[49] This task force would remain in the Adriatic, with availability varying between one and 96 hours' notice, to support operations ashore for the next three years, with HMS *Illustrious* finally leaving the Adriatic on 4 March 1996. It was one of three regular carrier deployments, with France and the U.S. inserting carrier task groups alongside shortly afterwards. Sustaining this deployment represented a considerable challenge, and success, for a Royal Navy with only three carriers, two of which were in commission at any one time, and only two air groups.[50] While the primary role of the task force was focused on the British Force (BRITFOR) of the UN Protection Force, it would have a much wider role in the Adriatic, with important implications for Sharp Guard.

The task force deployment fitted into the general pattern of increasing maritime and air operations around the former Yugoslavia in the first half of 1993. They were intended to intensify the pressure on combatants, particularly the Bosnian Serbs and Serbia. However, there was the chance that the augmentation might increase the risk to the deployed forces, UNPROFOR in particular, and also the Sharp Guard ships in Oparea Montenegro. The first commander of Britain's task force understood that his arrival offered both "potential help and potential complication."[51] Building on both informal contact and NATO commonalities, he noted it was quickly possible to establish the Adriatic-wide recognized air and maritime pictures, to cooperate in assembling them, and to exchange vital tactical information of mutual interest. In due course, units were also able

Naval Historical Branch, U.K. [a]

The frigate HMS *Broadsword* leads the Royal Navy's National Task Group in the Adriatic in 1993. The task group also comprises the aircraft carrier HMS *Ark Royal* and the RFAs *Olwen*, *Argus*, and *Fort Grange*.

to make use of each others' fuel tankers as well as the occasional exercise opportunity. Subsequent UKTG commanders worked to make cooperation more established. By mid-1993 the establishment of routine Adriatic coordination meetings between commanders afloat and their staffs had greatly enhanced the inter task group coordination. Modeled on similar allied meetings in the Arabian Gulf post-1991, these regular monthly meetings at the staff level produced excellent results in terms of coordination and training. Informal meetings between the commanders themselves took place on a regular basis.

A result of this interaction was the publication of a *modus operandi* by the commander of USN Task Force 60 (the carrier battle group of the U.S. Sixth Fleet) as a concept of operations. Based on NATO procedures, this document "laid the foundation for the remarkably smooth running situation of overlapping co-ordination, command and control."[52] An early benefit of this cooperation was a coordinated carrier program, which allowed a roulement, or rotation, of the carriers at varying degrees of notice, easing the strain on all the carrier groups. When there was some nervousness in France that such an arrangement implied commitments to support troops of another nationality that could not be agreed to at the task group level, the outcome was an agreement to coordinate plans as much as possible without the commitment to a formal roulement.[53]

The national task groups not only benefited from the Recognized Air and Surface Picture in the Adriatic provided by Sharp Guard and Deny Flight operations but also contributed to it. The inherent flexibility of naval platforms allowed them to rapidly "chop" between national and NATO commands in order to fill the most pressing requirements. The national groups also offered surface combat air patrols to embargo forces on the "front line" of Oparea Montenegro, with the RN providing Sea Harrier jets and Lynx missile armed helicopters either on station or on alert. Given the proximity of the carriers to the threatened sector, they provided a much faster reaction time and longer loiter than land-based assets, although the Sea Harriers also benefited from land-based air-to-air refueling. The carriers also provided coverage that was far less dependent on the weather given their ability to avoid the mist that frequently interfered with flying operations based in Italy.[54] Again, it was possible to provide this sort of contingency coverage, without controversy or national compromise, because of the close working relationships established and because of the enduring framework of NATO's Article 5, which meant that collective defense was uncontroversial.

Air cover was important in enhancing the deterrent against any FRY attack on the embargo forces. It operated in a manner similar to, if more visible than, NATO submarines, including those of the Royal Navy, which provided a more discreet deterrent and obtained indicators and warnings from close inshore.[55] These operations, and the constant training for them, were important for two reasons. First, they enhanced the force protection and sought to mitigate the consequences of any attack on embargo ships. Second, they provided a high level of readiness for contingency plan Wolf Pen—an attack on the FRY naval forces based in Kotor Bay. This contingency plan had the potential involvement of a wide range of NATO and national assets, including land-based air from Italy, which could have been launched in retaliation to a FRY naval or air attack on Sharp Guard or national forces.[56] Wolf Pen could also have been initiated as part of a general escalation in hostilities against alliance or UN forces, particularly if there had been any question of interference against NATO and national forces engaged in the support or evacuation of UNPROFOR. Thus the Sharp Guard and national task groups were able to closely align their tasks and interests in a case of extreme emergency.

Supporting national forces ashore was the main reason behind the deployment of both the British and the French carrier tasks groups.[57] The force was poised, as one commander wrote, in the most classic, most ancient—and in the future, probably the most likely—form of naval operations, with the Navy holding itself ready to support the land battle at short notice in whatever way the land forces required. The initial UKTG, which included more than 350 troops embarked on RFA *Argus*, was held ready to reinforce UNPROFOR offshore from the port of Split, the British logistic hub. The task group's equipment included six 105mm guns, 200 extra vehicles, and mortar-locating radar. The personnel included extra logistic and medical staff and the vital gunfire support team from 148 Battery, Royal Artillery, the joint team required to target naval gunfire ashore.[58]

The deployment reflected the perceived rise in tension in the Balkans as UNPROFOR's role spread in both breadth of deployment and mission. It was also ready to counter the possible Serbian reaction to the imposition of a no-fly zone, which was then being discussed.[59] The UKTG arrived on station off Split on 26 January; the first British soldier to be

Naval Historical Branch, U.K. [c]

RFA *Argus* alongside in Split, with British vehicles for UNPROFOR in the foreground. *Argus* performed a dual role as a logistical base for troops ashore and as an essential component of contingency plans for evacuation.

killed in action in Bosnia had died in Gornji Vakuf 13 days before.[60] The positioning of the UKTG offered an immediate and viable reaction force for enlarged intervention or the coverage of evacuation. Other options elevated the risk of holding the required forces too far back to assist when required, or committing combat forces whose very deployment could provoke action against UNPROFOR. The maritime deployment retained flexibility without commitment. When the situation improved, the majority of the personnel, and then the artillery, could be withdrawn—the guns after over three months on station—without any apparent retreat. For the next 30 months, a force package tailored to the situation was retained in shipping alongside at Split or offshore as required.

The maritime combat force package could also have been adjusted rapidly to supply the large number of transport helicopters essential to Commander British Force, who did not have enough transport to withdraw without this assistance. The aircraft carrier retained the ability to convert to the helicopter carrier role to support BRITFOR and, over time, was also able to provide command and control and medical facilities to the troops ashore. Similar arrangements were also practiced by the French, working out of their base in Ploce and, to a lesser extent, by the Canadian Navy, which was prepared to surge a force of destroyers, frigates, auxiliaries, and helicopters.[61] Such support also meant coordination of national plans. After a Dutch escort frigate joined the UKTG, the commander's directive about being prepared to assist was amended from just British to read UN troops.[62] In April 1993 *Ark Royal* was ordered to stand by to support Canadian troops in Srebrenica. Lacking in this period its own large-scale amphibious capability, by 1995 the Royal Navy was exchanging selected officers with the USN Mediterranean amphibious ready group in order to prevent any fade in skills. Also, by 1995 cross-deck exercises took place between the British, American, and French carriers and different national command assets were exchanged.

This extensive activity and contingency planning addressed what was a fundamental, grand strategic issue for the British government, which wanted to participate fully in UNPROFOR but also wished to minimize the risk of massive losses. This risk was inherent to UNPROFOR's situation as a lightly armed force surrounded by unpredictable armed factions. In December 1992, the prime minister had met with the Chief of the Defence Staff at Split about this issue, confirming the necessity of providing BRITFOR with the option of air and artillery support to allow reinforcement or cover evacuation. This strategic requirement was consistently maintained, with the U.K. Secretary of Defence stating in the spring of 1995 that it was essential that BRITFOR could be evacuated from Bosnia, preferably with its equipment.[63] Only maritime forces could be poised to fulfill this requirement. The relative viability of this option was well illustrated when NATO produced OPLAN 40104 in the spring of 1995, a study of an evacuation of all 40,000 UNPROFOR troops, largely by land routes. The plan assessed that such an operation would require extensive host nation support and would necessitate the introduction to theater of 60,000 NATO troops to execute it.[64]

An essential element of any operations, from spring 1993 onwards, was the provision of air support. The establishment of the no-fly zone was required not just to prevent the offensive use of FRY aircraft but also to provide clear skies for air support such as resupply and medical evacuation by helicopter. The no-fly zone also facilitated air intercept, reconnaissance, show of force, and close air support by fixed-wing aircraft. The constant availability of such support was particularly important to UNPROFOR given its isolation and the simultaneous lack of heavy weapons and exposure to them. Royal Navy Fleet Air Arm helicopters operating from both Split and afloat and Sea Harriers operating from the carriers formed part of this support for BRITFOR and wider UNPROFOR, as did other carrier aircraft. Symbolic of the shift of emphasis was the embarkation of a carrier-borne ground liaison officer beginning on 29 April, the first such appointment in 20 years. The flexibility of carrier air was also demonstrated, as it was able to offer sorties to NATO from what remained a national asset.

In these roles, the Sea Harrier's capabilities were enhanced by broader NATO air capabilities such as AWACS (airborne warning and control system) and tankers, but they also brought particular advantages similar to those they provided to Oparea Otranto.[65] The mobility of a floating airfield meant that Sea Harriers were both closer than land-based aircraft and less weather dependent, a significant factor given the weather vulnerability

Naval Historical Branch, U.K. [b]

Fleet Air Arm Sea Kings over Bosnia. These versatile helicopters fulfilled a wide range of roles, including resupply and casualty evacuation from both ships and shore.

A Fleet Air Arm Sea Harrier launches in the Adriatic. Naval Harriers demonstrated their capability in multiple roles during Operation Sharp Guard, flying more than 2,000 sorties.

of many Italian airfields, particularly for early morning coverage.[66] The Sea Harrier also had the advantage of being uniquely equipped to generate air intercept, close air support, and reconnaissance capabilities in the same sortie, a flexibility much appreciated by troops on the ground. By 1995 the Sea Harriers, which never numbered more than eight on deployment at any one time, had flown more than 2,200 sorties, roughly a third of all U.K. jet sorties in support of operations in Bosnia.[67]

Sea Harriers also participated in the final military stage of the Bosnian conflict when they flew in Operation Deliberate Force as part of the NATO bombardment of Serbian positions by air power and artillery. The artillery belonged to the Rapid Reaction Force, deployed from the end of May, which took up positions on Mount Igman above Sarajevo. The British guns and their crews were flown into Split and then secretly positioned on Mount Igman, but the ammunition, the heaviest element of their deployment, was immediately delivered from stocks held onboard the fleet stores ship RFA *Fort Austin* at Split.

The larger element of Britain's contribution to the Rapid Reaction Force was a brigade-size force. The choice had been between 3 Commando Brigade, Royal Marines, based partly afloat and partly in Split, and the British Army's 24 Airmobile Brigade, based entirely ashore with new facilities. The latter was chosen because there was a shortage of amphibious shipping for 3 Commando Brigade, and 24 Airmobile Brigade had more firepower, though not as much as the armored brigade the UNPRO-FOR commander would have preferred. The deployment of the brigade through Ploce took more than a month, was never fully completed, and was only possible through the loan of U.S. air and sealift resources. Croatia proved to be an awkward host nation, provoking Field Marshal Inge, Britain's Chief of Defence Staff, to state, "The Croats were bloody awful and wanted to make a lot of money."[68] The brigade took no part in Deliberate Force. Although its deployment was credited with some psychological effect on the Serbs, the principal analyst of the operation wrote that "as an exercise in practical power projection it left a lot to be desired."[69]

Although the commando brigade did not participate in Deliberate Force, Royal Marines played a prominent part in the operation. Lieutenant General Rupert Smith, the commander of UNPROFOR in Bosnia, had requested an operations staff to supplement his small peacekeeping command element. Because none was available from the British Army, one was formed from Headquarters Royal Marines as an administrative HQ under Major General David Pennefather, designated the Rapid Reaction Force Operations Staff (RRFOS). Pennefather stated that while he had no equipment he did have a tightly knit team.[70] Supplemented by French staff officers, British Army specialists and signalers, RRFOS developed the Air/Ground Operation Order in cooperation with Commander, Air Forces South. From 30 August RRFOS then coordinated the tactical level of the NATO campaign. While the campaign is often represented as being almost entirely airpower centric, General Smith emphasized the value of his artillery for its more enduring effect, one achieved by maintaining a maritime line of supply for the gunners' ammunition.[71] Indeed, during Deliberate Force more shells and mortar bombs were fired (1,490) than air weapons dropped (978).[72]

Some of the potential problems of land-based airpower also emerged during the brief campaign. The United States wished to deploy

F-117 Nighthawk stealth fighters to Italy in order to escalate their attacks against the Serbian air defense system. However, Italy withheld basing permission. This move was part of a wider pattern of Italian refusals during the campaign, which also affected the ability of Sea King airborne early warning helicopters from HMS *Invincible*, then staging through Brindisi, to improve their time on task providing support for Sharp Guard ships. The refusals derived from Italian dissatisfaction at not being a member of the diplomatic Contact Group on Yugoslavia, and the issue remained a potentially sensitive one, emphasizing that host nation support, even from a NATO ally, could never be taken for granted. The strikes were re-tasked to 13 USN Tomahawk land attack missiles (TLAMs), on board the Aegis guided missile cruiser USS *Normandy*, which could be fired from international waters without any impediment. The combination of the destruction caused and the specific weapon used, which the Serbs interpreted as an escalation that could target their leadership without restriction, tipped the Serbians into accepting a cessation of hostilities and negotiations at Dayton.[73]

Naval Historical Branch, U.K. [e]

The Rapid Reaction Force Operations Staff led by Major General David Pennefather was largely drawn from his closely knit team of Headquarters Royal Marines.

With the end of hostilities, the main task of RRFOS was preparing for the arrival of IFOR following the Dayton Peace Accords in December 1995. During this period there was a marked change of emphasis, moving from poise and contingency for withdrawal to presence and peace implementation. On 20 December 1995 the UKTG chopped to NATO command, and HMS *Illustrious* flew a month of supporting activity for IFOR's deployment. Rapid and decisive deployment of IFOR was seen as key to preventing any opposition to its arrival, and its establishment in theater required the presence and availability of seaborne air power, provided by the United States, Great Britain, and France. As a British defense minister put it, there was a

> . . . requirement quickly to deploy combat capable troops to help secure the ceasefire in Bosnia. . . . UK forces needed to move quickly into Bosnian Serb territory at the outset of the IFOR operation. . . . Their equipment went by sea. The decision not to move by land was vindicated by the significant delays experienced by other nations which chose that option.[74]

With the force established, which included land-based air, the naval forces could be released to national command, and *Illustrious* finally left the Adriatic on 4 March 1996.

Conclusion

Beyond outlining the full range of Royal Navy operations and what factors caused them to be effective, it is necessary to analyze the effects they created in the broader context of the conflict. Most Royal Navy activity during the conflict contributed to the enforcement of the embargo against FRY. In tactical terms there is no doubt this was successful, with commercial maritime traffic declining from late 1992 and, once appropriate UN authority had been granted, ceasing completely from summer 1993 until the sanctions regimes were lifted from late 1995 to mid-1996.

The extent to which this embargo affected Serbian and Bosnian Serb economic activity is debatable. There was certainly a high volume of cross-border land trade and black-market activity, particularly across the borders with Albania and the Yugoslav state of Macedonia. The Danube also provided an alternative route for bulk maritime traffic, but the parallel enforcement measures proved very effective against this route, with WEU police patrol boats additionally carrying out 6,748 inspections and discovering 422 infringements from summer 1993 onwards.[75] The net result of these measures was that, while trade continued, it was forced to use "break-bulk" means, limited to what lorries could carry, and at a fraction of the efficiency of bulk water transport.[76] For instance, matching the fuel carried on board MV *Gloria* would have required 8,000 lorry journeys.[77] This imposed high costs on the transit of goods and was a major determinant of hyperinflation in Serbia, which ran at up to 33 percent a day by August 1993.[78] This, by itself, was unlikely to compel policy changes in the Serbian elite, who could, in large part, insulate their lifestyle from the effects of sanctions. However, inflation was a significant and growing burden on their populations, particularly when trying to support the extra strains and consumption needed for major military campaigns. From 1992 to 1995 Serbian industrial production fell more than 50 percent, and the defeat of Serbian forces by the Croats during Operation Storm was partly attributed to their lack of supplies.[79]

Although the Royal Navy was not a major contributor to the overall air effort in terms of volume of sorties, the RN did provide a valuable contribution that was difficult to substitute. Providing a secure, mobile, and (relatively) weather-independent airbase close to the front line, the carrier was well placed for quick reactions and filling in the gaps of the flying program that land-based planes found difficult to execute. This capability was particularly significant given UNPROFOR's vulnerable position on the ground. The flexibility of the carrier was also demonstrated by its ability to convert to the helicopter carrier role, if required, and its ability to provide an acceptable venue for peace talks in 1993.[80] Similar advantages were also secured by the other carrier-operating allies.

Naval aviation also played a major role in the force protection of the ships on Sharp Guard's Oparea Montenegro, with the RN providing armed helicopters, airborne early warning helicopters, and fixed-wing coverage. As this role never had to be realized, it is all too easily forgotten, but it was important in enhancing deterrence and managing the risk to NATO ships, which had to deploy into a medium- to high-threat environment to be effective.

This role also had a strong, if subtle, connection with UNPROFOR on the ground. In order to provide reliable support to the ground forces, particularly in case of escalation, the NATO maritime and air forces had to be able to dominate and decisively defeat any Serbian maritime and air opposition. The force protection requirements of Sharp Guard and Deny Flight served both to protect enforcement ships and humanitarian relief flights and to maintain a capacity for immediate decisive intervention against air and naval threats *in extremis*. This capacity underlay options for the reinforcement or withdrawal of international forces on the ground.

A capacity for expansion, and particularly withdrawal, was a strategic requirement of the British government for the deployment and maintenance of the BRITFOR contribution to UNPROFOR. The only viable way to achieve both goals was through a maritime-supported base at Split. Again, this essential capability is all too easily overlooked, but was a prerequisite for strategic-level consent to operations on the ground. Moreover, at a time when it seemed feasible that NATO might fracture over Bosnia given the wide variety of opinions on possible action, alliance consensus over Sharp Guard, Deny Flight, and UNPROFOR operations had an additional strategic significance. These operations provided a tolerable minimum, in some ways a lowest common denominator that the allies could agree on, but one that also provided genuine effects in theater. The effects in the Balkans were both physical and psychological, demonstrating disapproval of Serbian behavior and providing an important measure of alliance unity.

There was a gradual improvement in the liaison between Britain's ground and maritime forces during the Bosnian campaigns as the ground forces came to realize, and the maritime forces to effectively demonstrate, the full range of support that could be provided from the sea. The fact that this recognition took time to develop was symbolic of the more limited interaction that most of the British services had experienced during the latter part of the Cold War when the scale of operations and the likely scenarios contemplated had envisaged most of the forces fighting complementary, but largely parallel, campaigns. The Bosnian operations were an important element in altering this perception, with an increasing emphasis on "jointery" in the British forces.[81] Much of this was reflected in the 1994 Defence Review, "Front Line First," which occurred midway through the conflict. This review is often represented as only a cost-cutting exercise, which damaged sustainability in areas like medical services. However, it also authorized important innovations such as the Permanent Joint Headquarters and the Joint Services Command and Staff College, as well as new equipment for the Royal Navy, such as TLAMs for RN submarines and a dedicated helicopter carrier (LPH).[82] These would prove central to future joint and combined operations. RN submarine-based TLAMs were used in the Kosovo campaign of 1999, and the LPH played a major role in Sierra Leone in 2000.[83]

If Bosnia was a driver for improvements in Britain's ability to operate its forces jointly, for the Royal Navy it was also a confirmation of the value of its investment in interoperability with its NATO and WEU partners. Long-term training, convergence, and familiarity, particularly in organizations such as SNFL, paid huge dividends for the relative ease with which combined operations were implemented off Yugoslavia. These operations, in turn, provided considerable improvements in the qualities and skills of all alliance navies. However, it is important to remember that the NATO/WEU maritime forces were able to develop their operations gradually and were never subjected to a live combat challenge.

The Adriatic operations of this period provide an excellent example of the utility of maritime power in operations short of all-out war. The Royal Navy deployed self-sustaining maritime forces in the theater of operations, in accordance with political direction, over a period of several years. It enforced the maritime embargo, while simultaneously remaining poised either to project additional power ashore or to withdraw, without the connotations of defeat or compulsion that apply to similar operations with land forces. In addition, it remained able to land, sustain, and reinforce land forces and was available, if necessary, for their evacuation.

The Royal Navy adapted quickly to the necessary procedural and technical complications of joint and combined maritime operations, but there was never any doubt that coordination, rather than regulation, was the right approach. The long tradition of cooperation at sea, vitally reinforced by the network of NATO training, communication, and familiarity, facilitated the human network of trust among the participants that formed the fundamental basis of success.

Chronology of Operations

July 1992 onward: Maritime Monitor, the NATO maritime surveillance operation in the Adriatic.

July 1992 onward: Sharp Vigilance, the WEU maritime monitoring operation.

November 1992 onward: Maritime Guard, the successor to Maritime Monitor. The operation name changed when UNSCR 787 allowed enforcement with minimal force.

November 1992 onward: Sharp Fence, the successor to Sharp Vigilance. The operation name changed when UNSCR 787 allowed enforcement with minimal force.

November 1992 onward: Grapple, the deployment of U.K. land-based peacekeeping troops in Bosnia. It was also the initial operation name for the deployment of U.K. Carrier Task Group 612.

November 1992–December 1995: Hamden, the operational name assigned to the involvement of all U.K. forces in the former Yugoslavia, whether land, air, or maritime.

April 1993 onward: Deny Flight, the UN-mandated NATO operation to enforce the no-fly zone.

June 1993 onward: Sharp Guard, the combined NATO and WEU maritime interdiction operation, successor to both Maritime Monitor/Maritime Guard and Sharp Vigilance/Sharp Fence.

August–September 1995: Deliberate Force, the NATO operation to bombard Serbian positions and infrastructure using artillery and airpower.

20 December 1995 onward: Joint Endeavor, the NATO operation to implement the Dayton Peace Accords.

Notes

1. For the major exception to this neglect, see Sean M. Maloney, *The Hindrance of Military Operations Ashore: Canadian Participation in Operation Sharp Guard, 1993–1996*, Maritime Security Occasional Paper No. 7 (Halifax: Centre for Foreign Policy Studies, Dalhousie University, 2000).

2. A chronology of operations is at the end of this paper.

3. For a fuller discussion of the effects based approach to maritime operations, see Colin S. Gray and Roger W. Barnett, eds., *Seapower and Strategy* (London: Tri-Service Press, 1989), and Stephen Prince, "Maritime Warfare, A Historical Perspective," in *Effects Based Warfare*, ed. Christopher Finn (London: HMSO, 2004).

4. For a concise history of the events, see Alastair Finlan, *The Collapse of Yugoslavia, 1991–1999* (London: Osprey, 2004).

5. Tim Ripley, *Operation Deliberate Force, The UN and NATO Campaign in Bosnia, 1995* (Lancaster: Centre for Defence and International Security Studies, 1999), p. 21 and chap. 14.

6. Rupert Smith, *The Utility of Force: The Art of War in the Modern World* (London: Allen Lane, 2005), 334.

7. This airbridge delivered nearly 16,000 humanitarian delivery sorties between 1992 and 1996. See Tim Ripley, *Air War Bosnia* (Shrewsbury, UK: Airlife, 1996), chaps. 2 and 3, and p. 105.

8. Maloney, *Hindrance of Military Operations Ashore*, 10.

9. "History of WEU," Part 4, Operational Role, Section B, Operations in the Context of the Yugoslav Conflict, 1992–1996, at http://www.weu.int/History.htm#4B, accessed 20 June 2006.

10. Denmark had previously deployed a small number of Leopard main battle tanks with its UNPROFOR contingent but this was very much an exception. See Ripley, *Operation Deliberate Force*, 40.

11. Rupert W. Murray, *IFOR on IFOR* (Edinburgh: Connect Publishing, 1996).

12. For the most convincing statement of this case, see James Gow, *Triumph of the Lack of Will, International Diplomacy and the Yugoslav War* (London: Hurts & Company, 1997).

13. Elizabeth M. Cousens and Charles K. Cater, *Towards Peace in Bosnia, Implementing the Dayton Accords* (London: Lynne Rienner Publishers, 2001), 54, 66.

14. Smith, *Utility of Force*, 335.

15. For instance, polling in America showed that some 70% of the U.S. public opposed sending U.S. troops to Bosnia. See Dana H. Allin, *NATO's Balkan Interventions*, Adelphi Paper No. 347 (London: Oxford University Press and International Institute for Strategic Studies, 2002), 41. In Germany only 14% of those polled supported German forces participating in a UN peace enforcement operation and in the UK, 59% were against military intervention. See Gow, *Triumph of the Lack of Will*, 173, 179.

16. Allin, *NATO's Balkan Interventions*, 28; see also Joyce P. Kaufman, *NATO and the Former Yugoslavia: Crisis, Conflict and the Atlantic Alliance* (Lanham, MD: Rowman & Littlefield Publishers, 2002), 100–129.

17. Allin, *NATO's Balkan Interventions*, 17.

18. Smith, *Utility of Force*, 337. France and then Britain were the largest troop contributors to UNPROFOR.

19. Gow, *Triumph of the Lack of Will*, 139.

20. Allin, *NATO's Balkan Interventions*, 35.

21. Smith, *Utility of Force*, chap. 9.

22. It should be remembered that UNPROFOR also operated in Croatia and that the UN Preventative Deployment was deployed on the Macedonian border.

23. UNPROFOR's total military strength never exceeded 40,000, and in November 1994 it was 38,130. See http://www.un.org/Depts/dpko/dpko/co_mission/unprofor_b.htm, accessed 10 September 2006.

24. Quoted in Ripley, *Operation Deliberate Force*, 26.

25. UNPROFOR's deployment in Bosnia was not without cost however. From 1992 to 1995, 167 members of UNPROFOR were killed in action. See Finlan, *Collapse of Yugoslavia*, 35.

26. Michael McConville, *A Small War in the Balkans* (London: MacMillan, 1986).

27. Maloney, *Hindrance of Military Operations Ashore*, 4–9.

28. SNFL is now known as Standing NATO Maritime Group 1. John Hattendorf, "NATO's Policeman on the Beat: The First Twenty Years of the Standing Naval Force, Atlantic, 1968–1988" in *Naval History and Maritime Strategy: Collected Essays*, ed. John Hattendorf (Malabar, FL: Krieger Publishing, 2000).

29. Canada, Germany, the Netherlands, the UK, and the U.S.

30. Vice Admiral Greg R. Maddison, Oral History (31D 6 MADDISON), 28 September 2005, Canadian War Museum, 3, 22.

31. Maloney, *Hindrance of Military Operations Ashore*, 21.

32. Ibid., 20.

33. For the Royal Navy, these scenarios had particular resonance given that the Royal Navy's Task Force of 1982 had come relatively close to shooting down a civilian airliner during its passage south to the Falkland Islands. See Sir Sandy Woodward, with Patrick Robinson, *100 Days: The Memoirs of the Falklands Battle Group Commander* (Annapolis, MD: Naval Institute Press, 1997), 102–4.

34. Maloney, *Hindrance of Military Operations Ashore*, 35, 42–43.

35. http://www.afsouth.nato.int/operations/SharpGuard/SharpGuardFactSheet.htm, accessed 10 September 2006.

36. Eric Francis Germain, "The Coming Revolution in NATO Maritime Command and Control," November 1997, at http://www.mitre.org/work/tech_papers/tech_papers_97/technet97/index.html, accessed 10 September 2006.

37. Quoted in web reference above.

38. Summary of discussion following a seminar on combined operations, chaired by Rear Admiral Alan Massey, Assistant Chief of the Naval Staff, UK Ministry of Defence, 23 February 2006.

39. Restrictions on German ships were relaxed from 1994.

40. Maloney, *Hindrance of Military Operations Ashore*, 16, 34.

41. The change in U.S. policy was an expression of domestic political pressure and consistent with the strategic policy preferences articulated above.

42. Maloney, *Hindrance of Military Operations Ashore,* 16–17.

43. Certain bulk fuel and wheat carriers could only be safely inspected in harbor, due to the fumes in their storage areas.

44. For an anecdotal account of a Royal Navy frigate on a Sharp Guard deployment, see Christopher Terrill, *HMS Brilliant: In A Ship's Company* (London: BBC Books, 1995).

45. Maloney, *Hindrance of Military Operations Ashore,* 29–30.

46. That is closer than 5,000 meters.

47. Maloney, *Hindrance of Military Operations Ashore,* 41–42.

48. http://www.afsouth.nato.int/operations/SharpGuard/SharpGuardFactSheet.htm, accessed 10 September 2005; Maloney, *Hindrance of Military Operations Ashore,* 52.

49. The national task group was initially part of Operation Grapple, later renamed Operation Hamden, with Grapple referring only to British ground forces.

50. Captain T. W. Loughran, "Operational Effectiveness and Resource Constraints—HMS Ark Royal in Operations Grapple and Hamden 1993/4," *Royal United Services Institute Journal* 140, no. 1 (February 1995): 45.

51. Rear Admiral Jeremy Blackham, "Maritime Peacekeeping," *Royal United Services Institute Journal* 138, no. 4 (August 1993): 22.

52. Eric Grove, "Navies in Peacekeeping and Enforcement: The British Experience in the Adriatic," *International Peacekeeping* 1, no. 4 (Winter 1994): 463.

53. Ironically, the RN found it harder to coordinate with the USN carrier program, not through any lack of willingness but because of the U.S. carrier's more global program—the carrier was required off Somalia in October 1993.

54. Loughran, "Operational Effectiveness and Resource Constraints," 46.

55. Maloney, *Hindrance of Military Operations Ashore,* 21–22.

56. Ibid., 22–23.

57. While there were no U.S. troops in Bosnia, USN forces maintained similar capabilities to intervene in support of forces ashore if required.

58. E. Fursdon, "Poised in the Adriatic," *Navy International* 98, no. 516 (May/June 1993): 170.

59. Ibid.

60. R. Fox, "Balkan Stew: British Forces in the Balkans—Keeping the Peace in Bosnia and Kosovo" in J. Thompson, ed., *The Imperial War Museum Book of Modern Warfare, British and Commonwealth Forces at War 1945–2000* (London: Sidgwick & Jackson, 2002), 336.

61. Maloney, *Hindrance of Military Operations Ashore,* 45–46.

62. Fursdon, "Poised in the Adriatic," 171.

63. Discussion broadcast in Episode Two of the BBC's *Defence of the Realm,* first broadcast on BBC1, 1996.

64. Ripley, *Operation Deliberate Force,* 70; Gow, *Triumph of the Lack of Will,* 274.

65. E. Grove, *Ark Royal: A Flagship for the 21st Century* (Portsmouth: HMS Ark Royal, 2001), 51.

66. Loughran, "Operational Effectiveness and Resource Constraints," 46.

67. *Statement on the Defence Estimates* (London: HMSO, May 1995), 50–51. One Sea Harrier was lost over Bosnia in April 1994 while flying a particularly hazardous CAS sortie for UNPROFOR. For the pilot's account, see Nick Richardson, *No Escape Zone* (London: Little Brown & Co., 2000).

68. Quoted in Ripley, *Operation Deliberate Force*, 137.

69. Ibid., 137–39.

70. Ibid., 136–37.

71. Smith, *Utility of Force*, 355.

72. Ripley, *Operation Deliberate Force*, 350–51.

73. Ibid., 285–86.

74. See the Right Honourable James Arbuthnott, MP, Minister of State for Defence Procurement, *Hansard*, 18 July 1996, pt. 12, col. 1334–5: Christopher Bellamy, *Knights in White Armour* (London: Hutchinson, 1996), 185, 228–29.

75. "History of WEU," 4B, accessed 20 June 2006. The UK provided three of the eight patrol boats used by the WEU and some training support.

76. For the economics of different modes of transport, see Robert Gardiner, ed., *The Shipping Revolution: The Modern Merchant Ship* (Conway's History of the Ship) (London: Conway Maritime Press, 1992).

77. Calculation provided by CJ4 Staff Branch, HQ International Security Assistance Force, Kabul, 30 September 2006.

78. Maloney, *Hindrance of Military Operations Ashore*, 53. See also *The Economist*, 10 September 1993, 60, which records August 1993 inflation in Serbia at 1,180%.

79. See *The Economist*, 31 August 1996, 44–45.

80. David Owen, *Balkan Odyssey* (London: Indigo Books, 1995), 233.

81. Blackham, "Maritime Peacekeeping," 23.

82. Tim Laurence and Stephen Prince, "The Continuing Transformation of Britain's Maritime Forces," *Royal United Services Institute Journal* 148, no. 2 (April 2003).

83. David Richards, "Operation Palliser," *Journal of the Royal Artillery* 127, no. 2 (Autumn 2000); Lee Willett, "From Tigre to Tomahawk: the Adriatic Revisited, 1999," in *Seapower Ashore*, ed. Peter Hore (London: Chatham, 2001).

CHAPTER 3

The U. S. Navy's Contribution to Operation Sharp Guard

Sarandis Papadopoulos

The end of the Cold War in 1991 loosed a violent mixture of nationalist ambitions in the Balkans, resulting in almost a decade of conflict in the region. The independence movements created five new states: Slovenia, Croatia, Bosnia-Herzegovina, Macedonia—which had declared independence in 1991 without going to war as a result—and the Federal Republic of Yugoslavia (FRY), which included Serbia and Montenegro, all inside the former Socialist Federal Republic of Yugoslavia. The creation of four of these states came at the cost of tens of thousands dead and as many as one million more victims of ethnic cleansing. Such baleful events demanded an international response, especially as the conflict threatened to expand beyond Yugoslavia, drawing in either Greece or Turkey, both NATO members. The political complexities, however, required nations, including the United States, to make a measured and discrete commitment, one admirably served by naval power.[1]

The delicate nature of intervening in the conflict posed severe challenges for the Western European Union (WEU), NATO, and the United Nations. Beginning in March 1992 member states contributed more than fourteen thousand soldiers to the United Nations Protection Force (UNPROFOR) in the Republic of Bosnia and Herzegovina, a force that grew to almost forty thousand by 1994.[2] In addition a small military observer force (including American soldiers) went to Macedonia, and NATO aircraft parachuted supplies to the beleaguered population and enforced a prohibition on military air activity over Yugoslavia (Operation Deny Flight).[3] The objects of these overlapping operations were to limit the violence within Bosnia-Herzegovina and deter Serbian aggression. When these failed to curtail the violence, the UN declared an embargo on the delivery of weapons into the former Yugoslavia. The international community eventually controlled shipments of all items save food and medicine.[4] The maritime enforcement of the arms embargo ultimately became known as Operation Sharp Guard.[5] Throughout the course of the three-year Balkan conflict, Provide Promise, Deny Flight, and Sharp Guard sought to limit the death and destruction wrought by the Yugoslav war.

It took time to establish a political climate that would support NATO using its armed forces, including a naval deployment in the Adriatic, to limit the Balkan conflict. The NATO alliance was created to defend member countries from invasion, not to intervene in a conflict "out of area."[6] The 1991–1995 Yugoslav war was also the first time NATO had to manage and carry out combat operations. As a result, it established a strategic framework incrementally.

Deployed to monitor the arms embargo against the Federal Republic of Yugoslavia, Standing Naval Force Mediterranean (SNFM, or STANAVFORMED) conducted the first NATO out of area operation, entailing peacekeeping and peace*making* duties.[7]

The sea forces conducting Operation Sharp Guard patrolled the Adriatic Sea near the Federal Republic of Yugoslavia in two zones. The first force assumed station in the narrow strait between the Albanian coast and Otranto, Italy. The second force monitored the Montenegrin shoreline and Serbian naval forces in their base at Kotor Bay, the country's only remaining port. The latter patrol area lay nearest to Serbian forces, and it was therefore considered the more dangerous operating zone.[8]

Yugoslavia's air, missile, and naval units never struck at the NATO/ WEU forces operating in the Adriatic Sea, yet they remained a potential threat to the vessels. In particular, the Balkan state's sea service had five small submarines (two of them modern), several modern frigates, and a flotilla of nine small missile boats plus several more torpedo and mine vessels.[9] These craft were available at the start of Sharp Guard, although the ships' operational capability declined as time passed. In addition, several batteries of SSC-3 Styx antiship missiles also posed a threat to the allied ships.[10] Given these threats the ships off the Montenegrin coast continually maintained a defensive stance with weapons kept on standby.[11]

In many ways Operation Sharp Guard played to the strengths of the NATO alliance, as the naval forces involved could be drawn from existing command structures. To respond to the needs of the two patrol areas, NATO shifted Standing Naval Force Atlantic (SNFL, or STANAVFORLANT) and Standing Naval Force Mediterranean to the Adriatic region.[12] With experience at working together, these forces provided the ongoing combat-credible presence that an effective embargo required. Leaders from the two standing naval forces and a Western European Union task group commanded in rotation. The three groups covered 12 patrol areas with one ship apiece.[13] Typically, two or three American warships served in the NATO commands.[14] In June 1993 the three task groups, two NATO and one WEU, formed Combined Task Force (CTF) 440, and the mission assumed the name Operation Sharp Guard.[15]

Established in January 1968, Standing Naval Force Atlantic constituted the principal multinational NATO response force during the last half of the Cold War.[16] Earlier attempts to create multinational ground formations, and an experiment with a U.S. Navy ship crewed by alliance personnel, had not proven successful. Intended from the outset to improve interoperability between alliance navies, SNFL also served as a fire brigade in case of emergencies. In peacetime, the usual five-ship standing force cruised the Atlantic Ocean so its multinational sailors could prepare for wartime antisubmarine and convoy missions. Command over SNFL rotated among the commanding officers of its constituent vessels. Fulfilling that role gave a Belgian, Canadian, or Danish officer the opportunity to oversee the work of German, British, and U.S. ships. As such it became an important test bed for developing the doctrine called for in Allied Tactical Publications and Experimental Tactics. The ships and crews assigned to SNFL learned how to work together in a manner unique to NATO navies and passed on those skills to their parent navies throughout the last half of the Cold War.

Standing Naval Force Mediterranean had a shorter life span than its sibling multinational force, having been established on 30 April 1992 with identical missions and similar composition as SNFL. It did, however, have a longstanding, if intermittent predecessor, NATO's Naval On-Call Force Mediterranean, first established in 1969 and frequently reconstituted thereafter. With this background, SNFL and SNFM were well prepared to execute the embargo mission that Sharp Guard presented them.

Naval forces drawn from the Western European Union formed the third contingent. This all-European task group exchanged ships for training and operations with SNFL and SNFM, except for Canadian and U.S. contributions that remained under NATO control.[17] The three naval contingents employed identical doctrine and shared information over the same systems. North American vessels never joined the WEU naval force, nor could their officers command it.[18] Despite different controlling authorities, the rules of engagement (ROE) employed by ships under WEU command did not vary from those operating under the control of NATO formations.

Organizationally, the forces committed to the Adriatic maritime interdiction operation fit neatly into the dual structures of the North Atlantic Alliance and the Western European Union. The ultimate local authority supervising the operations of Sharp Guard was NATO's Commander, Naval Forces South (COMNAVSOUTH).[19] Since the establishment of the command in 1967, the officer in that billet has been an Italian Navy vice admiral.[20] The arrangement placed the WEU ships in the NATO chain of command, and they sailed under the authority of the United Nations.[21] Under their operating authority, Sharp Guard surface ships could enter Montenegrin territorial waters, but did not do so.[22] Albania permitted Sharp Guard forces to operate in its territorial waters, and therefore cover the full width of the mouth of the Adriatic Sea.

Commander CTF 440 controlled Sharp Guard operations with subordinates designated Combined Task Groups (CTG) 440.1 off Montenegro, 440.2 in the Strait of Otranto, and 440.3 for training or port visits.[23] SNFL, SNFM, and WEU forces rotated through the task group roles. Finally, Sharp Guard patrol aircraft and submarines operated under their own parallel command authorities.

CTF 440 ships primarily undertook maritime interdiction operations (MIO). In June 1993 the NATO and WEU councils allowed the harmonization of tactics between the two organizations to carry out MIO in the Adriatic.[24] NATO/WEU ships patrolled the Adriatic looking for surface ships attempting to run the embargo. The warships would approach suspect vessels, interrogate them by radio as to cargo and destination, and when necessary board and search those deemed suspicious.

Combined training exercises helped build the effective allied interaction that took place during Operation Sharp Guard. In 1992, for example, U.S. Sixth Fleet ships took part in 57 multinational exercises.[25] The next year the number of exercises in the broader ambit of U.S. Naval Forces Europe dropped to 52, owing to a heavy operational commitment.[26] Most exercises were bilateral. They also included annual events such as Exercise Dogfish, a NATO antisubmarine practice. Dogfish 1993, for example, employed five nations' boats and nine countries' maritime patrol aircraft (MPA), including those of Canada, the United Kingdom, and the United States, notably stressing the importance of "communication," a necessary ingredient to the success of Operation Sharp Guard.[27] In 1994 the number of multinational events dropped to 51, 40 of them involving NATO nations and 11 with other countries in the Mediterranean and Black Sea regions. The annual report of the Commander in Chief, U.S. Naval Forces Europe, stressed that "Forward Presence = Combined Combat Effectiveness."[28] A similar tempo of combined training continued into 1995 and 1996. Clearly, the U.S. Navy and its NATO friends understood the importance of naval forces practicing together for shared, continuous, and sometimes harrowing operations in the Adriatic.

Combined training also helped build trust and forge a team out of Standing Naval Force Atlantic and the broader task force. In April 1993, as the UN Security Council worked out Resolution 820 for the arms embargo, Canadian Commodore Greg Maddison raised his flag on HMCS *Algonquin* as Commander SNFL, in Norfolk, Virginia.[29] Within days of assuming command, and as the squadron exercised off the Virginia coast in preparation for deployment, Maddison received orders to sail for the Mediterranean. Over the ensuing weeks, his ships trained as they crossed the Atlantic and drilled with the French, Spanish, and Portuguese navies as they sailed near Europe and into the Middle Sea. These exercises involving submarines and aircraft turned SNFL into a combat command. Echoing Admiral Horatio Nelson, Maddison later characterized the multinational ship commanders as "my band of brothers."[30] Without such practice, the admiral noted, "I would not have reported that we were operationally ready." His words offer ample testimony to the value of working together to build skills and confidence. As the Adriatic mission developed over the following year, replacement ships integrated themselves into an existing tactical framework set by SNFL and the other two task groups, learning the rules of the mission much in the same manner as new students entering a classroom.

Different National Priorities

Despite the recognized need to employ consistent rules of engagement for the entire Maritime Interception Force, the participating allied navies proved unable to do so in full. A key difficulty revolved around the employment of weapons, or the use of force, that made Sharp Guard a more intense operation. For warships assigned to both the WEU and NATO task groups, the rules allowed a variety of escalating levels of force.[31] Ships could fire warning shots with inert ammunition, and use inert or training rounds for nondisabling fire. Training ammunition would be employed for disabling fire, but only under the authority of the combined task group commanders.[32] Divergent allied practices over the use of force remained academic, however, because ships assigned to Sharp Guard never had to resort to firing on merchant vessels. Sharp Guard patrols discovered six vessels carrying prohibited goods, which they confiscated. No major ship successfully ran the arms embargo after April 1993.[33]

The three combined task groups of CTF 440 operated under the same rules of engagement, approved by NATO, though each nation announced its own particular reservations.[34] Commanders had to accommodate the different political sensitivities of each nation, but the familiarity built by training together allowed the staff officers planning operations to tailor roles to ships of different navies. This is not to suggest that operational limits hamstrung commanders or reduced the effectiveness of CTF 440. As Vice Admiral Maddison later noted in his oral history, Sharp Guard units employed "some of the more robust Rules of Engagement I have ever operated under."[35]

Only the task group commander could order a boarding or the firing of warning shots, but all ship commanders retained the authority to respond with force if fired upon.[36] Still, a degree of vagueness arose with the rules of engagement for Operation Sharp Guard. Subordinates often interpreted the rules in different ways, depending upon nationality. For example, one American warship commander hesitated to use force, when authorized to do so, out of concern for the political consequences.[37] As another example, American naval officers believed they could disable a ship by hitting its engine room, while Dutch officers believed they had authority to fire on the bridge. Together, these diverse practices created challenges for commanders on the scene.

As an operation conducted under UN authority, Sharp Guard was affected by changes in rules of engagement. UN Security Council Resolutions (UNSCR) 1021 and 1022 defined cargo prohibited by the embargo as heavy weapons, ammunition, and aircraft, but not small arms.[38] The nature of American participation in the sanctions also changed in early November 1994, when the rules of engagement became more complex. In response to pressure from members of the U.S. Congress, who wanted the embargo lifted against Bosnia-Herzegovina, the U.S. Senate passed the so-called Nunn-Mitchell Amendment.[39] The amendment expressly prohibited the employment of American military units, that is, ships assigned to Sharp Guard, from enforcing the embargo or diverting any ships headed for Bosnia-Herzegovina. Nunn-Mitchell compelled a change in the U.S. ROE. Nonetheless, U.S. naval vessels continued to prevent arms shipments to the Federal Republic of Yugoslavia and to the Bosnian Serbs as well. To accommodate the American political change, the task force commander assigned the U.S. ships to different roles in the operation, playing either an informational role or serving on picket duty identifying blockade runners.[40] Speaking in early 1995, Dutch Commodore Nicolas van der Lugt, then commander of Standing Naval Force Mediterranean, described the operational impact of the U.S. ROE change as "almost nil. The USN ships still continue to contribute to the maritime embargo against Serbia and Montenegro."[41]

Another problem stemmed from the security classification of all national rules of engagement, which prevented the sharing of their precise nature even with allied navies. In that sense, Operation Sharp Guard highlighted the limitations of standing NATO rules, codified in the Military Committee's document MC192/2 written for actions prior to a general war and not for protracted sanctions enforcement.[42] To lend an idea of what such a challenge could mean, years later the commander of Destroyer Squadron 16, a component of the U.S. Sixth Fleet, noted that the U.S. rules applicable for an exercise had been shared only at the staff level, building an "unrealistic" response.[43]

U.S. Navy Sharp Guard Operations

As the Federal Republic of Yugoslavia and its Serbian allies in Bosnia-Herzogovina considered the NATO/WEU force in the Adriatic a provocation, NATO naval commanders took additional steps to protect the Sharp Guard ships.[44] They employed a U.S. guided missile cruiser or destroyer, with the call sign Red Crown, under CTG 440.1 tactical control. The Red Crown ships, usually equipped with the Aegis battle management system, monitored aircraft flying over the Balkans.[45] These ships could identify friendly aircraft returning from Deny Flight or Provide Promise missions, transmitting contact information that would prevent any unneeded alarm among allied crews.[46] Given their more sophisticated sensors, processing power, and wider methods of communication, these ships could also coordinate the responses of all CTF 440 ships to blockade runners and proved an important asset throughout the maritime embargo.[47]

The air and missile defense of the NATO and WEU vessels, which tended to be surface combatants or antisubmarine vessels, depended upon the weapons, sensors, and battle management capabilities of the American Red Crown ships. Given the speed of the potential attackers, Red Crown ships operated at the center of CTG 440.1, completely covering its components.[48] While the possibility of FRY intervention, perhaps in the form of a strike by its two squadrons of MiG-29 interceptors or other jet aircraft, was remote, it could not be discounted.[49] Red Crown was vital protection for Sharp Guard units, and it remained in place even after the late-1994 change in American rules of engagement.[50]

Maritime patrol aircraft were another vital component of Operation Sharp Guard, providing extensive search support. Beginning in August

A P-3C Orion of Patrol Squadron 45 fires self-defensive flares as the pilot prepares for an overland surveillance mission in Bosnia-Herzegovina.

1992, flights originated from Sigonella, Sicily.[51] Commander, Area Air Resources Mediterranean controlled these patrols under the direct authority of COMNAVSOUTH.[52] At any given time roughly two-thirds of the MPA were U.S. Navy P-3 Orions, with one-third a mix of allied P-3s; French, German, or Italian BR 1150 Atlantiques; or RAF MR-2 Nimrods.[53] Because these aircraft were designed for antisubmarine work, the American planes originally carried the MK-46 torpedoes needed for antisubmarine warfare missions. During Sharp Guard, however, patrol planes switched to air-to-surface weapons, usually Maverick missiles, to address any challenge posed by merchant vessels. Typically one aircraft at a time flew a six-hour stretch over the Montenegrin patrol area while another observed the Otranto chokepoint, unless grounded for maintenance or by execrable weather.[54] The Montenegro patrols flew around the clock, while the southern flights provided coverage three-quarters of each day.

To further improve the "eyes and ears" of the multinational force, U.S. Navy EP-3 aircraft conducted daily reconnaissance sweeps over the Adriatic. A national asset, these aircraft flew so-called Indications and Warning (or signals) intelligence missions supporting Operation Sharp Guard.[55] The sophisticated receivers of these aircraft could pick up electronic emissions from the Federal Republic of Yugoslavia, either on the ground or at sea. A NATO-controlled E-3 Sentry airborne warning and control system (AWACS) aircraft, using Link 11, disseminated the information obtained by the EP-3 to the NATO/WEU operating forces.[56]

On a part-time basis, British, French, and American naval aviation units also supported Sharp Guard's maritime embargo mission. When sailing in the Yugoslavian theater, U.S. and allied aircraft carriers flew dozens of sorties daily to reinforce the embargo and carried out the other two UN-mandated missions.[57] Over the Adriatic these flights tended to be missions offered in support of Sharp Guard, and not directly controlled by COMNAVSOUTH. While probably less important than the maritime patrol aircraft to executing the sanctions mission, the armed carrier aircraft added a powerful presence to the embargo operation.

Along with allied vessels, one other type of U.S. naval unit consistently offered operational support to Sharp Guard. Under Commander, Submarines Mediterranean—a U.S. Navy officer with a NATO position— units of the submarine attack force sailed, under NATO operational control, beneath the surface of the Adriatic to monitor Yugoslav naval forces.[58] The embargo force therefore generally counted upon U.S. nuclear submarines to survey naval movements in the region.[59] With the authority provided by UNSCR 820, these nuclear vessels typically patrolled the area off the Montenegrin coast.[60] Other NATO submarines complemented the U.S. subsurface units, either to cover gaps in the American coverage or to broaden the area surveyed. American submarines provided two-thirds of the undersea coverage during the first thirty months of Operation Sharp Guard.[61] In general the submarines reinforced the search for illicit cargo vessels, but their prime mission remained notifying the surface ships in case of a sortie by the Yugoslav navy. NATO submarines watched and waited for those occasions when ships, especially one of the Yugoslav submarines, left port for practice, and did so without confronting any of the dangers a surface warship or aircraft would have faced.[62]

The integration of all intelligence sources regarding ship movements took place outside the immediate theater of Operation Sharp Guard. The procedure centralizing collection, combination, and production of data had its roots in the U.S. Navy's Cold War experience in tracking the Soviet navy and the development of the service's Ocean Surveillance Information System.[63] It provided information on vessels operating in a particular region, derived from all sources. During the Balkan crisis, the Fleet Ocean Surveillance Information Facility (FOSIF) in Rota, Spain, provided such information to the sanctions enforcement ships through a daily radio broadcast.[64] FOSIF originally offered information solely to American forces, but with the start of the embargo NATO authorities activated an existing memorandum of understanding, allowing the Rota installation to broadcast daily situation reports to Sharp Guard forces. Having a more complete picture of the maritime situation, the enforcement operation enjoyed a distinct advantage over ships attempting to run the blockade. This direct feed of American intelligence also reinforced confidence and trust among the enforcement task force units.

Guided missile frigate USS *Samuel B. Roberts*, center, and attack submarine USS *Baltimore*, top, pull along USS *George Washington*. The *George Washington* Battle Group has just completed a six-month Mediterranean deployment, participating in sustained operations supporting the NATO-led peacekeeping in Bosnia and the UN sanctions against Iraq.

All three parts of the naval command patrolled the waters of the Adriatic, searching for merchant vessels carrying contraband. A NATO/ WEU warship encountering a vessel challenged it and inspected it at sea for embargoed goods. When the searchers detected suspicious items, or an indication of something concealed on board, they diverted the vessel with allied personnel on board to the Italian port of Brindisi. Under the sanctions regime, CTF 440 ships prevented two vessels bearing oil and four carrying weapons from breaking the embargo.[65] Not only did the command physically stop attempts to run the UN arms and trade embargo, but it presented a deterrent, discouraging consideration of such an effort.[66]

The most dramatic case of an attempted blockade run took place in mid-1994 when the Maltese-registered oil tanker *Lido II* attempted to transport a large cargo to Montenegro.[67] The ship paused in Brindisi and then set sail—ostensibly for Albania—on the 1 May holiday. The ship carried 50,000 tons of oil. CTG 440.1 forces observed the ship headed for the Montenegrin port of Bar, about 40 nautical miles north of its declared destination.[68] When challenged, the merchant vessel announced a flooding emergency, prompting two Montenegrin tugs and a surface force of Yugoslav warships to sail to the putative rescue. The ensuing moments saw tensions rise as both the combined task group and Yugoslav forces went to general quarters, and NATO alert aircraft streaked in to support the surface ships. Averting a more direct confrontation, Dutch marines boarded the tanker, inspected the flooding problem, determined it to be fraudulent, and then ordered the ship to sail for Brindisi. The Yugoslav naval vessels backed away from the confrontation. The flexibility and responsiveness of the Sharp Guard embargo, including Red Crown coordination by the cruiser USS *Philippine Sea*, came through strongly in this incident.[69]

Conclusion

Operation Sharp Guard lasted for 43 months, from November 1992 to June 1996. NATO and WEU ships challenged 74,192 merchant ships and boarded over one-twelfth of them in the search for contraband.[70] The embargo enforcement groups diverted more than 1,400 ships for further

Nuclear-powered aircraft carrier USS *George Washington* and guided missile destroyer USS *Arthur W. Radford* conduct underway replenishment in the western Mediterranean Sea. The ships support both NATO peacekeeping missions in Bosnia in the Adriatic Sea and the UN-sponsored sanctions against Iraq in the Arabian Gulf, July 1996.

detailed inspection in Italian ports and identified the six violators of the UN sanctions. To do so, allied ships spent more than 19,000 days at sea, yielding a daily average of over 15 ships underway at any time. The maritime patrol aircraft flew more than 7,000 sorties, or more than five flights per day. Sharp Guard, NATO's first combat operation, was a large-scale and successful effort.

The top-level command arrangements created for Operation Sharp Guard reduced tensions stemming from the conflicting goals of the United Nations, which sought support for the peacekeeping effort, and the NATO objective of seeking to maintain a strong deterrent to a wider conflict.[71] The alliance's commitment to working through operational problems allowed the accomplishment of both goals. At the level of individual ships and crews, the ongoing sequence of exercises, in particular the workup training conducted by Standing Naval Forces Atlantic before the start of the mission, gave embargo participants the confidence they needed to continue working with allies. This combination of operational clarity and skilled tactical execution built a convincing deterrent, perhaps forestalling the eruption of a wider European war. By preventing delivery of heavy weapons and fuel, Sharp Guard offered a robust answer to the Balkan threat, demonstrating the resolve needed to limit the spread of the conflict. The limited naval operation had successfully played an important role in constraining a deadly civil war in the Balkans.

Notes

1. For a fuller exploration of this tension, see A. Vernon, *Defining the Decade: Military Operations and Political Constraints in the 1990s* (Alexandria, VA: CNA, August 2004), especially 13–15.

2. For the UN Protection Force's initial strength, see International Institute for Strategic Studies, *Strategic Survey 1991–1992* (London: IISS/Brassey's, May 1992), 37; for final strength, see International Institute for Strategic Studies, *The Military Balance, 1994–1995* (London: IISS/Brassey's, October 1994), 273–76.

3. *The Military Balance*, 275–76. The UN Preventive Deployment Force watched the Macedonian border. The airlift became Operation Provide Promise, and earlier names for the no-fly zone enforcement deployments were Sky Monitor and Sky Guard. See Michael Johnson, Peter Swartz, and Patrick Roth, *Doctrine for Partnership: A Framework for U.S. Multinational Naval Doctrine* (Alexandria, VA: CNA, March 1996), 138–39.

4. Specifically, UNSCR 713 (1991) prohibited military equipment shipments to the former Yugoslavia, and UNSCR 757 (1992) banned all trade to Serbia and Montenegro, save food and medical supplies. The UN Security Council authorized the use of military units to enforce the embargoes under Resolutions 787 (1992) and 820 (1993). See *The Military Balance*, 275.

5. Earlier names for Sharp Guard included Maritime Monitor, Maritime Guard, and Albanian Guard. Ibid.

6. Hennin Frantzen, *NATO and Peace Support Operations, 1991–1999: Policies and Doctrines* (London and New York: Frank Cass, 2005), 63–69. See also Dieter Stöckmann, "Koalitionsoperationen der NATO" (Paper presented to the 2001 meeting of the Clausewitz-Gesellschaft e.V.), 67–68, at http://www.clausewitz-gesellschaft.de/fileadmin/dokumente/ Gesellschaft/BC_2001.pdf, accessed 15 May 2006.

7. Frantzen, *NATO and Peace Support Operations*, 66.

8. G. A. S. C. Wilson, *Maritime Rules of Engagement: The European Perspective* (Alexandria, VA: CNA, July 1994), 61.

9. International Institute of Strategic Studies, *The Military Balance, 1992–1993/1993–1994/1994–1995* (London: IISS/Brassey's, Autumn 1992/October 1993/October 1994), 87–88/92/106 show consistent figures and reflect the decline in maintenance as well.

10. Chris Carlson, "Harpoon Scenario: Adriatic Apoplexy," *The Naval SITREP: The Journal of Naval Miniatures Gaming*, no. 21 (October 2001): 5–7.

11. Guy A. H. Toremans, "Operations in the Adriatic" (Interview with Commodore Nicolas van der Lugt, RNLN, Commander, Standing Naval Force Mediterranean) in *Naval Forces*

(2/95): 34. See also Greg Maddison, "Reflections on NATO and Naval Forces: Operations in the Adriatic," *Canadian Naval Review* 2, no. 1 (Spring 2006): 25–27.

12. The standing forces have also respectively been called STANAVFORLANT and STANAVFORMED with further name changes in late 2004 to Standing NATO Maritime Groups (SNMG) 1 and 2.

13. Gregory Swider et al., *Naval Contributions to Bosnian Operations* (Alexandria, VA: CNA, October 1995), 82, and Figure 8, 91 (Classified Document [CD]).

14. Ibid., 1 (CD).

15. Peter Hore, ed., *Royal Navy and Royal Marines Operations 1964 to 1996* (London: Maritime Strategic Studies Institute, July 1999), 95.

16. John Hattendorf, "NATO's Policeman on the Beat: The First Twenty Years of the Standing Naval Force, Atlantic, 1968–1988," in ed. John Hattendorf, *Naval History and Maritime Strategy: Collected Essays* (Malabar, FL: Krieger Publishing, 2000). See also "NATO Ministerial Final Communiqué," 13–14 December 1967, at http://www.nato.int/docu/comm/49-95/c671213a.htm, accessed 20 November 2006.

17. Wilson, *Maritime Rules of Engagement*, 59. The WEU comprised ten nations: Belgium, France, Germany, Greece, Italy, Luxembourg, the Netherlands, Portugal, Spain, and the United Kingdom.

18. Ibid., 60–62.

19. Ibid., 59.

20. See http://www.afsouth.nato.int/factsheets/navsouth.htm, accessed 15 June 2005.

21. Kathleen Reddy, "Operation Sharp Guard: Lessons Learned for the Policymaker and Commander" (Unpublished paper, U.S. Naval War College, Newport, RI, 13 February 1997), 8–9.

22. Swider et al., *Naval Contributions to Bosnian Operations*, 93 (CD).

23. Ibid., fig. 7, 89.

24. NATO/WEU Operation Sharp Guard, IFOR Final Factsheet, 2 October 1996, 6, at http://www.nato.int/ifor/general/shrp-grd.htm, accessed 28 November 2006.

25. Commander Sixth Fleet, "COMSIXTHFLT Command History Report," 18 February 1993, 22–23 (CD).

26. Commander in Chief, U.S. Naval Forces Europe/U.S. Commander, Eastern Atlantic, "Command History Report," 29 September 1994, III-33–III-39 (CD).

27. Ibid., III-35 (CD).

28. Commander in Chief, U.S. Naval Forces Europe/U.S. Commander, Eastern Atlantic, "Command History Report," 10 April 1995, III-28 (CD).

29. Vice Admiral (ret.) Greg R. Maddison oral history, 28 September 2005, Canadian War Museum, 7–10.

30. Ibid., 11.

31. Stacy Poe, "Rules of Engagement: Complexities of Coalition Interaction in Military Operations Other Than War" (Unpublished paper, U.S. Naval War College, Newport, RI, 13 February 1995), 12.

32. COMTRBATGRU INFO CNO, "ROE/Plain Language for Sharp Guard," 141841Z APR 95, 3, Folder "Sharp Guard, Provide Promise, Deny Flight 01 April 95–30 June 95," Box 2 of

3, CNO, DCNO (Plans, Policy & Ops) (N311), Archives NHHC. Live, explosive ammunition could only be used if authorized by COMVAVSOUTH, that is, a vice admiral (CD).

33. Reddy, "Operation Sharp Guard," 10; and Toremans, "Operations in the Adriatic," 34.

34. Maddison oral history, 15.

35. Ibid., 16.

36. Wilson, *Maritime Rules of Engagement,* 60; and Poe, "Rules of Engagement," 13.

37. Poe, 14.

38. IFOR Final Factsheet, 2.

39. Letter, Barbara Larkin, Acting Assistant Secretary of State to Rep. Lee Hamilton, 20 May 1996, at http://www.globalsecurity.org/military/library/congress/1996_cr/h960611a.htm, accessed 21 June 2005.

40. Department of State Daily Press Briefing, by Christine Shelly, 14 November 1994, at http://dosfan.lib.uic.edu/ERC/briefing/daily_briefings/1994/9411/941114db.html, accessed 21 June 2005.

41. Toremans,"Operations in the Adriatic," 34.

42. Wilson, *Maritime Rules of Engagement,* 3, 50.

43. Commander Destroyer Squadron Eighteen, "Rules of Engagement (ROE)," 22 February 1999, Navy Lessons Learned Database.

44. Swider et al., *Naval Contributions to Bosnian Operations,* 19 (CD).

45. On USS *Anzio,* an Aegis ship serving as Red Crown, see "COMSIXTHFLT SITREP for the Period 06 Mar 95–09 Mar 95," para. 11A. On USS *Kidd,* a non-Aegis ship with recent upgrades for Red Crown duty, see "COMSIXTHFLT SITREP for the Period 23 Mar 95–27 Mar 95," para. 27A. Both items contained in Folder "Sixth Fleet C.H. 1995 Folder 2 of 2," Post-1990 Command File, Archives NHHC (CD).

46. Swider et al., *Naval Contributions to Bosnian Operations,* 40–41 (CD).

47. USS *Arleigh Burke* (DDG 51), "HF Action Circuit and Link Management for Sharp Guard MIO," 7 August 1995, Navy Lessons Learned Database.

48. Swider et al., *Naval Contributions to Bosnian Operations,* 91–92 (CD).

49. Richard Heaton and Gregory Swider, *IW Applications: Iraq and Former Yugoslavia* (Alexandria, VA: CNA, August 1995), 10.

50. "COMSIXTHFLT SITREP . . ." *passim* for 1995, "Sixth Fleet C.H. 1995 Folders," Post-1990 Command File, Archives NHHC (CD).

51. Commander in Chief, U.S. Naval Forces Europe/U.S. Commander Eastern Atlantic, "Command History 1 January 1992 to 31 December 1992," 12 August 1993, III-7, Folder "Europe U.S. Naval Forces/Eastern Atlantic, CH 1993," Post-1990 Command File, Archives NHHC (CD).

52. For command relationships, see Figure 7 in Swider et al., *Naval Contributions to Bosnian Operations,* 89 (CD).

53. Typically three or four allied aircraft, roughly one-third of them UK or Canadian, and six to eight USN patrol aircraft; see "COMSIXTHFLT SITREP for the Period 29 Dec 94–02 Jan 95," para. G, Folder "Sixth Fleet C.H. 1995 Folder 2 of 2," Post-1990 Command File, Archives NHHC. See also International Institute of Strategic Studies, *The Military Balance,* 57. In the Canadian Forces the patrol aircraft similar to the P-3 is designated the CP-140 Aurora (CD).

54. Commander in Chief, U.S. Naval Forces Europe/US Commander Eastern Atlantic, "Command History 1 January 1993 to 31 December 1993," 29 September 1994, III-43, Folder "Europe U.S. Naval Forces/Eastern Atlantic, CH 1993," Post-1990 Command File, Archives NHHC. Swider et al., *Naval Contributions to Bosnian Operations*, 90, 92 (CD).

55. "COMSIXTHFLT SITREP for the Period 29 Dec 94–02 Jan 95," para. G.

56. Swider et al., *Naval Contributions to Bosnian Operations*, 94. Air Force EC-135s also flew such missions. See also USS *Arleigh Burke*, "HF Action Circuit and Link Management for Sharp Guard MIO" (CD).

57. Swider et al., *Naval Contributions to Bosnian Operations*, 41, 54–55 (CD).

58. Ibid., fig. 7, 89.

59. "COMSIXTHFLT SITREP for the Period 29 Dec 94–02 Jan 95," para. H, "Submarine Attack Force" (CD).

60. Swider et al., *Naval Contributions to Bosnian Operations*, 11 (CD).

61. See, for example, "COMSIXTHFLT SITREP for the Period 02 Mar 95 to 06 Mar 95," para. 7H, and "COMSIXTHFLT SITREP for the Period 08 May 95 to 11 May 95," para. 7H. See also Swider et al., *Naval Contributions to Bosnian Operations*, 51–52 (CD).

62. See examples in "COMSIXTHFLT SITREP for the Period 14–17 Feb 94," para. F; "COMSIXTHFLT SITREP for the Period 21–24 Feb 94," para. F; "COMSIXTHFLT SITREP for the Period 17–21 Mar 94," para. F; and "COMSIXTHFLT SITREP for the Period 09–12 May 94," para. F. All in Folder I "Sixth Fleet CH 1994," Post-1990 Command File, Archives NHHC (CD).

63. Christopher Ford et al., *The Admiral's Advantage: U.S. Navy Operational Intelligence in World War II and the Cold War* (Annapolis, MD: Naval Institute Press, 2005), chaps. 3 and 4, especially p. 44, 74–76.

64. Swider et al., *Naval Contributions to Bosnian Operations*, 55 (CD).

65. Ibid., 50 (CD).

66. Heaton and Swider, *IW Applications*, 27 (CD).

67. IFOR Final Factsheet, 2.

68. Swider et al., *Naval Contributions to Bosnian Operations*, 51 (CD).

69. "COMSIXTHFLT SITREP for the Period 09–12 May 94," para A, Folder I "Sixth Fleet CH 1994," Post-1990 Command File, Archives NHHC (CD).

70. All details taken or derived from IFOR Final Factsheet, 1 and 6.

71. Ettore Greco, "The Evolving Partnership Between the United Nations and NATO: Lessons from the Yugoslav Experience," n.d., 7, at http://www.nato.int/acad/fellow/95-97/greco.pdf, accessed 21 June 2005.

CHAPTER 4

The Combined Naval Role in East Timor

David Stevens

The management of the Coalition is the biggest issue.

—Commodore J. R. Stapleton, RAN, Naval Component Commander, Operation Stabilise

The successful INTERFET (International Force East Timor) deployment from September 1999 to February 2000 was about crisis intervention rather than outright conflict; its aim, to provide a peaceful and secure environment in which the United Nations could conduct humanitarian assistance and nation building. But for the Australian Defence Force (ADF), it remains a watershed, marking not only the largest single deployment of Australian military forces overseas since World War II but also the first time that Australia had provided the core force for a UN-mandated peace enforcement operation. Both aspects had more than transitory significance, for they demonstrated the willingness of the Australian government to employ the ADF offshore in a manner that few local defense analysts or policymakers had hitherto expected. Instead of operating in its traditional role of junior partner in either a U.K.-or U.S.-led coalition, in East Timor Australia acted as chief contributor and lead nation: "that nation with the will and capability, competence, and influence to provide the essential elements of political consultation and military leadership to coordinate the planning, mounting, and execution of a coalition military operation."[1]

Involvement in Operation Stabilise, as the INTERFET deployment was known, nevertheless, severely stretched the ADF's available resources and revealed a yawning gap between advertised and actual capability.

Evolving from the post-Vietnam War pullback from the Southeast Asian region, the existing "Defence of Australia" doctrine was "threat based" and had envisioned the ADF primarily providing defense-in-depth for the Australian mainland.[2] In effect, the high-technology assets operated by the Royal Australian Navy (RAN) and Royal Australian Air Force (RAAF) would allow control of Australia's sea and air approaches, leaving the Australian Army to deal with those enemy forces that managed to leak through the barrier.[3] Such a strategy left the army in particular with little capability for, or doctrinal interest in, the projection of military power at a distance. Yet, as the situation in East Timor developed into the most serious regional crisis since Vietnam, it seemed inevitable that Australia would need to intervene, and that to halt the escalating violence such intervention would need to be substantial.

From the start ADF planners recognized the need to assert INTERFET's authority across all levels of a fractured society, making face-to-face contact with both potential belligerents and local supporters vital. This practical need inevitably placed a high priority on assembling a broad-based coalition willing to deploy significant forces ashore.[4] The tendency at the time and subsequently to examine the operation primarily in terms of "boots on the ground" has, however, served to seriously skew our more general understanding of the part played by other force elements.[5] In fact INTERFET was very much a joint and combined force, and as its commander, Australian Army Major General Peter Cosgrove, unhesitatingly acknowledged, the naval presence was not "an incidental, nice to have 'add on'." Rather, he continued, "it was an important indicator of international resolve and most reassuring to all of us who relied on sea lifelines."[6] Yet more than this, the capability, responsiveness, and flexibility of coalition naval assets ensured INTERFET could operate in a secure environment, allowed in-theater mobility, and then offered continuing sustainment. "Mass," Norman Friedman underlines in *Seapower as Strategy*, "has to come by sea,"[7] and in terms of logistics support multinational sea power provided INTERFET's functioning foundation.

It is within this context of coalition interdependence, or "strength through diversity," that we can most usefully examine the combined naval role in East Timor. Australia did not have the maritime assets available to go in alone, even had such an option been desirable. Close to seamless cooperation, something that Western navies have long looked upon as operational bedrock, proved vital to provide appropriate capabilities and get the best out of individual force elements.

Background

Situated just south of the Equator between the Timor and Banda seas, the island of Timor is at the eastern end of the Lesser Sunda Archipelago and some four hundred nautical miles from the nearest large Australian port at Darwin. Mountainous, thickly vegetated and poorly developed, the island is about 470 kilometers long and 110 kilometers wide. Politically and culturally, it is divided into two. West Timor, a former Dutch colony, passed to the new Republic of Indonesia in 1949 with the dissolution of the Dutch East Indies. East Timor, on the other hand, had been colonized by Portugal. Not until 1975, following a regime change in Lisbon, did moves begin to replace the colonial administration with a popular assembly. In a sad foretaste of future events, Portugal proved unable to control the violent clashes between those East Timorese who sought independence and those who favored integration with Indonesia, and effectively abandoned the territory to civil war. On the pretext of restoring order, Indonesia invaded on 7 December 1975 and assisted the pro-integration parties with establishing their own provisional government. Ignoring calls by both the United Nations Security Council and the General Assembly to respect East Timor's territorial integrity, the Indonesian parliament formally incorporated the province into the Republic on 17 July 1976.[8]

Thereafter the General Assembly routinely reaffirmed the right of East Timor's 800,000 people to self-determination, but largely limited practical assistance to the promotion of dialogue between the various interest groups. These measures did little to quell local dissatisfaction with the profound social changes imposed by the imported Indonesian administration, or to prevent the province from remaining a serious internal security problem. The continuing large military presence not only overwhelmed any attempts at normality but also ensured that the Indonesian national armed forces

East Timor

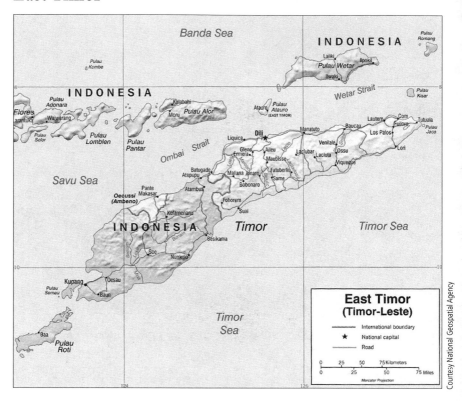

(TNI) dominated the development process.[9] Moreover, attempting to cut off pro-independence guerrilla groups from popular support, the TNI regularly resorted to a heavy-handed policy that kept international attention focused on Indonesia's poor human rights record.[10] Events such as the well-documented 1991 massacre in the East Timorese capital of Dili simply highlighted the depth of the continuing tragedy.[11]

The first real hopes for reform came with another external regime change. In May 1998 Indonesian President Suharto's 31 years of authoritarian rule came to an end, and the following month new President B. J. Habibie announced that his administration might be prepared to give East Timor special status within the Republic. Subsequent tripartite talks between Indonesia, Portugal, and UN Secretary-General Kofi Annan eventually reached agreement on the use of a direct ballot to determine

East Timorese willingness to either accept substantial internal autonomy or formally separate from Indonesia.[12] Responsibility for arranging the popular consultation fell to the UN, and in June 1999 the Security Council established the United Nations Mission in East Timor (UNAMET), involving up to 280 civilian police officers and 50 military liaison officers. UNAMET did not have a mandate to enforce security, but UN Security Council Resolution (UNSCR) 1236, adopted on 7 May 1999, had already stressed the Indonesian government's responsibility to ensure the safety of international staff and observers.[13]

At this time the TNI still maintained some 18,000 troops in East Timor. But far more volatile were the more than 20,000 members of various armed militia groups, who supported autonomy over independence and planned to influence the vote through a widespread campaign of intimidation. Command and materiel linkages between the TNI and militia were clear to outside observers, even if "the extent to which TNI's actions on the ground were sanctioned by, or ordered from Jakarta" remained murky.[14] The pro-independence FALINTIL (National Armed Forces for the Liberation of East Timor) guerrilla army, by contrast, could deploy just 2,000 men and was following a policy of restraint.[15] Militia activity became more intense during July 1999, with threats made against UNAMET staff and thousands of East Timorese forced to leave their homes. Despite a three-week delay caused by the community unrest, the ballot was held successfully on 30 August 1999. Some 95 percent of registered voters went to the polls, and more than 78 percent of these decided to reject the autonomy proposal and opt instead for independence.[16]

The result, however, sparked an escalating campaign of planned retributive violence.[17] Unwilling to accept their loss, militia groups, at times supported or sanctioned by Indonesian security forces, rampaged through towns attacking residents, burning homes, and destroying local infrastructure. Over the next few weeks several thousand East Timorese were murdered while another 500,000 fled to safety.[18] Indonesia emphatically denied any TNI involvement and initially opposed any suggestion of a foreign security presence, but its own attempts to restore order, including a declaration of martial law, had little or no effect. On 8 September, following the deaths of four local UNAMET workers, the UN announced a total withdrawal. Calls from the international community for action on the deepening humanitarian crisis grew more strident, and over the next week, the UN secretary-general maintained constant contact with President Habibie and those states likely to play a key role in mounting and supporting a peace-enforcement operation.[19] On 12 September Habibie bowed at last to the pressure and announced Indonesia's readiness to accept external assistance. Three days later the UN Security Council adopted Resolution 1264:

> *Determining* that the present situation in East Timor constitutes a threat to peace and security, [and] *Acting* under Chapter VII of the Charter of the United Nations. . . . *Authorizes* the establishment of a multinational force under a unified command structure, pursuant to the request of the Government of Indonesia conveyed to the Secretary-General on 12 September 1999, with the following tasks: to restore peace and security in East Timor, to protect and support UNAMET in carrying out its tasks and, within force capabilities, to facilitate humanitarian assistance operations; and *authorizes* the States participating in the multinational force to take all necessary measures to fulfil this mandate.[20]

The secretary-general had earlier invited Australia to lead the multinational force.[21] In officially announcing acceptance, Australian Foreign Minister Alexander Downer expressed his delight that the UNSC resolution was unanimous and strongly worded. Unusually for the UN, the mandate was "unambiguous and clear cut."[22] Indeed, in comparison with most other UN-sponsored missions, there were several remarkable features about the INTERFET deployment, not least the speed with which it was mounted followed by its clear and unqualified success. Elated by the partnership established between the UN and the people of East Timor, Secretary-General Annan soon proudly held up INTERFET as a model peace-enforcement operation.[23] For Australians, however, perhaps the most notable feature of Operation Stabilise was that the operation had taken place under their leadership.

Preparation and Planning

An archipelago comprising more than 17,000 islands, Indonesia is both the largest and most populous nation in Southeast Asia and shares with Australia more than a thousand miles of maritime boundary. As more than one foreign policy analyst has noted, Australia needs Indonesia more than

Indonesia needs Australia,[24] and this strategic reality was reinforced regularly in the security context. "Our defence relationship with Indonesia," noted the 1994 Defence White Paper, "is our most important in the region and a key element in Australia's approach to regional defence engagement. It is underpinned by an increasing awareness of our shared strategic interests and perceptions."[25]

Like most of the Western world, Australia, while expressing concern for humanitarian issues, had readily acquiesced to Indonesia's 1975 invasion of East Timor. Three years later Australia announced its decision to "recognize *de facto*" that the province was part of Indonesia.[26] Notwithstanding the objections of a vocal East Timorese lobby, Australian politicians had thereafter trod warily around the issue, seemingly unwilling to risk trade and security ties with their most important neighbor.[27] Even so, as evidence of the deliberate pattern of violence and intimidation mounted in the first months of 1999, the situation garnered increasing political attention. Buoyed by growing international and public demands for action, East Timor rapidly moved from its position as an irritant in the bilateral relationship to the top of Australia's regional foreign policy agenda.[28]

The flaring of ethnic tensions within several Indonesian provinces in the wake of President Suharto's departure had already raised Australian fears of a wider descent into lawlessness. President Habibie enjoyed an uncertain legitimacy in Indonesia, and as early as May 1998 the ADF became aware that it might have to deploy forces to evacuate Australian citizens working in the country.[29] By the end of the year Chief of the Defence Force Admiral Chris Barrie, RAN, had publicly warned that the ADF needed to be ready for a "very significant military operation . . . much more widespread than anything we might have contemplated 15 to 18 months ago."[30] Barrie gained agreement to raise the readiness and strength of certain ADF elements, and when announcing these measures in March 1999, Australian Defence Minister John Moore included East Timor in the context of regional contingencies that might arise at short notice. Moore noted that a peacekeeping mission was not yet in prospect, but added, "The Government's responsibility, and our intention is to be in a position to be able to respond effectively to a considerable range of possibilities."[31]

Indonesian authorities were not consulted on developing ADF plans, but discussions between Australia and possible coalition partners were already underway at various diplomatic and military levels.[32] An obvious first port of call was New Zealand, where the ANZAC tradition and long-standing cross-Tasman alliance had made the two defense forces highly interoperable.[33] Australia had yet to seek a definite commitment, but there seemed little doubt that New Zealand supported a substantial and fully cooperative effort. The chief of the New Zealand Defence Force, Air Marshal Carey Adamson, later acknowledged how his force elements had been chosen in consultation with Admiral Barrie, how they were readily placed under Australian control, and how close cooperation proved crucial to getting the best out of scarce assets.[34] Integration with the Royal New Zealand Navy was so close that the frigate HMNZS *Canterbury*'s commanding officer, Commander Warren Cummins, RNZN, later described how in practical terms his ship "became an Australian frigate."[35]

Coalition warships from Italy, Thailand, Portugal, and Australia crowd the wharf at Darwin, Australia.

Sea Power Centre–Australia

Given East Timor's geographical proximity to Australia, and U.S. pre-occupation with the campaign then underway in Kosovo, ADF planners expected practical support from the Northern Hemisphere to be far more limited. Ties with the U.S. were nevertheless exploited wherever possible. From an early date the U.S. military became involved in contingency planning,[36] and initial advice from Chairman of the Joint Chiefs of Staff General Hugh Shelton indicated that though the U.S. would not provide "shooters," assistance with logistics, intelligence, and communications was likely.[37] Such assurance, even without political agreement, comforted planners already identifying large gaps in Australian capability. By U.S. standards Australia maintains only a small force at high readiness, and the ADF was being thoroughly scoured for both deployable and enabling forces.

Sustainment was the most difficult issue facing ADF planners, and from an RAN perspective the most significant shortfall was in heavy sealift, in part due to the delays in modernizing two *Newport*-class amphibious transports purchased from the U.S. Navy in 1994.[38] This left only the heavy landing ship HMAS *Tobruk*, itself long overdue for an extended maintenance period.[39] In a hurried if significant addition to its force structure, in May 1999, the RAN commissioned HMAS *Jervis Bay*, an 86-meter, fast wave-piercing catamaran built for commercial ferry service and chartered directly from the builder. Although not acquired with East Timor specifically in mind, the voyage from Darwin to Dili and return was within *Jervis Bay*'s unrefueled range at 40 knots, and during Stabilise, she was to prove her worth time and again.[40] For a substantial military contingency, however, additional sealift capacity would be needed and must either come from other coalition partners or involve further short-notice commercial charters.

As the referendum drew closer, the ADF continued to turn over some of the "what ifs" attendant upon a Service Assisted Evacuation from East Timor, which had by now received the ADF code name Operation Spitfire. Most of the detailed work was done by the newly established Deployable Joint Force Headquarters (DJFHQ), an army organization located in Brisbane, which later formed the core of INTERFET's Joint and Combined Task Force Headquarters. DJFHQ and later INTERFET Commander Major General Cosgrove has admitted that this work "was far from the depth of planning desirable for an emerging military contingency."[41] But regardless of military prudence, Cosgrove understood that the Australian government and public, not to mention the international community, would expect any substantial on-the-ground presence in East Timor to be ready and inserted quickly. Hence DJFHQ simultaneously developed plans for a larger and longer-term peacekeeping-type commitment. In essence, Cosgrove took the high-end evacuation plan and modified it to require the insertion of a light infantry brigade through Dili, with the addition of some more robust capabilities and a logistics component.

Australian planners were already working with UN security staff and assumed that the ADF would lead any deployed multinational force.[42] But while they were aware of significant international lobbying by Australian and New Zealand diplomats, neither the expected composition nor structure of the force nor the extent and strength of the UN mandate could yet be guaranteed. Also uncertain was the level of cooperation to be expected either from Indonesian authorities or, more particularly, from the TNI, which at the very best would be uneven and might actually

HMAS *Jervis Bay* sails from Dili after delivering more INTERFET troops to East Timor.

be hostile. For the previous quarter-century the armed forces had been the primary implementers of Indonesian policy in East Timor. Control was now slipping from their grasp. Australia's leading role in bringing about this change appeared to most Indonesians as a departure from the previous stance of cooperation and understanding, and an act against their national pride.[43] Among other complications, this pervasive attitude meant that any deployed force would need to deal with a major public misinformation campaign generated by the Indonesian media, with flow-on effects into the region.

Australia's diplomatic maneuvering and operational plans needed to strike a careful balance, ensuring that Indonesian sensibilities were not directly offended, while adopting a firm posture that would help the TNI to withdraw in an orderly fashion. An important consideration was to secure a strong local component to legitimize Australia's leadership role, improve its regional image, and lend INTERFET credibility as a whole. Indonesia specifically asked for an ASEAN (Association of Southeast Asian Nations) presence in the force,[44] but determining how far these nations might commit posed problems. Joining INTERFET, after all, "would mean a departure from the principle of mutual noninterference by which ASEAN members had always been bound, politically and psychologically," and would be a considerable step for them to take.[45] As late as 14–18 September, Vice Chief Air Marshal Doug Riding, RAAF, was still conducting a "whistlestop tour" through Southeast Asia, attempting to influence the nature of the contributions and help shape the structure and capabilities of the force.[46] Results were mixed. Thailand announced on 16 September that it would provide INTERFET's deputy commander and ultimately sent some 1,600 troops, the largest national contingent after Australia.[47] The Philippines, by contrast, contributed a "humanitarian relief task force" to INTERFET and balanced this by sending a medical team to West Timor.[48]

The maritime component of Deployable Joint Force Headquarters had only been set up at Maritime Headquarters in Sydney in January 1999, and in late August a small planning team was assigned to assist with Operation Spitfire.[49] The bulk of the team received orders to move from Sydney to Brisbane on 7 September, just prior to the release of the Operation Stabilise warning order.[50] Thereafter DJFHQ (M) became the Naval

Component Command, "an 'Environmental Sub-Unit Command' under Commander INTERFET,"[51] and began planning in earnest for the larger operational commitment. Responsible for the command and control of maritime units assigned to INTERFET, the naval component immediately established connectivity with the various ships and headquarters organizations involved in the deployment. It then worked to develop the maritime concept of operations while simultaneously contributing to all parts of the joint and combined planning task. Notwithstanding the ADF's long-standing claim to be a joint organization, the army was not used to the other two services questioning what they were doing and why they were doing it. As such, a first step for the newly appointed Naval Component Commander (NCC), Commodore J. R. Stapleton, RAN, was to establish trust with Cosgrove, who had not previously worked with either

INTERFET Naval Component Commander, Commodore J. R. Stapleton, RAN, left, and his Chief of Staff, Commander Daryl Bates, RAN.

him or the Air Component Commander (ACC), Air Commodore Roxley McLennan, RAAF. Stapleton even recalls having to barge into his first joint planning meeting in Brisbane because he had not been invited to attend.[52]

The frenetic pace of early activity contributed to such oversights, but the separate commanders quickly established a good working relationship, as did their key staff officers.[53] Fortuitously, several in the naval component had already gained experience with Cosgrove's organization, having completed the planning and, more important, the CPX (Command Post Exercise) phase for Exercise Crocodile 99, a major Australian-U.S. joint event that had begun in August and was aimed primarily at improving interoperability.[54] This exposure proved extremely important to the successful planning and execution of Stabilise, for as one senior member of the naval staff observed: "The value of knowing your opposite number, the planning team, planning methods and knowing the requirements/ capabilities of the other services can not be underestimated [*sic*]."[55]

NCC's aim throughout Stabilise was to support the land forces in achieving their goals, which in the initial stages were based on the insertion of the maximum combat forces in the minimum time. To this end, early maritime planning focused on area surveillance, protection of the sea lines of communication to East Timor, and provision of appropriate sealift assets to bring in troops and heavy equipment. Key stakeholders readily appreciated these aspects of the maritime plan, but non-naval planners were found to be far less familiar with the importance of the naval role in many other areas, notably broader maritime tactical operations, combat support services, and port operations. It took time to establish a better understanding of naval capabilities throughout HQ INTERFET and for early and extensive consultation with the naval component to become a matter of course. The results were evident in some of the initial directives associated with Stabilise. *Tobruk*, for example, noted in her post-deployment report that these were largely land-oriented and did not consider maritime issues.[56] The joint task force commander, Captain (N) Roger Girouard, CF, similarly observed that, in comparison with a Canadian headquarters, at HQ INTERFET the air and naval components were essentially "add-on elements."[57]

As the coalition formed, it constantly reviewed plans, and teams from the participating nations provided advice on the assets assigned.[58] Identified capability shortfalls were passed up the command chain, and Admiral Barrie remained in constant touch with his foreign counterparts.[59] Yet, because the circumstances on the ground were both in crisis and constantly changing, even determining the overall operational framework for the deployment remained a challenge. Quickly appreciated by all was the absence of host-nation support, a situation worsened by the knowledge that what little infrastructure existed in East Timor was rapidly being destroyed. Nor would any commercial contractors be available in Dili, or indeed, any population center closer than Darwin. This latter aspect posed a significant problem for a moderate-size defense force like the ADF, which had generally expected to contract out many of its support tasks. The push during the preceding years to outsource noncore functions with the intention of improving the ADF's combat effectiveness also meant that essential trades ranging from cooks to terminal handlers were in short supply.[60]

INTERFET eventually included contingents from 22 nations, of which 10 provided naval assets as detailed in Tables 1 and 2. In terms of both hulls (22 vs. 14) and ship days in theater (971 vs. 784), the RAN would eventually be in the minority, but in the initial phase the naval force was primarily Australian. Ad hoc arrangements regarding command and control and other key issues would be required, but successfully operating with this coalescing multinational force was in no way daunting to Stapleton. His appointment as the Naval Component Commander derived from his existing role as Commodore Flotillas (COMFLOT), the immediate commander of the RAN's seagoing fleet. Like most RAN officers, he had spent much of his professional career working closely with allied and regional navies, including several years on exchange service. The Australian ships he had available had been involved in a succession of bilateral and multilateral exercises and were already worked up to a high efficiency level. Several members of the international contingent, notably New Zealand and the United Kingdom, had likewise been active in recent combined exercises in Australian waters. Stapleton had therefore just worked with them at sea, was aware of each ship's individual capabilities, and knew their commanding officers well.[61]

Table 1. Maritime INTERFET Coalition Vessels

Nation	Ship	Period allocated to INTERFET
Canada	*Protecteur* (AOR 509)	23 Oct 1999–23 Jan 2000
France	*Vendémiaire* (FFG 734)	20 Sep–17 Nov 1999
	Siroco (LSD 9012)	10 Oct–25 Nov 1999
	Prairial (FFG 731)	16 Oct–29 Nov 1999
	Jacques Cartier (LST 9033)	28 Nov 1999–12 Jan 2000
Italy	*San Giusto* (LPD 9894)	26 Oct 1999–15 Feb 2000
New Zealand	*Endeavour* (AOR 11)	21–24 Sep 1999, 28 Jan–23 Feb 2000
	Te Kaha (FFH 77)	19–26 Sep 1999
	Canterbury (FFH 421)	26 Sep–12 Dec 1999
Portugal	*Vasco Da Gama* (FFG 330)	16 Nov 1999–22 Feb 2000
Singapore	*Excellence* (LST 202)	10 Oct–27 Nov 1999
	Intrepid (LST 203)	10 Oct–13 Dec 1999
	Perseverence (LSL 206)	9 Jan–17 Feb 2000
Thailand	*Surin* (LST 722)	28 Oct 1999–23 Feb 2000
United Kingdom	*Glasgow* (DDG 88)	19–29 Sep 1999
United States	*Mobile Bay* (CG 53)	20 Sep–5 Oct 1999
	Kilauea (T-AE 26)	20 Sep–2 Oct 1999
	Belleau Wood (LHA 3)	5–28 Oct 1999
	Tippecanoe (T-AO 199)	16–24 Oct 1999
	San Jose (T-AFS 7)	25–31 Oct 1999
	Peleliu (LHA 5)	26 Oct–27 Nov 1999
	Juneau (LPD 10)	28–31 Jan 2000

Table 2. Maritime INTERFET – Australian Units

Ship	Period allocated to INTERFET
Anzac (FFH 150)	19–29 Sep 1999
Adelaide (FFG 01)	19 Sep–19 Oct 1999
Success (AOR 304)	19 Sep–28 Oct 1999
Darwin (FFG 04)	19 Sep–3 Nov 1999
Australian Clearance Diving Team Four	19 Sep–2 Dec 1999
Hydrographic Office Detached Survey Unit	19 Sep–2 Dec 1999
Tobruk (LSH 50)	20 Sep–6 Nov 1999
Balikpapan (LCH 126)	20 Sep–13 Nov 1999 8 Dec 1999–15 Jan 2000
Brunei (LCH 127)	20 Sep–17 Nov 1999, 8 Dec 1999–15 Jan 2000, 15–23 Feb 2000
Labuan (LCH 128)	20 Sep–14 Oct 1999, 10 Nov–8 Dec 1999, 19–23 Feb 2000
Jervis Bay (AKR 45)	21 Sep 1999–23 Feb 2000
Tarakan (LCH 129)	30 Oct–8 Dec 1999 13 Jan–16 Feb 2000
Sydney (FFG 03)	3 Nov–19 Dec 1999
Australian Clearance Diving Team One	2 Dec 1999–17 Feb 2000
Newcastle (FFG 06)	19 Dec 1999–26 Jan 2000
Betano (LCH 133)	19 Jan–19 Feb 2000
Melbourne (FFG 05)	20 Jan – 23 Feb 2000

Because Australia had taken the role of lead nation, by default the ADF's command structure became the coalition force command concept. In ADF parlance, Major General Cosgrove was the "supported" commander, leaving the non-deploying Commander Australian Theatre (COMAST), Air Vice Marshal R. B. Treloar, RAAF—the ADF's designated operational level commander—as the "supporting" commander. In consequence, RAN units destined for East Timor might be assigned directly to Commander INTERFET (Major General Cosgrove as CTF 645) or remain under the COMAST Maritime Commander (Rear Admiral J. R. Lord, RAN, as CTF 627). But in either case, they ended up working for Commodore Stapleton, who remained dual-hatted as both NCC (CTG 645.1) and COMFLOT (CTG 627.1). The command chain worked flexibly enough, but did blur organizational responsibilities for subordinates and hence could become confusing, especially for units from navies less familiar with RAN operations. It also necessitated the creation of a separate collective signal address, "MARITIME INTERFET," in order to direct all assigned maritime forces.

Some units from contributing nations were not allocated to either task force, meaning that NCC did not have operational control or even tactical control, but other command and control problems came directly from the diverse nature of the participants and the primacy of their own national objectives. Though all contributing nations were ostensibly deploying forces to help the East Timorese people, no member of the coalition wished to antagonize Indonesia unnecessarily or put at risk their

Coalition ships sit close off Dili Harbor: HMAS *Success*, HMAS *Adelaide*, and FNS *Vendémiaire*.

Sea Power Centre–Australia

own bilateral relationship. This consideration ensured Operation Stabilise maintained an overtly and highly sensitive political nature, and meant that all participants placed varying levels of restrictions on INTERFET tasking while retaining close contact with their own national command structures.

Most problematic for NCC were those units required to pass all tasking requests to home locations via their local national command elements in HQ INTERFET. Delays of up to three or four days were common, ruling out the possibility of any short-notice tasking. Following a request from Stapleton, most of the contributing nations soon allocated liaison officers to the component, greatly helping to reduce response times and improve relationships. Indeed, good working relationships were the catalyst for a well-coordinated effort, and from the beginning Stapleton understood that it could never be a matter of laying down the law. Rather he needed to chip away at any resistance by building up liaison. He therefore made a point of establishing contact with units even before they arrived. As part of the joining procedure, he would attempt to determine what capacity they brought, the rules of engagement (ROE) under which they intended to work, and the particular limitations (political or other) within which they needed to work.[62] The naval component staff would then produce an individual concept of operations for that unit.

An area needing especially close attention was the complex legal environment, which magnified the challenges involved in creating a cohesive operating framework.[63] Unlike other peacekeeping operations during the 1990s, notably the Kosovo deployment where the UNSCR expressly recognized the sovereignty of the Federal Republic of Yugoslavia,[64] the United Nations had never accepted Indonesian claims to sovereignty over East Timor. In fact, apart from Australia and the United States, all other nations contributing to INTERFET had taken a similar stance on East Timor, seeing it as a "UN-designated non-self-governing territory" under de facto Indonesian control.[65] This status immediately confused such issues as the legal status of East Timorese waters, and hence the delineation of the area of operations (AO), and had a direct impact on the supporting documents Australian authorities were producing on INTERFET's behalf. As the authorized ROE lacked any detail with regard to rights of navigation, maintaining consistency of approach could be difficult, particularly for those navies not used to operating in archipelagic regions. Comprehensive briefing and advice from NCC's legal officer became an essential component of the joining routine for all new arrivals.

An Australian naval task group commander is accustomed to operating with a small staff, but usually with backup provided by the ship in which the team is embarked. Because the RAN did not yet have available an appropriate afloat command platform,[66] Stapleton and his staff deployed ashore with the remainder of HQ INTERFET, and in this context had the smallest component command in terms of numbers of people and the largest in terms of assets. As deployed to East Timor, the naval component comprised only ten RAN officers and some six other ranks, with various coalition liaison officers coming and going throughout the operation as illustrated in Table 1. This small group eventually controlled a force of 35 warships, coordinated the effort of 8 other naval ships that operated purely in support of INTERFET, and assisted with the management of some 35 merchant ships.[67] In addition, from the day of insertion NCC became harbor master for all East Timorese ports, managing the entry into theater of all military vehicles, equipment, and personnel, and the port requirements for commercial shipping and vessels carrying internally displaced persons and humanitarian assistance.

Control and Insertion

With the determination that securing Dili would be the key to controlling East Timor, the date for INTERFET's insertion into the capital, D-day, was set for 20 September. In parallel with the final stages of the Stabilise planning process, naval forces began gathering in Darwin. The growing RAN and RNZN contingent was joined in mid-September by the Aegis guided missile cruiser USS *Mobile Bay* and destroyer HMS *Glasgow*. Already on Far East deployment, *Glasgow* was an obvious selection for the British. Commander in Chief, U.S. Pacific Command (USCINCPAC) Admiral Dennis Blair, USN, likewise diverted *Mobile Bay* from participation in Crocodile 99 soon after President Bill Clinton confirmed on 9 September that the United States would support an Australian-led peacekeeping force.[68]

Stapleton began briefing ship command teams on the broad outline of the maritime operational plan on 14 September, although the fluidity of the situation on the ground made matters interesting. Arriving in Darwin on 25 September, the multi-role vessel HMNZS *Canterbury* still found the state of affairs somewhat disorganized with operation orders and tasking messages at a minimum.[69]

Such criticism largely reflects the difficulty of rapidly bringing together an ad hoc coalition with minimal time to conduct negotiations or adopt framework documents. Cosgrove has recalled that "on the day of the operation, only a few of the likely force elements of INTERFET could be described with any accuracy or finality."[70] Notwithstanding *Mobile Bay*'s presence and the arrival of Commander, U.S. Forces INTERFET Brigadier General J. G. Castellaw, USMC, at Darwin on 17 September,[71] even the possible U.S. contribution was still being considered and would not be settled for some time. Some of the participation agreements were reportedly not concluded at all during the period of the INTERFET deployment.[72] Adopting a pragmatic approach was the only solution, with HQ INTERFET generally proceeding on the basis that an agreement was operative even though the contributing nation might not yet be a party.

Overall direction of Stabilise took several days to settle down, but the naval organization at least was already largely in place. The senior Australian unit, the frigate HMAS *Adelaide*, had been designated CTG 627.2 and composite warfare commander as early as 10 September.[73] This task organization was similar to that used in recent exercises and offered no surprises to the other navies then represented. The predominance of RAN and RNZN combat assets at this stage also made ROE for the task group quite manageable. One of the Naval Component Commander's responsibilities had been to ensure that authorized ROE were adequate for maritime purposes, and with a cohesive force and robust UN mandate this was not overly difficult.[74]

On 18 September *Adelaide* sailed her task group—comprising the frigate *Anzac*, replenishment ship *Success*, and landing ship *Tobruk*; the heavy landing craft *Balikpapan*, *Brunei*, and *Labuan*; together with the destroyer HMS *Glasgow* and the frigate HMNZS *Te Kaha*—from Darwin for the AO. The simultaneous departure of so many ships received extensive media coverage, effectively putting to rest any continuing speculation surrounding the insertion of INTERFET. Once clear of the harbor, the task group dispersed into distinct elements based on functional tasking, with escorts covering the logistic and amphibious units. Even as these units sailed, other INTERFET naval assets, including USS *Mobile Bay*, the small New Zealand tanker HMNZS *Endeavour*, the French frigate FNS *Vendémiaire*, and Australian frigate HMAS *Darwin* were already at sea just outside East Timorese waters.

In late August the Australian Maritime Commander, Rear Admiral Lord, had recalled *Darwin* from a Southeast Asian deployment and tasked her with participation in Operation Spitfire. Arriving in the waters off southeastern East Timor on 6 September, the frigate became the first coalition unit on station, and for the next 12 days patrolled a 60-by-20-nautical-mile box near the Wetar Strait.[75] Initially positioned to provide search and rescue, flight deck, and basic medical support for army helicopters transiting from Australia, *Darwin* was well placed to begin building and maintaining a comprehensive surveillance picture. Indonesian military assets showed interest, and pleasantries were exchanged, but by maintaining her station outside territorial waters the frigate was under no obligation to move. *Darwin* was also well positioned to escort the fast transport HMAS *Jervis Bay*, which on three occasions sailed briefly from Darwin with a ground security force embarked and ready to assist with the handling of evacuees. In the event, none of these additional support measures was needed, and RAAF and Royal New Zealand Air Force aircraft extracted safely almost 2,500 authorized personnel between 6 and 14 September.[76]

Following the announcement of INTERFET, TNI movements around East Timor increased, and interaction with coalition units became less friendly. In addition to the thousands of Indonesian troops still maintained ashore, military aircraft were active from airfields in West Timor, while at least two submarines, together with several logistic ships and surface combatants, operated off the coast. Early identification of all contacts was essential as the TNI seemed determined to make its presence felt. Some Indonesian warships, recalled Commander Cummins, "were more aggressive in their actions than others, they were all very quiet, they wouldn't talk and they wouldn't radiate and the first indication was generally a visual bearing and some of them got quite close especially at night."[77] Although mainstream thought in the TNI understood that mischance needed to be avoided, there were some in the TNI "who, for other reasons, were not as worried about that, and some whose sense of outrage clouded their judgment."[78] Without any means to identify these "rogue elements," coalition commanders had to consider all Indonesian military assets a potential threat until they retired from the area. At the same time, INTERFET aimed to avoid confrontation. Following advice to either maintain the status quo or just keep things calm, *Darwin* maintained her patrol in the lead-up to D-day, moving into the outer areas of her box to avoid misunderstandings but be able to maintain a comprehensive maritime picture.

As in most littoral operations, the greatest threat came from unalerted air contacts coming quickly off the coast, and it was now that the unique capabilities brought by individual coalition members could be readily appreciated. *Mobile Bay* entered the AO as the most sophisticated combatant available to the coalition. Although operational control remained firmly in U.S. hands, the ship readily provided extensive support to the maritime task group in a variety of intelligence-gathering and surveillance roles. Throughout her time in theater, the Aegis cruiser remained Air Warfare Commander and her weapons, sensors, and battle management systems "meant that the force could operate with a high degree of confidence, even without the continuous presence of friendly fighter aircraft."[79]

Mobile Bay did not operate alone, and during the initial insertion all coalition surface combatants and maritime patrol aircraft were effectively integrated and able to support an area wide surveillance picture through standard "LOCATOR" reports and Link 11. The vast array of sensors these units operated and, equally important, their ability to display, manipulate, and communicate the collected information provided INTERFET commanders with the tools to make educated decisions. There were problems, for example, in marrying the maritime surveillance picture with that on land, but the capability to detect and track multiple contacts in several dimensions, and for as long as was needed, ensured that INTERFET received a recognized picture extending out to at least 400 nautical miles from Dili. With this level of battlespace surveillance the likelihood of the force being taken by surprise was greatly minimized if not completely removed.

Although high-frequency Link operations were hampered by East Timor's mountainous geography, the linked picture was also relayed to mainland Australia via the OTCIXS (Officer in Tactical Command Information Exchange Subsystem) network to the Joint Intelligence Centre at HQ Australian Theatre in Sydney. Hence, when on 19 September Cosgrove flew into Dili for discussions with the senior TNI officer in East Timor, Major General Kiki Syahnakri, he arrived with a good understanding of the situation. Concerned by the time it might take to build up INTERFET combat power ashore, Cosgrove made clear his requirements for airfield and port use and deployment areas. Indonesian authorities seemed taken aback by the size and rapidity of the intended deployment, but as a result of these discussions Cosgrove was able to make his insertion plan a little less confrontational, delaying slightly the immediate deployment of the Australian Army's Black Hawk helicopters.[80]

The first few days of the operation were nonetheless tense. The situation ashore was highly charged, and Cosgrove placed great reliance on an assortment of coalition warfighting capabilities. Adopting what he has described as "a Rooseveltian approach" ("Speak softly and carry a big stick."), Cosgrove acknowledged the advantage INTERFET gained from "the persuasive, intimidatory or deterrent nature of major warships."[81] The Operation Stabilise execution order went out late on 19 September, and the following dawn, the residents of Dili awoke to find the destroyer *Glasgow*, frigates *Anzac* and *Darwin*, and the tanker *Success* just off the harbor. *Darwin* detached to patrol the western approaches, while *Anzac*, assuming the role of Dili Guardship, provided close escort protection for *Success*. An hour later the first of 15 RAAF and coalition C-130 transport aircraft allocated for the initial insertion of land forces arrived at Dili airport.[82] Small parties of INTERFET Special Forces first secured the airport and then began moving into the devastated and still burning town. Later in the day Major General Cosgrove and his command element arrived to set up HQ INTERFET, although it was not fully established until 25 September.

Sea Power Centre—Australia

A chartered merchant ship unloads army vehicles at Dili.

On 21 September, watched closely by a number of Indonesian naval vessels at anchor and alongside, the coalition amphibious group arrived at Dili to begin landing INTERFET's heavy equipment. Special Forces had already secured the wharf and, while clearance divers worked quickly to remove a wreck placed by the Indonesians at the bottom of the berth, a Hydrographic Office Detached Survey Unit (HODSU) conducted a rudimentary survey of the port approaches to confirm navigational safety.[83] Unloading began at dawn and by sunset the entire port was open and a beach landing site had been cleared and was operating. That same day *Jervis Bay* completed the first of her ferry runs from Darwin to Dili to add bulk to the troop buildup.[84] With more than 3,000 troops and their equipment landed by air and sea within the first 48 hours, the initial insertion was robust, rapid, and clearly professional, helping to make the force appear larger than it actually was. But it was at the port, rather than at the more remote airfield, that this demonstration of efficient and determined operations made the greatest impression. Thousands of civilian and military onlookers were left in no doubt either about INTERFET's intentions or the fact that the TNI were no longer in control.[85]

These first amphibious lodgments also added emphasis to the necessity of protection operations. As necessary the movements of high-interest contacts, such as the two Indonesian submarines, were continuously observed and surveillance responsibilities handed over between coalition units.[86] There was no illumination by fire-control radars, but the coalition's seamless monitoring left no room for waywardness. During the first few days *Anzac, Glasgow,* and *Darwin* received additional support from *Adelaide, Te Kaha,* and *Mobile Bay,* which, when not providing close escort to and from Darwin, patrolled the eastern and western approaches to Dili. The impact these large, gray, and obviously well-armed assets had on the many observers ashore should also not be underestimated. Purely through presence, the coalition's maritime forces plainly demonstrated both international resolve and INTERFET's ability to defend itself at its most vulnerable time. The Canadian CJTF commander put it succinctly:

> . . . an armada is still an impressive and intimidating sight. The coalition's massed tonnage and naval might in the approaches to Dili helped convince the TNI and the Government of Indonesia that the international community had in fact ranged itself in full support of an independent East Timor, in a way that coalition forces ashore could not. Sea power as a diplomatic force is alive and well.[87]

Other coalition commanders went further. Air Marshal Adamson, for one, concluded that the reason the Indonesian military threat "didn't become anything more than just a threat . . . was because of the strong and vigorous naval presence we had right from the beginning."[88] Most important, this deterrent effect was present irrespective of an individual coalition unit's national ROE. An outside observer could not miss seeing that INTERFET had brought along the capability to provide an overwhelming response to a threatening action. This display limited what potential belligerents could do, as they had no way to determine what they might get away with. Militia provocations and challenges to INTERFET's authority did take place ashore, but they were invariably low-level, cautious, and unorganized, doing nothing to prevent INTERFET from gaining and maintaining the initiative.

In effect, the presence of maritime forces provided INTERFET with a multidimensional protective umbrella, or "ring of steel,"[89] as Commander

Cummins described it—one that limited the possibility of external interference and directly empowered land force commanders, allowing them to concentrate on the mission at hand. Equally significant, high-end combat capabilities combined with the inherent mobility of maritime forces went far toward making the coalition presence seem ubiquitous. Moreover, should the situation ashore ever have become untenable, the naval component formed the only credible basis for an emergency extraction plan. Together these factors were tremendous confidence builders for INTERFET forces as a whole, and the Naval Component Commander ensured they were maintained for as long as was needed.

Implicit in all this maritime activity was the requirement for sustained high-level interoperability. "INTERFET," as one New Zealand academic study concluded, "functioned in the crucial first week because the Australian armed forces could interoperate with diverse contingents drawn from Britain, France, New Zealand and the United States."[90]   In the maritime environment interoperability was best evidenced in the vital role of Dili Guardship whose responsibilities included allocating force protection for sealift and sustainment assets, developing and maintaining the recognized maritime and air picture, and acting as local warfare commander. During the first critical week the role routinely passed between the different combatant units of the RAN, Royal Navy, and U.S. Navy.[91] Confidence in the easy transfer of such responsibilities can only be obtained from common operational doctrine and close familiarity among units. As highlighted by Captain James Goldrick, then the director of the RAN's Sea Power Centre, frequent, challenging, and realistic "bi-lateral and multi-lateral exercises pay huge dividends in this regard," allowing mutual experience to easily translate into the operational sphere.[92]

Interoperability also provides context for understanding connectivity with information and intelligence sources. Here the C4I (command, control, communications, computers, and intelligence) support provided by U.S. forces played a pivotal role, with USCINCPAC's Defense Information Systems Network (DISN), MSQ-126, arriving at Darwin with 18 personnel on 19 September.[93] A U.S. fleet systems support asset designed for rapid deployment to provide DISN services for early-entry forces, the MSQ thereafter "provided DSN (Defense Switched Network), NIPRNET (Non-Classified Internet Protocol Router Network), SIPRNET, video, GCCS (Global Command and Control System), and AUTODIN (Automatic Digital Network) messaging."[94] For the Australian Naval Component Commander, the U.S.-sponsored GCCS, a successor to the Joint Operation Tactical System, proved to be an invaluable command analysis tool and secondary communications system. Through GCCS, the naval component had both effective situational awareness and a ship-shore communications system working before midnight on D-day, a remarkable achievement. Indeed, because most other systems ashore took time to establish, ship systems at first provided the backbone of INTERFET communications, and because he had ready access, the Naval Component Commander initially had a far better intelligence picture than anyone else in HQ INTERFET.[95] In a practical sense this meant that workarounds, such as Stapleton hand-carrying information to Cosgrove, were sometimes necessary.

The safe insertion of INTERFET had been achieved, but there remained much to accomplish. Even as INTERFET deployed, those opposed to East Timorese independence completed the final acts of their "scorched earth" policy, and few buildings in Dili remained habitable. On 28 September a Canadian Strategic Reconnaissance Team arrived and gave a sobering description of the situation:

> Flying into Dili, a coastal town ringed by substantial hills, fires were still evident and a smoke haze was everywhere. The city was partially alight, while half remained occupied by the TNI. At the west end, refugees were crowded into standing room only in an old warehouse, unsure of whether to fear a resurgence of TNI/militia outrage or believe the disinformation about the "murdering INTERFET killers and rapists." Troops and trucks and firepower were everywhere, but given that the heights were not yet secured, the vulnerability of INTERFET's toehold in East Timor was also evident. Militia soldiers were known to be present, although the town remained largely deserted. The militia's bounty on the INTERFET leadership demanded robust personal security. The TNI remained in large numbers, notionally restricted to the barracks, but they and the

gunboats and submarines in the area made it clear that Indonesia was still interested in what was going on and that a turn for the worst could get ugly very fast.[96]

While the TNI remained in strength, INTERFET would find it difficult to concentrate on the militia, but working to the coalition's advantage was Australia's previous investment in its military relationship with Indonesia. Built up through many years of close professional contact, the TNI's leadership had a clear understanding of the ADF's competence, effectiveness, and determination. There was enough mutual respect, and indeed friendship, at senior levels to allow each side to understand the other's way of thought and how each would respond. This was nowhere more apparent than in the discussions that took place between Rear Admiral Lord and his Indonesian counterpart, Commander Western Fleet, on the continued presence of Indonesian surface and subsurface units in the vicinity of East Timor.[97] By keeping the TNI fully briefed on INTERFET's intentions and registering concerns directly with the appropriate Indonesian commander, INTERFET ensured that there was "a predisposition to talk through issues rather than shoot through them," and this dialogue continued through to the end of the operation.[98] On 24 September Indonesia lifted martial law and began their military pull out from East Timor. By 31 October this withdrawal had effectively been completed.

Consolidation and Sustainment

The initial focus on the insertion of INTERFETs combat forces soon gave way to the consolidation phase of Operation Stablise, aimed at allowing UN operations to continue and INTERFET support to build up. At the outset Major General Cosgrove had ordered that INTERFET elements would not attempt to live off the local economy, therefore everything had to be brought in. Often there were up to 18 commercial ships in Dili harbor and two to three shipping movements a day, "an important reminder," as one assessment noted, "that effective sea lift in strategic terms rests even more upon the ability to access commercial tonnage than it does upon military vessels."[99] Protection of sea lines of communication thus remained an important maritime task throughout the operation and was achieved mainly through constant monitoring and patrols. A warship, for example, would maintain visibility on each merchant ship from the time it entered the AO until it anchored, offering chartered shipping a welcome measure of reassurance.

The absence of local infrastructure remained a challenge, and the inability of chartered shipping to load and unload without access to suitable wharfage and specialized handling equipment was a severe constraint. In fact, the inadequacies of the port facilities, lack of lay-down space, and movements of equipment all conspired to slow down and sometimes halt the flow of supplies.[100] Nevertheless, the Dili airfield had similar difficulties and, unlike the port, had to shut down at night.[101] Logisticians well understood that sealift was far more efficient and effective for force sustainment and the final balance was clear. The 11 nations contributing to the Coalition Airlift Wing flew 3,400 sorties, carried 9,500 tons of freight, and transported 38,000 passengers,[102] yet more than 91 percent of cargo and most of the passengers delivered to East Timor came by sea.[103]

Hence, even as the intensity of the maritime tactical situation reduced, the transport and amphibious capability of the maritime forces became more important. Throughout the first month, thousands of troops poured into Dili as did heavy equipment, fuel, and supplies. Once INTERFET had established its authority in the capital and its surrounds, coalition ground forces moved out to take control elsewhere, which Cosgrove labeled an "oil spot concept."[104] In addition to occupying the smaller inland towns the operational strategy required three major troop lodgments to be mounted from Dili. The first two aimed to prevent the militias using Indonesian West Timor as a safe base from which to foray into East Timor. Operation Lavarack, which began on 1 October, secured the northwestern half of the inter-Timor border. It was followed five days later by a major landing at Suai on the south coast, Operation Strand, which eliminated the militia presence in the southwest border region. The last major lodgment, Operation Respite, which began on 22 October, aimed to relieve the geographically isolated Oecussi enclave—a district on the northwest coast separated by some eighty kilometers of Indonesian territory from the rest of East Timor and overflowing with refugees.[105]

Throughout these operations coalition maritime capabilities, and above all amphibious units, proved essential to any realistic efforts to make land forces mobile over long distances. Although the initial insertion might be by troop-carrying helicopter, heavy equipment invariably came over the shore, as did follow-on logistic support.[106] After the initial Suai landing, *Tobruk* conducted four return trips from Darwin to Suai, during which she transported almost two thousand tons of cargo and 642 soldiers. Each of these "Military Sealift/Amphibious lodgements" was, as noted in *Tobruk's* post-operational narrative, "definitely an Allied affair: *Tobruk* transported cargo and troops from Australia, New Zealand, Canada and Ireland, while being escorted by or working in concert with Australian, Canadian, French, New Zealand, United Kingdom and United States warships and aircraft."[107]

Lodgment was not without difficulties, particularly at Suai where the majority of Canadian and New Zealand equipment was found to be containerized, "irrelevant," as the Canadian CJTF noted, "in a third-world country with no handling capacity."[108] The initial solution entailed mid-stream offloading by craning the containers from *Tobruk* into a heavy landing craft for subsequent pick-up by a side-loading truck. Although just workable in benign sea states, the procedure was neither efficient nor particularly safe. Far preferable was the use of heavy lift helicopters to pick up containers directly from *Tobruk's* deck, but these were a rarity among the coalition, particularly at sea. Indeed, only U.S. forces possessed the necessary rotary-wing assets. On 29 September U.S. Secretary of Defense William Cohen advised Australian authorities that the amphibious assault ship USS *Belleau Wood* would provide heavy lift capabilities with its U.S. Marine Corps CH-53E Super Stallion helicopters.[109] Without these aircraft, the unloading operation might take two to three days; with their assistance, it could be achieved in less than seven hours.[110]

Belleau Wood, complete with a contingent of Marines from the 31st Marine Expeditionary Unit (MEU) arrived in the AO on 5 October and was relieved by USS *Peleliu*, with a contingent of the 11th MEU on 26 October. Although U.S. policy aimed to minimize its footprint ashore,

Sea Power Centre—Australia

The heavy lift ship HMAS *Tobruk* approaches Dili wharf to unload her cargo of Australian Army vehicles and equipment.

participation by these large and highly capable units offered a significant show of force at a critical time. They not only affirmed the unmistakable U.S. backing as INTERFET established control of the border with West Timor but also showed real depth to the multinational forces committed. At least one analyst has argued that without these vessels, "the speed with which INTERFET expanded its authority would have been significantly retarded."[111] Although the long-term contribution made by RAN assets cannot be overlooked,[112] without doubt the continuing U.S. involvement offered unmatched political leverage and stands as a useful example of naval presence used for commitment rather than purely for security reasons.

Meanwhile, for the coalition's surface combatants and their organic aircraft, the maintenance of a "presence factor" also continued as a major consideration in planning, with Cosgrove using these units as symbols of his seriousness and intent up until INTERFET's last day in theater.[113] From the time of an individual troop insertion until final withdrawal, a frigate would remain on patrol within sight of the shore as the Local Area Warfare Commander. Providing what was termed "constructive reinforcement," the ship offered cover as necessary, together with health support services, aeromedical evacuation, air mobility operations, and lily-pad and refueling support for army helicopters.[114] Sustained presence was particularly important during the initial surveillance and intelligence-gathering missions ashore, for on at least one occasion a Special Forces patrol got in over its head and required extraction.[115]

Direct fire support was never required from any of the offshore guardships but remained readily available throughout, while the focus on the safe delivery of logistic supplies never lessened. Multisensor surveillance also remained crucial, but even low-technology capabilities proved useful, since deep water existed quite close to the shore, and ships were often used to provide additional visual surveillance of the surrounding coastal area.[116] One of the later arriving warships, the frigate HMAS *Sydney*, reported that her "highly visible presence" as Oecussi Guardship in November–December 1999 "provided the local population, Land Component personnel and ship's Humanitarian Assistance teams great reassurance. In addition it provided a strong deterrent to any militia who may have been observing INTERFET activity from the hills surrounding Oecussi."[117]

Already assuming equal importance for the forces afloat was the provision of "morale support" or hotel services. As most of the soldiers initially landed were combat troops, they had little capacity for other tasks. To many Australian army commanders, it came as a revelation that warships could offer a welcome and needed respite from the hot, dry, and dusty living conditions their personnel experienced ashore.[118] *Tobruk*, for example, when either alongside or at anchor, "offered recuperation services of showers, laundry facilities, fresh meals, temporary air conditioned comfort, e-mail and Interflora facilities."[119] Her arrival was often described as a "God Send" by the forces ashore, and during her two-month deployment more than 1,800 troops used her onboard services, while she continuously sent ashore snack and barbecue packs and fresh provisions.

Sea Power Centre—Australia

The INTERFET force hits the beach at Suai in the southwest corner of East Timor. HMAS *Labuan,* HMAS *Brunei,* and HMAS *Balikapan* provided the force with the capability to make a beach landing to offload their vehicles. HMAS *Tobruk* moved hundreds of troops from Dili to set up a permanent security presence in the border town.

By the end of October, 10,238 coalition personnel had been deployed to the AO, and in practical terms INTERFET had returned peace and stability to some 80 percent of East Timor. UNSCR 1264 had agreed that INTERFET should be replaced as soon as possible by a UN peacekeeping operation and invited the secretary-general to plan and prepare for such a deployment. The combination of INTERFET's rapid progress and the decision, on 19 October, of the Indonesian People's Consultative Assembly to recognize East Timor's independence allowed for the establishment of the UN Transitional Administration in East Timor (UNTAET) on 25 October. UNSCR 1272 (1999) endowed UNTAET with "overall responsibility for the administration of East Timor" and empowered it "to exercise all legislative and executive authority including the administration of justice."[120] INTERFET's transition to UNTAET did not begin, however, for another three months with the final transfer of responsibilities taking place on 23 February 2000.[121] Thereafter INTERFET forces either moved to the UNTAET command structure or redeployed to home locations.

In the meantime, with the level of maritime warfare tasks relatively low, the majority of the Naval Component's effort went toward logistic sustainment of the land forces, together with engineering repair services and mobility tasks around the AO.[122] To simplify reporting and tasking, the Naval Component had by this stage been functionally subdivided into five broad elements: Alpha—Dili Guardship, Bravo—Amphibious and Afloat Support, Charlie—Escort Duties and Suai Guardship, Delta—Oecussi Guardship, and Echo—Rest and Recreation visits to Darwin.[123] In effect, within the AO a three-layer approach existed:

> In the inner harbour and local coastal area there were very small amphibious ships that the Australians have, the LCHs. There were a number of other nations who brought in similar size ships and so they were providing the local coastal and small port re-supply around the coast. Then you had the middle layer of the large amphibious ships that were doing the big haulage backwards and forwards from Darwin. Everything worked in and out of Darwin. There was a steady stream of ships coming in and out around the coast and they were providing the bulk stores, which were then off-loaded onto the smaller stuff or ashore. Then in the outer perimeter you had the warships that were providing the Dili guardship for escorts and that type of stuff and the command and control facilities as well.[124]

The approach of the wet season in November threatened to further complicate movement in the AO. The south coast of Timor experiences an average of three cyclones per year which, even without these heavy monsoonal rains, make the few East Timorese roads and airfields unusable.[125] This left seaborne resupply to regional centers as the only viable solution, one that might be better described, to paraphrase recent U.S. Navy "Sea Power 21" concept developments, as "inadvertent Sea Basing."[126] Cosgrove was typically straightforward about the "crucial nature" of this relationship: "We surrounded East Timor with floating warehouses, gas stations, air ports and docks and motels. It would have been a real struggle to maintain tempo and achieve sustainment ashore, without our afloat logistic capability."[127]

Dependence on offshore support was nowhere more apparent than in the provision of fuel. Although there was some fuel ashore, it belonged to the Indonesians and neither the INTERFET command nor the UN was willing to touch it. Thus, for the first three months of the operation, naval units were the only source of the diesel (F76) and aviation (F44) fuel that the coalition consumed at some thirty thousand liters a day.[128] The lack of facilities to transfer fuel ashore was a particular weakness, and fuel from the available tanker was initially transferred to a dump ashore using collapsible fuel drums underslung from an RAN Sea King helicopter. Fuel trucks were brought into the theater only in mid-October, and these were then carried to the tanker using a landing craft. Neither of these techniques was overly efficient, being described as "akin to filling tanks by buckets."[129] Moreover, as the force dispersed, the need for fuel broadened geographically, and so the complexity of fuel distribution increased as did reliance on the available tanker. The maintenance of adequate fuel stocks required close liaison among the environmental component commands, offering another insight into the importance of the wider coalition contribution.

Until mid-October, *Success* and *Endeavour* were the only tankers available to INTERFET, and with *Success* required to remain in the AO to provide fuel ashore, *Endeavor* maintained a shuttle service. A typical return run from either Singapore or Darwin saw *Endeavour* deliver 150 tons of aviation fuel and 2,200 tons of diesel fuel to INTERFET and then conduct replenishments of fuel and provisions with coalition surface combatants.[130] Just before departing for home on 20 October, *Endeavour* topped up the tanks of the incoming Canadian replenishment ship HMCS *Protecteur*.

In welcoming *Protecteur*, Rear Admiral Lord highlighted traditional linkages: "Your arrival brings a welcome boost to the INTERFET afloat support forces and adds another important element to the international communities [sic] response to East Timor. The long and successful association between our two navies will ensure your rapid integration with the INTERFET maritime forces."[131] *Success* was in need of a maintenance period, however, and about to follow *Endeavour* out of the AO. What Lord had not highlighted was that *Protecteur* would soon become the naval component's only tanker and thus a potential single point of failure for the entire operation.[132] Particularly noteworthy in this context is that the early Canadian vision for *Protecteur*'s employment was based not on maritime replenishment, but on her sister ship HMCS *Preserver*'s experience in Somalia in 1993 and other missions in Florida and the Bahamas. *Protecteur* was to be "relatively Dili-centric, providing a medical team ashore, humanitarian aid and to serve as a floating command post for the Canadian Joint Task Force Commander."[133]

That *Protecteur* could easily absorb a significant role change reinforced Captain Girouard's assessment that she "was a viable and flexible platform for the mission envisaged."[134] During her time in the AO, *Protecteur* also assumed the duties of Task Group Logistic Commander, responsible for ordering supplies and coordinating their provision for the whole of the naval task force. But once an element of routine had set in, humanitarian projects did receive a greater level of priority. In fact, from the earliest days of Stabilise naval specialists had gone ashore as work parties to clean and repair buildings, construct ablution facilities, undertake plumbing and electrical services, and assist terminal handlers with the offloading of military cargo. HQ INTERFET and its barracks were only rendered habitable through the efforts of naval shore parties.[135]

As INTERFET facilities ashore improved, these parties changed focus to assist with rebuilding the civilian infrastructure. A number of nongovernmental organizations, or NGOs, had arrived in INTERFET's wake, but none had the resources or people to achieve much more than food distribution until after December 1999.[136] Because the visibility of humanitarian assistance compared with other activities was disproportionately high in the eyes of higher authority and the media, the Naval Component Commander ensured that each coalition unit had the opportunity to put such parties ashore.[137] By the end of the operation naval units had expended more than 20,000 hours of humanitarian assistance, saving lives and providing shelter to many thousands of East Timorese.

Coalition Observations

INTERFET was a strong coalition and the system, although set up hurriedly, worked well, but several issues deserve further comment. First is the importance of nurturing the coalition itself. The ad hoc nature of the

INTERFET structure made for a complicated operational environment, not made easier for other national components by the fact that, in the first instance, the HQ INTERFET staff was almost completely Australian. Clearly, the personality and political skills of the force commander were crucial.[138] Bringing a welcome breath of cultural reality to purely technological considerations of interoperability, Cosgrove has remarked how managing the relationships among the different coalition partners not only took up a great part of his day, but "were absolutely key to success":

> The robust and rough and ready lip service we pay to the interoperability issues between proudly different, but vastly similar, national and military cultures such as those of the USA and Australia does not ring true when the potential combined force has a different make-up. Platitudes such as "fish or cut bait" or "if it's too hot in the kitchen . . ." don't mean much if the coalition won't form, or if having formed, won't work. We have all been working on these relationship issues for decades, so I'm not saying we're starting from scratch but if the requirement is for true burden sharing then part of the burden is a sensitivity to accompany our clear and fierce mission focus.[139]

Commodore Stapleton and his successor, Commodore B. D. Robertson, RAN,[140] have likewise observed that coalition management was their biggest issue, and they took great care to foster their areas of the relationship matrix.[141] Convoluted national command and control systems and limitations on tactical control could make flexible tasking difficult, but to avoid any impression that his was a purely Australian headquarters, Stapleton had made liaison officers an integral component from an early stage. These officers in turn formed a key part of the individual network of connectivity maintained by each national element and proved vital to the Naval Component Commander when negotiating workarounds. It must be noted, however, that the presence of so many nationalities also caused security problems. The importance of the Global Control and Command System during INTERFET's insertion has been mentioned, but its continued use became impossible once coalition officers joined the NCC staff full time. In effect, because he could not have ashore all the communications gear he needed, NCC had to "dumb down" as

INTERFET became more multinational. Fortunately, he could "smart up" again simply by going back on board a RAN ship.

Communications nevertheless had to be maintained across the force, and here coalition building from a naval perspective had a distinct advantage. In an interview published in the December 1999 edition of *Proceedings,* Australian Chief of Navy Vice Admiral David Shackleton elaborated on some of East Timor's early lessons. These, he noted, were "typical": "navies can meet almost anywhere. You can talk on a radio and you can set up an arrangement." "Navies," he continued, "are very good at forming and doing business in a coalition way that I think armies and air forces find difficult."[142] The INTERFET experience reinforced the points that language problems tend not to be significant at sea, and that the NCC could construct a force that communicated because all the naval elements had common operating procedures. If there was ever any doubt, then the message could always be sent in plain English, albeit with increased possibility of compromise.

At the same time, operating with a disparate force that included both high- and low-capability navies meant that there were multiple levels of interoperability to consider. The Australian Navy, as Shackleton also noted, has "to be interoperable with just about everybody."[143] In practice, NCC had to be able to communicate both up and down. Yet, even for the RAN and U.S. Navy, despite years of working together and operating compatible equipment, high-level interoperability did not just happen. One might have expected cryptographic commonality to be a C4I staple, but even this aspect was found to require an inordinate amount of time and effort.[144] Only the willingness of individual units to remain flexible and adapt to changing circumstances brought success. Because the naval component operated as an "aligned" rather than an "integrated force," the same need for individual flexibility also became necessary when determining relationships between ships. *Darwin*'s post-deployment report notes that any problems in this regard "were quite manageable," but adds that this was "due to the dedication of involved personnel to get the job done." [145]

Notwithstanding such efforts, each nation, and indeed each ship, presented different challenges. The Royal Thai Navy's logistic ship *Surin* (LST 722), to take one example, arrived in a poor materiel state and required a long maintenance period in Darwin before being operationally employed.

Meanwhile some vessels, or at least their commanders, appeared to prefer port visits to NCC's operational tasking, and long or unpredictable periods of "national tasking" often severely limited their utility.[146] National restrictions relating to the carriage of specifically "military" materiel vice "humanitarian" stores and equipment further limited the usefulness of some of these deployed ships. The French government, for instance, was one of the first to offer naval units to the coalition but had decided that "its response would be humanitarian" and therefore only assets to support such efforts would be deployed.[147] These sorts of national constraints meant that capabilities brought to, or weighting within, particular task elements were sometimes less than desired and at other times disproportionately heavy. Thus too many surface combatants in lieu of logistic support units, when transport resources were stretched to the limit in the latter phases, on occasion reduced the NCC's ability to relieve assigned units and provided redundancy.[148]

Differences in approach among individual units became a critical consideration in this context. The Naval Component Commander experienced no problems tasking the New Caledonia-based landing ship, FS *Jacques Cartier*. By contrast, her predecessor, the larger FS *Siroco*, had arrived directly from France with significantly different procedures. Apparently unaware that Darwin was a commercial rather than a naval port, *Siroco* initially claimed she could not accept a lower priority for loading and would therefore sail for Dili with significantly less cargo than planned. As the Australian Defence Force had no influence over routine commercial shipping, and the NCC had allowed *Tobruk* to depart the AO only after the French had formally signed up to the task, there was no slack to play with. Only by sending the French national commander from Dili to Darwin was the problem eventually resolved. Not surprisingly, the NCC noted in a brief to the Australian Maritime Commander: "Owing to the political complexities and diverse nature of the forces involved, tasks which would normally be conducted without detailed planning or instructions require high levels of liaison and monitoring."[149]

Finally, mention must be made of ROE, which within an ad hoc multinational operation are generally likely to be more contentious than in a formalized alliance such as NATO.[150] From the beginning of Operation Stabilise all commanders recognized that national policies might not always coincide. Even the deployed U.S. forces had severe limitations on the equipment they could use, where they could (or, more important, could not) go, and what they could do.[151] All units felt able to decline a tasking if they perceived it to be in conflict with national foreign policy or ROE. At the same time, the NCC recognized that some nations were not as advanced on this issue as others and had yet to develop a mature ROE framework. If time allowed, an individual commander would refer the matter in dispute to the relevant national command element in HQ INTERFET for resolution. If the problem could not be resolved here, it would then be passed to national headquarters at home.

Nevertheless, the risks to coordination, timing, and readiness within the force were real, and once more a pragmatic approach proved essential. The answer was always to match forces with activity, allowing INTERFET needs to be satisfied without compromising unique national interests. The Singaporeans, for example, were exceptionally keen to assist the coalition. At the same time, as a member of ASEAN, they were extremely sensitive to regional perceptions and did not wish to appear as a big international player. The three Singapore Navy LSTs were therefore given the role of providing a continuous ferry service from Darwin to Dili. Although relatively low key, they worked in tandem with other coalition sealift assets, and their contribution remained instrumental in establishing the land component of INTERFET ashore. Remarking on "the ease with which the Singaporean Navy slotted into the Coalition, particularly the way in which they related to the RAN," Commodore Robertson gave most credit to the RAN's long-running program of regional engagement.[152] In this sense, Australia was able to bring a valuable partner into the coalition in a manner that might not have been so easy had another nation with global responsibilities, and the associated negative undertones, provided the lead.

The main lesson here is that ships are self-contained; hence, units without appropriate ROE, capabilities, or skill sets can, if required, be isolated to some extent. This tactical separation potentially reduces the need of the commander to provide a level of supervision that might drag away more capable assets from where they are needed most. Even ashore, Cosgrove deliberately divided East Timor into more and less difficult areas, ensuring that tough areas, such as those on the borders, were handled only by forces with the requisite skills and experience for "peace making" rather than "peace keeping."[153] In many respects, however, this was only workable because the higher-level threat failed to materialize, for as one of the first detailed studies of the operation pointed out:

> A truly multinational and ad hoc peace-enforcement force with a diverse membership is workable only if the mission does not involve high-intensity operations against competent opponents employing sophisticated weapons offensively. In this sense INTERFET was fortunate not to encounter opponents that were willing to wage war against it in a more effective manner. It should also be pointed out that it was possible to be misled as to the apparent ease by which INTERFET established its authority. The determination and efficiency that characterized INTERFET operations, particularly on the border, in the Oecussi enclave and in the vicinity of Dili rapidly nipped any opposition in the bud. If anything the firm response and coherent policy of the force demonstrated that in order to make a force multinational without sacrificing functional interoperability, a limited number of countries need to accept responsibility for the conduct of any offensive operations that need to be undertaken.[154]

In East Timor as so often elsewhere, the military commander needed access to a balanced set of joint capabilities. Yet apart from the United States, few nations today could ever hope to mount such an expeditionary force. Hence the key for all INTERFET commanders was to get the individual members of the coalition working as much as possible as a unified force. In reality, the breadth of maritime tasks undertaken during Stabilise could not have been achieved without contributing nation support. This holds true from both a practical and political perspective, for there were always two dimensions to the operation: what INTERFET was actually doing, and what it was perceived to be doing. The upshot of all this was that the naval component needed to be not just interoperable and cohesive but flexible and willing to compromise. The NCC and his staff maintained a constant balancing act. Dealing with both bilateral and a multilateral relationships, they had to remain focused on the success of the INTERFET mission while ensuring that each national contingent achieved its political objectives.

Conclusions

Operation Stabilise was a success, but in historical terms the insertion and sustainment of INTERFET was by no means an enormous undertaking. No matter how well led and implemented the actual operation, the fact remains that the ADF was stretched to the breaking point in providing a small division-size expeditionary force only some four hundred miles from Australia: 24 hours by sea, 90 minutes by air. Success, therefore, might equally be attributed to external factors, especially two critical ones: Indonesia's decision not to oppose the coalition, and U.S. political support. In view of the importance of such outside issues in shaping the operational environment, a common observation has been that fortune smiled on INTERFET.[155] Dili to Darwin was just within the ADF's capabilities, no threat—human or natural—disrupted INTERFET's supply lines, all essential units managed to stay operational, and Australia's friends proved willing to cooperate. Stabilise also began at just the right time, with Exercise Crocodile 99 establishing good working relationships among the individual service planners and smoothing the integration of the component commands.

But one should not forget that diligence is the mother of good fortune. Multinational interoperability provided INTERFET's lynchpin, and at a fundamental level Stabilise worked because disparate forces could function together to share the operational burden. Importantly, this interoperability came about not just through advanced technological compatibilities but also from person-to-person links. Thus crucial to implementing the operation were the ADF's deliberate efforts to develop relations with both regional states and allies. This was nowhere more obvious than in the maritime arena, which possessed the added benefit of the Western world's long-practiced policies of naval cooperation. Many years of joint training, standardized doctrine, familiarity with each other's ways and habits, and compatible equipment ensured that coalition navies achieved and sustained the required levels of interoperability. This competence and the ability of ships to carry out a large number of disparate activities simultaneously for extended periods ensured that the Australian Navy could call on its core coalition partners with a level of confidence unmatched by other environmental components.

The views presented in this chapter are those of the author and do not necessarily represent those of the Royal Australian Navy or the Australian government.

Notes

1. "The Lead Nation Concept in Coalition Operations," MWG Report to the Multinational Interoperability Council, 20 December 2000.

2. For the official view, see Commonwealth of Australia, *Defending Australia: Defence White Paper 1994* (Canberra: Australian Government Publishing Service, 1994).

3. David J. Campbell, "Maritime power and the Australian Defence Force," in *Maritime Power in the 20th Century: The Australian Experience*, ed. David M. Stevens (Sydney: Allen & Unwin, 1998), 249–58.

4. Alan Ryan, *Primary Responsibilities and Primary Risks: Australian Defence Force Participation in the International Force East Timor*, Land Warfare Studies Centre, Paper No. 304, Canberra, November 2000, 39–42.

5. A member of the Australian public was quoted during the Sydney INTERFET welcome home parade as saying: "I didn't know the Navy was in Timor." Cited in Paul G. Kinghorne, "OPERATION STABILISE—Australian Naval Participation in East Timor," *Naval Supply Newsletter*, June 2000, 25.

6. Peter Cosgrove, "The ANZAC Lecture at Georgetown University," *Journal of the Australian Naval Institute* (April–June 2000): 9.

7. Norman Friedman, *Seapower as Strategy: Navies and National Interests* (Annapolis, MD: Naval Institute Press, 2001), 3.

8. For an East Timor chronology, see http://www.un.org/peace/etimor/Untaetchrono.html, accessed 20 April 2006.

9. TNI (Tentara Nasional Indonesia).

10. For an insightful and detailed summary of the TNI's multifaceted role in East Timor, see Robert Lowry, *The Armed Forces of Indonesia* (Sydney: Allen & Unwin, 1996), 151–62.

11. On 12 November 1991 Indonesian troops fired upon a peaceful memorial procession to a cemetery in Dili that had turned into a pro-independence demonstration. More than 271 East Timorese were killed. Total East Timorese casualties during the 1975–1999 Indonesian occupation have been estimated at between 100,000 and 200,000.

12. "Question of East Timor," Report of the Secretary-General, 5 May 1999, at http://www.un.org/peace/etimor/docs/UntaetDr.htm, accessed 20 April 2006.

13. For the text of the resolution, see http://www.un.org/peace/etimor/docs/UntaetDrs.htm, accessed 20 April 2000.

14. *East Timor in Transition 1998–2000: An Australian Policy Challenge*, Department of Foreign Affairs and Trade, Canberra, 2001, 61.

15. Peter G. Edwards and David Goldsworthy, eds., *Facing North: A Century of Australian Engagement with Asia*, vol. 2, *1970s to 2000* (Melbourne: Melbourne University Press, 2003), 236.

16. Report of the Joint Standing Committee on Foreign Affairs Defence and Trade (JSCFADT), "A Visit to East Timor: 2 December 1999," Parliament of the Commonwealth of Australia, Canberra, December 1999, 46.

17. Militia goals included removing the foreign presence, wreaking vengeance on proindependence supporters, and sending a warning to other Indonesian regions with secessionist movements. See Edwards and Goldsworthy, *Facing North*, 245.

18. East Timorese casualties in the wake of the referendum have been variously estimated at between 1,400 and 30,000.

19. For the text of Kofi Annan's press statements during this period, see http://www.un.org/News/ossg/sg/pages/speeches_search.html, accessed 20 April 2006.

20. For the full text of the resolution, see http://www.un.org/peace/etimor/docs/UntaetDrs.htm, accessed 20 April 2006.

21. Kofi Annan made the approach to the Australian prime minister on 6 September 1999. See Edwards and Goldsworthy, *Facing North*, 248.

22. JSCFADT, "Visit to East Timor," 50.

23. Ryan, *Primary Responsibilities and Primary Risks*, ix.

24. See, for example, Carl Thayer, "Australian Perceptions and Indonesian Reality" (Lecture at the New Zealand Institute of International Affairs [Dunedin Branch], Hocken Hall, The University of Otago, Dunedin, 12 May 1988).

25. *Defending Australia: Defence White Paper 1994*, 87.

26. Cited in Edwards and Goldsworthy, *Facing North*, 217.

27. As late as December 1998, Prime Minister John Howard had reaffirmed Australian support for Indonesian sovereignty, although he admitted that "a decisive element of East Timorese opinion is insisting on an act of self-determination." See Edwards and Goldsworthy, *Facing North*, 228.

28. Edwards and Goldsworthy, *Facing North*, 216.

29. David M. Horner, *Making the Australian Defence Force* (Melbourne: Oxford University Press, 2001), 9.

30. "Massive plan to evacuate 10,000," *Age* newspaper, Melbourne, 16 December 1998.

31. ADF Media release MIN067/99, 11 March 1999.

32. Ryan, *Primary Responsibilities and Primary Risks*, 39–41.

33. The ANZAC (Australian and New Zealand Army Corps) tradition arose from the amphibious landing at Gallipoli on 25 April 1915.

34. Interview with Air Marshal Carey W. Adamson, 31 January 2002, RNZN Museum. Copy held by Sea Power Centre–Australia (SPC–A).

35. Interview with Commander Warren M. Cummins, 15 February 2000, RNZN Museum. Copy held by SPC–A.

36. "How Cosgrove led his warriors for peace," *Sydney Morning Herald*, 31 January 2000.

37. Adamson interview, 31 January 2002.

38. HMA Ships *Kanimbla* (ex-USS *Saginaw*) and *Manoora* (ex-USS *Fairfax County*).

39. "Operation Stabilise," *The Navy: Magazine of the Navy League of Australia* 62, no. 1 (January–March 2000): 3–10.

40. Brian D. Robertson, "Not Learning the Lessons of Operation Stabilise," *Journal of the Australian Naval Institute* (April/June 2000): 11.

41. Cosgrove, "The ANZAC Lecture," 6.

42. Edwards and Goldsworthy, *Facing North*, 241.

43. In an apparent response to Australia's role in the East Timor crisis, on 16 September 1999 Indonesia abrogated a bilateral defense treaty signed in 1995.

44. ASEAN comprises Brunei, Cambodia, Indonesia, Laos, Malaysia, Myanmar, Philippines, Singapore, Thailand, and Vietnam.

45. Edwards and Goldsworthy, *Facing North*, 250.

46. Ryan, *Primary Responsibilities and Primary Risks*, 40.

47. By mid-November 1999 Australia's commitment ashore had reached approximately 5,500 troops. See Horner, *Making the Australian Defence Force*, 22.

48. Edwards and Goldsworthy, *Facing North*, 252.

49. Kinghorne, "OPERATION STABILISE," 24.

50. The ADF contribution to East Timor actually took place under the banner of Operation Warden. Operation Stabilise was the coalition aspect.

51. Bradley A. White, "Maritime Operations in East Timor: The HMAS MELBOURNE Experience," *Journal of the Australian Naval Institute* (April/June 2000): 16.

52. Interview with Commodore James R. Stapleton, RAN, December 2004, Naval History & Heritage Command (NHHC), Washington, DC. Copy held by SPC–A.

53. Robertson, "Not Learning the Lessons of Operation Stabilise," 10.

54. Commonwealth of Australia, *Defence Annual Report 1999-2000* (Canberra: Defence Publishing Service, 2000), 270.

55. Kinghorne, "OPERATION STABILISE," 24.

56. HMAS *Tobruk*, "Operational Report 18 Sep 99-05 Nov 99," 5 November 1999, SPC–A.

57. Captain (N) Richard Girouard, "Op Toucan," *Maritime Affairs* (Fall 2000): 27.

58. For example, U.S. INTERFET liaison officers deployed to Brisbane on 31 August 1999. See Lyle M. Cross, Randy P. Strong, and Dave Delauney, "EAST TIMOR: A Case Study in C4 Innovation," *CHIPS—The Department of the Navy Information Technology Magazine* (Winter 2003), at http://www.chips.navy.mil/archives/03_winter/webpages/timor.htm, accessed 14 February 2006.

59. Adamson interview, 31 January 2002.

60. Kinghorne, "OPERATION STABILISE," 24.

61. Stapleton interview, December 2004.

62. Ibid.

63. For a detailed discussion, see Michael Kelly, Timothy L. H. McCormack, Paul Muggleton, and Bruce M. Oswald, "Legal aspects of Australia's involvement in East Timor," *International Review of the Red Cross*, no. 841, 101–139.

64. UNSCR 1244 (1999).

65. Kelly et al., "Legal aspects of Australia's involvement in East Timor."

66. *Manoora* and *Kanimbla* have since taken on the role of command ship, with both vessels effectively performing this task during Operations Enduring Freedom and Iraqi Freedom.

67. Robertson, "Not Learning the Lessons of Operation Stabilise," 10.

68. For an Australian perspective on the development of U.S. involvement in East Timor, see Edwards and Goldsworthy, *Facing North*, 248–49.

69. Cummins interview, 15 February 2000.

70. Cosgrove, "The ANZAC Lecture," 7.

71. Cross et al., "EAST TIMOR: A Case Study in C4 Innovation."

72. Kelly et al., "Legal aspects of Australia's involvement in East Timor."

73. HMAS *Adelaide*, "Report of Proceedings–September 1999," 12 October 1999, SPC–A.

74. Discussion with NCC Chief of Staff in 1999 Captain Daryl W. Bates, RAN, 21 February 2006.

75. Peter G. Lockwood, "RAN Participation in East Timor: Perspective from HMAS *Darwin*" (Presentation at 2001 King Hall Naval History Conference, Canberra, 27 July 2001). Copy held by SPC–A.

76. David Wilson, *Warden to Tanager: RAAF Operations in East Timor* (Maryborough, Queensland: Banner Books, 2003), 9.

77. Cummins interview, 15 February 2000.

78. The Brisbane Institute, "Questions to Major-General Cosgrove," 16 May 2000, at http://www.brisinst.org.au/resources/cosgrove_peter_cos.html, accessed 20 April 2006.

79. James V. P. Goldrick, "East Timor," *Journal of the Australian Naval Institute* (April/June 2000): 25.

80. Interview with Major General Peter Cosgrove, December 1999[?], RNZN Museum. Copy held by SPC–A.

81. Cosgrove, "The ANZAC Lecture," 9.

82. Wilson, *Warden to Tanager*, 13.

83. Like the clearance divers, the three-man HODSU was embarked in *Success* and called forward as soon as a special forces presence was established in the port precinct.

84. *Jervis Bay* averaged three trips per week between Darwin and Dili. Up to the end of February 2000 she had carried 10,740 passengers, 447 vehicles, and 2,505 tons of cargo. See HMAS *Jervis Bay*, "Report of Proceedings–February 2000," 6 March 2000, SPC–A.

85. Stapleton interview, December 2004.

86. HMAS *Adelaide*, "Report of Proceedings–September 1999."

87. Girouard, "Op Toucan," 29.

88. Adamson interview, 31 January 2002.

89. Cummins interview, 15 February 2000.

90. Centre for Strategic Studies (CSS), "Strategic and Military Lessons from East Timor," Strategic Briefing Papers, vol. 2, pt. 1, February 2000. See http://www.vuw.ac.nz/css/docs/Strategic_Briefing_Papers/Vol.2%20Feb%202000/East%20Timor.pdf, accessed 1 May 2006.

91. HMAS *Anzac*, "Report of Proceedings–September 1999," 6 October 1999, SPC–A.

92. Goldrick, "East Timor," 25.

93. "Special Navy comm unit supports the East Timor peacekeeping force," at http://www.gcn.com/print/vol18_no33/749-1.html, accessed 16 May 2006.

94. Cross et al., "EAST TIMOR: A Case Study in C4 Innovation."

95. Stapleton interview, December 2004.

96. Girouard, "Op Toucan," 26–27.

97. Interview with Commodore James R. Stapleton, RAN, 3 November 2000, RNZN Museum. Copy held by SPC–A.

98. Cosgrove, "The ANZAC Lecture," 6.

99. Goldrick, "East Timor," 24.

100. Girouard, "Op Toucan," 27.

101. Stapleton interview, December 2004.

102. Peter J. Criss, "Air Operations in Australia's Defence," *United Service* 52, no. 3, 25.

103. 91.7 percent by weight and 93.2 percent by volume. See Kinghorne, "OPERATION STABILISE," 26.

104. The "oil spot" concept entails establishing dominance in key locations from which the surrounding and interconnecting areas are influenced and subsequently controlled.

105. For details of these operations, see Ryan, *Primary Responsibilities and Primary Risks*, 74.

106. All beaches used for logistics were first swum by clearance divers and surveyed by HODSU to establish their suitability.

107. John M. Pritchard and Peter D. Arnold, "A Much Neglected Lady Proves She Can Still Deliver the Goods: HMAS TOBRUK's role in Operation Spitfire/Warden/Stabilise," *Journal of the Australian Naval Institute* (April/June 2000): 21.

108. Girouard, "Op Toucan," 28.

109. "Operation Stabilise," *The Navy*, 7.

110. "Stallion lifts a series of firsts," *Navy News Special INTERFET edition*, December 1999, 13.

111. Ryan, *Primary Responsibilities and Primary Risks*, 80.

112. *Belleau Wood*'s team assisted on 23 October and offloaded 22 ISO 20-foot containers. A similar operation, on 29 October, using *Peleliu*'s team offloaded 16 ISO 20-foot containers. It is worth noting that the remaining 101 containers carried by *Tobruk* during the operation were offloaded using her own crane. See Pritchard and Arnold, "A Much Neglected Lady Proves She Can Still Deliver the Goods," 21.

113. Robertson, "Not Learning the Lessons of Operation Stabilise," 12.

114. White, "Maritime Operations in East Timor," 17.

115. Girouard, "Op Toucan," 27.

116. Cummins interview, 15 February 2000.

117. HMAS *Sydney*, "Conduct of a Surveillance and Presence Mission," 3 December 1999, SPC–A.

118. See, for example, "Interview with Vice Admiral David Shackleton," U.S. Naval Institute (USNI) *Proceedings* (January 2002): 62; and White, "Maritime Operations in East Timor," 18.

119. Pritchard and Arnold, "HMAS TOBRUK's role in Operation Spitfire/Warden/Stabilise," 21.

120. For the full text, see http://www.un.org/peace/etimor/docs/UntaetDrs.htm, accessed 20 April 2006.

121. Although the INTERFET handover began on 1 February 2000, UNTAET had already initiated operations and established the basic elements of its administrative structure.

122. Robertson, "Not Learning the Lessons of Operation Stabilise," 12.

123. White, "Maritime Operations in East Timor," 16.

124. Cummins interview, 15 February 2000.

125. Robertson, "Not Learning the Lessons of Operation Stabilise," 14.

126. See http://www.nwdc.navy.mil/Concepts/Sea_Basing/SeaBasing.aspx, accessed 2 May 2006.

127. Cosgrove, "The ANZAC Lecture," 9.

128. Figure cited in John Crawford and Glyn Harper, *Operation East Timor: The New Zealand Defence Force in East Timor 1999–2001* (Auckland: Reed Publishing, 2001), 74.

129. Robertson, "Not Learning the Lessons of Operation Stabilise," 12.

130. "Operation Stabilise," *The Navy*, 6.

131. Message, Maritime Commander Australia to HMCS *Protecteur*, 200616ZOCT 99, SPC–A.

132. Girouard, "Op Toucan," 28.

133. Ibid., 26.

134. Ibid.

135. "Working Party Joins in Spirit," *Navy News Special INTERFET edition*, December 1999, 7.

136. Robertson, "Not Learning the Lessons of Operation Stabilise," 13.

137. Stapleton interview, December 2004.

138. Ryan, *"Primary Responsibility and Primary Risks,"* 28.

139. Cosgrove, "The ANZAC Lecture," 7–8.

140. Robertson assumed duties as NCC from November 1999.

141. Stapleton interview, December 2004.

142. "Australian Operations in East Timor," Interview with Vice Admiral Shackleton, USNI *Proceedings* (December 1999): 4.

143. "Interview Australian Chief of Navy," USNI *Proceedings* (January 2000): 57.

144. Extract from HMAS *Darwin*, "Post-deployment report," 6 November 1999, SPC–A.

145. HMAS *Darwin*, "Post-deployment report."

146. Kinghorne, "OPERATION STABILISE," 29.

147. "France moves quickly on UN request," *Navy News Special INTERFET edition*, December 1999, 11.

148. Robertson, "Not Learning the Lessons of Operation Stabilise," 10.

149. "Brief to Maritime Commander visit to East Timor," 18 October 1999, East Timor File, SPC–A.

150. Eric S. Miller, *Interoperability of Rules of Engagement in Multinational Maritime Operations*, CRM 95–184 (Alexandria, VA: CNA, October 1995), 14.

151. Discussion with Captain Daryl W. Bates, February 2006.

152. Robertson, "Not Learning the Lessons of Operation Stabilise," 11.

153. Cosgrove, "The ANZAC Lecture," 7.

154. Ryan, *"Primary Responsibility and Primary Risks,"* 64.

155. General Cosgrove himself has noted the "ever present part that luck played." See Cosgrove, "The ANZAC Lecture," 9.

CHAPTER 5

A Limited Commitment to Ending Civil Strife: The U.S. Navy in Operation Stabilise

Sarandis Papadopoulos

The defining characteristic of naval operations in the post–Cold War world is their direct link to events ashore. Given the predominance of Western maritime strength, few states would choose to challenge the ships of Australia, Canada, the United Kingdom, or the United States, especially when operating in concert with one another. Mindful of the changing nature of operations afloat, the sea services of these four countries, along with those of eight other nations, supported a United Nations intervention to quell civic strife in East Timor, many of whose people sought independence from the much larger Indonesia. Operation Stabilise, conducted in late 1999, stands out as a key example of how naval capabilities can help resolve conflicts on land.

East Timor had been a territory of Portugal until 1974, when a newly democratic Lisbon government ended its control of the colony and an East Timorese government took power.[1] Indonesia, glimpsing an opportunity to gain control of what its more extreme nationalists called the "27th province," occupied East Timor in 1975 and only added to the tensions there. A November 1991 massacre in Dili, the capital, by troops of the Indonesian National Armed Forces, or TNI, began to turn international opinion against the occupation.[2] Compounding the strife, a severe regional economic decline began in 1997, drawing U.S. government attention. Following the collapse of the dictatorship of President Suharto, in 1999 new President B. J. Habibie allowed a referendum in East Timor on independence from Indonesia. Pro-independence forces won the plebiscite, but militia groups loyal to Jakarta and rogue TNI elements threatened a breakdown of law and order.[3] The United Nations stood determined to prevent widespread banditry and killings by intervening with military force. Such a force would interpose itself between the Timorese population and potential attackers.

Australia proved key to bringing in the U.S. government to support the East Timor operation. Leadership from Canberra was essential as the post–Cold War world saw humanitarian and peacekeeping forces increasingly assembled on a regional basis and operating under UN auspices.[4] In this case, Australia assumed the status of lead nation, a role allowing a more limited U.S. government commitment, with its forces playing a supporting role.

The UN-sponsored plebiscite took place on 30 August. More than 78 percent of the East Timorese rejected circumscribed autonomy within Indonesia, instead demanding outright independence.[5] A series of attacks on the pro-independence supporters in East Timor began the next day by militia members working with Indonesian military support. Beginning on 8 September, Australian and New Zealander military aircraft evacuated UN observers and refugees from the trouble zone, making the mission of the armed services a humanitarian one.[6] At the time, United Nations observers reported that TNI soldiers were aiding the pro-Jakarta militia members who attacked the Timorese.[7] Given the prospect of large-scale massacres, the Canberra government suggested it would enthusiastically welcome any form of American support for a UN-mandated peacekeeping force to enforce the withdrawal of Indonesian troops.[8]

On 15 September 1999 United Nations Security Council Resolution (UNSCR) 1264 requested the deployment of military forces to the troubled island, specifying that the soldiers shield residents of East Timor and establish peace and security there.[9] Under the authority of the United Nations, ships from Australia, Canada, Great Britain, and the United States, along with four other nations, initially supported land forces ashore, eventually drawn from 20 nations' armed services and police forces.[10] Troops of the 3rd Brigade, Australian Army, reinforced by British and New Zealander units, first began landing in Dili on 20 September.

Additional contingents of soldiers and police landed over the next three weeks, raising the number of personnel on the island to more than 8,000.

By authorizing intervention "to restore peace and security," UNSCR 1264 effectively created a peace*making* mission under Article 42 of Chapter VII of the UN Charter.[11] The mandate was, therefore, politically robust. The command became the International Force East Timor, or INTERFET.[12] Indonesian troops began withdrawing westward by sea three days after international forces first landed in Dili. Once again, securing sea control—accomplished through common doctrine, familiarity inculcated through training, and interoperable command, control, and communications—allowed naval forces to assist land power in separating violent groups ashore.

The U.S. Commitment

One should view the East Timor intervention against the backdrop of the region's political importance to the United States and its peacekeeping operations worldwide. While the crisis drew headlines in the United States, Southeast Asia attracted little interest among Americans as a prospective theater for the commitment of large combat forces.[13] Given the heavy demand for U.S. military forces elsewhere, Washington made clear its disinclination to deploy sizable forces to East Timor.[14] Instead, American sentiment favored a constrained military obligation. On 29 September 1999 U.S. Secretary of Defense William Cohen summed up the prevailing sentiment: "We are not the world's policeman, and we do not seek to fulfill that role. What we do seek is to promote stability and democracy wherever we can and in whatever capacity we can, and we are in a supportive role right now."[15] American forces would participate but in a limited manner.

The operational reason for the low U.S. Navy commitment lay in the sea service's tempo in peacekeeping and enforcement actions. During spring 1999 three American aircraft carrier battle groups (CVBGs) and an amphibious ready group (ARG) were committed to combat actions against the Federal Republic of Yugoslavia. The eight-week-long Operation Allied Force, followed up by a long-term ground commitment, involved American forces in the effort to prevent ethnic cleansing in Kosovo.[16] During the year another CVBG and an ARG remained committed to supporting maritime interdiction operations in the Middle East and enforcing the no-fly zone over Iraq in Operation Southern Watch. The commitment of another ARG to Turkey for earthquake relief in August and September 1999 further strained U.S. naval resources.[17] The U.S. Navy would have been hard pressed to deploy large forces in support of the East Timor intervention.

At the same time 1999 saw the United Nations engaged in the second-largest number of peacekeeping operations in its history, straining member nation resources.[18] Thus few countries could spare troops for intervention in East Timor. The Australian commanders of Operation Stabilise would have to leverage every asset at their disposal.

The unstable Timorese situation into which American service members stepped compelled them to tread a fine line between conflicting requirements. INTERFET called on U.S. personnel to serve as part of a multinational force working under a UN mandate. As participants in Stabilise they operated under the direction of a foreign commanding officer, Major General Peter Cosgrove of the Australian Army. The Americans therefore had to adapt to unfamiliar command, control, and planning practices conducted by a "bewildering" array of actors.[19]

Indonesia and Timor

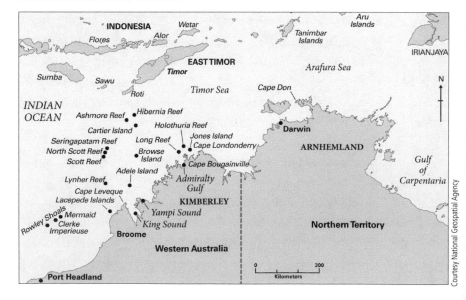

Intervening in East Timor would place the Americans in risky circumstances. The outside intervention had begun with regional nations, Australia and New Zealand, performing a humanitarian mission. Given the chaos developing on the ground in East Timor and indeed throughout Indonesia, the Americans realized they might find themselves working in an unstable "failed state" instead.[20] The U.S. government wanted to avoid a situation in which a humanitarian operation deteriorated into a civic breakdown as seen earlier during the Somali and Rwandan crises, with the intervention forces on the ground, including Americans, too few in number to handle a collapse of internal security.[21] For that reason U.S. leaders decided to limit their commitment ashore.[22]

The uncertain nature of the American commitment to INTERFET meant the Navy and Marine Corps forces had only a vague idea of their mission off Timor. During the summer of 1999, U.S. military staff members planned a set of responses to an evolving "situation in Timor" that paid close attention to questions of intelligence, geography, and the supply constraints.[23] Even after the intervention began, Marine Brigadier General John Castellaw, commander of the U.S. Forces INTERFET, remarked to a *Washington Times* reporter on 30 September 1999, "We are proceeding without a plan, doing our best as it's been laid out."[24] Such indistinct responsibilities, both before and after the start of Operation Stabilise, would call for adaptability on the part of U.S. forces.

Castellaw laid out four goals for U.S. forces in the region, conforming to the overall INTERFET mission and his own national instructions, while retaining the greatest degree of initiative possible:

1. Establish a comprehensive force protection plan.

2. Minimize the footprint and exposure of U.S. forces in Dili (and other sites within East Timor).

3. Rapidly introduce unique U.S.-only capabilities.

4. Commander, INTERFET remains in charge.[25]

The general's intent conformed to his politically mandated instructions and acted as informal rules of engagement for the American ships assembling off the coast.

Brigadier General Castellaw's orders also reflected the U.S. determination to play a noncombat role in East Timor.[26] More important, his goals maximized the ability of U.S. forces to protect themselves, especially from the highest potential threatening source, the Indonesian Navy. The American commander had no reasons to expect a direct confrontation with the Indonesians but had to consider the possibility. With those priorities, the general could remain confident that his forces would provide unique capabilities to INTERFET and General Cosgrove without putting themselves at risk ashore.[27] It was an impressive balancing act.

Subordination in a foreign-led operation did raise structural and doctrinal questions for the U.S. forces committed to East Timor. Castellaw's stricture on the deployment of forces ashore reflected the political guidance of President Bill Clinton and the U.S. National Security Council (NSC). Meeting on 16 September, the NSC mandated an American supporting role, with no more than 250 personnel on the ground.[28] Apart from a small team in Dili, and a number of Air Force transport aircraft flying between Darwin and Dili, the only other U.S. presence in the region would be Navy ships and embarked Marines. Under existing doctrine the Americans would have designated their units a "Joint Task Force," incorporating different service elements and a planning staff under the command of a U.S. officer.[29] Instead, Admiral Dennis Blair (Commander in Chief, U.S. Pacific Command) and Castellaw termed the American contingent a "Joint Force," reflecting a multiservice composition but without mandating the staff members that joint doctrine demanded. Adding a staff would have pushed the personnel numbers above the maximum set by the NSC.[30] Calling the U.S. group a joint force also enabled it to work under the operational control of the foreign-headed INTERFET.[31] U.S. Navy ships were *not* assigned to the joint force but designated "Joint Task Force–Timor Sea Operations," probably because their crew numbers would also have exceeded the personnel ceiling. These units reported directly to Castellaw. American naval forces added their considerable capabilities to the UN operation but did not compromise U.S. government political restrictions.

U.S. Forces Participate in Stabilise

Despite their relatively small numbers, the U.S. Navy ships available for Operation Stabilise made a significant contribution, for their crews held several advantages that made them familiar with allied tactics and doctrine. Initially, the sole American warship available in the region was the guided missile cruiser USS *Mobile Bay*, engaged with the Royal Australian Navy in Exercise Crocodile '99. The ship's fortuitous presence in a scheduled exercise allowed the crew to accustom themselves to Australian military procedures, giving them confidence in the force they supported. Better, the ship's parent command, U.S. Seventh Fleet, had two years earlier identified several incompatibilities between the American and Australian planning processes.[32] After working with the same Australian command participating in the East Timor operation—the 3rd Infantry Brigade—lessons-learned reports had identified differing national approaches to preparing amphibious landings. The reports suggest that the two navies possessed background information helpful for quickly resolving the incompatibilities. Finally, Major General Cosgrove offered another, personal, counterbalance to any lack of familiarity between the American and Australian forces: in 1979 he had graduated from the U.S. Marine Corps Command and Staff College.[33]

Mobile Bay offered unique capabilities to the maritime component of INTERFET. In particular, she was an Aegis combat system-equipped cruiser, ideal for gaining a comprehensive understanding of the air and ocean environment around Dili.[34] Locally acquired data could be combined with intelligence details from outside the theater delivered through the ship's Trojan Spirit II satellite communication systems.[35] Once collated, *Mobile Bay*'s Link-16 system could automatically share information with the other warships through their compatible Link-11 systems, relying on a process called "concurrent interfacing."[36] Further complemented by information acquired by a U.S. EP-3 Aries electronic intelligence aircraft based near Darwin, Australia, the cruiser offered a comprehensive understanding to the international force.[37] No other ships in INTERFET could build such a complete air picture, and the ground forces committed to the operation certainly had nothing comparable in their inventory for sharing combat data. The cruiser therefore served a vital purpose in its ability to warn UN forces of potential threats from the air or sea.

The U.S. Military Sealift Command also supported INTERFET. With a civilian crew, the USNS *Kilauea*, a 20,000-ton ammunition ship, left Exercise Crocodile '99 to support Operation Stabilise.[38] While not employed as a cargo vessel, *Kilauea* operated from her enclosed hangar two CH-46 Sea Knight helicopters, aircraft capable of moving up to 10,000 pounds or 25 people by air.[39] The ship could offer a mobile, self-supporting floating air base, a so-called lily pad, wherever and whenever the UN force required one. Helicopters based on board also made the 500-mile transit from Darwin to East Timor.[40] Initially, *Kilauea* and *Mobile Bay* constituted Joint Task Force–Timor Sea Operations.

As the international force expanded its control of East Timor, a U.S. amphibious warfare ship, USS *Belleau Wood*, pitched in to support Operation Stabilise. In reality a small aircraft carrier, the ship carried much of the 31st Marine Expeditionary Unit (MEU), built around a reinforced infantry battalion.[41] She arrived off East Timor around 1 October, and *Belleau Wood*'s embarked aircraft, from Marine Medium Helicopter Squadron 265, offered a reinforced heavy-lift air group crucially important to the INTERFET force.[42] The squadron operated a mix of CH-46 and CH-53 Sea Stallion machines ideally suited to moving heavy payloads.[43] Transport planes based in Australia could deliver only a limited supply of food by parachute to the island's civilian population. The CH-53s, in contrast, moved large amounts of food by air from ships offshore. Sea Stallions of USS *Peleliu*, another amphibious ship of the *Belleau Wood* class, alone delivered more than 1.5 million pounds of humanitarian supplies and equipment in one month. Helicopters could also avoid the already overburdened and violence-prone mountain roads and deliver cargoes directly to isolated villages. The Marine units prevented more extreme hunger among the people, of whom more than 200,000 were refugees.[44]

By and large the ground components of the MEU, as well as most U.S. forces, did not go ashore. Indeed, some additional command and control elements worked in Darwin. The 130 or so Americans in Dili provided intelligence, communications, and civil affairs support for the

USMC photo

Assigned to Fleet Surgical Team 5 aboard USS *Belleau Wood,* Navy physician Lieutenant Commander Sara H. Arnold administers medicine to an East Timor child. Arnold was among the many doctors from the *Belleau Wood* Amphibious Ready Group who took part in humanitarian visits in East Timor after civil strife in that country.

international force headquarters.[45] The limited ground commitment conformed to Brigadier General Castellaw's goals of maintaining force protection and keeping a small footprint on the ground in East Timor. It also reflected the U.S. government's desire to provide limited support to the United Nations and back up the operation's lead country, Australia.[46]

Belleau Wood's arrival off East Timor came at a crucial time in Operation Stabilise. Some nations contributing to INTERFET, such as New Zealand, lacked the logistical means needed to support their forces "over the shore," that is, directly from ships at sea.[47] Similarly, the Canadian Forces did not posses a single amphibious vessel capable of supporting the reinforced infantry company committed ashore. The Canadians relied on aircraft and other nations' shipping to move soldiers and deliver supplies. The Australian supply capabilities became stretched to the limit as they attempted to make up for other nations' lack of resources. Major General

Cosgrove considered the supply services provided by Australian sources to have operated "well above design capability."[48] But American military airlift offered an important, perhaps vital, margin of support. In the words of Defense Secretary Cohen, the U.S. airlift became a "force multiplier," allowing the peacekeeping operation to continue.[49]

Despite logistical limitations, on 10 October General Cosgrove sped up the timetable for sealing the border with Indonesia's West Timor province. He saw an opportunity to end the violence and accelerate the occupation of all East Timor. The general deployed an Australian infantry battalion by air to a series of border villages, effectively preventing infiltration by pro-Indonesian militia members.[50] The rapidity of these troop movements proved key to the UN force's success in protecting the civilian populace from militia attacks and stood in contrast to the deliberate buildup of some other multilateral operations.[51] In doing so, however, the general placed one-third of his infantry in exposed positions that were hard to supply with the limited number of Australian helicopters available. Resorting to U.S. Marine Corps helicopters allowed Cosgrove to make the move with a higher degree of confidence for distant deployment and resupply missions.[52] The multilevel flexibility of the UN units, especially the operational mobility enabled by naval forces, came through strongly in this phase of the Timorese operation.

When *Mobile Bay* departed Indonesian waters on 26 October, *Belleau Wood* assumed responsibility for all American support for Operation Stabilise, including command, control, and communications.[53] In early November, the amphibious warfare ship headed home to Sasebo, Japan, for a long-overdue operational pause. *Peleliu* deployed from the Arabian Gulf as a replacement and served for another month as the American warship hosting the largest transport helicopters. In January 2000 the smaller amphibious transport dock ship USS *San Antonio* and the embarked Marines supported the same mission during the UN force's occupation of the "Oecussi enclave," an outlying segment of East Timor separated by 50 kilometers of Indonesian territory.[54] Finally, the USNS *San Jose*, an auxiliary fleet support ship, relieved *Kilauea* to maintain supplies for the peacekeepers.

Following the completion of INTERFET's mission on 23 February 2000, the UN transferred authority to a police force with a more modest mandate. The United Nations Transitional Administration in East Timor (UNTAET) would operate with up to 8,950 military personnel, plus 200 military observers and 1,640 police.[55] These peacekeepers would complete execution of Operation Stabilise. Only a small number of American service members remained ashore in East Timor throughout the peacekeeping mission. A contingent of 30 military personnel, under a parallel U.S. command structure and employing national rules of engagement, worked on the ground alongside UNTAET, while American warships periodically visited for transport, humanitarian, or civic assistance missions.[56] A reflection of the considerable stretch confronting the U.S. armed services, the limited number of Americans on the ground fulfilled the demands placed upon them, while maintaining a low profile.

Operational Challenges

U.S. Navy forces encountered logistical difficulty in making wholesale deliveries of supplies to East Timor. In large measure this challenge stemmed from the episodic nature of the deployment, marked by intermittent activity

USN photo, Lt. Lisa Brackenbury

The amphibious assault ship USS *Belleau Wood*, which provided American support for Operation Stabilise, heads to her new homeport of San Diego, California, August 2000.

and long lulls. As a result minor shortages arose. For example, in October, *Mobile Bay* reported a shortage of F44 aviation fuel, resulting from its extensive support for helicopter flights to destinations far inland from the ship. Indeed one report submitted by the cruiser labeled F44 a "rare commodity in theater," and requested an oiler to resupply the naval forces committed to INTERFET.[57]

Retail delivery of supplies also became complicated during Operation Stabilise. The absence of a joint task force as the designated administrator of such deliveries proved one reason for the shortfall.[58] Because the U.S. force did not include a supply vessel, the lack of some spare parts became a problem. For common supply items the Australian logistical chain could support the U.S. ships, but items exclusively used by the Americans had to come directly from national sources. Ordering the items by satellite telephone or email proved straightforward. But Singapore and Guam, both more than 1,500 kilometers distant, constituted the nearest American supply depots, and no regularly scheduled vessels steamed from there to support the two U.S. ships.[59] Neither the Navy supply system nor the regional bases formally knew the warships' location, leading to one order of items being shipped by air to Sasebo, Japan, rather than to Guam. Consequently, *Mobile Bay*'s crew called for replacements for damaged items (casualty reports, or "CASREPs"), either by satellite telephone or email, and had them transported to Australia because the "husbanding agent in Sydney will know where the ship is."[60] Operating outside of the customary U.S. command structure compelled the Americans to improvise a workable supply system.

The 130 Americans making the ground-based communications and intelligence commitment to INTERFET, critical to mission success in East Timor, also required logistics support.[61] The communications and personnel were flown in from Darwin, 800 kilometers away, by just four medium-range aircraft. Naval units offshore kept the personnel supplied for two months.

Delivery of medical care to the U.S. personnel who were rushed to the tropical region of East Timor proved difficult.[62] Malaria was a constant worry, especially for helicopter crews who flew to points throughout the island. Uniforms treated with permanent insect repellent were in short supply, and service members considered their insect repellant unsatisfactory.[63] The preventive medical staff and other naval medical personnel recognized these deficiencies and recommended several measures for later deployments to tropical regions, especially those afflicted by civil unrest that often limited the access to public health.

Toward the end of the deployment, Commander Seventh Fleet noted his dissatisfaction with the meteorological support provided by *Belleau Wood* and *Peleliu*. Given INTERFET's dependence on aerial delivery of supplies, quick collection and delivery of meteorological data were essential to the safe operation of helicopters and fixed-wing aircraft in East Timor.[64] Heightening his concern was the possible development of fierce tropical cyclones that begin hitting the region in November. The meteorological teams took anywhere from three to seven days to fully develop their understanding of the region's weather, too long to determine the meteorological effects on Operation Stabilise.[65]

Assessment

Measured in terms of the goal to clear Indonesian troops from East Timor and establish an independent government based in Dili, INTERFET and UNTAET were unqualified successes. Allied forces protected the local population from further massacres while suffering few casualties of their own. That the force accomplished its mission by overcoming the obstacles of distance and political constraints makes its success all the more impressive.

From the U.S. perspective, Operation Stabilise yielded outstanding results. Working within a narrow set of political restrictions, American military forces provided vital support to INTERFET forces in East Timor. On the political side, the presence of U.S. Navy warships and aircraft as well as a small ground contingent signaled the importance Washington placed on the success of the Australian-led UN mission. That presence also served as a brake on the destabilizing activities of the militias, bandits, and even the Indonesian armed forces. From operational and tactical standpoints, the American naval presence was equally crucial. U.S. Navy units provided a comprehensive and robust picture of the air and sea around East Timor, offered helicopter transport to points throughout the country, served as floating bases just offshore, delivered food and other supplies to coalition troops and starving Timorese villagers, and conducted a full range of command, control, communications, intelligence, and civic action services. Despite some challenges delivering spare parts, medical care, and meteorological analysis, the U.S. Navy satisfied the need to minimize the American commitment to the region, while it helped establish the independence of East Timor and deliver its people from civil chaos.

Notes

1. http://www.un.org/peace/etimor/UntaetB.htm, accessed 25 January 2006.

2. Larry Dinger, "East Timor and U.S. Foreign Policy: Making Sausage" (Unpublished paper, National War College, Washington, DC, 2000), 2–3, at http://www.ndu.edu/library/n2/n005603D.pdf, accessed 26 October 2005. American opinion on East Timor proved quite polarized in the 1990s; see Noam Chomsky et al., "Ending 20 Years of Occupation: East Timor and U.S. Foreign Policy," Columbia University, 9 December 1995, at http://www.zmag.org/chomsky/talks/9512-timor-etan.html, accessed 27 October 2005.

3. Dinger, 3–5. Concern of the United Nations dated from December 1975 when the General Assembly had passed a resolution calling for East Timorese self-determination. See A/Res/3485 (XXX) "Question of Timor," 12 December 1975, at http://daccess-ods.un.org/TMP/4636015.html, accessed 27 October 2005.

4. Ian Clark, "Why the 'World's Policeman' Cannot Retire in Southeast Asia: A Critical Assessment of the 'East Timor Model'" (Unpublished master's thesis, U.S. Naval Postgraduate School, Monterey, CA, June 2002), 7–9. The same impulse compelled the West European Union to commit ground troops to the former Yugoslavia as part of UNPROFOR, and naval forces to Operation Sharp Fence, both in 1992.

5. On the plebiscite, see http://www.un.org/Depts/dpko/missions/unmiset/background.html, accessed 25 January 2006. See also K. Day, "Australian Peacekeeping Operations in East Timor," May 2000, 1, at http://www.ngic.army.smil.mil/products/htf/NGIC-1122-0041-00/art3.htm, accessed 5 December 2005.

6. Clark, "Why the 'World's Policeman' Cannot Retire," 10.

7. http://daccessdds.un.org/doc/UNDOC/GEN/N99/262/20/PDF/N9926220.pdf?OpenElement, accessed 25 January 2006.

8. Dinger, "East Timor and U.S. Foreign Policy," 5.

9. For the Security Council resolution, see http://www.un.int/usa/sres1264.htm, accessed 16 December 2005.

10. Listing of forces taken from "Riots, Rebellions, Gun Boats and Peace Keepers: East Timor," at http://www.britains-smallwars.com/RRGP/EastTimor.html, accessed 21 November 2005.

11. For the charter, see http://www.un.org/aboutun/charter/index.html, accessed 23 January 2006.

12. INTERFET forces executed Operation Stabilise, while Australian forces employed the operational name Warden for their contributions.

13. Alan Ryan, "Australian Army Cooperation with the Land Forces of the United States: Problems of the Junior Partner," Land Warfare Studies Centre, Working Paper No. 121, January 2003, 20.

14. On the questions addressed to U.S. President Bill Clinton regarding an American ground force presence in East Timor, see *Public Papers of the Presidents of the United States: William J. Clinton, 1999*, book 2 (Washington, DC: Government Printing Office [GPO], 2001), 1514, 1526, 1528, 1546.

15. As quoted in James Hessman, "U.S. Escalated Support for INTERFET Mission," *Sea Power* 42, no. 11 (November 1999): 30.

16. H. H. Gaffney et al., *U.S. Naval Responses to Situations, 1970–1999* (Alexandria, VA: CNA, December 2000), 61–66.

17. William Cobble et al., *For the Record: All U.S. Forces' Responses to Situations, 1970–2000* (Alexandria, VA: CNA, June 2003), 107.

18. James Dobbins, "The UN's Role in Nation-Building: From the Belgian Congo to Iraq," *Survival* 46, no. 4 (Winter 2004–05): 82.

19. USS *John S. McCain*, "Operational Groups," Navy Lessons Learned Database, 14 April 2000.

20. Clark, "Why the 'World's Policeman' Cannot Retire," 4.

21. On the inadequate force levels in Somalia, see Dobbins, 85. On the direct comparison to Rwanda, made by the President of the United States, see *Public Papers of the Presidents: William J. Clinton, 1999*, book 2, 1542.

22. Debra Beutel, "A JTF In Support: How U.S. Forces Can Achieve Success *by Influence*" (Unpublished paper, Naval War College, Newport, RI, 10 May 2002), 10.

23. U.S. Forces INTERFET, "Operation After Action Report. Part I: Executive Overview," 11 February 2000, 2.

24. As quoted in Beutel, "A JTF In Support," 10. Brigadier General Castellaw was Deputy Commander, 3rd Marine Expeditionary Force.

25. As listed in Beutel, "A JTF In Support," 11.

26. Excerpt of interview with Lieutenant General John Castellaw, October 2006, n.p. I am indebted to Dr. Nathan Lowery, U.S. Marine Corps Museum, for providing me with this source.

27. On the U.S. providing transportation, communications, and intelligence support for Operation Stabilise, announced on 13 September 1999, see *Public Papers of the Presidents: William J. Clinton, 1999*, book 2, 1528.

28. James Glynn, "Operation Stabilise: U.S. Joint Force Operations in East Timor" (Unpublished Master of Military Studies thesis, U.S. Marine Corps Command and Staff College, 20 April 2000), 12–13. Linda Kozaryn, "U.S. Limits Assistance to East Timor," suggested the limit was 200 personnel; see Armed Forces Information Service, 17 September 1999, at http://www.defenselink.mil/news/Sep1999/n09171999_9909162.html, accessed 25 January 2006.

29. Glynn, "Operation Stabilise," 5.

30. Ibid., 17.

31. Ibid., 19.

32. See Commander Seventh Fleet, "Australian Defense (*sic*) Force Battle Procedure Not Compatible with U.S. Expeditionary Forces Doctrine," Navy Lessons Learned Database, 4 May 1997.

33. See Major General Cosgrove's biography, at http://www.awm.gov.au/people/1070841.asp, accessed 1 February 2006.

34. I am indebted to Dr. David Stevens of the Sea Power Centre–Australia for pointing out this unique U.S. Navy contribution to Operation Stabilise, in conversations in July 2005.

35. Glynn, "Operation Stabilise," 8, 9, especially n. 7.

36. On the operational particulars of Link-16 ships, see Aegis Program Manager, Logicon Inc., *Understanding Link-16: A Guidebook for New Users* (San Diego, CA: Logicon Tactical Systems Division, April 1994), 7-2-7-7, A-10–A-11.

37. "Operation Stabilise After Action Report," 5.

38. Ibid., 3.

39. For USNS *Kilauea*, see http://www.msc.navy.mil/inventory/ships.asp?ship=kilauea&type=AmmunitionShip; for the lift capacity of a CH-46, see http://www.globalsecurity.org/military/systems/aircraft/ch-46.htm, both accessed 20 January 2006.

40. "Operation Stabilise After Action Report," 3.

41. On USS *Belleau Wood* and the 31st Marine Expeditionary Unit (Special Operations Capable), see letter, President Clinton to Speaker of the House of Representatives J. Dennis Hastert, as required by the War Powers Resolution, in United States, President William J. Clinton, "A Report Regarding Forces in East Timor," 8 October 1999, House Document 106-141 (Washington, DC: GPO, 1999), 1.

42. There is some confusion on the arrival date of USS *Belleau Wood*; Glynn, "Operation Stabilise," 6–7, reports her arrival as 5 October. The *Dictionary of American Naval Fighting Ships* lists a 14 September arrival, with helicopter missions beginning on 1 October, the date I have elected to use. See http://www.history.navy.mil/danfs/b4/belleau_wood.htm, accessed 20 January 2006.

43. James Folk and Andy Smith, "A LOGCAP Success in East Timor," *Army Logistician* 37 (Jul/Aug 2000), at http://www.almc.army.mil/ALOG/issues/JulAug00/MS566.htm, accessed 16 December 2005.

44. Numbers vary; see the 12 September entry at http://www.un.org/peace/etimor/Untaetchrono.html, accessed 24 January 2006.

45. See Kozaryn, "U.S. Limits Assistance." INTERFET's American headquarters staff came from all four U.S. services and rotated through in sequence. For example, Army 11th Signal Brigade troops replaced Marines of the 11th MEU in the communications work for INTERFET. See "Operation Stabilise After Action Report," 7, 33–34. For an Indonesian view of U.S. military strength, see "Indonesia: US Merely Sends Communications Personnel for INTERFET," *Antara* (29 September 1999): 1.

46. See the comments of Admiral Dennis Blair, Commander in Chief, U.S. Pacific Command, 24 September 1999, as quoted in "Operation Stabilise After Action Report," 24.

47. Air Marshal Carey Adamson, New Zealand Defence Force, "East Timor," (Brief to Chiefs of Defence Conference 2000, on humanitarian operations and multilateral efforts in East Timor), 2. Copy in author's files.

48. As quoted in Clark, "Why the 'World's Policeman' Cannot Retire," 30.

49. For Cohen, see Douglas Gillert, "U.S. Support Increases to East Timor 'Operation Warden,'" Armed Forces Information Service, 29 September 1999, at http://www.defense.gov/news/Sep1999/n09291999_9909292.html, accessed 25 January 2006. Lieutenant General Castellaw applied the same metaphor; see Beutel, "A JTF In Support," 12.

50. "Operation Stabilise After Action Report," 6.

51. Day, 3. On the contrast between the UNTAET experience and other UN operations, see Colm Mangan, "Multi-national Commitments to Peace Support Operations. A small state's experience" (Presentation at the International Commission of Military History Colloquy, Potsdam, Germany, 25 August 2006), 3.

52. "Operation Stabilise After Action Report," 7; and Beutel, "A JTF In Support," 12. With the departure of the U.S. Navy ships, four contractor-flown aircraft replaced their helicopters starting in November 1999. See Folk and Smith, "A LOGCAP Success."

53. http://www.history.navy.mil/danfs/b4/belleau_wood.htm, accessed 15 December 2005.

54. "Operation Stabilise After Action Report," 10–11, 35.

55. President William J. Clinton, "Periodic Report of the U.S. Military Force in East Timor," 25 August 2000, House Document 106-288 (Washington, DC: GPO, 2000), 1. For slightly varying numbers, see UNTAET Press Office, "Fact Sheet 2: UNTAET Basic Facts," April 2002, http://www.un.org/peace/etimor/fact/fs2.PDF, accessed 31 January 2006.

56. President William J. Clinton, "A Report Regarding Forces in East Timor," 25 February 2000, House Document 106-203 (Washington, DC: GPO, 2000), 1–2.

57. USS *Mobile Bay*, "Fuel (F44) In Theater," Navy Lessons Learned Database, 2 October 1999.

58. One Marine Corps major characterized the combat service support of U.S. forces as "inefficient" and created "from scratch." See Glynn, "Operation Stabilise," 20–21.

59. USS *Mobile Bay*, "Logistics," Navy Lessons Learned Database, 2 October 1999.

60. Ibid.

61. Lynn Cross et al., "East Timor: A Case Study in C4I Innovation," *CHIPS: The Department of the Navy Information Technology Magazine* (Winter 2003): 30, at http://www.chips.navy.mil/achives/03_winter/PDF/timor.pdf, accessed 30 November 2006.

62. "Operation Stabilise After Action Report," 33; Navy Environmental and Preventive Medicine Unit 6, "Lessons Learned from Operation Warden/Stabilise, 28 September to 17 December 1999," copy in author's files.

63. Navy Environmental and Preventive Medicine Unit, "Lessons Learned," 2, 3, 6, 7.

64. Commander Seventh Fleet, "Pacific METOC Conference Hot Wash Up Report," Navy Lessons Learned Database, 2 December 1999.

65. Ibid. On the Australian cyclone season, see http://www.bom.gov.au/info/cyclone/, accessed 27 January 2006.

CHAPTER 6

The U.S. Navy's Role in Coalition Maritime Interception in Operation Enduring Freedom, 2001–2002

Jeffrey G. Barlow

Initiating Operation Enduring Freedom

On the morning of 11 September 2001, hijackers seized four American airliners in flight and used them as weapons against United States high-value targets. Two airliners were crashed separately into the Twin Towers of the World Trade Center in New York City, igniting raging fires that eventually caused the structures to implode cataclysmically. A third passenger plane was crashed into the Pentagon, breaching a side of the massive building and starting extensive fires. The fourth aircraft, which headed to Washington, D.C., toward what was believed to be a major political target (possibly the White House or the Capitol), crashed into a field in southwestern Pennsylvania during a struggle between the passengers and the hijackers for control of the plane. In all, nearly 3,000 people were killed. Within a day of the attacks, American intelligence agencies had linked the coordinated strikes to the al-Qaeda terrorist organization led by Osama bin Laden, which used territory in Afghanistan as its base of operations.

On 12 September the United Nations Security Council passed Resolution 1368 condemning the terrorist attacks. NATO's North Atlantic Council acted that same day, invoking Article 5 of the Washington Treaty, which states that an attack on one member is an attack on all. In a similar fashion, the ANZUS allies, agreeing with the United States and Australia that Article 4 of the ANZUS Treaty applied to the terrorist attacks against New York City and the Pentagon, invoked their treaty obligations to support the United States.[1] In Central Command's area of responsibility (AOR), 12 September was the day that the USS *Enterprise* carrier battle group had been scheduled to out-chop, having been relieved on station by the USS *Carl Vinson* carrier battle group. Under the circumstances, *Enterprise's* departure was cancelled. With this change in plan, General Tommy R. Franks, Commander in Chief, U.S. Central Command (USCINCCENT) had an available naval force of 25 ships, 177 aircraft, and 18,000 personnel on station in the North Arabian Sea, ready if needed to undertake combat operations.[2]

In the days following the 11 September attacks, Afghanistan's Taliban government refused repeated demands by the U.S. government either to turn over Osama bin Laden or to close down the al-Qaeda terrorist training camps operating on its territory.[3] It quickly became evident to President George W. Bush, and his senior foreign policy and defense advisors, that only military action would compel the Taliban's compliance. Since Afghanistan lay within Central Command's AOR, Secretary of Defense Donald Rumsfeld directed General Franks on 12 September to prepare a series of "credible military options" ranging all the way up to full-scale combat operations for dealing with Osama bin Laden, al-Qaeda, and those who facilitated their terrorist activities.[4]

On 14 September the United States Congress passed a joint resolution (S.J. Res 23) authorizing the President of the United States "to use all necessary force against those . . . [who] aided the terrorist attacks." When signed into law four days later, it furnished the Defense Department with the authority to prepare a military response to the terrorists' 9/11 attacks. This initial American response to terrorism was designated Operation Enduring Freedom (OEF) on 25 September.[5]

On 21 September General Franks briefed President Bush on possible operations that Central Command (CENTCOM) could conduct, including a proposal to destroy the al-Qaeda network inside Afghanistan and topple the Taliban regime that was supporting it. When, a few days later, this proposal became Franks' recommended military course of action, Secretary Rumsfeld approved it. Franks briefed the plan to President Bush on 2 October. Bush, after approving the plan, directed that combat operations begin on 7 October.[6]

Forging Coalition Support for OEF

On 3 October 2001 Air Force General Richard B. Myers, Chairman of the Joint Chiefs of Staff, authorized CENTCOM to conduct exploratory military-to-military discussions with the many countries that had expressed a willingness to take part in Operation Enduring Freedom. Interestingly, the week before, General Franks had requested the assignment to CENTCOM of military forces from the United Kingdom.[7]

The following day, at the request of the United States, the NATO allies expanded the list of options that the alliance could take in the campaign against terrorism. They agreed upon eight specific actions that included enhancing intelligence sharing related to terrorist threats, replacing assets in NATO's area of responsibility to cover those assets withdrawn to support operations against terrorism, and allowing the United States and other allies access to ports and airfields on NATO-member territory (including refueling evolutions) during antiterrorism operations. These actions put operational teeth to the alliance's earlier invocation of Article 5 of the Washington Treaty.[8]

On 7 October, the day the initial American air strikes took place in Afghanistan, President Bush delivered an address to the nation. He told the American people:

> On my orders, the United States military has begun strikes against al Qaeda terrorist training camps and military installations of the Taliban regime in Afghanistan. These carefully targeted actions are designed to disrupt the use of Afghanistan as a terrorist base of operations, and to attack the military capability of the Taliban regime.
>
> We are joined in this operation by our staunch friend, Great Britain. Other close friends, including Canada, Australia, Germany and France, have pledged forces as the operation unfolds.[9]

Shortly after the president's speech ended, British Prime Minister Tony Blair publicly announced Britain's military participation in the strikes, telling reporters in a press conference held at 10 Downing Street, "I can confirm that last Wednesday the US Government made a specific request that a number of UK military assets be used in the operation which has now begun. And I gave authority for these assets to be deployed. They include the base at Diego Garcia, reconnaissance and fighter support aircraft and missile firing submarines. Missile firing submarines are in use tonight."[10]

NATO announced on 9 October that its Standing Naval Force Mediterranean (SNFM), then participating in Exercise Destined Glory 2001 off the southern coast of Spain, would be ordered to the Eastern Mediterranean to conduct maritime presence operations in support of the international campaign against terrorism.[11] Although the operation, designated Active Endeavour, formally began on 26 October, it actually had started on 6 October when SNFM headed east.[12] One of the force's important roles was checking the origin and destination of ships sailing through the Suez Canal.[13]

British support for an increased naval presence in OEF gathered steam during October 2001. Three Royal Navy submarines—HMS *Triumph*, HMS *Trafalgar*, and HMS *Superb*—were already in the AOR. And, in fact, the missile submarines *Triumph* and *Trafalgar* had been involved in launching Tomahawk land attack missiles (TLAMs) against al-Qaeda and Taliban targets in Afghanistan since the commencement of OEF.[14] Fortuitously, during September and October 2001, a sizable U.K. maritime task group (in the largest deployment of British forces overseas since the Falklands War) was participating in Saif Sareea II, an exercise with the Omani armed forces as a part of the Royal Navy's overall Exercise Argonaut 2001.[15]

On 26 October, a Ministry of Defence spokesman told the House of Commons:

> Our current forces are primarily configured to assist in the coalition's air campaign. That campaign will continue and develop over time and so must the capabilities that we assign to it. We have therefore

decided to create a large and rebalanced force in the region. . . . What I can do is describe the forces that we will reassign to Operation Veritas from Exercise Saif Sareea 2 [II] when the exercise finishes next week.

Those forces will comprise the following: the aircraft carrier HMS *Illustrious*, which will be re-equipped for helicopter operations; the assault ship HMS *Fearless*; a submarine presence able to launch Tomahawk missiles [HMS *Triumph* and HMS *Trafalgar*]; the destroyer HMS *Southampton*; the frigate HMS *Cornwall*; seven Royal Fleet Auxiliaries—the RFAs *Sir Tristram, Sir Percivale, Fort Victoria, Fort Rosalie, Bayleaf, Brambleleaf* and *Diligence*; and four additional support aircraft consisting of Nimrod maritime patrol aircraft and Hercules transport planes.[16]

Rear Admiral James Burnell-Nugent, who had been commanding the maritime portion of Exercise Saif Sareea, was assigned command of the naval task force.[17] The overall British contribution to OEF was designated Operation Veritas. The Type 23 frigate HMS *Kent*, the first of the British surface ships participating in Saif Sareea to detach for service in the Arabian Gulf, became the new Armilla Guardship. The frigate carried out the role of maintaining a permanent British naval presence in the Gulf and undertook maritime interception operations (MIO) in support of UN Security Council Resolutions (UNSCRs) 661 and 665.[18]

Kent was on station and conducting MIO as early as 8 October. The British task force headed by HMS *Illustrious*, however, did not begin operations in the AOR as part of the coalition naval forces until early December 2001.[19] A portion of this delay was likely due to issues relating to the British rules of engagement (ROE) for Operation Enduring Freedom.

Australia, like the United Kingdom, responded quickly to the terrorist attacks on 9/11. By 18 September, Royal Australian Air Force personnel on exchange duty with the U.S. Air Force were flying in combat air patrols over the continental United States. And, as of that date, the Australian government had authorized Australian Defence Force exchange personnel attached to American military services to deploy with U.S. forces on operations, both inside the United States and abroad.[20]

On 16 October, in response to President Bush's request the day before that Australia activate its commitment to join the coalition force, Australian Prime Minster John Howard publicly detailed his country's contribution to Operation Enduring Freedom. The deployed naval portion of the Australian Defence Force consisted of a task group comprising an amphibious command ship, the LPA HMAS *Kanimbla* (a converted former U.S. LST) equipped with organic helicopter support; an escorting frigate, HMAS *Adelaide*; and a second frigate, HMAS *Sydney*, with embarked helicopter capability, directed "to assist in the coalition's protection of shipping effort."[21] In point of fact, however, *Sydney* was being sent to the region as a relief for the guided missile frigate HMAS *Anzac*, which was already operating in the AOR as part of the Maritime Interception Force (MIF), enforcing UN sanctions against Iraq.[22] The prime minister noted that the bulk of the Australian forces committed would be deployed by mid-November 2001. The Australian military contribution to OEF was designated Operation Slipper.

Sydney, because of her requirement to relieve *Anzac* in theater, was dispatched separately to the Arabian Gulf by Maritime Headquarters after she completed her OLOC (Operational Level of Capability) workup and assessment. She arrived on station on 9 November 2001. In the meantime, the task group consisting of *Kanimbla* and *Adelaide* readied for deployment. The task group commander, Captain Allan Du Toit, and his staff joined *Kanimbla* on 31 October. Following completion of its workup in the waters of the Western Australian Exercise Area, TG 627.1 left Australia on 16 November, headed for the Gulf. Following a fueling stop and short final workup period at Diego Garcia, the task group sailed on 29 November 2001 for the Middle East area of operations (MEAO). *Kanimbla* and *Adelaide* entered the MEAO on 2 December and passed through the Strait of Hormuz four days later.[23]

The United States' third major coalition partner, Canada, also responded quickly to the 9/11 terrorist attacks in New York City and at the Pentagon. The Canadian government sought to demonstrate its support by furnishing a "fast, visible reaction." On 7 October Canadian Prime Minister Jean Chrétien stated that his country would furnish a range of sea, air, and land forces to the coalition being formed to fight terrorism.

The following day, Minister of National Defence Art Eggleton laid out the military forces that would be provided for the country's participation in the antiterrorist campaign, to be designated Operation Apollo. He noted that Canada would commit one-third of its warships, six aircraft, and a portion of Joint Task Force (JTF) 2—its antiterrorist unit—to the effort.[24]

With specific regard to the ships involved, the first to be sent to the Gulf was the Canadian patrol frigate *Halifax*, which was already serving with the Standing Naval Force Atlantic.[25] Because NATO had invoked Article 5 of the Washington Treaty, the Ottawa government believed this action lent legitimacy to its decision to redirect the ship elsewhere. *Halifax* was immediately dispatched to the Gulf region, arriving there the last week of October. Meanwhile, the Canadian Navy was ordered to assemble a task group for service in the CENTCOM area of responsibility. Commodore D. W. Robertson and his staff, embarked in the Tribal-class guided missile destroyer HMCS *Iroquois*, departed on 17 October from Halifax with the task group's two other ships, the patrol frigate HMCS *Charlottetown* (which had just returned from the region in July) and the resupply ship HMCS *Preserver*. Following several days of working-up exercises, the command sailed for the Gulf. The Canadian task group had in-chopped the CENTCOM AOR in mid-November, and by the following week steamed in the North Arabian Sea off the Pakistani coast, serving as the escort for the U.S. Marine amphibious ready group (ARG) preparing to conduct operations into Afghanistan.[26]

The final Canadian warship to arrive in the Gulf during 2001 was the West Coast-based patrol frigate HMCS *Vancouver*. On 30 October, she departed Esquimalt and headed south to San Diego to integrate into the USS *John C. Stennis* carrier battle group. On 12 November 2001, following a week of working up, the *Stennis* force, with *Vancouver* serving as part of the escort, sailed from San Diego for Southwest Asia. The command in-chopped the CENTCOM AOR on 15 December, and *Vancouver* was detached to operate in the North Arabian Sea.[27]

In addition to the major coalition partners, an impressive number of other countries contributed warships or other forces employed in the CENTOM AOR in maritime tasks during Operation Enduring Freedom. These included Bahrain, France, Germany, Greece, Italy, Japan, the

Netherlands, Poland, and Spain. France, for example, provided a carrier battle group (CVBG) built around the nuclear carrier *Charles de Gaulle* to support combat operations in the North Arabian Sea. Germany sent a force of three frigates and a supply ship that operated in the Horn of Africa region. Italy furnished its only carrier battle group, built around the aircraft carrier *Garibaldi*, which like the French CVBG operated in the North Arabian Sea. And although Poland had no ships in the AOR, it supplied a special forces unit that served as boarding teams for maritime and leadership interceptions in the Northern Arabian Gulf and North Arabian Sea.[28]

Maritime and Leadership Interdiction Operations

At the time operations against al-Qaeda and Taliban forces in Afghanistan began in October 2001, American warships and those of certain coalition navies had been carrying out maritime interceptions in support of UNSCRs 661 and 665 for some 11 years. The year before, at the time of the tenth anniversary of the first UNSCR maritime interception operation in connection with the embargo of Iraq, it was determined that since the start of such operations in August 1990, U.S. and coalition warships had queried 29,307 merchant ships, boarded 12,763 of these vessels, and diverted 748 of them for inspection in ports of coalition countries.[29] And during calendar year 2001 alone, forces employed in MIO had conducted 2,570 queries of merchantmen and 1,276 boardings, and had diverted 95 of them for inspection.[30]

General Franks' Theater Campaign Plan for Operation Enduring Freedom defined U.S. Central Command's mission in the following manner: "to destroy al Qaeda; to end support of terrorism by states and non-state organizations; to eliminate terrorist access to weapons of mass destruction to provide military support to humanitarian operations; and, once these objectives were achieved, to prevent the re-emergence of terrorism."[31] The campaign plan was to be carried out in four phases— Phase I, "Setting Conditions for Initial Operations"; Phase II, "Initial Combat Operations"; Phase III, "Decisive Combat Operations"; and Phase IV, "Sustainment and Prevention of Terrorist Re-emergence."[32]

In preparing for pending operations in his AOR, General Franks reorganized his theater command structure according to functional componency. He assigned Vice Admiral Charles W. Moore Jr., commander of the U.S. Naval Forces Central Command (COMUSNAVCENT) and the U.S. Fifth Fleet, as Combined Forces Maritime Component Commander.[33] COMUSNAVCENT's own area of responsibility included the Arabian Gulf, Arabian Sea, Gulf of Oman, Red Sea, and portions of the Indian Ocean (an area of some 7.5 million square miles, or almost three times the size of the continental U.S.).[34]

On 1 November 2001 USCINCCENT promulgated the second of three operations orders connected to military operations in Afghanistan.[35] The operation order noted, "We are now transitioning to Phase II-Stage 2 (Continued Operations)." It specifically tasked COMUSNAVCENT with a number of missions, including the following: "[Maintain] maritime superiority to ensure uninterrupted access and movement through the Arabian Gulf and [support] CJFSOCC [Combined/Joint Forces Special Operations Component Commander] by conducting precision strikes against al Qaida, Taliban C2, and Taliban military targets. . . . Support CJFACC [Combined/Joint Forces Air Component Commander] with aircraft sorties to include strike, CAS [close air support], and counter-air missions . . . [and] Conduct maritime intercept missions."[36]

In the months before the events of 9/11, the Fifth Fleet generally was a force numbering around twenty ships, including an aircraft carrier battle group—with an air wing composed of 85 or more planes—and an amphibious ready group. The number of assigned personnel was on the order of 15,000, with some 1,000 of these stationed ashore. Because of the ramp up of naval forces engendered by Operation Enduring Freedom, however, the number of U.S. and coalition warships in COMUSNAVCENT's area of responsibility grew to as many as 130 ships; up to 70 were U.S. Navy warships.[37]

Fifth Fleet was organized into nine task forces: TF 50 (Battle Force), TF 53 (Logistics Force), TF 54 (Submarine Force), TF 55 (Middle East Force), TF 56 (Special Tasks), TF 561 (SEAL Force), TF 57 (Maritime Patrol Force), TF 58 (Amphibious Force), and TF 59 (Coalition Integration

Force).[38] Vice Admiral Moore established Task Force 50 shortly after 9/11 to furnish the required command structure for the several carrier battle groups operating in the North Arabian Sea. The initial Commander Task Force (CTF) 50 was Rear Admiral Thomas E. Zelibor, on board USS *Carl Vinson*.[39] Although Task Force 50's principal effort was conducting air operations into Afghanistan, its supporting tasks included the protection of the amphibious ready groups and the Combat Logistics Force, maritime interception, and support to MIO and to intelligence, surveillance, and reconnaissance operations in the Horn of Africa region.[40]

As had been the case in the 11-year period before September 2001, MIO forces focused on containing the oil-smuggling operations from Iraqi ports. Under UNSCR 986 (14 April 1995), Iraq had been permitted to use the profits from the sale of its oil for in-country humanitarian relief (designated the Oil-for-Food Program). If Iraq could get around this closely monitored program by allowing its oil to be shipped illegally by third parties, it stood to make a substantial amount of untraceable income that could be used for any purpose, including beefing up its rearmament efforts. The source for both the legal and illegal oil coming out of Iraq was the Mina al-Bakr Oil Terminal, located at the mouth of the Khawr Abd Allah—a bight at the head of the Arabian Gulf where the territorial waters of Kuwait, Iraq, and Iran converge.[41] The principal destination for the smuggled oil was the United Arab Emirates (UAE), south of Qatar on the Saudi Arabian peninsula. Alternative destinations that were less frequently used were the port of Bandar Abbas in Iran and ports in Yemen, Pakistan, and India.[42]

In early October 2001, the NAVCENT staff drafted a position paper (in message form) on the potential use of coalition naval forces in follow-on operations relating to OEF. It postulated that coalition forces in support of Enduring Freedom could contribute to a variety of missions like ongoing maritime interception actions, logistic support, escort operations, and future operations against terrorists operating outside of Afghanistan. With respect to ongoing maritime interceptions, the paper specifically noted, "These will be in support of U.N. Security Council sanctions on Iraq and will require both surface combatants and patrol boats with boarding teams capable of non-compliant boarding and maritime patrol and reconnaissance aircraft."[43]

During November 2001, as OEF ground operations caused the loss of Taliban control in major Afghan cities, General Franks, Vice Admiral Moore, and their staffs began analyzing the effect this would have on the leadership of the Taliban and al-Qaeda. It quickly appeared that both al-Qaeda leaders and Taliban government officials would possibly attempt to flee first into Pakistan from Afghanistan and then escape from the former by sea or air to countries where they could seek refuge. Commander Task Force 50, for example, postulated that in such an event Osama bin Laden and other senior al-Qaeda members would attempt to escape to countries such as Somalia, Sudan, Yemen, the Philippines, Indonesia, and Malaysia, using small watercraft such as dhows or helicopters, small planes, or possibly commercial flights.[44]

At this time U.S. naval intelligence estimated that as many as 25 vessels were associated in some way with bin Laden and al-Qaeda. These ships were assessed as being generally engaged in legitimate shipping activity in the Red Sea, the Gulf of Aden, and other Middle Eastern waters, but were thought possibly also to have been chartered by or carried cargo for al-Qaeda.[45]

CTF 50 decided to draft an operational plan that maximized the employment of U.S. and coalition naval forces to seal off terrorist sea and air escape routes emanating from southern Pakistan. This necessitated expanding the existing NAVCENT maritime interception operations to include seizure of escaping terrorists. The new mission was designated "leadership interdiction operations" (LIO).[46]

Commander Destroyer Squadron 9, embarked in the carrier *Carl Vinson*, was initially designated as the commander for leadership interdiction operations. Eventually, in addition to the U.S. Navy, the navies of four coalition partners—the United Kingdom, Canada, France, and Italy—took part in LIO patrols, which began in the Gulf of Oman on 23 November 2001 and commenced in the North Arabian Sea six days later.[47]

The LIO rules of engagement authorized coalition warships to stop and visit non-government vessels based on "reasonable suspicion." While the rules permitted the coalition ship commander to query such vessels and conduct consensual visits, COMUSNAVCENT had to authorize the use of disabling fire to force a vessel to stop. American LIO rules of engagement allowed coalition warships to search and seize nongovernment vessels based on what was called "actionable intelligence"—defined as sufficient indicators for a reasonable person to believe the vessel is "actively supporting international terrorism" (i.e., transporting Taliban leaders or al-Qaeda terrorists). However, boarding of suspicious warships

Gulf of Oman

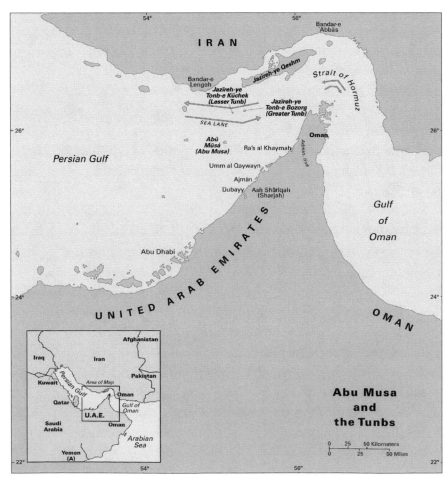

or government vessels would only be allowed based on actionable intelligence, and nonconsensual boardings could only be undertaken with authorization from the U.S. Secretary of Defense.[48]

Halifax, the first Canadian ship to in-chop the AOR during Operation Enduring Freedom, began operating initially as a Strait of Hormuz escort. She transitioned quickly, however, into patrolling for oil smugglers along the coast of the UAE.[49] Before leaving Canadian waters, Commodore Robertson had resisted having his task group take on maritime interception force duties, and so he and the Canadian staff had agreed on a fleet protection role for his ships.[50] Accordingly, when the Canadian task group in-chopped, it had been assigned responsibility for serving as the defensive escort for the U.S. ARG operating off Pakistan. This situation changed, however, once leadership interdiction operations were initiated, and the Canadian government authorized more robust rules of engagement to clarify noncompliant boarding tactics in connection with these new operations.[51]

Because of the increased strain due to the combination of MIO tasks in the Arabian Gulf and LIO tasks there and in the Arabian Sea, Vice Admiral Moore decided in early February 2002 that the span of control was simply too great for the existing sea combat commander to oversee everything. Accordingly, after consulting with Commodore Robertson, he granted Robertson the coordination authority for the Gulf of Oman sector "west of 60E," the Southern Arabian Gulf, and the Strait of Hormuz escort operations. Therefore, during February and March 2002, the Canadian task group commander led a multinational task group composed of Canadian, French, British, U.S., and other warships based in the Gulf of Oman.[52] In April he turned over his command to his successor, Canadian Commodore Eric Lehre, who continued the coalition coordination tasking.[53] When the Australian task group in-chopped the AOR, the Australian government still had not decided how this force should be employed operationally. Therefore, when its ships arrived in Bahrain, there was no authorization "for any kind of a mission," in the words of the then commanding officer of *Kanimbla*, Commander David McCourt, RAN.

Ships from allied navies of the United States, France, the United Kingdom, the Netherlands, and Italy steam in parade formation during Operation Enduring Freedom, 18 April 2002.

Nonetheless, because McCourt anticipated that boarding parties from his ship eventually would be used for MIO, he enrolled his personnel in the MIO school at Bahrain.[54] In the meantime, Captain Du Toit, the task group commander, met with the Fifth Fleet commander, Vice Admiral Moore. As Du Toit recalled:

> [Moore] was particularly keen for the RAN to assume a significant warfare command role and for *Adelaide* and *Kanimbla* to be gainfully employed in the Northern Arabian Gulf (NAG) along with *Sydney*, as part of the MIF. He also recognized that *Kanimbla* was ideally suited to fulfill the role of Maritime Interception Operations (MIO) command ship. His views were strongly influenced by the recent success of *Anzac*'s deployment and a brief visit to the MEAO by the Maritime Commander Australia and MCC AST [Maritime Component Commander Australian Theatre], Rear Admiral Geoff Smith, in late September [2001], during which potential tasking for RAN units was discussed.[55]

It was following a U.S. request and advice from the Chief of the Defence Force that the Australian government agreed to make the task group available for maritime interception operations. In addition, Captain Du Toit was directed to assume the role of Maritime Interception Commander, in charge of enforcing UN sanctions against Iraq. This assignment was rotated monthly with Captain David Jackson, USN, Commander Destroyer Squadron 50, with *Kanimbla* being employed as the MIO command ship. On 5 December 2001, the operational control of Du Toit's task group was handed over to CENTCOM's Combined/Joint Force Maritime Component Commander.[56] *Kanimbla* and *Adelaide* first sailed for COMISKEY—the MIO holding area located less than 100 miles off the Iraqi coast—and spent days doing merchant ship clearance operations. They then moved to the middle of the Arabian Gulf and conducted MIO.[57]

The success of coalition maritime interception operations under these command arrangements was demonstrated by the high level of continuing merchant vessel queries and boardings. In November 2001 coalition forces queried 237 ships, boarded 113 of these, and diverted five to COMISKEY. In January 2002 the numbers had risen to 366 ships queried, 132 boarded, and six diverted. And in March 2002 the MIF warships queried 331 vessels, boarded 122, and diverted two.[58]

During the first five weeks that leadership interdiction operations were being carried out, coalition warships made more than 2,500 queries

Sailors from guided missile destroyer USS *Hopper* and coastguardsmen prepare to board a dhow suspected of smuggling oil out of Iraq. Boarding teams conducted maritime interception operations, searching for contraband cargo aboard merchant ships in the Arabian Gulf. The MIO coalition effort enforced a UN Security Council Resolution imposed against the Iraqi government after the 1991 Gulf War.

of suspicious ships by radio or visual signal. These queries had resulted in five consensual boardings and one nonconsensual boarding. LIO conducted in the Arabian Sea was complemented at the same time by intelligence, surveillance, and reconnaissance operations carried out in the waters surrounding the Horn of Africa. By March 2002 coalition warships had successfully carried out some 7,244 LIO queries and conducted 47 boardings of suspect vessels.[59]

Conclusions

The coalition navies involved in maritime and leadership interdiction tasks during OEF worked smoothly together. This was particularly true with the navies of the United States, Great Britain, Australia, and Canada. The individual allied navies had been exercising together with the U.S. Navy regularly during the past several decades. Furthermore, they shared communication systems such as COWAN (Coalition Wide Area Network) that allowed ready communication between the ships of the four navies.

Nonetheless, the interaction among the four navies was not completely seamless. They each had to function under separate national rules of engagement, and these ROE differed from each other in the restrictions they imposed on actions by the respective navies. NAVCENT's staff found that the strictures of the Royal Navy's rules of engagement, for example, made it difficult for the British to integrate easily into the MIO effort. As a February 2002 debriefing of NAVCENT's N3 (Operations) staff revealed, the constraints imposed by the ROE handicapped the Royal Navy's ability to take part in the Task Force 50 effort. One American staffer noted, "UK – they let TF50 go thru process & then back away → know they can't do it [.]"[60]

For their part, American commanders in the CENTCOM AOR found that the high classification of U.S. planning information dramatically slowed their ability to share the details of operational plans and intelligence with their coalition colleagues during the initial period of the commitment of forces. As analysts for the Office of the Chief of Naval Operations' Deep Blue planning organization commented in their post-conflict assessment of the strengths and weaknesses of the U.S. Navy in OEF, "Countries will not relax or adjust their national rules of engagement if the U.S. Navy will not tell them what they might be called

Crewmembers from guided missile cruiser USS *Thomas S. Gates* conduct MIO training at sea. These sailors boarded and inspected vessels to ensure they were in compliance with UN resolutions pertaining to Iraq and not carrying illegal cargo, October 2002.

upon to do."[61] In its January 2002 review of the situation, the NAVCENT staff suggested a way around the problem: develop "a 'Releasable' synopsis of the operational plans and ROE, which could be used to brief and inform potential coalition partners."[62]

Ultimately, the fact that the maritime interception effort proved as successful as it did during OEF, despite such drawbacks, was a testament to the enduring value of the training provided by the multinational naval exercises and bilateral task group workups that the U.S. Navy and its major allied partners had participated in over the previous half century. As sailors similarly familiar with both the rewards and perils of regular and even continuous operations at sea, they knew how to broker among themselves the informal means of cooperation that enabled their forces to overcome the rigidities imposed by differing national conceptions of how best to respond to the war on terrorism.

The author made full use of both classified and unclassified material from the U.S. Navy, the U.S. Department of Defense, and other U.S. government agencies and activities. Although the classified information cited or quoted in this chapter was reviewed, subsequently declassified, and cleared for open publication by the Department of Defense's Office of Security Review, the classified documents used in drafting the chapter retain their original security classifications.

Notes

1. Declassified information from document entitled "Operation ENDURING FREEDOM," n.d. [early February 2002], [1]; NAVCENT Operation Enduring Freedom Records, Archives Naval History & Heritage Command (NHHC); declassified information from Robert J. Schneller Jr., "OEF Handbook," 25 September 2003, 4, Archives NHHC; and Australian Ministry of Defence Media Release from the Ministry of Defence website entitled, "The Australian Defence Force's response to September 11," Departmental 463/02, 6 September 2002, 1; Operations Subject Collection, Aviation Archives NHHC.

2. Document entitled "NAVCENT TOP 25 EVENTS," n.d. [late January 2002], [1]; NAVCENT Operation Enduring Freedom Records, Archives NHHC; and declassified information from "Operation ENDURING FREEDOM," [1].

3. Letter, Ambassador John Negroponte, Permanent Representative of the United States of America to the UN, to the President of the Security Council, S/2001/946, 7 October 2001, quoted in "Operation *Enduring Freedom* and the Conflict in Afghanistan: An Update," Research Paper 01/81 (London: International Affairs & Defence Section, House of Commons Library, 31 October 2001), 9.

4. Schneller, "OEF Handbook," 12, citing Bob Woodward, *Bush at War* (New York: Simon and Schuster, 2002), 43–44; and Statement of General Tommy R. Franks, Commander in Chief, U.S. Central Command, House Armed Services Committee, 27 February 2002.

5. Schneller, "OEF Handbook," 8. The original name—Operation Infinite Justice—had been changed in response to protests by Muslim groups. See also U.S. Department of Defense News Transcript: "DoD News Briefing – Secretary Rumsfeld," 25 September 2001, 1; Operations Subject Collection, Aviation Archives NHHC.

6. Schneller, "OEF Handbook," 14, citing Statement by General Franks, 27 February 2002.

7. Declassified information from document entitled "CJFMCC MAJOR MILESTONES [–] OPERATION ENDURING FREEDOM," n.d. [early February 2002], 1; NAVCENT Operation Enduring Freedom Records, Archives NHHC.

8. NATO Press Release 2001/138, 8 October 2001, quoted in "Operation *Enduring Freedom* and the Conflict in Afghanistan: An Update," 29; and article from NATO's AFSOUTH website

entitled "NATO and the Scourge of Terrorism: OPERATION ACTIVE ENDEAVOUR," 20 February 2002, 2; Operations Subject Collection, Aviation Archives NHHC.

9. Bush's Address to the Nation, 7 October 2001, quoted in "Operation *Enduring Freedom* and the Conflict in Afghanistan: An Update," 14.

10. Blair's Press Conference, 7 October 2001, quoted in "Operation *Enduring Freedom* and the Conflict in Afghanistan: An Update," 14–15.

11. NATO Press Release, 9 October 2001, quoted in "Operation *Enduring Freedom* and the Conflict in Afghanistan: An Update," 30; and "NATO and the Scourge of Terrorism: OPERATION ACTIVE ENDEAVOUR," 1–2.

12. "NATO and the Scourge of Terrorism: OPERATION ACTIVE ENDEAVOUR," 2.

13. Article from the Royal Navy's website entitled "Exeter Is Back," 29 January 2002, Operations Subject Collection, Aviation Archives NHHC.

14. Article from the British Ministry of Defense website entitled "Operation *Veritas*—British Forces," 6 November 2001, 1, Operations Subject Collection, Aviation Archives NHHC.

15. Article from the Royal Navy website entitled "RFA Ships Play Major Role in Oman," 23 October 2001, 1, Operations Subject Collection, Aviation Archives NHHC.

16. House of Commons Debate, 26 October 2001, quoted in "Operation *Enduring Freedom* and the Conflict in Afghanistan: An Update," 27.

17. "Operation *Enduring Freedom* and the Conflict in Afghanistan: An Update," 27.

18. List from the British Ministry of Defence website entitled "UK Forces participating in Exercise *Saif Sareea II*," 20 September 2001, 1; article from the Royal Navy portion of the Ministry of Defence website entitled "Operations: Armilla Patrol," 1–2, 7 January 2003, 1–2; and article from the Royal Navy website entitled "Gulf Patrol—Kent Hands Over to Portland," 2 February 2002, all in Operations Subject Collection, Aviation Archives NHHC. The submarines *Trafalgar* and *Superb* that also had been participating in Exercise Saif Sareea II had been detached at the beginning of October to take part in the opening stages of OEF. See "UK Forces participating in Exercise *Saif Sareea II*," 2. The Armilla Patrol had been established in 1980 at the beginning of the Iran-Iraq War in order to ensure the safety of British-flagged merchant ships operating in the region. "Operations: Armilla Patrol," 1.

19. Declassified information from the "Coalition Ships" pages of NAVCENT's Ship Employment Schedules for 1–31 October 2001 and 1–31 December 2001; NAVCENT Operation Enduring Freedom Records, Archives NHHC.

20. "The Australian Defence Force's response to September 11," 1–2.

21. "Operation *Enduring Freedom* and the Conflict in Afghanistan: An Update," citing an Australian Ministry of Defence Press Release, 16 October 2001; and two, short news clips from the Australian Ministry of Defence website—"The Australian contribution [to Operation Enduring Freedom]," and "Amphibious Transport (LPA)," both 11 December 2001; Operations Subject Collection, Aviation Archives NHHC.

22. Post-Command narrative by Commodore Allan Du Toit, Royal Australian Navy, of his tour as the Australian Task Group Commander in the Arabian Gulf during "Operation Slipper," n.d., Enclosure 3 to Australian document NA(W) 2-5/4716, 22 March 2005, 13; Curator Branch Collections, NHHC. *Anzac's* participation in the MIF was as part of Australian contribution to the UN sanction enforcement regime, designated Operation Damask by the Australian government.

23. Post-Command narrative by Commodore Allan Du Toit, 13–14.

24. Article from the Canadian Forces website entitled "Backgrounder: The Canadian Forces' Contribution to the International Campaign Against Terrorism," BG-02.001f, 7 March 2003, 2; Operations Subject Collection, Aviation Archives NHHC; "Operation *Enduring Freedom* and the Conflict in Afghanistan: An Update," citing a Canadian Department of Defense press release, 8 October 2001; and Robert H. Caldwell, "The Canadian Navy, Interoperability, and USN-Led Operations in the Gulf Region from the First Gulf War to 2002," chap. 7 herein, 217.

25. The last Canadian warship in the Gulf, HMCS *Winnipeg*, had departed for home in early August 2001. Caldwell, chap. 7 herein, 219.

26. "Backgrounder: The Canadian Forces' Contribution to the International Campaign Against Terrorism," 3; and Caldwell, chap. 7 herein, 220.

27. "Backgrounder: The Canadian Forces' Contribution to the International Campaign Against Terrorism," 3–4; and Caldwell, chap. 7 herein, 228, citing Richard Gimblett, *Operation Apollo: The Golden Age of the Canadian Navy in the War Against Terrorism* (Ottawa: Magic Light Publishing, 2004), 52.

28. Report from the White House website entitled "Campaign Against Terrorism [:] A Coalition Update," 26 March 2002, 7–9; and explanatory list from the CENTCOM website entitled "Comprehensive List of Support for War Against Terrorism from some Coalition Partners as Compiled by the DoD," 7 June 2002, [6]–[7], [9], [12], [15], and [18]; both in Operations Subject Collection, Aviation Archives NHHC.

29. Schneller, "OEF Handbook," 46, citing Edward J. Marolda and Robert J. Schneller Jr., *Shield and Sword: The United States Navy and the Persian Gulf War* (Annapolis, MD: Naval Institute Press, 2001), xv. This book is a reprint of the original book published by the Naval Historical Center (now Naval History & Heritage Command) in 1998, with minor changes in wording.

30. Table entitled "Calendar Year MIO Totals," 4 May 2002; NAVCENT Operation Enduring Freedom Records, Archives NHHC.

31. Declassified information from Schneller, "OEF Handbook," 14–15, quoting the "CFC OEF Theater Campaign Plan," 26 November 2001.

32. Declassified information from Schneller, "OEF Handbook," 15.

33. Declassified information from Thomas Bowditch, David Taylor, and Alarik Fritz, *Maritime Command Relationships in OEF* (Alexandria, VA: CNA, August 2002), 3.

34. Briefing delivered by Captain Thomas A. Yeager, USNR, and Commander Daniel H. Struble, USNR, *Operation ENDURING FREEDOM: COMUSNAVCENT and FIFTH Fleet Documentation Team*, at the Naval Historical Center, 5 June 2002, 3 (notes appended to slide labeled "Naval Forces Central Command—5th Fleet"); collection of miscellaneous OEF materials assembled by Robert J. Schneller Jr., NHHC.

35. Declassified information from Schneller, "OEF Handbook," 19. The first OPORD had been issued on 25 September.

36. Declassified information from Schneller, "OEF Handbook," 20, quoting CJFC OPORD 02-02.

37. Yeager and Struble Briefing, *Operation ENDURING FREEDOM: COMUSNAVCENT and FIFTH Fleet Documentation Team*, 4 (notes appended to slide labeled "Task Force Organization").

38. Declassified information from Schneller, "OEF Handbook," 28.

39. Yeager and Struble Briefing, *Operation ENDURING FREEDOM: COMUSNAVCENT and FIFTH Fleet Documentation Team*, 5 (notes appended to slide labeled "CTF 50—Striking Forces").

40. Declassified information from Schneller, "OEF Handbook," 28–29, citing CTF-50 Campaign Plan.

41. Declassified information from Schneller, "OEF Handbook," 39–40.

42. Ibid., 40, citing Brief, Multinational Interception Force Operational Update for the UNSCR 661 Committee, 5 November 2002.

43. Declassified quote from draft message from COMUSNAVCENT to USCINCCENT MacDill, regarding C/JFMCC procedures for the assignment of Coalition LNOS [naval liaison officers] to the C/JFMCC Headquarters in Bahrain, Z Oct 01, 2–3; Schneller, OEF Collection.

44. Declassified information from Schneller, "OEF Handbook," 47, citing CTF-50 CONOPS Brief on Leadership Interdiction, n.d.

45. Ibid., 47, citing Brief, Japanese Task Group In-chop Conference, 4 December 2001.

46. Ibid., 47–48, citing CTF-50 CONOPS Brief on Leadership Interdiction.

47. Ibid., 48, citing CFMCC OEF SITREP 231903Z NOV 01; and (for commencement of Gulf of Oman LIO), "NAVCENT TOP 25 EVENTS."

48. Ibid., 49, citing Brief, "Global War on Terrorism: Expanding Maritime Interception Operations," 19 January 2002.

49. Caldwell, chap. 7 herein, 222.

50. Ibid., 219.

51. Ibid., 219, 223.

52. Ibid., 232.

53. Ibid., 240.

54. Captain David McCourt, RAN, interview with Robert H. Caldwell and Jeffrey G. Barlow, 27 July 2005, HMAS *Stirling*, Perth, Australia.

55. Post-Command narrative by Commodore Allan Du Toit, 14.

56. Ibid.

57. McCourt interview. The location of the COMISKEY holding area is discussed in Michael Martinez, "A Strike Against Iraqi Smuggling: When the Navy rounds up ships for inspection, it holds them in the Persian Gulf 'Comiskey," *Chicago Tribune*, 18 January 2003, as taken from the DOD *Early Bird* website.

58. "COALITION MIO STATISTICS," NAVCENT Operation Enduring Freedom Records, Archives NHHC.

59. Declassified information from Schneller, "OEF Handbook," 49, citing Brief, "Global War on Terrorism: Expanding Maritime Interception Operations," and Daily Watch File Folder, TFCC Watch Officer Files, COMUSNAVCENT N3 materials.

60. Unclassified note in NAVCENT Debrief by Captain J. A. Wombwell, USNR, 24 February 2002, unnumbered page, notebook labeled "NAVCENT Brief Notes"; NAVCENT Operation Enduring Freedom Records, Archives NHHC.

61. Declassified information from Schneller, "OEF Handbook," 103, quoting Brief, Deep Blue, "Course Corrections for the Global War on Terrorism," 20 March 2002.

62. Ibid., 102, quoting [NAVCENT] Brief, "Welcome Defense Science Board Task Force," 7 January 2002.

CHAPTER 7

The Canadian Navy, Interoperability, and U.S. Navy-Led Operations in the Gulf Region from the First Gulf War to 2003

Robert H. Caldwell

Introduction

The navy matters in Canada. More often than not, since the Second World War, Canadian national and naval concerns have coincided with broader Anglo-American interests, as demonstrated in the Arabian Gulf region for the past 15 years. It was no accident that Canada contributed the first coalition task group after the 9/11 attacks, for she had participated in the worldwide surge of U.S. Navy–led maritime surveillance and interdiction operations throughout the 1990s.

The aim of this work is to examine interoperability and to identify lessons learned from the Canadian naval experience conducting interdiction and escort operations in the Gulf region between 1991 and 2003. The underlying premise is that nothing was sold out, that interoperability with the U.S. Navy neither caused nor resulted in any Canadian surrender of sovereignty thwarting its ability to make choices for the future with regard to multinational relations. Indeed, this study's premise is just the opposite: that the Canadian Navy's considered and conscious decision to seek interoperability with the U.S. Navy in the early 1990s actually increased the range of options available to the government of Canada when it faced the question of what to do following the attacks of 11 September 2001. Contrary to what some would argue, the evidence suggests strongly that naval interoperability served Canadian interests as a nation-state because sea power—and the projection of influence from the seas—has different effects than the application of air and land power. Simply put, the navy's interoperability provided profound benefits to Canadians that far outweighed putative risks to the nation's autonomy as a sovereign state capable of multinational relations with choices for the future.

This study is a narrow history of a medium-size navy's experience in modern warfare. It is deliberately written with the interests in mind of young men and women of the Canadian Navy and the allied navies, who it is hoped will find the lessons useful.[1] Still, it does not claim to be exhaustive because we have concentrated on a wide theme, *the relevance of navies and interoperability*, which allows the reader a glimpse into how the Canadian Navy responded to changes between 1991 and 2003.

Sea Control

Sea control is a modern term understood throughout NATO; nevertheless, using the term requires care by historians. For example, in current publications sea control is listed as one of the four roles of maritime forces, separate from command of the sea, sea denial, and maritime power projection. Sea control "allows the use of the sea in specified areas for specific periods of time . . . the level of sea control required will be a balance between the desired freedom of action and the degree of acceptable risk. Sea control comprises the control of the surface and subsurface environments and the airspace above." In context, while maritime power projection utilizes power *from* the sea, sea control operations "are purely naval in nature" because they are conducted *at* sea; while they may influence the shore, they do not touch it directly.[2]

By nature, sea control operations "are static and conducted using long-range surveillance and airborne weapon delivery systems over large areas of sea . . . to allow a mobile force, under afloat command with its layered defences of moving close and distant screens, to pass through areas of operations . . . without mutual interference or fratricide." Standard NATO doctrine sets out five elements to sea control operations. The first is "Establishment and Maintenance of a Recognized Maritime Picture"

(RMP), described as a "picture of the surface, air, and sub surface situation," which is gathered in all maritime operations, "ranging from peacetime through increasing tension to hostilities."[3] In other words, the RMP is an agreed-upon and—if it is to be useful—shared sense of situational awareness based on information and intelligence of all kinds that gives those in charge the confidence that they are unlikely to be surprised.

A concomitant of sea control operations are maritime interdiction operations (MIO). In NATO these operations are described under five headings, building up from "seaborne enforcement" to "interdiction of enemy forces," "interdiction of commercial shipping," "embargoes and quarantine," and finally "blockade." NATO indicates that interdiction of enemy forces "can be conducted against warships and aircraft at sea and in harbour or other shore bases. Denying an adversary the ability to use the maritime portion of [an operational area] . . . hampers attempts at manoevre from the sea and frustrates sea control and sea denial operations." Interdiction of commercial shipping is considered a "strategic/operational activity designed to erode an opponent's ability to conduct armed conflict. At the operational level, loss of supplies could severely limit the mobility and firepower of an opponent as well as affecting morale."[4]

Commodore Eric Lehre, the second Canadian Task Group commander to serve in the Gulf in 2002, considered traditional sea control to be his "dominant task, even though it was never stated in orders." His Canadian and coalition ships could not conduct "sanction enforcement or peacekeeping" until they had "built a maritime picture of the area" and deployed their ships and aircraft "to control what goes on it." Lehre mused that the term sea control is avoided in our "gentle, coalition-building, cooperative approach to life," no matter how essential it might seem to be.[5] Interoperability was linked to sea control, and the degree of interoperability determined the extent to which the Canadian Navy could influence and contribute to these operations.

Command and Control

The American, British, Australian, and Canadian navies fully understood standardized NATO command and control arrangements used at sea in the 1990s. *Command* meant the "authority vested in an individual of the armed forces for the direction, coordination, and control of military forces." *Control* expressed the "authority exercised by a commander" over part of the activities of subordinate organizations . . . not normally under his command, which encompasses the responsibility for implementing orders and directives. All or part of this authority may be transferred or delegated." For example, *tactical control* was considered to be the "detailed and, usually, local direction and control of movements or maneuvers necessary to accomplish missions or tasks assigned."[6]

The Origins of an Interoperable Paradigm

During the Second World War Royal Canadian Navy (RCN) escorts sailed with U.S. Navy ships, and vice versa, on convoy protection tasks in the Battle of the Atlantic. After the war, cooperation continued. For example, in 1947 the RCN adopted U.S. Navy communications systems, which enhanced interoperability during the Korean War and the Cold War. Korean operations were important. The RCN provided individual fleet destroyers to the United Nations naval coalition from 1950 to 1955, and while they were highly effective, the *political* significance of the RCN effort was diluted because the ships, deployed individually, were not "recognizable" as a distinct Canadian contribution.[7] Thus Canadian naval officers began to craft a new approach that stressed both interoperability and maximum national visibility, which could be achieved through group-level missions, and not simply individual ship tasks.

* * *

Throughout the mid-1960s the United Kingdom withdrew from its security responsibilities "east of Suez,"[8] and the United States was required to replace the British obligations, particularly to ensure "the stability and security of the strategically vital Persian Gulf region."[9] The Americans have intervened with military force in the Gulf region three times in the past 26 years. These interventions included operations against Iran in the 1987–1988 Tanker War, against Iraq in the 1990–1991 Gulf War,[10] and again in Iraq in 2003. Americans have played a vital role in all of these operations, particularly between 1991 and 2003, and allied navies have reinforced U.S. Navy task forces in these latter actions.

Canada did not participate in the Tanker War, the outcome of which shaped relationships in the region.[11] The war began with a deterioration of relations between the United States and Iran in 1979. By late 1987 tensions had arisen between Iran, already at war with Iraq, and the smaller states in the Gulf region supported by the Americans, the British, and many western European states. These nations deployed naval forces in late 1987, and by early 1988 deployments included the "United Kingdom's ten-ship *Armilla* Patrol and two Dutch, two Belgian, seven Italian, and thirteen French ships," including a carrier.[12] On 18 April 1988 the U.S. Navy fought its largest surface action since the Second World War and destroyed "about half" of the Iranian navy, while Iraq, America's ally, kept up pressure against the Iranians on land. On 18 July 1988 the Iran-Iraq War—and the first U.S. Gulf war—ended in defeat for the Iranians.[13]

Two years later, however, Canada rapidly supported American and allied military intervention against Iraq in the Gulf region. Canada's largest military contribution to the 1990–1991 Gulf War was a naval task group commanded by Captain (N) Duncan E. "Dusty" Miller, with his staff, in the antisubmarine destroyer (DDH) HMCS *Athabaskan*. They were accompanied by HMCS *Terra Nova*, a destroyer escort (DDE), and a fleet replenishment ship (AOR), HMCS *Protecteur*. One of the navy's four powerful Tribal (or *Iroquois*) 280-class destroyers, *Athabaskan* had not been modified by the TRUMP (Tribal [class] Update and Modernization Project) and reclassified a DDG.[14]

By December 1990 the Canadian Task Group was conducting Multinational Interception Force (MIF) operations with the American and coalition naval forces in the northern Gulf region. Nevertheless Commodore Ken J. Summers, the commander of Canadian Forces Middle East, perhaps remembering the Korean experience, sought a role at the group level that ensured Canadian recognition. The Americans readily agreed to the Canadian request to protect the Combat Logistics Force (CLF), which consisted of the supply ships that accompanied each U.S. Navy battle group as well as the British, Dutch, and Australian naval forces. The Canadians parlayed the CLF escort task into a fleet logistics coordinative mission, and in early January 1991 the U.S. Navy designated

Captain Miller as a subordinate warfare commander "in his own right: UNREP Sierra."[15] By 19 January, Miller and his staff were "coordinating the activity of some ten escorts and twenty auxiliaries."[16]

Over a decade later Commodore Summers summed up the experience:

> In hindsight, one can argue that the Gulf War ended the Canadian Navy's pre-occupation with [antisubmarine warfare] . . . and ushered in a new era [emphasizing] . . . the utility of a sea control, multi-role capable, coordinating navy able to partake and provide the lead in coalition naval operations against today's asymmetric threat. This has been a positive change and it was great to be part of that paradigm shift.[17]

The Canadian effort to coordinate logistics for the large and diverse fleet demonstrated high interoperability, and when combined with the navy's speed of deployment, both capabilities provided the government with options. Canadian historians have concluded that the government "got exactly what it wanted: an active but limited participation in the Coalition that was conducted at arm's length from direct American control, and to a degree to which a middle power with a limited defence budget can realistically aspire in the expensive high-technology business of modern war."[18]

1991—HMCS *Huron* and the Second Maritime Commanders (MACOM) Conference

Huron, an unmodified Tribal 280-class DDH, was ordered to replace *Athabaskan* in late February 1991 to impose the "continuing U.N. sanctions against Iraq, and to assist the Department of External Affairs in re-establishing a Canadian diplomatic presence in the Region."[19] Although *Huron* was to enforce UN sanctions, the historical report from the ship stated that this "did not occur once during *Huron's* tenure, and the ship simply identified and tracked what little peaceful merchant shipping braved the unsure waters of the Gulf."[20] At the time interdiction operations remained in a passive and largely ineffective mode.

Following her next patrol *Huron* hosted the Second MACOM Conference, where coalition naval forces' commanders gathered "to discuss the overall maritime strategy and policy for naval forces operating in the Gulf in support of United Nations efforts against Iraq." Commander R. H.

Melnick, the commanding officer of *Huron*, chaired this historic meeting. Eleven nations were represented from the multinational force: Australia, Bahrain, Canada, Denmark, Italy, Japan, Kuwait, Spain, the United Arab Emirates (UAE), the United Kingdom, and the United States.[21] Their senior naval officers met to discuss two types of future operations: interception of merchantmen and mine countermeasures.

Rear Admiral R. A. K. Taylor, USN, Commander Task Force (CTF) 152 spoke first, and while he admitted that interception operations had been "extremely effective in the Arabian Gulf (AG) and the Red Sea (RS)," he noted the operations were "an expensive and resource-intensive method of enforcing sanctions against Iraq." The result had been an "overburdening of naval assets in the enforcement of sanctions," and so the "value of using military forces in the RS and AG has been eclipsed" by events following the war. For example, Taylor stressed the importance of monitoring Iraqi shipping: "The most important variable in the equation is when Iraq will again be allowed to participate in foreign trade. The importance of this is that 60% of profits from international trade will pay war reparations and the remaining 40% will contribute to the restoration of the Iraqi economy."[22] Concluding, Taylor *discouraged* intervention operations and suggested that the coalition navies advise their "respective governments" to consider terminating "sea-based operations in favor of simplified ashore methods."[23]

Clearly the Americans wanted change, and Taylor offered three nonmaritime options:

- Precertification of cargo at a loading point.
- Inspection of cargo at Aqaba (requiring the consent of Jordan).
- Inspection of cargo at the Jordanian/Iraqi border (which eliminates adverse effects of boarding vessels on the Jordanian economy).[24]

Commodore P. J. Cowling, RN, Commander Task Group (CTG) 321.1 echoed the American view but reminded the coalition navies that he spoke for the Western European Union. He agreed with Taylor on the gloomy future of intervention operations, arguing that "the military task is virtually impossible . . . because of the number of ports available for trade around the [Arabian Gulf] . . . the difficulty in maintaining a real-time picture of merchant shipping due to a lack of available military assets, and the selective implementation of the embargo." Cowling summed up the situation in June 1991:

> The Western European Union . . . meeting in Paris had agreed that embargo operations could cease forthwith . . . it remains up to the individual governments . . . to support this position and to decide how to reallocate resources . . . a number of nations see their objectives in the Gulf as not being totally reliant on embargo operations. The mere presence of military forces has resulted in a renewal of confidence as seen by an increase in merchant traffic and a decrease in insurance rates. The value of reassurance and stability provided by this presence must be considered as a worthwhile objective within the AG and taken into account when determining priorities.[25]

Each coalition naval representative spoke briefly, and all agreed with the Anglo-American view on reducing maritime interception operations in the region. Both the Australians and the Canadians claimed that they were committed until September 1991, and only the Americans advised that their presence in the region would continue "indefinitely."[26]

Two weeks later *Huron* departed, and Canada's naval contribution to the Gulf ceased. Nevertheless a powerful precedent had been set, and the nation's participation with her coalition partners was popular with the Canadian public. Canadians associated the navy with the Gulf region, and as the region mattered, so did the navy. Moreover, because of the television coverage of the war, as well as the positive press about her naval contribution, Canadians had become accustomed to naval forces serving alongside the Americans in the region.

1992—HMCS *Restigouche*

Notwithstanding the recommendations of the Second MACOM Conference, eight months later *Restigouche*, a west coast, steam-turbine destroyer escort commissioned in 1958, was tasked to join the Multinational Interception Force to enforce UN Security Council Resolutions (UNSCRs) 661 and 665 against Iraq. Commanded by Commander D. Baltes, she represented the last of the postwar steam ships to serve in a war zone.

Restigouche came round to Norfolk, and in March 1992 joined two U.S. Navy ships en route to the Gulf. Together they practiced boarding operations and exchanged "ideas and exercise procedures."[27] This informal grouping of a Canadian ship with American ships, designed to ensure interoperability, was simply an extension of Canadian-American cooperation that had continued since the Second World War.

A month later *Restigouche* joined the navies of Australia, France, and the United States operating at the entrance to the Gulf of Aqaba. Initially she was assisted by the United States Coast Guard and then settled into the daily routine of boardings. She inspected 18 vessels by the end of April, and on 4 July, her last day of operations, she conducted her 125th boarding.[28]

Despite the change in policy and practice, *Restigouche's* mission was highly successful and she sustained the Canadian profile in the Gulf region. She had formed important ties with the U.S. Navy, continuing the precedent of training with American ships on passage to their operational area, as had been done during the Korean conflict. Clearly the navy— now in receipt of its first *Halifax*-class Canadian patrol frigate (CPF) and TRUMPed DDH 280s—was in step with the government, and both were keen to maintain a visible presence in the region. *Restigouche* represented the prototype single-ship deployment for a worldwide surge in U.S. Navy-led maritime surveillance and interdiction operations, and these operations would inform Canadian foreign and naval policy throughout the 1990s.

1993–1994—Haiti

Concurrent with initiatives to participate in interdiction operations in the Gulf region, the Canadian Navy and the government participated in similar American-led operations in the Caribbean.

In late 1990 Jean-Bertrand Aristide was elected president of Haiti; however, he was deposed and exiled in September 1991. For the next two years the Organization of American States (OAS) and the Security Council of the United Nations tried to stabilize the deteriorating situation in that country.[29] An enforced embargo was an option, and in December 1992 Canadian Prime Minister Brian Mulroney proposed a multinational blockade force made up of ships from "Canada, the United States, France and Venezuela."[30]

Various measures and sanctions were imposed against the anti-Aristide regime. The OAS and the Security Council decisively approved resolutions including imposing "maritime interception to enforce the embargo."[31] The Americans designated the operation Forward Action, and they commenced operations, which were *joint*, involving other services, as well as *combined*, bringing in the armed forces of other countries.

In September 1993 a Canadian naval task group consisting of HMC Ships *Preserver, Fraser,* and *Gatineau* sailed for the Caribbean to participate in "exercises," while the UN began to tighten up its relationship with Haiti.[32] On 15 October the Canadian group was deployed into Haitian waters as part of Forward Action. Their orders were to "establish an immediate Canadian presence, to enforce UN sanctions, and to assist in the evacuation of Canadian and other foreign nationals."[33]

The Forward Action Task Force would "hail, board, examine, and divert ships not in compliance with U.N. sanctions." Canadian ships and helicopters could enter Haitian airspace and territorial waters without clearance and fire warning shots if the situation warranted.[34] The effort gained momentum, and "20 ships from France, the United States, Argentina, the UK, the Netherlands and Canada" conducted interdiction operations.[35] The Canadian Task Group commander sometimes headed the patrol force, "coordinating the actions of all surface and air assets to achieve mission objectives." These responsibilities paralleled those of Commodore Greg R. Maddison, the Canadian commander of NATO's Standing Naval Force Atlantic (SNFL), who was conducting coalition interdiction operations at the same time in the Adriatic.[36]

Canadian ships served in the interception force until maritime interdiction operations ceased on 1 October.[37] United Nations Mission in Haiti deployed the following year, and Aristide, in exile in Montreal, Quebec, returned as the lawful president of Haiti.[38] Having gained additional experience with the U.S. Navy, the Canadian Navy welcomed the opportunity to coordinate operations on its behalf.

1994—Defense Policy, Task Groups, New Ships, and Revised Operational Training

During the 1990s the Canadian government had supported fundamental changes to the navy, and all emphasized interoperability with the U.S. Navy. The 1994 Canadian "White Paper on Defence" stated clearly that Canada would maintain a general-purpose, combat-capable naval task group on the east and west coasts, each consisting of a maximum of "four combatants, either destroyers, frigates or submarines, with a support ship and appropriate maritime air."[39] The navy's goal was to prepare to deploy, or redeploy from other multilateral operations, a single element or the vanguard of a task group "within three weeks," and then sustain the group "indefinitely in a low threat environment."[40]

Concurrently, Canadian sailors were receiving 12 new helicopter-equipped, *Halifax*-class frigates (FFHs)—CPFs—designed in the 1970s and built in the 1980s and 1990s. These frigates, with their Sea Sparrow close-range, surface-to-air missiles and Harpoon antisurface missiles, complemented the Standard 2MR long-range air-defense capability in the four *Iroquois* 280-class DDGs, which acted as flagships. The rebalancing of its assets between the east and west coasts prompted one naval analyst to claim that the "Canadian Navy came of age in the Asia-Pacific region in the post–cold war era."[41]

At the same time the navy revised its operational training emphasis. During the Cold War the Canadian Forces Maritime Warfare Centre (CFMWC) had conducted the annual MARCOT (Maritime Coordinated Operational Training) exercise, which was the most advanced level of training for MARLANT (Maritime Forces Atlantic). It was based on the Soviet naval threat in the Atlantic. The navy's experience in "peacekeeping"— as well as in the Gulf War—had "re-initiated" the need to "operate more effectively in a joint and combined context." In 1996 CFMWC, following the direction of Commander Maritime Command (MARCOM), changed the MARCOT exercise to reflect "the growing importance of littoral operations, especially those taskings relative to peacekeeping missions." CFMWC addressed the interoperable requirement by arranging for Commodore Donald P. Loren, USN, Commander Destroyer Squadron

(COMDESRON) 28, and his staff to provide the exercise opposition force. All participants benefited from the "challenging boarding scenarios for the Maritime Interdiction Operation," which was conducted "24 hours a day in almost all weather conditions."[42]

The main lesson learned on MARCOT 96 was that "there were problems . . . [and] differences in ROE [rules of engagement] . . . philosophies . . . [which] were common to all . . . a great deal of effort was devoted to harmonizing the NATO Joint and Combined ROE (JROE) for all services." The exercise proved the need to widen the "base of awareness and experience . . . to matters related to U.N. operations," and it highlighted the requirement for "better comprehension of matters such as international humanitarian law, joint and combined [ROE] . . . prudent and equitable use of force when dealing with belligerents in an intrastate conflagration, and understanding how to be an effective and active participant in attempts to limit, control, or end a conflict."[43]

Thus, through the 1990s, the absence of a bipolar world, the new defense policy, the patrol frigates, and combined training all contributed to a renaissance in the Canadian Navy. Balance and connectivity were the overriding principles, and by design, the navy was perfectly positioned for emphasis on interoperability. MARCOT exercises after 1996 marked a new operational mindset and concern for rules of engagement; moreover, single-CPF deployments with the U.S. Navy to the Gulf region demonstrated an arc of increasing responsibility and a reputation for effectiveness.

Single-CPF Deployments to the Gulf Region

1995—HMCS *Fredericton* and HMCS *Calgary*

Quality counts, but with the government focused on the situation in Haiti and the Adriatic, no Canadian warships were sent to the Gulf region between *Restigouche*'s departure and the spring of 1995. Even then, the first Canadian ship to return to the Gulf, *Fredericton*, commanded by Commander K. D. W. Laing, was not assigned to a coalition task group and conducted no operations during her four-week stay in March and April. Instead, by supporting various diplomatic and trade initiatives, *Fredericton* demonstrated a Canadian presence.[44]

Five months later Canada recommenced interdiction operations against Iraq. The government commissioned *Calgary*, a Canadian patrol frigate, on 12 May 1995.[45] Her commanding officer, Commander G. A. Paulson, the former executive officer on *Huron* during her deployment to the Gulf region in 1991, sailed his new ship to the Gulf following workups. The deployment of *Calgary* was definitive, and she served as a test bed for closer integration with the U.S. Navy.

Calgary did not practice with American ships, but trained on her own, and began her first operational patrol into the Northern Arabian Gulf (NAG) on 14 August. Her operations were controlled in the area by Commodore C. I. Lundquist, USN, COMDESRON 21, who directed *Calgary* into the forward patrol area, which covered the Shatt al-Arab (SAA) waterway, "the major routing for traffic in and out of Iraqi ports." Twelve miles from the coast of Iraq "the challenges . . . were . . . extensive; hugging the territorial limit while navigating amongst wrecks, shallows, and unreliable navigation aids."[46] Remaining outside "the territorial limit of Iraq," she completed her last patrol on 27 September.

> *Calgary* reported that by "day one" she had been seamlessly integrated into the Fifth Fleet Area of Operations. . . . The second challenge . . . was the MIF operations themselves. The confined operating area, navigational hazards, proximity to potential hostile nations, routine difficulties conducting hailings, smugglers, and sanction violators using the cover of darkness were . . . challenges . . . [and] the deep draft of the U.S. Navy combatants does not allow them to operate at the mouth of the KAA [Khawr Abd Allah] or SAA. *Calgary*'s position at the tip of the spear successfully ensured day and night coverage of Iraqi waterways.[47]

On 1 October 1995 *Calgary* departed the Gulf for the NATO Standing Naval Force Mediterranean (SNFM), where she went on station "twelve miles off the Montenegran coast" until mid-November.[48] Her deployment set a further precedent, participating in operations in the Gulf region as well as in the NATO Adriatic blockade off the Balkans, discussed elsewhere in this book.

1997—HMCS *Regina*

It fell to the largest navies to maintain a continuous presence in the region, and there was no Canadian deployment between 1 October 1995 and 6 April 1997 when *Regina* entered the theater. But as we have seen during that period, the navy had actively studied the problems of littoral operations and the means of ensuring heightened connectivity with coalition partners. It was therefore entirely appropriate that *Regina*, commanded by Commander T. H. W. Pile, was the first Canadian ship to work up and deploy with a U.S. Navy group specifically constituted for Gulf operations. The process began in January 1997, three months before her arrival, when *Regina* trained with the Pacific Middle East Force (PACMEF) 97-1, which formed a surface action group specifically tasked for interdiction operations under Commodore M. E. Duffy, USN, COMDESRON 9. Their training emphasized "multi ship scenarios and interdiction operations including boarding and hailing exercises focusing on multinational interdiction . . . operations and related boarding and hailing exercises."[49]

On 12 April *Regina* sailed north from Bahrain into the Northern Arabian Gulf patrol areas. Now under operational command of Fifth Fleet, *Regina* worked "directly for the Maritime Interdiction Operations (MIO) commander COMDESRON 50, Commodore J. F. Herger, USN."[50] *Regina* considered herself an "aggressive MIO unit" hailing many vessels and actually boarding nine ships "on her first patrol."[51] She conducted six patrols in the Northern Arabian Gulf. *Toronto Star* journalist Martin Regg Cohn, who was embarked on the second patrol, described interdiction operations as a

> repetitive, at times tedious process. Hailing ships, boarding boats, measuring fuel tanks, checking documentation. It is, very likely, the future of the Canadian Navy. Shooting wars don't happen very often, and Canadians usually keep their distance. But embargoes of the sort imposed on Iraq since the Persian Gulf War—currently, only medicine and prescribed quantities of oil for food are allowed in— are the wave of the future, says Pile. For pacifists and policymakers who prefer embargoes to shooting wars, maritime interdiction operations are the method of choice for retaliating against belligerent

or wayward nations. Blockades are an act of war under international law, and they require naval power to enforce them. . . . Tensions are inevitable . . . because 20 American warships are parked in Iran's neighborhood. . . . *Regina* is on a U.N. approved mission, but it remains on guard, caught between the Iraqis and the Iranians.[52]

The U.S. task group departed on 2 July, and *Regina* detached from her American consorts on 20 July as she approached Esquimalt. She had sailed 41,329 nautical miles and logged "57 boardings compared to her [Southern Arabian Gulf] counterparts cumulative total of 63." Demonstrating high interoperability with the U.S. Navy, she had completed the first deployment—from start to finish—with an American tactical group into the region.[53]

1998—HMCS *Toronto*

The next Canadian ship to serve in the Gulf region was *Toronto*, an east coast CPF, and the government deployed her to reinforce a UN-sponsored escalation of military force in the region.

Through the autumn of 1997, and into the early months of 1998, relations had deteriorated between Iraq and the United States and her allies. Both sides fought tit-for-tat over the expansion of the allied no-fly zones, conducted as Operations Northern and Southern Watch. By late 1997 Iraq had restricted access to the United Nations Special Commission (UNSCOM) weapons inspectors, and the United Nations, and Canada, stood foursquare behind the Americans. In January 1998 the Canadian government reinforced an allied buildup of military strength with her navy and air force.[54]

Toronto, under Commander B. J. Johnson, was already at sea in the eastern Atlantic, having worked up and fitted out in January 1998 to operate with NATO's Standing Naval Force Atlantic.[55] Thus, at 2000Z hours, 10 February, *Toronto* received a signal detaching her from SNFL and ordering her "to proceed at best speed to the Arabian Gulf to aid in the enforcement of U.N. Sanctions against Iraq." This no-notice tasking arose because, *Toronto* noted, "rising tensions between Iraq and U.N. Arms Inspectors had escalated to a point that Canada had decided to join a Coalition Task Force being formed in a show of force against Iraq."[56]

Incoming briefings by Commander, U.S. Fifth Fleet and his staff prepared *Toronto* for future interdiction tasks in the northern areas. Joining the USS *George Washington* carrier battle group on 7 March, she began her first patrol, and the following morning conducted her first boarding.[57]

Eventually there were close to "50 coalition ships and submarines, and some 200 naval aircraft" deployed, and the Royal Navy sent Her Majesty's Ships *Invincible* and *Illustrious*.[58] On 15 May *Toronto* departed the Northern Arabian Gulf, having demonstrated an important precedent in interoperability: a Canadian patrol frigate in a high readiness state—with only a minimum of specialized training—could effectively conduct interdiction operations with an American battle group in the Gulf region.

1998—HMCS *Ottawa*

A year later *Ottawa*, a west coast CPF, underwent extensive training for interdiction operations. In November 1997 *Regina* briefed her on her recent experience, and *Ottawa*'s commanding officer, Commander J. R. Bergeron, and his operations staff attended "a conference in San Diego in preparation for battle group deployment."[59] *Ottawa* was the second ship to work up with the U.S. Navy, but she would be the first ship to train with a carrier battle group preparing for operations in the Gulf following the escalation of hostilities in early 1998.

Ottawa trained extensively with the USS *Abraham Lincoln* carrier battle group.[60] Conducting her first maritime interdiction operation patrol from 5 to 17 August, she integrated easily into the complicated special operations in the Northern Arabian Gulf. When she sailed homeward, *Ottawa* had conducted more than 105 hailings and 35 boardings.[61] The ship's deployment reflected a trajectory of increasing responsibility in proportion to the Canadian Navy's efforts to ensure interoperability with the U.S. Navy.

1999—HMCS *Regina*

Regina served a second tour in the Gulf region, this time under Commander J. W. Hayes. Similar to *Ottawa*'s experience, she worked up with an American group on the West Coast, training with the USS *Constellation* carrier battle group from February until they sailed together in June 1999. *Regina* conducted patrols and operated in the northern holding areas; also, she participated in operations that involved multinational forces deploying close inshore in the extreme northern sector of the Gulf. Her historical report read:

> [The] . . . multinational force consisting of *Regina,* a U.S. Navy Seal team, two U.S. ships, a New Zealand ship and some Kuwaiti naval and coast guard vessels deployed under the cloak of darkness. . . . Only some 20 miles off the Iraqi coast, well within their missile range, these ships in turn launched their RHIBs [rigid hull inflatable boat] to take down and seize simultaneously three surprised cargo and oil smugglers that attempted to sneak past U.N. checkpoints enroute to accommodating ports in the Gulf. *Regina*'s RHIB, directed to its target by a U.S. Navy helicopter using only its infrared camera, captured a smuggler and escorted it to a holding area to await further processing.[62]

In November *Regina* returned home with the battle group.[63] For the second time in just over two years, she had reinforced the trust and interoperability required by American-led multinational forces in the Gulf.

2000—HMCS *Calgary*

Calgary sailed for the region in June 2000 under Commander T. M. Howard. Carrying on the tradition of high Canadian-American interoperability, she joined and trained with PACMEF 00-3, a small U.S. Navy task group consisting of USS *Milius,* an *Arleigh Burke*–class destroyer, and USS *Oldendorf,* a *Spruance*-class destroyer.[64]

The ships worked up in accordance with the group training program, and the three commanding officers conferred in a nightly "fireside chat." Each ship took a turn commanding various evolutions and maneuvers, and the commanding officers emphasized the tactics required for interdiction operations. On these exercises *Calgary* and her two U.S. Navy consorts agreed upon technical and communications arrangements to ensure a high level of interoperability.[65]

Calgary achieved one of her key objectives—"integration with American units"—by resolving "differences in procedures and interpretation of references" between the two navies.[66] Ship officers continued to review rules of engagement in preparation for briefings from a Canadian Forces lawyer, who joined the ship in the Far East and remained with her until the first MIO patrol. The lawyer's role was to advise on legal matters "such as territorial waters, ROEs, self-defence and use of force." [67]

Upon *Calgary*'s arrival, American briefings by Commander, U.S. Naval Forces Central Command and his staff in Bahrain reviewed all aspects of operations in the region. Following these meetings, *Calgary* conducted mothership and guardship duties, while she continued hailing contacts and pursuing suspicious vessels in the northern and southern Arabian Gulf. Mothership tasks were based upon "Health and Comfort Inspections" in which coalition ships inspected vessels waiting in holding areas and, where necessary, distributed food and water to them. More urgently, however, *Calgary*'s noncompliant boarding team, along with a second team from other ships, often stood by "to board smugglers coming out of the Khawr Abd Allah." It was assumed that these teams would take responsibility for a vessel already boarded. During such evolutions the temperature was in excess of "44 [degrees C] and a Humidex which reached 62 [degrees] each day," a measure of their strenuous nature.[68]

For those sailors still on board since *Calgary*'s first tour in 1995, the shallow waters off the KAA were familiar, although their tasks had become more intense to halt the Iraqi oil shipments banned by the United Nations. By the end of September, in the suffocating heat and stifling humidity, *Calgary* kept to a routine of hailing, tracking, boarding, and serving as mothership and guardship by day, while at night she conducted sweeps through the northern patrol areas. These night sweeps were timed to have the ship back in the northernmost holding area, operationally named COMISKEY, at first light "to conduct queries and boardings as necessary . . . under United Nations Security Council Resolution (UNSCR) 986."[69] Based on the shared misery of these circumstances, Americans and Canadians had formed a tight bond.

By late 2000 the Canadian Navy had relearned many valuable lessons about close-in operations in the Khawr Abd Allah. *Calgary* had reinforced the Canadian precedent by operating in circumstances that linked connectivity, rules of engagement, and interoperability in complex combined operations. She had gained high trust from the American and coalition navies.

2001—HMCS *Charlottetown* and HMCS *Winnipeg*

During summer 2000, *Charlottetown*, an east coast frigate commanded by Commander M. F. R. Lloyd, was ordered to prepare for Gulf region operations with the USS *Harry S. Truman* carrier battle group scheduled to deploy in early 2001, first to the Mediterranean for several months and then to the Arabian Gulf to conduct interdiction operations against oil smugglers. *Truman* is a *Nimitz*-class supercarrier, and *Charlottetown* was the first east coast ship to serve in such a carrier group.[70] The other surface ships included USS *Mitscher*, an *Arleigh Burke*-class destroyer; USS *Carr*, an *Oliver Hazard Perry*-class frigate; and USS *Bighorn*, an oiler.[71]

Arriving in the Mediterranean on 21 January 2001, the battle group remained in that theater for almost three months, conducting exercises with Standing Naval Force Mediterranean and U.S. Sixth Fleet forces.[72] Lieutenant Commander Ian Anderson, one of the operations room officers in *Charlottetown*, noted that they "spent several months training before moving through the Suez Canal and into the Arabian Gulf."[73]

Concurrently, Canada made another important decision: the nation would *increase* her naval presence in the region. *Winnipeg*, under Commander K. E. Williams, departed Esquimalt on 15 March 2001 to join the USS *Constellation* carrier battle group in the Hawaiian operational area. In addition to the "*Connie*," the battle group included USS *Chosin*, a *Ticonderoga*-class cruiser; USS *Benfold*, an *Arleigh Burke*-class destroyer; USS *Kinkaid*, a *Spruance*-class destroyer; USS *Thach*, an *Oliver Hazard Perry*-class frigate; and USS *Rainier*, a fast combat support ship.[74] These ships were *Winnipeg*'s consorts for the next six months.

Connie's tasks were formidable because the U.S. Navy viewed operations in the Gulf as part of "the forward deployment strategy that has characterized American foreign and defence policy objectives for the past decade." Forward deployment tasks included "patrolling the no-fly zone over southern Iraq . . . [and] projecting power and providing air support when required." At the same time coalition ships in the battle group operated in "a presence role to support the UNSCRs,"[75] and *Winnipeg*'s mission was to deploy with American forces for "operations in the Arabian Gulf in support of U.N. sanctions against Iraq."[76]

En route *Winnipeg's* crew prepared for operations in the Gulf by finalizing communications arrangements and conducting lectures on force protection and rules of engagement.[77] As the battle group transited toward Australia, *Winnipeg* was appointed on-site commander for a successful surface firing exercise. The American habit of delegating responsibility to *Winnipeg* continued, and the commanding officer was appointed the surface action group commander in charge of a sub-group sailing to Adelaide.[78]

Winnipeg undertook tasks typical for most Canadian or American surface ships in a carrier battle group prior to 9/11. She concentrated on building a recognized maritime picture using "satellite, air and other CVBG assets," and identifying tankers and merchant vessels, which were tracked and hailed when they entered international waters. The vessel's response to a set of hailing questions determined further action—perhaps a boarding operation.[79] Once more the Gulf environment at the height of summer was arduous, with the temperatures over 40 degrees Celsius. At one point *Winnipeg* was anchored in water that was 34 degrees Celsius.[80]

In mid-April, while awaiting the final installation of updated communications technology known as the Coalition Wide Area Network (COWAN), Commander Williams placed a liaison officer on board *Constellation*.[81] A Canadian legal officer, who had joined in Adelaide, accompanied Williams in rules of engagement discussions with the battle group staff.[82] Concurrently, *Winnipeg's* officers lectured on "Gulf geopolitical issues as well as the customs and religions of the area."[83]

Boarding operations were the bread and butter of interdiction work. Once in the Indian Ocean, *Winnipeg* began "visit, board, search and seizure" training with her battle group. While all coalition ships carried "basic security detachments" to conduct consensual boardings, some American ships embarked special teams that were prepared for opposed boardings. A typical Canadian frigate had only one boarding party, at times divided into smaller teams, but there was only one group to draw from, whether the boarding task was "non-cooperative or consensual."[84]

At the end of April *Charlottetown*, sailing in the *Truman* battle group, conducted her first MIO patrol in the Northern Arabian Gulf, "enforcing U.N. sanctions against Iraq."[85] Concurrently, *Winnipeg* noted that she was at her highest operational tempo, "ready to commence operations,"[86] and on 30 April *Winnipeg* and the *Connie* battle group changed operational command to Fifth Fleet.[87] As *Winnipeg* approached the Strait of Hormuz (SOH), the embarked legal officer intensified briefings on rules of engagement. Because *Charlottetown* was in the area, Commander Williams in *Winnipeg* watched her first patrol closely, and he "made a number of adjustments to my Security Teams/Boarding Party as a result," reporting:

> [O]perational planning is underway on board to ensure the ship is fully prepared for MIO ops as well as Mothership duties. Extra rations and water are being procured alongside Bahrain to replenish ships in holding areas that are about to run out shortly after my arrival in [the Northern Arabian Gulf]. I have also started a "cost capture" process to track all costs. . . . New ROE authorization [was] received clarifying all of my concerns/issues. . . . Support by the embarked JAG advisor continues to be excellent. I have forwarded new ROE to C5F [Fifth Fleet] and CCDG 1 [Commander Cruiser Destroyer Group 1, probably acting as CTF 50].[88]

Charlottetown's second and final MIO patrol was conducted from 16 to 31 May, and during it she remained very busy carrying out "91 hails and 28 boardings . . . for a total of 151 hails and 52 boardings."[89] She passed through the Suez Canal with her consorts *Mitscher* and *Carr* and entered Halifax on Canada Day, 1 July 2001. *Charlottetown* had completed a successful and eventful voyage and remained at a high state of readiness in the east coast task group.

In early May *Winnipeg* continued to patrol by day and night in the Southern Arabian Gulf (SAG), as well as near Iranian and Iraqi territorial waters in the northern end of the Gulf, which was "the choke point for vessels entering and exiting the main waterways of Iraq . . . [where] numerous shoals and isolated dangers . . . make navigation a challenge."[90] By 26 May there were six coalition warships in the north, and the operational tempo slowed down. Thereafter a special operation was planned for a three-day period to reduce the flow of oil smuggling. *Winnipeg* described these operations, in which her boarding teams intercepted known oil smugglers, and once boarded, they turned the ship over to another ship's security team so that *Winnipeg* could return and apprehend another vessel. The suspect vessel was escorted to where it was "searched during daylight hours." This tactic was successful in the past, but at this time "no smugglers tried to leave Iraq's internal waters."[91]

The number of patrolling warships fell in early June, and based on *Winnipeg's* stellar performance over the two-month period, Canadian-American interoperability had reached a new high. For example, the commanding officers from *Chosin* and *Kinkaid* met with Commander Williams to address the demands posed by the need to secure large numbers of diverted vessels. Their ships were "running out of equipment to support the numerous security teams." As well, because every waiting merchant ship required a small security detachment, the commanding officers found it difficult to keep their boarding teams intact in order to clear nonsmuggler vessels quickly.[92]

As a result, by 4 June, *Winnipeg* was "now in charge of nine diverted vessels and their security teams."[93] Her duties also included coordinating the assets of two American warships to manage the inspections of newly intercepted vessels. This was the first time that a Canadian ship in the region—without the formal appointment of the on-site commander—had been responsible for an operational site where U.S. Navy ships were deployed.

Concurrently, special operations planning continued, and again *Winnipeg* was a key participant. The operations were successful; by 20 June there were 17 diverted and detained vessels. All of them carried illegal Iraqi oil, and as a result of the high number of vessels waiting, mothership duties increased dramatically.[94]

On 16 July *Winnipeg* departed Dubai for her fifth patrol and this time claimed another first. The Canadian frigate reported that she was appointed

> "XM" or *On Site Commander in the NAG. This will be a first for a Canadian Warship.* Duties will involve compiling, coordinating and disseminating information to other ships under our control in the

NAG to ensure that MIO is conducted efficiently and effectively. *Winnipeg* will also assume mothership duties that will allow for an overall coordinated effort between detecting, boarding, inspecting and caring for smugglers [emphasis added].[95]

Winnipeg continued to coordinate routine and special operations in the north, as well as to conduct noncompliant boardings. As planning recommenced, she remained in command. Williams and his staff received specialist advice on "the capabilities and limitation of each special unit and how they are best used." The commanding officers of *Chosin, Kinkaid, Thach,* and the frigate USS *Nicholas* were briefed by Williams and his augmented staff on board *Winnipeg.*[96]

Handing over her appointment and special interdiction planning responsibility to *Chosin* on 24 July, *Winnipeg's* operational record revealed 61 boardings, including 4 noncompliant boardings, as well as 194 hails, 77 security team deployments, and 162 health and comfort inspections.[97] She entered Esquimalt at 0945 Friday, 14 September 2001, three days after the shattering attacks on the northeastern United States by al-Qaeda.

Winnipeg's experience demonstrates Canadian interoperability in the region prior to 9/11. She and the ships in the *Constellation* battle group had established firm sea control in the complex and shallow waters in the Northern Arabian Gulf in the summer of 2001, and as we will see, after 9/11 the American, British, and Australian navies sustained this level of control.

While interoperability on these patrols had been highly effective, the recognition of international waters was the most "controversial difference" between Canadian and American operational policies. This divergence lay in the method of determining how international waters are defined. Canada uses a "straight line," or "baseline" method, because the Iraqi and Iranian coastlines are "deeply indented and cut into," while the Americans measure from "the low-water line along the coast." Both are valid UN methodologies, but Canadians were sensitive to claims of territorial waters because of their own arctic sovereignty policy. Thus their ships were not able to operate in certain areas near the coast in the upper shallow waters of the northern Gulf. Consequently, Canadian ships had to work harder, keeping just outside of territorial waters, and they were responsible for "50 per cent of interdiction in the area."[98] Canadian statistics, before and after 9/11, are impressive.

Aside from the exceptional ability of Commander Williams and his crew, COWAN was the single most important contribution to Canadian–U.S. Navy interoperability. In his post-deployment report Williams noted:

> The success of COWAN/SIPRNET [Secret Internet Protocol Router Network] . . . firmly established this as the way ahead for the Canadian Navy–U.S. Navy interoperability . . . [we] must continue to push for expansion in the fitting of the COWAN system in U.S. Navy ships, especially those deploying for operations with Canadian units and for dedicated U.S. Navy shore support. . . . [These measures] will go a long way to progress interoperability between the U.S. and Canadian Navies and minimize the delay in SIPRNET/COWAN replication.[99]

In summary, in 2000 and 2001 *Calgary, Charlottetown,* and *Winnipeg* experienced a heightened level of intensity during their Gulf work, and the lessons identified by the ships' companies were outstripping staff ability to collate and disseminate information to new ships working up. *Calgary's* experience had been acute, and *Winnipeg's* more so a year later because frequently she had been appointed on-site commander. During the last deployment she had figured prominently in establishing sea control in the northern Gulf region.

Yet all the Canadian single-ship missions prior to September 2001 could claim to be highly interoperable success stories based on the Canadian multipurpose boarding party, the ships' diving teams, constant attention to rules of engagement, and their crews' overall competence. High trust was achieved, and the Americans in the Gulf allowed the Canadians "access to certain information," which might otherwise have been withheld. As well, these operations forced the Canadian Navy "to keep pace with security and defence advances," and "by demonstrating its ability to work with the U.S. Navy, the Canadian Navy establishe[d] that it can work with anyone."[100] Although we cannot tell, the Americans probably appreciated being seen with close allies, and the Canadian Navy's long association with the U.S Navy made her a natural ally.

A year to the day after her return on 15 September 2001, *Winnipeg* sailed from Esquimalt to return to the region in support of American interdiction operations.[101] During Commander Williams' 30-month tour commanding the ship, he and his crew had been at sea for a total of 18 months.[102] In early 2004 Williams, by then a naval captain, received Canada's Meritorious Service Medal for "his contributions . . . during his first deployment to the Gulf." He accepted the decoration and noted that his achievements were "due in large part to the valiant men and women with whom he has served. . . . Grey matter has no rank and some of the best ideas . . . were from some of the junior guys on the ship."[103]

The Canadian Navy on the Eve of 9/11

Interoperability and Information Technology

During the 1990s military analysts and scholars developed an unproven theory of war known as network-centric, or network-enabled warfare, the result of emerging information technologies creating the widely heralded "Revolution in Military Affairs."[104] All navies faced a simple dilemma: keep current with the U.S. Navy or be left behind. In response, the Canadian Navy sought and sustained the highest state of interoperability with the Americans[105] and throughout the decade fitted their ships "to the world—that is U.S. Navy—standard." By 2001 the Canadian Navy was the most interoperable medium-size navy in the world.[106]

Canada had kept abreast of rapid advances in American naval information technology through four related developments: a forces-wide "strategic imperative" of interoperability, continuous review of rules of engagement, integration of Canadian frigates directly into American groups,[107] and knowledge of current NATO and American doctrine and technology. There was, however, a fifth source: AUSCANNZUKUS (Australian, Canadian, New Zealand, United Kingdom, United States) agreements by which the countries shared information in communications and intelligence, particularly through the use of SIPRNET and the development of COWAN and recognized maritime picture-building systems.

Through the 1980s, the American, British, Canadian, and Australian (ABCA) and Royal New Zealand navies shared information through the ABCANZ-5 Information Exchange Project, which allowed them to keep up to date with fast-developing information technology. That project expired in May 1992. The U.S. Navy also had developed a "NOFORN" system known as the SIPRNET, which had "a revolutionary impact on the planning and conduct of operations within the U.S. military."[108] SIPRNET was understood to be a secret-level American-eyes-only network; nevertheless, the minutes of the United States Military Communication-Electric Board, dated 7 November 1995, declared that "connections to agencies of foreign governments are permissible through the use of approved security devices employed on each foreign connection to the SIPRNET. These security devices must be in U.S. controlled spaces."[109]

In 1997 the AUSCANNZUKUS navies agreed upon the Multilateral Master Military Information Memorandum of Understanding, which allowed them to establish an Information Exchange Annex in May 2001. This combined naval staff effort had a clear aim: to improve interoperability between the ABCA navies.[110]

Probably as a result of the AUSCANNZUKUS developments early in 2001, by September of that year the Americans had evaluated and approved the Cooperative Engagement Capability (CEC) designed "to coordinate threat decisions in real time." CEC sought to "distribute fire control quality information to participating nodes" so that targeting information could be shared within national or multinational commands. At the same time, the U.S. Navy began to take advantage of the "opportunities offered by the Internet to enhance the transmission of information."[111] Thus, by 9/11, there were three secure Internet-based systems in place, two American and one Canadian, and each exploited "the Internet to improve the flow of information."

After SIPRNET, the second U.S. system was COWAN, a communications means that permitted the establishment of a common operational picture at a coalition "secret" level. Separated, though not entirely, from the SIPRNET by software firewalls and gateways, COWAN was an American development, worked up with "Australia, Canada and the UK," allowing "coalition e-communication and data transfer at net-centric warfare standards. . . . [COWAN] enabled those countries to access and contribute information as well as respond to tactical directions and intelligence as it was developed."[112] COWAN was initially introduced in the multinational Rim of the Pacific (RIMPAC) exercise series, and then spread more broadly.[113] The third system was the Canadian-only MCOIN III, just as SIPRNET was an American-only system.[114]

Concurrently, the Canadians had kept up with recognized maritime picture-building capabilities. By 2001 they were well equipped to develop, maintain, and react to the "overall operational picture in the AOR [area of responsibility]," relying on Link 14, Link 16, the Global Command and Control System, satellite modems, and wide bandwidth.[115] Canadian Task Group commanders learned to manage information flow and bandwidth, allowing them to link into higher level American surveillance, warning, targeting, and control systems without becoming overwhelmed.[116]

In the Gulf region the Americans and Canadians had overcome difficulties with the fitting of the high-speed, satellite-carried, "secure E-Mail system—Cowan." Releasability issues, which had always been a problem, were mostly solved with the use of this system. By 2002, Commodore Lehre remembered that "no other nation had fit Cowan in its ships or trained to its demanding standards as fully as we had."[117]

The View of Commander, Maritime Forces Pacific in 2000

In February 2000 Rear Admiral Ron D. Buck, RCN, Commander, Maritime Forces Pacific addressed a conference on future maritime war hosted by the Royal Australian Navy in Sydney. The RAN published the work in early 2001, and Buck, who had been promoted to vice admiral in December 2000, was appointed Chief of Maritime Staff (CMS) in June 2001. Thus before 9/11, Buck demonstrated a sound grasp of future interoperable requirements, as well as the importance of information technology on naval command, control, and operations. He reminded his readers that

> Canada has been involved in virtually all recent maritime coalition
> activities including the Gulf War, the Adriatic, ongoing operations in
> the Gulf which includes integration into United States carrier battle
> groups, and INTERFET in East Timor. Interoperability is bread and

butter to the Canadian Navy and it is seen as being essential. . . .
Interoperability with the U.S. Navy should be the fundamental C4I
goal of any nation that operates or is likely to operate with the U.S.
Navy. . . . What the Canadian Navy must now do is to ensure that
it evolves its at-sea systems to have secure e-mail, web-based data
sharing, the recognized maritime picture using GCCS–M imagery
[see below], and collaborative planning tools.[118]

The admiral was satisfied with communications systems *ashore*, based
on the Global Command and Control System–Maritime (GCCS–M),
and he knew that his *at-sea* "seamless connectivity" was under way.
Realistically, the Canadian goals were to provide

- high data rate connections between systems ashore and afloat,
- full support for internet protocol technology,
- support to all relevant types of information,
- compatibility with current and emerging open systems
  standards, and
- sufficient bandwidth to support increasing data rates.[119]

Vice Admiral Buck was optimistic that bandwidth and communications
architecture difficulties could be worked out because he and his staff had
detected a change in American attitudes towards their security policy,
releasability, and increased interoperability. He claimed that

the importance of the effort now being made by senior U.S. Navy
commanders to deliver on commitments to allies should not be
understated. It is inherent within the policy [since 1995] . . . that
there has been a major shift in the U.S security culture: from one that
assumes, as a first premise, that nothing is releasable, to one which
assumes release may be acceptable unless there is national reason
not to do so.[120]

The admiral warned, moreover, that while the "AUSCANNZUKUS
Naval Command, Control and Communications Board is a useful
interoperability forum . . . it lacks 'teeth' when compared with the North
Atlantic Treaty Organization." He considered that other opportunities
were available, including "joint warrior interoperability demonstration,
multinational task group exercises, RIMPAC exercises, and BattleLab

experiments. These are but a few of the vehicles and opportunities . . . to make interoperability a reality."[121]

Vice Admiral Buck's remarks were prescient. Considering the challenges that lay ahead—before the 9/11 attacks—he declared, "Global interoperability must therefore be the goal, but it can only be achieved with a paradigm shift. Being interoperable with the U.S. is therefore the singular most important issue now facing all navies in regards to C4I if they wish to provide a core contribution to coalition warfare."[122] Dramatically, a few months later, the 9/11 tragedy provided the necessary paradigm shift.

In summary, in September 2001 Canadian flag officers and group commanders on each coast possessed a powerful combination of recognized maritime picture-building capabilities, supported by an advanced secure Internet communications system. Canadian ships stood in the front rank with the United States Navy, and were able to assume a major role in any American sea service area of operation.[123] As the aftermath of the 9/11 attacks proved, this capability mattered a great deal, and the navy provided the government with strong options for support to the United States.

The Interoperable Paradigm Expanded: Leadership Interdiction Operations and the Campaign against Terrorism

"Canada contributed the first coalition TG to arrive in CENTCOM AOR."[124]

"The USN OPANAL cell in USS Stennis *conducted a study that showed that the efficiency of the hailing regime doubled when the Canadian CTG ran the ships in the Gulf of Oman."*[125]

When the 11 September attacks occurred, the Canadian government reacted decisively and instinctively: a four-ship naval task group and a maritime patrol aircraft detachment were sent in support of United States combined operations in the Gulf region. A fifth ship, HMCS *Vancouver*, deployed with the *John C. Stennis* carrier battle group based on pre-9/11 plans to have a single Canadian frigate train with the Americans for maritime interdiction operations, in accordance with long-standing UN Security Council resolutions.

Arriving just over two months after the event, the Canadian Task Group was the first allied naval force to reinforce U.S. Navy and Royal Navy forces in the region. During the first rotation *seven* Canadian ships were deployed. The east coast fleet provided five of the seven, because, in accordance with Defence Planning Guidance, that part of the service was responsible for maintaining the navy's high readiness task group. Operations in response to the 9/11 attacks, named Apollo by the Canadians and Enduring Freedom by the Americans, would continue with six-month rotations of ships, often with staggered arrival and departure times, until the middle of October 2003. The rotations, known as "Rotos," were numbered beginning with Roto Zero.

On arrival, Canadian staffs confirmed a fleet protection role with the Americans, and a new form of interception—Leadership Interdiction Operation (LIO)—was added to the range of sea control tasks. More robust rules of engagement to clarify noncompliant boarding operations were authorized. Affairs moved rapidly, and by early February 2002 these types of interception operations blurred together, and the Americans reorganized

The Canadian patrol frigate, 12 of which were commissioned from 1992 to 1997, was the backbone of Canadian maritime interdiction operations in the Gulf region before and after 9/11. HMCS *Vancouver* is seen here with a hovering Sea King helicopter.

command arrangements for both operations. The Canadians were given the coordinating responsibility for the Southern Arabian Gulf, the Strait of Hormuz, and the Gulf of Oman (GOO), and thereafter they coordinated all interception operations—maritime and leadership—and escort operations for the U.S. Navy in this critical sector of the operational area.

* * *

Following the 11 September attacks, for the first time in its history, NATO implemented Article 5 of the collective agreement known colloquially as "an attack on one is an attack on all." The Canadian government wanted a fast and visible reaction, but its navy had no ship in the Gulf region, *Winnipeg* having departed for Esquimalt in early August.[126] The frigate *Halifax*, however, was at sea in the eastern Atlantic with NATO's Standing Naval Force Atlantic, and redeploying *Halifax* offered the government an easy option: Canada could quickly contribute a modern and well-connected ship to augment American antiterrorist efforts. The government chose this option because speed and commitment counted, and *Halifax*, led by Commander P. Ellis, was immediately re-tasked to sail east on her own. As in the First Gulf War, the navy had demonstrated that it could react faster, and with higher interoperability, than the other two Canadian services.

Reinforcing the trust established with the Americans over the previous decade, National Defence Headquarters and the government planned further contributions to fight terrorism in southwest Asia. The United States Central Command (USCENTCOM) area of responsibility was huge. Encompassing 25 countries, it contained the three "most critical choke points" known to mariners: the Suez Canal, the southern entrance to the Red Sea (Bab al-Mandeb), and the Strait of Hormuz.[127] Vice Admiral Greg Maddison, Deputy Chief of Defence Staff (DCDS), remembered that the planning process was based on two respective Canadian and American questions: What is it that you need? And what have you got? All coalition navies understood that while the Northern Arabian Gulf and the Strait of Hormuz required coalition ships in or near them, a wider sea control screen was required along the Iranian coast and south to the Horn of Africa. To satisfy the need, many options were open.[128]

By early October the government had directed that the navy dispatch the east coast task group, consisting of Commodore D. W. Robertson and his staff embarked in *Iroquois*, as well as *Charlottetown*, the frigate that had just returned from the Mediterranean and Gulf region three months earlier, and *Preserver*, a fleet replenishment ship. *Iroquois*, the DDG namesake of the 280 (Tribal) class, was an ideal command and control platform for the commodore and his staff. As the Canadian commitment to the war was planned to increase, the DCDS established an operational commander—Commander, Canadian Joint Task Force–South-West Asia—alongside Central Command headquarters in Tampa, Florida. The Canadian headquarters would also act as the National Command Element (NCE).

At his headquarters in Halifax, Rear Admiral M. B. MacLean, MARLANT, had directed that Commander J. B. McCarthy, commanding *Preserver*, initiate planning for a possible humanitarian deployment to New York, as well as working up for sea operations. McCarthy also examined options that could be "made available to the Canadian government for a naval response to the war on terrorism should the Canadian government decide" to pursue this alternative.[129] On 7 October *Preserver* received a warning order to sail in ten days, Canadian Thanksgiving weekend leave was cancelled, and the crew completed "a huge amount of work . . . including ammunitioning and fuelling."[130]

In *Charlottetown* feelings were mixed. She had returned from the Gulf on 1 July. On receipt of the warning order, her preparations included installing COWAN, which her crew knew was essential for operations with the U.S. Navy. Ten days later *Charlottetown*, still under Commander Lloyd, slipped to sail eastward, this time in the company of *Iroquois* and *Preserver*.[131]

Once at sea, Commodore Robertson was concerned about the level of connectivity. In his group war diary he noted in operational shorthand:

> **19 Oct 01.** Improvements have been realized in C4I connectivity as result of efforts at sea and ashore.

> **20 Oct 01.** First Phase of Round Robin trg [training] complete. Op Apollo sea trg det now in IRO [*Iroquois*] . . . C4I connectivity improved in all TG [Task Group] ships.

DND Photo HS2005-0152-01a

As Deputy Chief of Defence Staff, Vice Admiral Greg Maddison coordinated the Canadian response to the global terrorist threat following 9/11. As Commander, Standing Naval Forces Atlantic in 1993–1994, he designed and directed the operations for the NATO and Western European Union maritime interdiction forces for Operation Sharp Guard in the Adriatic.

23 Oct 01. TG training progressing well in all areas.

25 Oct 01. Final phase of trg progressing well.[132]

Cruising ahead of the task group, *Halifax* wasted no time in the Mediterranean. She had degaussed in Augusta, Sicily, on 13 October and proceeded to Souda Bay, Crete, to embark stores and equipment.[133] On 18 October *Halifax* sailed for Suez now "fully equipped" with the necessary supplies for sea operations in the Gulf.[134] She transited the Suez Canal four days later and arrived in Bahrain for her in-chop briefing with the U.S. Fifth Fleet on 31 October.[135] Commander Ellis remembered feeling that his ship had "assumed the role of the vanguard of the Canadian Forces. . . . We were the first allied warship to join the . . . [USN-RN-RAN] coalition. And although we were the first, by the time we left to return home [in mid-March] . . . there were about 60 ships in that operational theatre, from 10 different nations."[136]

Halifax sailed from Bahrain on 3 November, integrating perfectly into the American operational area, and she immediately began interdiction patrols in the Gulf of Oman. On 7 November the COMDESRON 50 chief of staff continued to brief the commanding officer on operations in the operational area.[137] Several days later *Halifax* was conducting her first mission: a Strait of Hormuz escort, followed by oil smuggling patrols off the coast of Fujairah, on the east side of the UAE, where "much time was spent identifying the hundreds of tankers bunkering and anchored."[138] The operations that Canadians had always prided themselves on—Arabian Gulf naval intelligence gathering—had begun again. This time there was a difference: operations were not being conducted *vide* UN Security Council resolutions.

In the early days of her deployment, *Halifax* received various escort and interdiction tasks throughout the region. A new issue arose, however, unrelated to the war on terrorism: Indian-Pakistani tensions increased, and *Halifax* found herself

> tasked to maintain the Recognized Maritime Picture. . . . Her main advantage as a Canadian warship was being a fellow Commonwealth member to both sides and thus able to mediate less obtrusively than an American or even British warship. In

the process, the signal processing and tracking capability of . . . [her] combat systems were proven to be superior in some respects . . . to . . . next-generation generation systems. *Halifax* was able to provide observations on Indo-Pakistani air and submarine movements that were especially important to the Coalition effort.[139]

The 21st of November was decisive in the history of Canadian naval operations. On that day, Commodore Robertson met with Vice Admiral Charles W. Moore, USN, in Bahrain. Moore was triple-hatted as commander of the U.S. Fifth Fleet, the MIF, and Naval Forces Central Command (NAVCENT) in U.S. Central Command's advanced headquarters in Bahrain. Well prepared for the meeting, Robertson was "pleased that operational background material . . . [had been] provided by *Halifax* . . . [and the] NCE. . . . While there was little that was new, the briefings were well done and the face-to-face contact allowed many issues to be resolved, or put them well on the way to resolution, including . . . [arrangements to ensure a high level of interoperability]."[140] The Canadians arrived well prepared.

Robertson met with Moore for about 40 minutes, and the two commanders concentrated on the likely task of defending the amphibious ready group (ARG), as well as interdiction doctrine and tactics. Admiral Moore defined a leadership interdiction operation as "first and foremost an information operation," and both commanders agreed that while "we couldn't impose ourselves on every ship . . . coming through" the operational area, we could "get the word out that there were ships present." Robertson considered he was "pretty comfortable with how the leadership interdiction operations would be run," and he now had a solid sense of what the Fifth Fleet expected of his group. In particular, Robertson understood the distinction between MIO and LIO, and he recalled that "although the Commander Fifth Fleet . . . had not authorized disabling fire or non-disabling fire in its entire three years in command for MIO against Iraqi sanction violators . . . he was willing to approve that in a heartbeat when dealing with a potential LIO candidate on which he had really good intelligence . . . or on which there was a very high area of suspicion."[141] The rules of engagement changed in the new environment.

The meetings at Fifth Fleet headquarters provided essential guidance for future Canadian operations, as Robertson remembered:

[T]here was an opportunity to find out . . . what the [ARGs] were
going to be doing . . . [in] the upcoming op [RHINO] . . . that
would take the marines ashore and eventually to Kandahar . . . [this
provided an understanding of] how long the amphibs would be
there off the coast . . . [and for example] why they would be pretty
tightly tethered to that place reducing the operational and tactical
flexibility that one might otherwise want to have of just being able to
get out of the way.[142]

This background would prove to be useful as relations between India and
Pakistan deteriorated through the following month.[143] By the third week
of November 2001, Commodore Robertson, Amphibious Support Force
Defense Commander, was deploying the Canadian Task Group into the
North Arabian Sea—east of the Gulf of Oman—to protect the large U.S.
Marine ARG that was to conduct operations into Afghanistan from south
of the Pakistani Coast.[144]

To review command appointments and relationships, Vice
Admiral Maddison directed the overall Canadian contribution through
Commodore J. J. P. Thiffault, the double-hatted officer in Tampa
commanding the Canadian Joint Task Force–South-West Asia and
heading the National Command Element. Thiffault executed operational
and national command of Commodore Robertson's task group designated
CTG 307.1. The Americans had designated the Gulf region as part of the
USCENTCOM area of responsibility, and all naval forces were controlled
by the U.S. Fifth Fleet in Bahrain. In the AOR the U.S. Navy had designated
the Canadian group as CTG 50.4, and the group was detached under the
tactical control of their Task Force 50. Robertson was appointed a sea
combat commander and tasked with protecting the ARG based on the
U.S. amphibious assault ships *Peleliu*, *Bataan*, and *Whidbey Island*.

As part of the screen, Robertson remained in the operational area with
the amphibious forces,[145] and he was well aware that his mission involved
intense intelligence gathering—collating all sources of information in order
to produce an effective recognized maritime picture to ensure sea control.
Moreover, Robertson knew the risks that the U.S. Navy "was willing to
take with sailors both in the MIO operations in the NAG and indeed [for

LIO] down to the Gulf of Oman."[146] For the next few months his group "tracked coastal naval forces" and monitored several Indian surface groups, including—four months later—"the 10 ships of the INS [Indian Naval Ship] *Virat*'s carrier battle group that passed through the Gulf of Oman in March [2002] en route to port visits in the Arabian Gulf."[147]

* * *

At the same time, HMAS *Sydney*, a frigate in the *Oliver Hazard Perry* class—*Adelaide* class in Royal Australian Navy terminology—arrived in the Northern Arabian Gulf ahead of a RAN task group, and on 9 November she relieved HMAS *Anzac*, the namesake of her FFH class, commanded by Captain Nigel Coates. *Sydney* formed Task Group 627.4 and was tasked to relieve *Anzac* for Maritime Interception Force operations "as part of the enforcement of United Nations sanctions against Iraq."[148]

Sydney, under Commander D. W. Bates, RAN, remained in the Northern Arabian Gulf until the Australian task group arrived in early December. The timely arrival of warships experienced with MIO, and who had been included in AUSCANNZUKUS information-sharing agreements, greatly enhanced operations in the region.[149] The RAN task group, TG 627.1, was "chopped [to] Operational Control of the Combined Joint Force Maritime Component Commander U.S. Central Command (CJFMCC–CENT) on 5 December for MIF operational tasking." The task group comprised the amphibious transport ship HMAS *Kanimbla* and the frigate HMAS *Adelaide*, with Captain Allan Du Toit, RAN, embarked with a staff on *Kanimbla*, as a tactical warfare commander.[150] Commander David McCourt, RAN, commanded *Kanimbla*.

Du Toit remembered:

The Commander U.S. Naval Forces Central Command and U.S. Fifth Fleet Commander C5F, Vice Admiral Moore, was particularly keen for the RAN to assume a significant warfare command role, and for *Adelaide* and *Kanimbla* to be gainfully employed in the NAG along with *Sydney*, as part of the MIF. He also recognized that *Kanimbla* was ideally suited to fulfill the role of Maritime Interception Operations (MIO) command ship. His views were strongly influenced by the recent success of *Anzac*'s deployment and a brief visit to the MEAO [Middle East Area of Operations] by the Maritime Commander Australia and MCC AST, Rear Admiral Geoff Smith, in late September, during which the potential tasking for RAN units was discussed.[151]

It was decided that command in the Northern Arabian Gulf would be shared by American and Australian commanders. Du Toit assumed "the role of Maritime Interception Commander (MIC), enforcing the long-standing U.N. sanctions against Iraq. This was to be effected on a monthly rotational basis with . . . COMDESRON 50, Captain David Jackson, utilizing *Kanimbla* as the MIO command ship." [152] The American officer would therefore manage the effort from the deck of a RAN ship.

Although U.S. Navy–RAN command relations in the Northern Arabian Gulf seemed perfect, low connectivity forced a revision. Captain Du Toit retained the appointment of MIC, but he was to command "from a U.S. unit." Du Toit recalled that he "assumed duties as the MIC and CTU 50.0.9 (XJ) from CDS 50 on 5 January 2002, initially embarked in the *Spruance*-class destroyer USS *John Young* (Commander Tim Smith) and later in her sister ship *Elliot* (Commander Jerry Provencher)." [153]

Du Toit described the training process that his ships underwent in early December 2001:

> Following "Inchop" briefings in Bahrain and boarding party and container climbing training for all boarding parties, the TG sailed for the NAG on 12 December 2001 to join *Sydney* for MIF operations. The boarding party training conducted by the U.S. Coast Guard detachment at the so-called "MIO University" in Bahrain was further consolidated by two days of assisted compliant boarding familiarization training with the COMISKEY (MIO holding area) guardship in the NAG, prior to conducting solo operations.[154]

The Australians made rapid progress at interdiction tactics. Du Toit recorded that each of the three Australian ships

> conducted MIO with two twelve-person boarding parties, which were capable of up to Level Two non-compliant boardings (NCBs). These teams . . . could be inserted into a target vessel by [boat] . . . by day or night or by Helicopter Fast Rope Insertion by day only.

In addition, *Kanimbla* created a third boarding party from the embarked EOD detachment that also had a very useful night-time helicopter insertion and seize capability, with no contributing nation possessing a similar capability. [155]

The Australians had moved fast, completing the U.S. Navy and U.S. Coast Guard training quickly, and they left no doubt that they intended to operate effectively in the hazardous Northern Arabian Gulf.

* * *

About a thousand nautical miles east, the U.S. Marine Corps ARG operated just outside the 12-mile limit of Pakistan's territorial waters. A range of threats was presented to these large, undefended, high-value forces, and for the next two months Commodore Robertson and the Canadian Task Group coordinated their surface and air defense. Rules of engagement and territorial waters limits were examined, and the Canadian operations concentrated on seaward defense, "which essentially meant that we would identify all contacts that closed the ARG to ensure that they did not present a threat."[156] *Charlottetown*'s crew took pride knowing that she was "the first to assume the duties of ARG escort" and that "Canada was the first country to arrive in theatre."[157]

By 7 December *Halifax* had joined the Canadian group, and the commanding officer noted that his fellow Canadian commanding officers agreed on the complexity of the problem:

> Essentially all boardings aiming to capture Taliban/Al Aqaeda combatants . . . will be based on actionable intelligence. It is possible that *Halifax* could be ordered to conduct a compliant boarding on a cooperative vessel, but that would only occur in the absence of actionable intelligence . . . such a boarding would be part of the information campaign to advertise that the coalition is here and that there is no escape by sea.[158]

Concurrently, *Preserver* was placed under tactical control of the Fifth Fleet Logistics Force—CTF 53. On completion of her deployment, *Preserver* had conducted

> more than 120 replenishments at sea with ships from Canada, the U.S., France, Australia, the U.K., the Netherlands and Italy, transferring

almost 27,000,000 litres of fuel and 1380 cargo pallets equaling 203,192
kilos of stores. At the same time she also participated in the general
surveillance and LIO effort, including two boardings—this in contrast
to the auxiliaries of practically every other navy that avoid engagement
in such "combat" operations.[159]

HMCS *Vancouver*, the west coast CPF sailing with the *John C. Stennis*
battle group as part of the pre-9/11 single-frigate deployments, was the next
Canadian ship to arrive in-theater. She was commanded by Commander J.
T. Heath. The Chief of Maritime Staff ordered her planned deployment to
continue, notwithstanding *Stennis* was re-tasked to participate in the air
war against the Taliban in Afghanistan. The battle group in-chopped on
15 December, and *Vancouver*, no longer required as an escort, conducted
a variety of interdiction operations as an interoperable problem-solving
reserve for CTF 50.[160]

On 19 December Vice Admiral Buck, now Chief of Maritime Staff,
was interviewed by Steve Madely of station CFRA–AM in Ottawa. The
admiral's remarks were significant because he used the term "maritime
interdiction operations" for the first time, and he provided the public with
a clear sense of what his men and women were facing at sea.

> We are actually doing a number of things. We are clearly providing
> protection to not only the aircraft carriers in the region but also
> . . . the Amphibious [Ready] Group, which landed Marines . . .
> we are conducting throughout the region what is called maritime
> interdiction operations . . . we have a complete picture of all vessels
> moving, and surveilling [*sic*] them for any suspicious activity . . . if
> there is suspicious activity . . . [we coordinate] with our other allies
> the appropriate action to ensure that we know what they're up to.

The reporter asked if that meant "actually boarding them," and the
admiral replied, "as we have been doing over the years, we do maritime
interdiction and, yes, that could include boarding." Their discussion then
focused on boarding policy and tactics.[161]

The CMS succeeded in keeping his remarks general, particularly
when he was asked about operational areas: "there's also an ongoing
action throughout the region . . . in support of U.N. sanctions. So there's

DND Photo HS-032613d74

Vice Admiral Ron Buck, Chief of Maritime Staff, left, presents Petty Officer 1st Class Michael Cooper, physician's assistant, with the South-West Asia Medal on HMCS *Fredericton* on 10 June 2003. The ship was deployed in the Canadian-commanded Task Force 151 in the Gulf region. In charge of the Canadian Navy on 9/11, Vice Admiral Buck oversaw the navy's high tempo operations in the region until November 2003.

a variety [of operations] . . . going on but those are the two main areas . . . there's a number of . . . operational zones and areas . . . that we have been working in for a number of years . . . we have a very good picture of what's going on."[162] Vice Admiral Buck accurately stressed the high level of interoperability. He reminded the reporter of the "common operating procedures, doctrine and training," which allowed the Canadians "to move seamlessly into this coalition activity." [163]

Buck also made clear that he would sustain the high tempo. In early December a fourth frigate, HMCS *Toronto*, sailed from Halifax to join the Standing Naval Force Atlantic deployed in the eastern Mediterranean and relieve American ships, which in turn were redeploying to the Gulf region. Later *Toronto* would be tasked away from SNFL to serve as the sixth Canadian ship in the region since 9/11.[164]

RAN operations had proceeded apace, and Captain Du Toit continued as Maritime Interception Commander sharing command of MIF operations in the Northern Arabian Gulf with COMDESRON 50. On 5 January 2002 he took his turn, embarked in *John Young*, a *Spruance*-class destroyer. Du Toit controlled "units from Australia (HMA Ships *Adelaide*, *Kanimbla* and *Sydney*) . . . the United Kingdom (HM Ships *Kent* and *Fearless*) . . . [and the U.S. Navy ships] . . . *Jarrett* and *Leyte Gulf*." He retained the MIF responsibility until 6 February when he returned it to the American destroyer squadron commander. Du Toit considered his command

> an important event, as it was the first time in the 12-year history of the MIF that a non-U.S. officer had assumed command of multinational MIF operations in the NAG. . . . This event was positively and extensively reported in the media back in Australia, which, because of the secrecy surrounding our deployment, provided the first real news for our families and friends, of what we were actually doing.[165]

Off Pakistan, the Canadian Task Group continued its ARG defense operations into January 2002, and then the operational situation changed. Withdrawing al-Qaeda and Taliban forces had been denied access to the Pakistani coast, so they moved westward into Iran, using Iranian territorial waters to flee across the Gulf of Oman and the narrow Strait of Hormuz. As a result leadership interdiction operations intensified.

* * *

On 20 January "CBC Newsworld" led with an exclusive story direct from *Iroquois* in southwest Asian waters. Captain C. L. Mofford commanded the ship. Anchor Alison Smith introduced the story with a pointed criticism of the navy: "Since it left in October, we haven't heard a lot about the naval task force [and] . . . the ships of Operation Apollo. Well, that's about to change. Tonight the first television report from on board."[166]

Rob Gordon of CBC Halifax was never shy about reporting naval matters. At sea in *Iroquois*, he spoke to the Canadian public dramatically and positively about the realities of naval life during the war on terrorism:

Sunrise on a foreign sea, a familiar sight now for 1200 Canadian sailors who left Canada three months ago. The five warships of this fleet are isolated and self-sustaining. Some of the sailors haven't set foot on dry land since they started patrols in the Arabian Sea. . . . The Canadian Navy has some of the hard slogging in the war on terrorism . . . backing the attack, escorting other coalition ships and re-supplying them, and defending U.S. carriers. . . . In front of us, two American warships as escorts. . . . This is the Strait of Hormuz, a narrow passage through which all ships coming in and out of the Persian Gulf must pass. . . . That makes the Canadians nervous . . . Canadian ships are vulnerable to terrorist attack . . . with few welcoming ports, the Canadians have been forced to spend a record amount of time at sea.[167]

Rob Gordon filed a second story the following day, and the "Newsworld" anchor in Canada again criticized the navy for what the network saw as a lack of information provided to the public. The anchor declared that "back in October when the ships sailed off [there was] . . . a lot of flag waving and all sailed off into obscurity. They are out in the middle of the sea. We've lost touch with them. What are they doing out there?" Gordon now was more than ready to answer this question, telling the Canadian public why, in the opinion of the CBC, the navy had released so little information.

Well, that's a funny thing. We all know since September 11th, it's a brand new world . . . for the Canadian Navy. Normally on missions . . . the press can go and see what they're doing. It hasn't happened this time. It's really because of the new world. As you know, the Canadian Navy is very small and it was designed really to hunt Soviet ships and fight in the Atlantic Ocean if the Cold War ever got hot. The mission they're on right now is not like that. They're not worried about being attacked by submarines. But they are worried about a guy in a boat— 15 foot boat with explosives as what happened with the USS *Cole* last year. What they've done is try to keep their movement secret. Not discuss what port they're in or out of and in fact, won't discuss what port they're using. Their missions are escort missions, working with the U.S. Navy and the U.S. aircraft carriers, escorting fuel ships and food and ammunition to and from the Persian Gulf and the Arabian Sea area.[168]

There was no mention of Canadian interoperability or operational responsibility.

On 6 February Commodore Robertson recorded that command arrangements required alteration due to the increasing pace of maritime and leadership interdiction tasks. He remembered:

> Throughout January, my American counterparts had been examining options for improving the ongoing Leadership Interdiction Operations across the theatre. They were not obtaining the coverage they thought possible and the span of control was too great for the Sea Combat Commander to easily improve the results. Additionally, communications with a widely dispersed coalition force were difficult, and yet the Sea Combat Commander, being borne in an aircraft carrier that had to remain in the optimum position for air operations, was unable to move to any other operating areas. The best solution was one that would see a part of the region taken over by a local commander. In discussions we agreed that the [Canadian Task Group] . . . would be well suited to taking on the leadership of operations from the Southern Arabian Gulf, through the Straits of Hormuz and into the Gulf of Oman.[169]

Thus, in early February, the U.S. Navy again demonstrated their respect for the capabilities of the commodore and his staff by granting them the tactical authority that had been discussed the previous month. The Canadians would coordinate sea control operations for the Gulf of Oman sector "west of 60E" and the Southern Arabian Gulf, and escort tasks through the Strait of Hormuz. Their command callsign was Charlie Zulu, "CZ," and they would remain in control of this critical operational sector—bracketing the Strait of Hormuz—until mid-2003. As Robertson put it, "for the months of February and March, the [Canadian Task Group] led a multinational task group of coalition ships in that area. . . . In total some 16 ships and aircraft from 8 countries (Bahrain, Canada, France, Germany, Italy, the Netherlands, United Kingdom, and the United States) participated in what amounted to a multinational task group based in the Gulf of Oman."[170]

To review leadership relations, by February 2002 CZ was still a formation under the national command of the Canadian Joint Task Force–South-West Asia and the National Command Element, headquartered in Tampa. In the U.S. Central Command operational area the Canadians were under local, or tactical control of Commander Task Force 50, who had further detached the group to the control of CTG 50.6, an American commodore, who was the overall sea combat commander. Thereafter, until later in the year, the Canadian Task Group coordinated maritime and leadership interdiction operations for CTG 50.6. In summary, the Americans had delegated to the Canadians the unceasing grind of coordinating scant resources for maritime and leadership operations south of the Northern Arabian Gulf area, which allowed the U.S. Navy to address wider issues, such as eventualities east of 60 degrees,[171] as well as sea control of the NAG for reasons other than interdiction operations.

On assuming command on 7 February, Robertson quickly sensed the difficulties in allocating resources between MIO and LIO requirements, as well as providing intelligence to build the recognized maritime picture. He reported in operational shorthand that the "First 24 hrs as GOO cdr is indicative of pull between LIO (Priority Tasking) and MIO, as ships have been retasked to be able to position VAN [*Vancouver*] to conduct surveillance of . . . [a suspected MIO vessel]. Pursuing an aggressive fly programme over coming days will cover LIO tasking and establish traffic patterns in GOO and through . . . SOH." These were early days for his new responsibility, and Robertson noted that as CTG 50.6 clarified leadership operations, the Canadian area of responsibility for the Gulf of Oman would be "more clearly" defined.[172]

Coincident with these developments, Captain Tom Yaeger, USN, from the Naval Historical Center (redesignated the Naval History and Heritage Command in 2008) in Washington, D.C., was conducting an oral history project with the Operational Documentation Detachment, Fifth Fleet.[173] On 12 March he visited the Canadian fleet replenishment ship *Preserver*, and he interviewed the commanding officer, Commander J. B. McCarthy. Yaeger covered much background material with his questions, and his interests were the main components of sea control: intelligence sharing within the coalition, interoperability, and connectivity. McCarthy was particularly outspoken on the latter.

> We're all aware in the Canadian Task Group that there is a communications linkage . . . that we are unable to [use, because] . . . SIPRNET . . . is a U.S. national [system]. . . . For allied ships . . . [and] coalition ships . . . there is what we call COWAN, which is a Coalition Wide Area Network . . . conceived on the west coast . . . [MARPAC] . . . ships are more familiar with it. We were given the capability for [COWAN] . . . before we sailed from Halifax but it has been, in my view, a slow process getting other coalition partners to hop on that . . . we've probably come a long way since we arrived in theatre in having more U.S. Navy assets that we can talk to directly, electronically as opposed to just by voice circuits or message traffic.[174]

McCarthy described the difficulties of relying on new communications systems at the expense of the old.

> [M]essage traffic is much less reliable, particularly with coalition partners and, in my view, particularly with U.S. Navy ships. . . . Very frequently we'll [conduct replenishment at sea (RAS) planning] . . . two days before by a priority or immediate message . . . [however some] ships won't have that. I think it's because there is such a reliance now on the immediate communications . . . I don't have that level of confidence that I used to have . . . if I send a priority message.

McCarthy was clear in the interview what he needed to improve logistics planning at sea.

> I would love to have either a Chat or a direct e-mail connectivity with CTF 53. . . . We have no chat capability except with our liaison officer . . . but we do have an internet E-mail connectivity . . . sporadic[ally]. . . . There are some U.S. ships we manage to achieve E-mail connectivity with and some we do not. . . . I think it will be an enormously useful tool if all coalition ships can speak to each other on a common electronic net, like some kind of a chat or at least E-mail. . . . [What we need is] . . . a system where you can reliably call up another unit . . . and get word to them. . . . I would prefer it to be more real time and expeditious.[175]

Captain Yeager questioned McCarthy on intelligence relating to target ships, and McCarthy, a former destroyer captain, knew exactly what he needed, for *Preserver* was "only authorized to do unopposed boardings, which translates into consensual boardings" in U.S. Navy terms. His operations team followed the "list of suspicious indicators, and used that as our measurement criteria when we hail vessels and board them . . . if the master is happy to have us aboard then there's really no . . . concern . . . we're . . . extremely careful. . . . I have not been particularly uncomfortable in sending seamen away in anything we've been asked to do."[176] Intelligence information allowed McCarthy to manage the risk to his boarding teams.

Summarizing his experience, McCarthy noted:

> [T]here were some growing pains with the whole command and control issue when we first arrived that we worked out with 53 and with the Canadian Task Group commander. My sense . . . is that *Preserver* is more integrated into the CTF 53 organization than are the naval support assets of the other coalition partners. . . . I think our task group commander made a conscious decision that we wouldn't go that way although the temptations sometimes to draw us back into the national umbrella have been quite strong . . . we have been almost an integral part of the CTF 53 organization and that's worked out well . . . that . . . expanded our horizon because it's obviously been a much bigger organization that we've been working in than we would ordinarily have in the national context which has been good for us, invigorating for us and just generally a positive and worthwhile experience for us.[177]

Together, Commodore Robertson and McCarthy understood the right balance in operational relations with the Americans.

On lessons learned, McCarthy emphasized the benefits of deploying single patrol frigates as part of U.S. Navy battle groups, which had provided visible evidence of Canada's interest in sustaining interoperability. He then advised that

> we have been fairly proactive in sharing with them observations and lessons learned from working in a very diverse . . . support

environment as opposed to the more focused Canadian task group environment. . . . We're hoping that those types of things will be absorbed in the overall statement of requirements for the ships . . . [which stresses] our interoperability with the U.S. Navy that maybe other navies aren't able to achieve. . . . We're always pretty comfortable to work with the United States Navy and I think can easily slide into something like this. It's just adapting to a much broader picture . . . that we need to do better but I think we're capable of it and prepared for it. . . . Nevertheless, I think we have achieved quite a high level of interoperability. There are no other navies that I know of that actually can have a warship assigned as part of a battle group . . . we've been doing that for some time . . . [for example] *Vancouver*. . . . So we know . . . interoperability is important. I think all our future planning is based on using that as . . . criteria. . . . On the policy side, of course, that gets into the political realm where obviously there will be convergences and divergences of views and strategic objectives.[178]

A day earlier, on 11 March, Commodore Robertson had also briefed Captain Yaeger on connectivity, the provision of intelligence, and rules of engagement. After three and a half months, he had no trouble coordinating these different demands. Like McCarthy, Robertson stressed the need for a common SIPRNET–COWAN "communications system" for all coalition ships. He suggested that the system be adapted beyond the ABCA group, so that other nations, like the Netherlands, could communicate easily in ad hoc coalitions. He put his point plainly: "If things are going to become dangerous you need to know that . . . [a] captain has got all the same information as the other participants."[179]

Robertson emphatically stressed the legal implications of MIO and LIO work in the Gulf region. In his mind, although the coalition was conducting a war against terrorism, the laws of armed conflict still applied to Canadian ships. For example, he and his captains had to consider "obligations under international law," and they had to

come to one's own decision about whether a vessel really has . . . [an] enemy character [and] . . . whether one has reasonable grounds to take action against the vessel. . . . We haven't encountered this problem but there is clearly the potential that American intelligence methods could say that . . . [a vessel] has hostile intent. Or indeed has enemy character, in this case we will say al Qaeda on board. . . . That vessel has to be dealt with. The Canadian question would be "OK fine how do you know that?" Because unless I'm convinced under international law, I can't take action . . . intelligence isn't perfect. . . . Imagine . . . being in a coalition navy and taking military action . . . [for example, using] disabling fire. . . . [We are] answerable to the Canadian and the international community about why . . . [we] took that action. And because "the Americans said so" won't necessarily . . . [clear us]. . . . The real issue is can we get . . . connectivity with more of the countries.[180]

Connectivity, in other words, was not just a tool that made operations more efficient because it simplified problems of command and control; it was also critical for the exercise of rules of engagement by Canadian sailors who were responsible to their government for their actions. Connectivity meant sharing resources and information, in an atmosphere of trust, to allow nations to exercise sovereignty even while deeply embedded in a coalition led by the world's sole superpower.

Despite justifiable concerns over releasability, Commodore Robertson was fundamentally satisfied with the arrangements. Moreover, LIO was working despite the initial misgivings of many participants, and afterward Robertson commented positively on this new genre of operation.

When the concept of establishing an LIO regime based on consensual boardings was proposed, a number of us had the same reservation. It did not seem likely that a regime based principally on the cooperation of merchant masters rather than U.N. Security Council resolutions would work. We thought it would be quickly proven impotent, but we were wrong. More than 100 vessels of all sizes were boarded by the coalition forces thanks to cooperation of their masters. . . . The result of an interesting idea by the U.S. Navy was that a regime of a type not previously employed was successfully established.[181]

* * *

The next year, the Maritime Interception Force in the Northern Arabian Gulf continued to conduct interdiction operations in support of the various UNSCRs mandating oil-related economic sanctions on Iraq. In early March 2002 Captain James Goldrick, RAN, took command of the MIF, replacing Captain Allan Du Toit.

Goldrick had taken over Du Toit's effective command arrangements within Fifth Fleet, and a separate Australian "National Commander" had been appointed, which allowed him more time to focus on operations. Goldrick retained the mission of reducing "the incidence of oil-smuggling from Iraq." He considered that he had "sufficient—but only just sufficient—forces to maintain a continuous cordon around the Khawr Abd Allah."[182]

As the MIF commander in the northern area, Captain Goldrick reported no legal challenges, but in the spring of 2002, he expressed concern about future American intervention operations:

> [T]he U.S. Navy had additional items on their agenda and . . . it took me time, new as I was to the Gulf, to understand . . . what the real implications of that were. For example, the U.S. Navy priority was to have an appropriate presence in the Northern Gulf to support Operation Southern Watch, the air defence and air movement problem. They also had to have a sufficient presence to be ready to strike Iraq if the situation required. Although we had no visibility of this, it was quite clear they were spending a lot of time thinking about the issues of any campaign that might be ordered against Iraq.[183]

Goldrick revised his MIF operational concept to meet these circumstances, and he grasped the military advantages, for future operations, that would result from UNSCR sanction enforcement.

His problem in the northern area was that a substantial outflow of oil left the Khawr Abd Allah every day. The amount was "the equivalent of a medium-sized oil tanker," and he knew that

> some had to be going out in the motor dhows, but only a proportion. Although we were watching for breakouts, the number we detected or had direct evidence of simply didn't match the outflow. I formed the view that we were not catching all the smugglers because we simply were not aware of all the smuggler movements. In my judgement we were all relying too much upon electronic detection methods, both passive and active, and failing to appreciate the smuggling organisation was capable of exploiting *a gap of only a couple of hours in our coverage* . . .

Crewmembers from HMCS *Toronto* assist a dhow with mechanical troubles in the Gulf region, 14 March 1998. Prior to 9/11 interdiction operations under various UN Security Council Resolution mandates were less warlike and closer to police operations.

we had the number of ships, the combinations of rules of engagements and the physical capabilities to actually maintain a 24-hour a day, seven days a week, twelve months a year close-up surveillance of the KAA. *That was the only thing that was actually going to stop the tanker traffic outright, and we implemented that change.* . . . I had a lot of work to do, not so much within the force, but outside it. Such issues as disposition planning, rotations of ships, replenishments and weapons firings all required consideration. Timings had to be carefully worked to make sure that somebody was always close up to the KAA . . . *we ended sitting up there close because Anzac and* [Du Toit's] *group had brutalised the opposition, were in a blockade mode. We had less boardings than before and less boardings than after, when the dhows became the target* [emphasis added].[184]

Goldrick commented on the propensity to ingest statistics at the expense of analyzing effects:

When you get people going on about how we did X numbers of this, and X numbers of that, and X numbers of the other [that is]

... viewed as a measure of success, as opposed to the *effect* you are trying to achieve ... it was only when intelligence came through that the amount of loading actually happening inside Iraq had dropped from about 50% to about 10%, that people were able to see that the blockade—where nothing seemed to be happening—was achieving the desired effect. We were able to see the major and direct effect on ... [Iraqi] morale.[185]

By sustaining sea control of the Khawr Abd Allah in support of UNSCR sanctions, the Australian task group in the Northern Arabian Gulf was also preparing the approaches for coalition military operations.

Balanced Forces and Steady States: A Perfect ABCA Paradigm

"Use the LIO model as practiced in the GOO for world-wide application—overall 'CZ' has it right."[186]

By late January 2002 Commodore Robertson and his ships had established sea control between the Southern Arabian Gulf and Gulf of Oman, and they enjoyed the respect of the U.S. Navy and coalition navies operating throughout the Gulf region. The Canadians achieved this level of success through effective intelligence-gathering, enforcing the maritime right of transit, and coordinating escorts, while demonstrating care over Iranian-claimed waters in these hazardous and contentious areas.[187]

On 1 April Commodore Robertson handed over command of the Canadian Task Group to Commodore Eric Lehre. On 2 May HMCS *Algonquin*, the commodore's command ship, had arrived, and by June *Ottawa* and *St. John's* had relieved the earlier frigates. *Protecteur*, the Canadian west coast replenishment ship, had replaced *Preserver* in the AOR. Soon after the takeover, Lehre reported his group had "firmly taken charge of the SAG/SOH/GOO sector in a manner not matched by any other national sector commander. Coalition units that used to breeze through the area in transit to and from the Gulf now check in, join our COMPLAN [communications plan] and Link, and are tasked. Everyone checks in with Charlie Zulu."[188]

Lehre was well aware that his operational waters—east and west of the Strait of Hormuz—were critical to the security of the massive area of responsibility, and vital specifically to Operation Enduring Freedom and the war on terrorism. This sector required the Canadians to control "most of the escape routes, while also being close enough to carry out escort duties through the Strait," and they were also in a "good position to 'back stop' against Iraqi oil smugglers" leaving the Gulf region.[189] To oversimplify, sea control of the operational area depended on the Canadians in the center.

To Lehre's northeast, the combined U.S. Navy–RAN–RN task group designated "XJ" functioned in the Northern Arabian Gulf, conducting interdiction operations *vide* United Nations resolutions. We have seen how Captains Du Toit and Goldrick worked against Iraqi oil smugglers who used Iranian territorial waters to slip past the interdicting coalition ships,[190] and from time to time a Canadian frigate served in their task group. To Lehre's south, a third task group operated off the Horn of Africa, "as it was believed Al Qaeda was preparing to re-establish bases there," having lost maneuver room in Afghanistan. This sector was usually commanded by a German or Spanish naval officer.[191]

The Canadian Task Group was able to sustain sea control in their area by using all available coalition surface ships, maritime patrol aircraft, and briefly a French submarine. These assets were "easily integrated" into the task group because of the high Canadian connectivity, the standardization of NATO procedures, and recent training in Submarine Element Coordination. Lehre noted that the submarine proved "one of our best sources for information . . . as she could manoevre to the limits of international waters right off their ports, giving us significant advance notice" of go-fast smugglers. These high-speed small craft were open boats, varying in length around 15 to 20 feet, and powered by large outboard motors. They carried human cargoes of transient workers across the Gulf of Oman. Like surfaced U-boats in the Second World War, their wakes were seen before their hull silhouettes.[192]

Sea control allowed Commodore Lehre to coordinate his main missions, whether leadership and maritime interdiction tasks or Strait of Hormuz escorts. Throughout 2002 LIO remained the prime mission for the task group "to either deter or apprehend Al Qaeda members attempting to flee Afghanistan using maritime routes for escape." Thousands of contacts were identified daily, from large merchant ships, through dhow-class vessels, to go-fasts. High-grade intelligence was required to selectively hail and board contacts suspected of carrying al-Qaeda. Here, the speed of maritime patrol aircraft and shipborne helicopters "greatly aided this effort by being able to intercept, check, and in some cases challenge" suspect vessels. Photographs of suspicious persons were taken with digital cameras and passed to nearby warships. COWAN allowed these images "to be matched against a large terrorist database, and any requirement for clearance or further action would be radioed back to the task group commander."[193]

Periodically CZ loaned a CPF to XJ to conduct MIO in the Northern Arabian Gulf, and in early April, *Ottawa* distinguished herself in a dramatic night noncompliant boarding of the oil smuggler *Rooa*: "In one sudden blinding flash of search lights . . . [*Ottawa*] . . . executed a take down of the vessel so swiftly the smuggling crew could not close down the vessel or mount a defence."[194]

Strait of Hormuz escorting required cool command and thorough training due to the high numbers of go-fast craft in the strait. As Lehre described it, "the local smugglers and their Go Fasts had the same appearance and were often operated with the same 'devil may care' attitude as a potential suicide boat, frequently closing our ships at speed to within hundreds of yards . . . the ships themselves were forced to fire warning shots to keep the most foolhardy Go Fasts outside of two hundred yards." In order to counter this persistent threat with balanced responses, rigorous training in applying rules of engagement was conducted from the task group commander down to "ship level, and within the ship between command and weapon crews."[195]

The coalition rules of engagement were complicated, and they were based on two national authorities: the mandate to conduct "non-consensual, or forced, boardings," and permission to detain "suspected terrorists found by our group efforts." In the latter case, "only the U.S. and Canadian ships were so authorized."[196] Lehre claimed that after his high connectivity, Canadian ROE were the most significant contributors to success: "Robust ROE . . . allow one's ships to fully contribute and not be forced to call in an ally when things get exciting.... For the TG commander, the differences that robust ROEs make are profound.... He cannot order a coalition ship working for him to do a task that the commander's own national ROE do not allow. Thanks to our strong Canadian ROE our TG Commanders were not put into that situation."[197]

These "robust" rules of engagement, it bears repeating, were not the internal product of the Canadian forces, but reflected the Government of Canada's continuing strong commitment to assist its allies in the war against terrorism.

To conduct his operations, Commodore Lehre usually had "four to seven units" assigned to him, plus he used "coalition units transiting the area ... to join in LIO/RMP Building." Lehre, a signals specialist, reported in early April that because of the high connectivity within the Canadian ships, they were the "glue that binds the coalition forces." COWAN, in his opinion, was "simply outstanding. It is the most reliable of the long-haul comm paths. The U.S. Navy is quickly realizing its value and it is the centre piece of the GOO architecture." Lehre added that "with virtually instantaneous comms," he was able to relay direction "to any of the coalition ships."[198]

The CZ capabilities were now well known to the coalition, and Commodore Lehre reported that "CTF 50 values our ships and our current efforts in the ... SAG/SOH/GOO. Our interoperability, our robust ROE, our RMP, and our Boarding expertise are simply not available in any other coalition partner."[199] By the end of May, Lehre advised that the Americans earlier had "predicted the Europeans would start drawing down," and they hoped "to fall back to a solid AUSCANUS core to keep the MIO/LIO operations running. This drawdown has happened and we remain at strength. This is noticed, as is our aggressiveness, our unequalled interoperability and robust ROE."[200]

* * *

In June 2002, at the height of the Canadian Navy's ascending trajectory of effectiveness in the Gulf region, Vice Admiral Buck hinted at an earlier whiff of Canadian interservice rivalry: "Eight months ago I was sarcastically asked what the naval role in land-locked Afghanistan would be. The answer, as we have seen, is clear." The admiral's response was not puffery and he was not gloating. He knew that geography had made the "Canadian military forces expeditionary," and that the navy, the smallest of the three services, had provided "the ability for Canada to execute its foreign policy options according to its own timetable rather than at the convenience of others."[201]

Buck reinforced this point, declaring that "many Canadians—and in particular the Canadian media—tend to measure military operations in terms of soldiers and green vehicles. Yet, Canada's expeditionary capability of first resort has been and is today its navy. A small but capable, multipurpose navy allows Canada to engage and, if need be, intervene. This has been our history, it is our present, and it will likely be our future." The admiral was right, the navy was Canada's best expeditionary capability, and no other service could claim this distinction. Buck's statement followed his affirmation that the navy was doing the "heavy lifting" in the campaign against terrorism, because "we have the equipment, the doctrine, the connectivity and procedures that make us key, integral players . . . we are there because we are good."[202]

Canadian operations remained upbeat. In June, and again July, Commodore Lehre's command ship, the DDG *Algonquin*, intercepted several suspected al-Qaeda terrorists.

Lehre's July report reflected a golden age for the Canadian Navy in the Gulf region. The statistics were impressive. Using the American Secretary of Defense's brief of 1 July, he reported some of the results in Table 1. [203] Lehre pointed out that the Royal Navy had less connectivity, and HMS *Cumberland*, a Type 22 frigate, had only recently installed COWAN. CTF 50 placed high value on the Canadian group because "Canada's interoperability with the U.S. Navy remains unmatched by any coalition navy." Lehre had established COWAN contact "with the next SCC" in the *Abraham Lincoln* carrier battle group, en route to relieve the *John F. Kennedy*, and this would allow the relieving group commander, Commodore Dan Murphy, to monitor "XZ-CZ chat."[204]

Table 1. Post-9/11 Coalition Interdiction Statistics–July 2002

	Ships Queried		Consensual Visits
	1 July 2002	**15 July 2002**	**1 July 2002**
Coalition Total	14,651[a]	15,667	166[b]
Coalition Navies:			
Australia	68		c
Canada	6,027	7,715[d]	101
France	1,422		1
Greece	560		6
Italy	1,860		29
Netherlands	1,563		12
Spain	65		c
UK	322		c
USA	2,754		17

[a]Approximately 65 queries a day. Many ships were queried more than once.
[b]Approximately one or two a day.
[c]Statistics not available.
[d]49.2 percent of the coalition total.

The small-boat trade in "people smuggling" had also decreased, and Lehre noted that their sortie rate was "77 in April, 44 for May, 17 in June, 34 in July and 12 so far in August."[205] Lehre complimented Canadian maritime patrol aircraft, noting that they "continue to excel in supporting LIO,"[206] and he suggested that the increase in July may have been due to improved "MPA coverage and more ships operating in the GOO." Overall, the commodore knew that they were intercepting most small boats "headed south (loaded) compared with those who later headed north (empty)."[207]

As for Strait of Hormuz escort tasks, since April, the group ships had escorted "64 unarmed or lightly armed" vessels of high value, with Canadians participating in 21 of these operations. Lehre noted that "warning shots and/or flares were fired on several of the early transits to successfully deter high speed craft—usually smugglers . . . but none have been fired during this period."[208]

Lehre was most pleased with the integration of high-speed communications that greatly enhanced his intelligence-gathering capability, which had "gained high praise with our U.S. Navy [commanders]." He reported that CTF 50 had urged Vice Admiral Timothy J. Keating, CENTCOM's Naval Component Commander in Bahrain, to utilize the "excellent analysis from 'CZ' staff and include MV/Dhow and Go Fast traffic analysis. . . . Use the LIO model as practiced in the GOO for world-wide application—*overall CZ has it right* [emphasis added]."[209]

Also in July, Commodore Lehre provided a detailed update on the communications capabilities of his command, and once more COWAN was his battle-winning favorite.

> It is now clear there is an inner and outer core of naval participants in OEF [Operation Enduring Freedom]. The inner has Cowan and Siprnet. The rest don't and are out. This is not good for Canada nor anyone else. . . . The most obvious costs are that the others are not as effective. . . . Cowan is a better choice . . . most in the . . . [*Abraham Lincoln* carrier battle group] . . . will be so fitted. Some of the RAN are fitted and the UK ship is howling for activation of his Cowan . . . [account]. So expect short term gains within the AUSCANUKUS or Cowan A Group . . . what this theatre really calls for is Cowan (C for Coalition) . . . part-time dial-up participants are not worth our trouble. Come with a leased channel and 24/7 Cowan connectivity or don't come at all.[210]

Lehre concluded with a summary of the remarks he used when he spoke to the messes of his ships.

> I now make it clear they are serving in the best medium power navy in the world. Few navies receive anything like the support from home . . . we have no in-theatre bases . . . our . . . [maritime patrol aircraft] . . . skill is unmatched be it in crew skill or outright determination. . . . Third, our helos are old but they fly longer days than any other and achieve hail rates that often are higher than some other nation's ships. . . . Fourth, our ships . . . C4I [command, control, communications, computers and intelligence] fits are unmatched by anything short of a U.S. Navy cruiser or DDG 51 [USN *Arleigh Burke*–class destroyer]. The most competent of our coalition ships has declined to take on the acting SAG . . .

[Commander] . . . role that our own CPFs execute flawlessly. No one can compete with the LIO . . . products we develop onboard and this was acknowledged by CTF 50. Fifth, only the U.S. Navy exceeds our Op Tempo . . . the brief to the U.S. Sec Def I quoted in my last sitrep still remains true today. With five nations regularly tasked to LIO duties, Canadian ships still provide 50 pct of the hails and 63 pct of the boardings. Our . . . [naval boarding parties] . . . are unmatched and our AOR is now providing hailing and CV rates equal to some nations['] frigates while also serving as the only Arabian Gulf oiler. . . . All in all, the navy has no peer competitors.[211]

In August Commodore Lehre reviewed the impressive operational statistics for the group in his final report, simplified at Table 2.[212]

Table 2. Canadian Interdiction and Escort Statistics—31 August 2002

	Ships Queried	Consensual visits	SOH escorts
Coalition Total	18,577	235	66*
Canadian Navy	8,998 (48.4%)	146	21

*Unarmed or lightly armed coalition ships.

Plans for War Alter the Paradigm

In fall 2002 the operational paradigm east of Suez began to shift. Talk of war and invasion increased, and the UN Security Council debated new resolutions against Iraq. The Americans moved additional forces north to bring pressure against the regime. Because the "vast bulk of the material" had to funnel through the Strait of Hormuz, that move increased the need to secure its approaches.[213]

On 4 September Commodore Lehre handed over command to Commodore Dan Murphy. Lehre reported that the task group had closed the al-Qaeda and Taliban maritime escape routes, and they "appear to have been successfully deterred."[214] Concurrently, the volume of merchant vessel traffic in the Canadian sector increased, and on 9 October the threat was maximized when al-Qaeda widened the war by attacking the French oil tanker *Limberg* in the confined Strait of Bab al-Mandeb, off Aden. More pressure was placed upon the Fifth Fleet's coalition navy to escort high-value ships through the Strait of Hormuz, and the Canadian Task Group commander assumed added responsibility to ensure sea control of his critical sector.[215]

* * *

At the end of October 2002, Captain Peter Jones, RAN, took command of his task group and the maritime interception forces in the Northern Arabian Gulf. Jones relieved Captain Peter Sinclair, RAN, who had replaced Captain James Goldrick. Jones knew that COMDESRON 50, sharing command with him for maritime interception operations, was war-planning in Bahrain at U.S. Fifth Fleet headquarters. He suspected that this would mean maximum sea-time, and it proved so—"from the end of October until early April we were at sea for all but about 14 days."[216]

* * *

Before September 2002, Commodore Murphy had spent five months at the U.S. Central Command headquarters in Tampa as the "principal staff officer for Canadian joint operations." He and the commander of the Canadian Joint Task Force–South-West Asia, Commodore Pierre Thiffault, along with British representatives, had been the only non-Americans allowed to attend the daily video teleconference held by General Tommy Franks, the CENTCOM commander. Those in attendance included representatives from the "CIA, Special Forces . . . and the Pentagon."[217] Murphy described the "strategic context" he faced from September to February 2003 during his five months as task group commander: "1. the USS *Cole* bombing, 2. the MV *Limberg* bombing, 3. the Bali bombing, and 4. the Mombassa bombing. Three of these four significant terrorist events perpetuated by Al Qaeda occurred in the CENTCOM area of operations where Canadian ships and aircraft contributed; and three out of four of them occurred during Roto 2."[218]

With the third task group, Murphy commanded within the framework established in late 2001; that is, his operational control authorities were U.S. Vice Admiral Timothy Keating in Bahrain, as well as the "carrier-based Task Force Commander at sea," call sign "XZ." During his five-month tour, XZ commanders were embarked on, respectively, the carriers *George Washington*, *Abraham Lincoln*, and *Constellation*. Murphy continued the Canadian policy of complementing his COWAN capability with liaison officers in the XZ carrier and at NAVCENT headquarters in Bahrain.

These officers provided him and his reduced staff—he commanded in CPFs, first *St. John's* and then HMCS *Montreal*—with "immediate access to the Sea Combat Commander and the intelligence to support my piece of the tactical puzzle."[219]

Concurrent with American, British, and Australian war planning, Commodore Murphy, with American authority, began to coordinate the

> efforts of our other Coalition partners who, like Canada, would not provide military support for potential operations against Iraq—not even UNSCR work. They were in theatre strictly for Op Enduring Freedom. That's why Canadian connectivity through . . . [COWAN] . . . was so important in providing a U.S. bridge to the anti-terrorism coalition, and contributed to the view that Canada was well placed and most capable of doing more.[220]

Throughout late 2002 and early 2003, Murphy worked with coalition commanding officers on four critical aspects of Gulf region operations: "differing national ROE, small boat attack guidance, night-time small boat transits, and oil smuggling consolidation ops."[221] He was assisted by CP-140 Aurora maritime patrol aircraft, and he noted: "The maritime picture building they were able to do, and the illegal oil smuggling consolidation they were able to uncover, was incomparable," leading to the boarding of vessels of greatest interest.[222]

The commodore summed up his tour, stressing the recurrent and impressive Canadian interdiction statistics, as well as the importance of COWAN:

> From September to December 2002, the Coalition's 238 boardings were twice the number of boardings done . . . during the previous 8 months. Canadian ships accounted for half of those. . . . That translated into effective deterrence. We locked-up that body of water so tight that terrorists had difficulty finding boats to get out of Pakistan. . . . We tripled the number of [SOH] escorts from [the previous task group]. Ninety escorts were conducted from September to January [2003] that provided COs with their most challenging moments: assessing hostile intent from crossing . . . Go-Fasts. . . . [The Americans] approved my handling of that assignment without reference to the Sea Combat Commander. We contributed

well to maritime intelligence with . . . surveillance . . . by remaining
completely interoperable with our U.S. Navy operational controllers
in the [CVBGs] and in NAVCENT HQ . . . through Cowan.[223]

* * *

By January 2003 Iraqi naval ships were maneuvering into a wartime
posture in the Northern Arabian Gulf. Captain Jones recalled that these
ships, as well as Saddam Hussein's yacht and various big ships, which
had been "holed up in Umm Qasr, came down the river [the Khawr
Abd Allah], and then went up the Shatt al Arab to Al Basrah." The result
was that he, as Maritime Interception Force commander, became a local
surface warfare commander. Following his guidance, the Australians tried
to "tidy up the local air warfare command." Their vulnerability was serious
because the task group was so far north that the Aegis cruisers could not
provide coverage to counter an air or missile attack. In Jones' opinion, it
was doubtful that air defense forces "would pick up a missile being fired
from the Al Faw Peninsula with a one-minute time of flight to a ship in
the northern area."[224]

At the same time, the Australians considered options for their ships
in the event of war with Iraq, and they began working on the aim: "What
do we want to achieve as a navy?" The RAN changed its operational and
national command structure and concentrated on how to *sustain* sea
control in the Northern Arabian Gulf. At stake was their hard-fought
control of the shallow-water KAA area. They knew that

> success to date had been based on . . . [interdiction] . . . so close
> inshore, in the shallow water, that if you drew away the critical mass
> of shallow-water draught ships, the effort was going to move back.
> Therefore you were effectively going to lose sea control, which had
> been so hard won. This would have opened up an opportunity for
> the Iraqis to mine the northern areas, and adopt a sea denial strategy,
> which could have impeded coalition operations.[225]

Task Force 151, Liberation of Iraq, and Drawdown

When Commodore Roger Girouard replaced Commodore Murphy
on 13 January 2003, he was well aware that the Canadians "were highly
regarded and widely respected in Coalition Combined and Joint

Operations."[226] He also knew that an invasion of Iraq was imminent. No one knew exactly when war would occur, but everyone was certain that it would start before the crippling heat of spring and summer.

During the first two months of his command, the Canadian government pursued a policy of seeking United Nations approval for coalition military action against Iraq. Concurrently, the navy developed an array of options upon which the government could base future Canadian policy in the region. These choices ranged from participation in the potential Operation Iraqi Freedom, the liberation of Iraq, to remaining in Operation Enduring Freedom in Afghanistan while not openly participating in operations against Iraq. Canada's effective role in the First Gulf War coordinating coalition Battle Force resupply—12 years earlier—stood as a clear precedent for a future Canadian mission at the formation level. A command ship, the DDG *Iroquois*, was readied to deploy to the Gulf region in early 2003.

Together, the U.S. Navy, RN, and RAN faced northward and prepared for the invasion. Their task force emptied the KAA and Umm Qaasr area of Iraqi naval vessels, dhows, and steel-hulled shipping. Captain Jones, commanding the Australians, was clear on why they succeeded:

> [W]e had exerted sea control and had exerted it for so long that the Iraqis were prevented from taking the initiative. Our control of the sea denied the Iraqis the ability to lay defensive minefields even in their own waters. They tried to lay some fields covertly but these efforts were thwarted through our control of the sea. I think this is a great example of sea control and the importance of the blockade.[227]

The rapid flow of events in Girouard's first two months was marked by two decisive moments in Canadian naval relations with the U.S. Navy, as well as with the Canadian government. On 7 February the combined efforts of staffs at all levels accomplished a conclusive step in the Canadian experience in the region: Commodore Girouard's command would be raised to task force status, designated TF 151, and the Canadian operational area would expand north to almost the Saudi Arabia–Kuwait border—to 28°30′ north.[228] Thus, although not officially part of the allied coalition formed to invade Iraq and topple Saddam Hussein, the Canadians now controlled the southern edge of the coalition's operational area.

The second event on the eve of war was important because it represented the first—fortunately brief—setback in Canadian–U.S. naval relations. In defining the navy's role in the region, the Canadian government changed its rules of engagement concerning "any Iraqis taken prisoner in the act of escaping by sea." The revised direction was clear: prisoners were not to be passed on to the Americans. Girouard saw for the first time Canadian-American relations severely tested. At once he noticed an "immediate and perceptible cut-off of access to certain elements of intelligence," and he remembered that

> because we were not signed on to Op Iraqi Freedom . . . there was a separate communications plan the Aussies and Brits and the Americans were on that we were not, and that meant that there were pretty important nuggets of information that we were not by default privy to. . . . At the end of the day we were certainly given the information to do our job, but there were times we were not 100 per cent sure that we had all of the information we needed. It was not the most comfortable way to be doing business at that time.[229]

Operation Iraqi Freedom began on 18 March, and the Canadians continued to coordinate the three previous coalition Operation Enduring Freedom operations: MIO in their expanded area south of the much-reduced Northern Arabian Gulf sector, LIO in the Gulf of Oman, and escorts through the Strait of Hormuz. At the end of March, for a brief period, there were five Canadian warships operating in the region. *Montreal* and *Winnipeg* had deployed in September as part of Roto 2—Girouard commanded from the former—and they were briefly held over, while *Regina* had arrived on 15 March as a Roto 3 ship. *Iroquois*, the DDG command ship, and *Fredericton* were on station two weeks later.[230] The United States ambassador to Ottawa, A. Paul Cellucci, attempting to bring balance to the situation, did not hesitate to compliment the Canadian contribution:

> [W]e are disappointed that some of our closest allies, including Canada, have not agreed with us on the urgent need for this military action against Iraq. But Canada remains a crucial partner in this global war on terrorism, and we are grateful for that. Canadian naval vessels, aircraft and military personnel continue anti-terrorist operations in the Persian Gulf. . . . Ironically, *the Canadian naval*

DND Photo HSO-34004-52

A boarding party from HMCS *Regina* alongside a merchant vessel in the Gulf region, 6 April 2003. In a typical post-9/11 Canadian leadership or maritime interdiction operation, this team was fortunate to have both a rope ladder, known as a jumping ladder, and a rigid accommodation ladder.

> *vessels, aircraft and personnel in the Persian Gulf I mentioned earlier who are fighting terrorism will provide more support indirectly to this war in Iraq than most of the 46 countries that are fully supporting our efforts there* [emphasis added].[231]

By 3 April Commodore Girouard had transferred his staff to *Iroquois*, commanding the task force from the larger ship. As operations continued, Girouard noticed that relations with the U.S. Navy warmed again, and by the middle of April, both navies were operating as closely as in the past. Hard-won trust could be suspended over differing politics, but because it had been so deeply implanted, it easily survived such interludes.

* * *

A few days later Captain (N) Paul A. Maddison, commanding officer of *Iroquois*, wrote the family network for his crew:

> All in *Iroquois* are very well. Last week we embarked the Task Group Commander and his staff, who transferred over from *Montreal*...this was the reason that *Iroquois* deployed—to provide the Commodore with the command and control capability that is unique to *Iroquois* class of ships. It was equally gratifying to be the agent of *Montreal*'s relief. . . . They have done a superb job since deploying nearly seven months ago, and we in *Iroquois* are inspired by the high standards of operational excellence that they have set.

On 23 April Maddison reported that the "tempo has quieted somewhat recently due mostly to reduced traffic in the GOO," and later he mused from his ship that "coalition forces that are forward deployed and leading from the front are perhaps the forces that are best poised to meet combined national security objectives while acting globally. This sounds quintessentially Canadian—multilateral engagement that positively influences global stability." He was right, for Canada's contribution signified a prevailing and popular interest in coalition operations in the Gulf region.[232]

* * *

Throughout May 2003 the region was strangely quiet. There was no longer an illicit Iraqi maritime traffic in oil, and the routes for shipping traffic that required a Strait of Hormuz escort changed from south to north, while terrorist movement from north to south declined. Leadership interdiction in the Gulf of Oman was reduced to maintaining a presence, and the operational terms changed: LIO became a form of MIO for Operation Enduring Freedom, to distinguish these operations from Operation Iraqi Freedom.

Twelve years of grinding UN interdiction operations aimed at Iraq had come to an end, and by June the Americans, Canadians, and coalition allies planned a drawdown of their maritime forces in the region. *Regina* was short-toured, arriving back in Esquimalt on Canada Day, 1 July 2003.

On 15 June Canadian Joint Task Force–South-West Asia ordered Commodore Girouard to disband TF 151, which ended more than four months of coalition task force command. Commander H. T. Harsch, *Fredericton's* commanding officer, was authorized to serve as Southern Arabian Gulf Commander, similar to the pre-9/11 leading role when *Winnipeg's* commanding officer had been appointed on-site commander in the Northern Arabian Gulf.[233] Harsch was pleased with the way that his combat team and his ship "embraced the extra work involved" as SAG Commander. He had found the responsibility "interesting and challenging" and recorded that

> the Americans were extremely pleased with our performance in this role, indeed they were effusive in their praise for the ship. They were also easy to work for in that they provided clear strategic direction, and then pretty much left it up to me to execute. At any one time we had up to five Coalition warships under my command, but usually it was . . . two or three. . . . It was clear to me that the forces in the Gulf Region were attempting to maintain the same level of oversight, but with a fraction of the assets . . . we did what we could.[234]

Calgary arrived in the region on 1 August, and on the 8th she assumed duties from *Fredericton* as SAG Commander.[235] Eight days later she was granted a second Canadian appointment, CTF 307, Commander Task Force Operation Apollo. Her commanding officer, Commander D. M. Mackeigan, humorously noted, "I need a new ballcap" to represent his new role.[236] *Calgary* served in these capacities until 18 October, departing on 1 November. Although the Gulf region remained quiet, *Calgary* had conducted 24 boardings and 92 SOH escorts of her own, and had coordinated dozens of operations in the region.[237]

Upon *Calgary's* arrival in Esquimalt, Vice Admiral Buck summed up her experience, considering it a microcosm of over two years of Canadian naval operations in the Gulf region.

> You are the sixteenth Canadian warship to return from Operation Apollo, this essential campaign against terrorism, and you are also the last one. It is a period that saw 16 ships and 4100 sailors deployed in support of this operation—a . . . [decisive] undertaking that had not been seen since

the Korean War. You have made a huge commitment to the success of this operation, made a huge difference. You have done the heavy lifting.[238]

He was right. Operations after 2001 had led to the collapse of Iraq in 2003, and in May of that year UNSCR 1483 was approved "under enormous pressure from the U.S." This UNSCR removed all the United Nations monitors from Iraq, eliminated the "661 Committee," which had managed the Oil-for-Food Program; suspended the role of the United Nations Monitoring, Verification and Inspection Commission, its disarmament agency; and eliminated any international oversight of oil sales or disposition of oil proceeds. In theory MIO had ceased. The resolution also endorsed the "Occupying Authority" status of the U.S. and Britain in Iraq. A year later the United Nations approved another "multinational force," and according to one expert, this "left the U.N. role in Iraq's troubled political transition undefined."[239]

* * *

In 2004 the "Oil-for-Food" scandal was released as a headline story implicating the United Nations as scapegoat for a failed and corrupt program. The resulting blowback has revealed that while oil exports were being interdicted and inspected at sea, the Americans and British at the UN allowed oil to be exported to Jordan and Turkey overland, without any monitoring.[240]

In summary, after Ramadan in late 2002, with Iraqi oil continuing to move overland, but with no further smuggling activity, a point was reached where Maritime Interception Force operations were no longer necessary to enforce sanctions at sea. Nevertheless, the naval forces in the Northern Arabian Gulf remained, for they provided sea control in the shallow and complex maritime approaches to Iraq. The effects of that control shaped two contingencies. First, Iran was denied the opportunity to demonstrate a maritime presence in the Gulf region. Second, sea control permitted a clear coalition attack into the Khawr Abd Allah, the Shatt al-Arab, al-Faw, and upstream to Basra in order to force regime change in a benighted nation that had already suffered so much under Saddam Hussein's rule, as well as from sanctions approved by the Security Council.

Observations and Comments on the Future

Observations

During the 1990s, following their experience in Korea, the Cold War, and the First Gulf War, the Canadian Navy did not think small. The service evolved into an "adaptive and hybrid" maritime arm: a blue-water force with four guided missile destroyers and 12 shallow-draft Canadian patrol frigates plus support ships. All proved highly capable of conducting littoral operations. Interoperability with American forces was set as a goal, and Canada's west coast fleet was augmented to balance with naval forces on the Atlantic coast. NATO and ABCA Quadripartite agreements were in place, and the navy gained firsthand experience in the Adriatic and the Caribbean, and from many single-frigate deployments in the Gulf region. These operations required three capabilities: recognized maritime picture-building, high connectivity with evolving American information technology, and government-supported rules of engagement.

Connectivity was necessary to ensure an easy transition into command relations with the Americans, themselves governed by strict rules of engagement and releasability regulations. The Canadians acquired and used Link 11, Link 16, SIPRNET, and COWAN—the basic communications pillars of naval network-centric warfare—before and after 9/11. They also stressed the human side of connectivity, embedding commanders, staffs and liaison officers, where possible, alongside American commanders. The crucial influence that the liaison officers provided and the evolving role of legal officers, who were embarked on frontline Canadian ships before and after 9/11, require further examination.

Gulf region operations synthesized the navy's decade of force restructure and developing interoperability with the U.S. Navy, especially their emphasis on connectivity and rules of engagement, and the Canadians achieved a high reputation in the process. Their paradigm of "high interoperability equals increased options" offered the government a wide set of choices after 9/11. For example, once the Canadian Task Group had arrived in late 2001, it operated in four different command relationships. The group first provided defense to the amphibious ready group, operating under the tactical control of the carrier groups with the designation Amphibious Support Force Defense Commander. In January 2002, when they were authorized their own operational area and designated CZ, they controlled all interdiction operations in a vast area comprising the Southern Arabian Gulf, the Strait of Hormuz, and the Gulf of Oman. They worked in Task Force 50 under the tactical control of a sector control commander (SCC). The approach of war caused a further change, and by December 2002 the Canadian group was no longer linked to an SCC but dealt directly with TF 50. In February 2003 the Canadian group commander was elevated to task force commander status, heading newly formed Task Force 151.

Clearly, the harmony between the Canadian government's desire to be seen as useful and the navy's willingness to assume risk had produced robust rules of engagement, and the Canadian coordination of the Southern Arabian Gulf, Strait of Hormuz, and Gulf of Oman was, by any standards, a good fit. It was an ideal operation for an aggressive pair of well-connected frigates with the appropriate ROE, commanded by a senior officer and staff in a guided missile destroyer, which was the perfect command platform for interdiction operations. The wider Canadian command and control arrangement—fully embraced by the Americans— was linked to Ottawa through their task force headquarters at CENTCOM in Tampa and augmented by an extensive liaison officer system throughout the Gulf region, ensuring that the Canadians had the ability to make their own decisions.

Nevertheless, periodic problems occurred, and this author does not wish to leave an impression that all was well the entire time. The Americans, however, always found a way to make coalition efforts function. Problems were worked around or worked out. Setbacks—almost all of them concerning connectivity—were seen and solved as they arose.

As operations began in November 2001, Commodore Drew Robertson remembered how important his connectivity proved to be:

> [T]he latest Coalition Wide Area Network . . . gave me connectivity
> with the U.S. Navy at-sea commanders that no other nation had.
> This connectivity was vital to our being able to take on a coalition
> leadership role in the Gulf of Oman and make the contribution we did.
> It also gave me much better insight into the U.S. Navy commanders'

intentions—and so an ability to examine those intentions from a Canadian viewpoint.[241]

In other words, high connectivity provided options for Canada. More broadly, the increased information flow did not—and probably still does not—completely ease the problem of command at sea. Commodore James Goldrick reaffirmed that "there are times when the situational awareness of the higher command is greater than those on scene. The dilemma, as it has ever been for the remote commander, is in being sure that this is really the case and not an illusion."[242]

While Canadians understood that keeping current with American information systems was a critical requirement for them, so was the understanding and pursuit of the nontechnical notion of trust. Trust with the U.S. Navy was tested with each new deployment, and Canadians had learned that "information-sharing protocols must be re-brokered for each deployment. Sometimes gaining access is a question of proving one's bona fides to the battle group; sometimes the battle group staff is simply unaware what information has been passed, or is otherwise available, to the Canadian ship."[243]

After 9/11 the Law of War and International Maritime Law were brought into question as they applied to the Gulf region and the so-called war on terrorism. It was a chaotic time, with the established tenets of military thought turned upside down, perhaps best summed up by Admiral Percy Fitzwallace, the fictional chairman of the Joint Chiefs of Staff in a 2002 episode of "The West Wing": "I can't tell when it's peacetime and wartime anymore."[244]

Almost at once the Canadian Navy grasped these developments in modern warfare. Commodore Robertson and his three successors stressed the legal implications of sea control work. In Robertson's mind, although the coalition was conducting a war against terrorism, extending beyond the bounds of the Westphalian state system, the international Laws of Armed Conflict nevertheless still applied to Canadian ships. For example, we saw that he and his captains had to consider "whether one has reasonable grounds to take action against the vessel" because they were "answerable to the Canadian and the international community . . . and because 'the Americans said so' won't necessarily . . . [clear us]."[245]

All the Canadian group commanders understood the clear relationship between balance, trust, connectivity, and knowledge. In post-9/11 operations trust was needed as much as technology. Canadians learned that to be interoperable meant giving whatever you have to give. Trust was derived from the generous sharing of knowledge. Americans like and respect such knowledge, and Canadians gave it freely, knowing that acts of generosity will be reciprocated by American acts in return, again increasing trust. If Americans trust a navy, they will give it responsibility. This relationship provided the Canadian government with options, and not surprisingly they chose to assist the Americans with a significant naval force until mid-2003. Lesson learned: you can't surge trust.

In the 2001–2003 period Canada was acting like a good world citizen but at the same time keeping her options open. Naval interoperability was essential to pursue this policy of flexible choices. We had to participate, but at the same time we had to act in a manner Canadians wanted. This imperative was not articulated until several years later by a young scholar, Jennifer Welsh, who suggested that Canada should think

> more strategically about its role internationally. And a strategy requires choice: not being all things to all people. Not trying to steal a newspaper headline on every national issue. But choosing those areas where we want to make a contribution and where we are willing to apply our resources (human as well as financial) to make a difference. Designing such a strategy requires three steps: re-examining our values, articulating our interests, and focusing and prioritizing our activities.[246]

In essence, Welsh advocated a sovereign nation's right to do that what it prefers, and turn away from that which it does not want to do. But any action requires tools, and for some, using military tools represents a loss of sovereignty because they are invariably employed alongside others' forces. Sovereignty is therefore lost in the exercise of sovereignty, at least to the most rigid critics of coalition military operations. The reality of the events shown in this chapter is quite different. Between 1991 and 2003 the Canadian Navy achieved a high standard of interoperability with the U.S. Navy *at no risk to its sovereignty*. Government policies remained clear and firm, they were known by those who had to implement them, and they were implemented at no risk to the Canadian Navy's ultimate operational effectiveness in support of Canada's allies.

The Canadian Navy had proved its value to Canada and to the U.S. Navy. Although Canadian flag officers and staffs confronted a different world after 2001, in the previous decade they had gotten things right. They did not face a steep learning curve in confronting the challenges of that new world because, first, they had command experience and sea service in the Gulf region; second, they knew what was expected of them; and finally, they fitted in by knowing exactly what options were open.

Naval Thought and Canadian Policy

What is the significance of Gulf region operations? Perhaps naval thought can help us understand the experience as it applies in a 21st-century world recently described by James Boutilier:

> The Europeans have moved into a post-modern age, where, weary of centuries of internal conflict, they have begun to forfeit Westphalian notions of national sovereignty voluntarily and to seek some larger sense of community. The European Union, with its rather effete and self-denying responses to international threats, stands in stark contrast to the robustly self-confident nationalism appearing in East Asia . . . [which is] a complex arena—historically, geographically, and jurisdictionally. China and India have become unabashedly Mahanian in their pursuit of naval power to deal with these challenges, by adopting the "great battle fleet" concepts described by the 19th century American sea power advocate, Admiral Alfred Thayer Mahan. In psychological terms, they are exhibiting the will to rule, something the Europeans have lost and the Americans are tiring of.[247]

For Western navies there is no agreement on a higher theory of war. In September 2005 Sir Michael Howard declared that theorists are "divided between those who maintain that war will be transformed by a 'Revolution in Military Affairs' created by information technology, and those who believe that 'irregular warfare' will make such technology obsolete. We shall see."[248]

With the future uncertain, naval theorists have stressed the prominence of maritime forces. They are correct to do so.

In early 2005 historian Geoffrey Till emphasized navies for the future because the "global sea-based system based on the merchant ship and the container . . . is essentially transnational . . . [this system] is under permanent threat." Till argued that economic interdependence and reduced geographic distance means that what happens "over there matters . . . to us here."[249] Supporting this assertion, Professor Colin Gray stated in the same year that a "cardinal benefit of sea-based power is that its exercise as threat or in action does not depend upon the prior assent of local polities. Naval vessels are sovereign territory." He added that the United States "understands that it must maintain a globally dominant navy. It cannot function as guardian of world order, or even just protect its vital interests, unless it enjoys the ability to assert and defend the sea control it will need in order to secure access to distant landmasses." Gray argued that "American defence analysts do not anticipate that future warfare will see a return of blue-water combat, with states contesting for control, even command, of the sea. However the U.S. ability to exploit its control of the sea for influence upon the land will be opposed vigorously in some contexts." It remains to be seen how our fleets will look as they adapt into forces that are purpose-built to conduct "intense combat in the littoral region, as the superpower would strive to enforce strategic access to problem areas ashore, including very deep ashore."[250]

Geoffrey Till offered a possible glimpse of the future by reminding us that navies "are being required to act together in common cause to project military power ashore, particularly in expeditionary operations at a distance from the home base." Navies will have to "shift priorities from the sea to the land, from power at sea to power from the sea." Till also warned of challenges to "traditional naval ways of doing things and some ancient naval expectations about operational independence and freedom of maneuver."[251]

Till's remarks reflect the lack of settled war theory, the reality of modern sea use, the importance of information technology, and the influence of American notions of intervention. These circumstances probably will continue to shape medium-size navies like Canada's. For example, most navies will transform, becoming more expeditionary as they equip for missions to support the projection of power ashore. Command arrangements may change as well. By 2006 there were at least three Canadian studies examining the results of task group operations in the Gulf region after 9/11, and these studies will, no doubt, add to future decisions on command, control, and communications architecture.[252]

And what of interdiction operations? A hundred years ago Alfred Thayer Mahan wrote in his definitive article, "Blockade in Relation to Naval Strategy," that "whatever the number of ships needed to watch those in an enemy's port, they are fewer by far than those that will be required to protect the scattered interests imperiled by an enemy's escape."[253] Citing Mahan, Professor Roger Barnett of the U.S. Naval War College has observed that future blockade operations should seek to control shipping or the shipment of contraband at the source rather than at the destination. Effective Canadian shallow-water interdiction operations in the Northern Arabian Gulf prior to 9/11 and RAN operations in the spring of 2002 prove Barnett and Mahan to be right. We should, however, be clear on why this was so: the navies had sought high connectivity, and their governments had provided robust rules of engagement, and only because of this combination was interoperability high enough to make these operations possible.

By the summer of 2005 two key appointees—the Director Maritime Policy (DMP) and the Chief of Maritime Staff—had published their views on the imperatives facing the Canadian Navy. Both opinions represented current uncertainties as well as lessons learned from the Gulf region. Captain (N) P. C. Avis, DMP, set forth the new national security challenge:

> The terrorist has changed the battlespace . . . [for] Maritime Security. Since the struggle against international terrorists doesn't focus on sovereign states in particular, the battlespace becomes equally local and federal, domestic and international, sensational and commonplace . . . informational and ephemeral . . . terrorists own the timeline. . . . The emphasis . . . must [be] . . . on finding the terrorist and understanding his plan before he executes.[254]

At the same time Vice Admiral M. B. MacLean, Chief of Maritime Staff, stressed interoperability and transformation. He asserted that "interoperability to me is ... an understanding of how your partners do ... business."[255] The admiral warned of future change from "a Cold War 'blue water' escort force to an expeditionary 'green water' coastal or 'brown water' amphibious force."[256]

On 12 May 2008 Prime Minister Stephen Harper unveiled a defense policy for Canada, the *Canada First Defence Strategy*. It called for new naval equipment to include "joint support ships" and "arctic/offshore patrol ships." As well as strengthening security "at home," Harper emphasized that the policy would ensure that Canada would remain "a robust and reliable contributor to international security and humanitarian missions." [257]

Part of these future operations are coalition blockade actions— under whatever name they will go by: interdiction, interception, sanction enforcement, antipiracy, or arctic patrols. They will remain a prime role for a future Canadian Navy conducting preemptive operations. Our surface ships, particularly the DDG Tribals with a 50-foot height of eye, will continue to prove invaluable in waters like the Gulf region where threats are asymmetric, shipping traffic is heavy, vessel identification is difficult, and early warning is required. New developments such as low-orbit satellites, line of sight technologies, and unmanned aerial vehicles will improve information gathering in busy foreign littorals,[258] and in home waters high-frequency surface wave radar systems will provide "surveillance up to 200 nautical miles off the east and west coasts."[259] Nevertheless, complicating these technical developments is a new threat— cyber war—and naval reaction to this prospect.[260]

Sea control and interoperability—the two Canadian specialties in the Gulf region—are concomitants of green, brown, and arctic water operations, and navies conducting them will have to maintain "sea control in the narrow seas and littoral against everything from shore-based aviation, missiles, and artillery, through mines, coastal submarines, and fast attack craft, to swarming attacks from terrorists on jet skis."[261]

Final Comments

For more than 20 years the Canadian Navy has progressively built a base of professional expertise now embedded at all levels of training, leadership, and technical equipment acquisition throughout the service. This knowledge of U.S. Navy–led coalition operations can serve the government as a building block for the future, whatever it may hold.

Between 1991 and 2003 the navy had learned to sustain naval interoperability and prepare for sea control operations with balance, trust, high connectivity, and continued service in the Gulf region as well as in NATO deployments. Based on the past, we should continue taking nothing for granted and deliberately work at sustaining connectivity at every opportunity. This may mean revising agreements and arrangements, for each single Canadian patrol frigate that sails with an American group begins from a *tabula rasa*. Interoperability has to be constantly re-brokered, and also marketed. This is not stated in a negative sense; it is merely the start point to understanding how the Americans do business.

The Canadian Navy, in this author's opinion, must unflaggingly argue the clear linkage between high interoperability and greater options for its government in future operations in a troubled world. Moreover, the argument must be made for Canadian naval contributions to be at task group level in order that their political significance is not diminished.

In keeping with these notions, the Canadian government must understand seven fundamental characteristics of modern naval war. First, Canada will never fight alone overseas, she will always operate in a coalition. Second, we have been, and will continue to be, in a struggle for public opinion from local to global levels. Third, the events since 2001 probably will not shape future warfare in a logical, linear continuation. Instead, war in the 21st century will be more or less the same for naval commanders, who, for example, will continue to question whether the situational awareness of higher commanders is greater than those on site. Fourth, wherever ABCA navies sail, sea control will be maintained. Drawing from that control, gathering and sharing intelligence, staying abreast of events, and reacting quickly to new information will determine the effectiveness of future naval operations. Fifth, Canada's sailors, based on the Gulf experience, will have to remain connected, and must also keep "the lure of technology in perspective . . . realizing that the human component is the key to adaptability."[262] Sixth, naval vessels are sovereign territory, and task group commanders and ship commanding officers need robust rules of engagement—the property of the government—for them to sail where they can help the most, regardless of nationality or concern for who commands. Finally, you cannot surge trust, and medium-size navies when deployed in coalitions achieve more than when they stay at home and study, or "game," new developments. Omitting any one of these fundamental characteristics to realize a fiscal or political saving will only reduce the effectiveness of any future naval operation.

Appendix

Legal Matters: Use of Force, Territorial Waters, and Rules of Engagement

The Gulf region is a surreal place. Westerners sense a dreamlike feeling when faced with the dramatic difference between rich and poor, opulent excess, wide cultural differences, and seemingly erratic and impulsive behavior of the local people. At times ideas, actions, and activities like naval and military operations take on a bizarre quality that is difficult to explain in American, British, Canadian, and Australian terms. The result can reshape our thinking: the circumstances are surreal and bizarre, so why should the law matter? In fact, the Gulf region experience has taught us that the law does matter, and governments, not navies, approve rules of engagement.

Rules of engagement were always in two parts: territorial waters issues and rules governing use of force for boarding and inspections, particularly for noncompliant boardings. Legal matters are not solved quickly in any navy, certainly not as quickly as doctrine, tactics, and equipment can be adapted to new situations. Between 1991 and 2003 Canadians enhanced their interoperability by continuously reviewing their rules of engagement to ensure international law was respected when using force in interdiction operations. Legal officers began to serve at sea with the single-CPF deployments in 2000. There were no major difficulties before or after 9/11, and Canadians learned that revising ROE was a challenging aspect of interoperability. The lesson for future operations was clear: legal matters take time and there probably will be a period of duplication and confusion.

Prior to 9/11, Canadians clarified their noncompliant boarding (NCB) policy during the aggressive American initiative taken in the spring and summer of 2001 to defeat Iraqi oil smugglers in the Northern Arabian Gulf. Indeed, the commanding officer of *Winnipeg* commanded NCB operations in these shallow and contested waters between Kuwait, Iraq, and Iran several months before 9/11.

In late 2001 the Taliban were defeated in Afghanistan, yet there was no land force cutoff plan, and an ad hoc naval screen was formed quickly across the maritime approaches to the region. By January 2002 leadership interdiction operations had developed as an operational concept separate from the customary UNSCR maritime interdiction operations. LIO provided the coalition navies with a legitimate reason for emphasizing their rules of engagement, and therefore interoperability, with the U.S. Navy, beyond UN sanction work.

The Australians, heavily committed to leadership interdiction operations in the Northern Arabian Gulf after 9/11, never had a problem justifying operations beyond traditional maritime interception operations. For them, aggressive interdiction operations with the Americans established textbook sea control in the northern area, and this proved to be decisive a year later. The Canadians, in late 2001 and early 2002, briefly had two sets of rules of engagement, one each for maritime and leadership interdiction operations; however, with government approval these were soon blended together.

By March 2002 Commodore Robertson, the first Canadian group commander, and Canadian staffs in Tampa and Ottawa had confirmed common rules of engagement for post-9/11 operations anywhere in the region. Robertson remembered later:

Canada's ROE gave us more latitude than any other navy except the U.S. Navy. Had the coalition been left with the lowest common denominator as our collective ROE, the coalition would have been restricted to military operations in Afghanistan and nothing beyond surveillance would have been possible at sea. Happily . . . we all knew each others' limitations and the commanders were able to allocate and employ forces with those limitations. . . . What was vital to the operation was that countries shared their ROE, and that as a minimum all ships had the ROE to defend other coalition naval forces, and this we had.[263]

What concrete lessons can we derive from this experience? To summarize, operators will figure out what they need to do, while lawyers will generally only review options and decide what is legal and not base judgments on operational needs. Naval and military lawyers are not proactive—they do not normally anticipate operations, revising engagement rules ahead of time as a contingency plan. Military lawyers tend to be reactive, and they propose revisions to these rules for government approval only when faced with new circumstances. Navies have to find ways and means to shorten response time, and naval planning and deployment must be done in lockstep with legal planning. The main lesson here is obvious: interoperability with the U.S. Navy—and the legal implications for the government—must be emphasized at all times, during periods of routine training as well as deployments, in order to give the government time to approve rules of engagement.

Notes

1. In 2011 the name Royal Canadian Navy was reintroduced. For the historical approach used in this work—an operational theme—we are indebted to Jeremy Black's introduction in his *World War Two: A Military History* (New York: Routledge, 2003), xi–xii.

2. *Allied Joint Maritime Operations* (NATO, April 2004): 1-8, 1-9 (hereafter *AJP 3.1*).

3. *AJP 3.1*, 1-10, 1-11.

4. Ibid., 1-11.

5. Commodore Eric Lehre and CPO2 Doug McLeod, "Canadian Naval Task Groups in Op Apollo," *The Maritime Warfare Bulletin/Le Bulletin de Guerre Maritime* (Halifax: 2003): 105 (hereafter Lehre and McLeod, "Canadian Naval Task Group in Op Apollo," *MWB*).

6. U.S. Department of Defense, *Dictionary of Military Terms: Joint Chiefs of Staff* (1990), 101, 112, 385.

7. Major Jean H. Morin and Lieutenant Commander Richard H. Gimblett, *Operation Friction 1990–1991: The Canadian Forces in the Persian Gulf* (Toronto: Dundurn Press, 1997), 179.

8. For the Royal Navy background on some operations between 1958 and 1961, see Naval Staff History, *Middle East Operations—Jordan/Lebanon—1958, Kuwait—1961* (London: MOD, 1968). We are indebted to the Naval Historical Branch in the United Kingdom for drawing this work to my attention.

9. Kenneth M. Pollack, "Securing the Gulf," *Foreign Affairs* 82, no. 4 (July/August 2003): 2.

10. Michael A. Palmer, *On Course to Desert Storm: The United States Navy in the Persian Gulf* (Washington, DC: Naval Historical Center [NHC], 1992).

11. Canadian naval forces were not deployed to the Gulf region, probably because, for one reason, in late 1987 and early 1988 the Canadian Navy was preoccupied, alongside the U.S. Navy, with Operation Bandit, the deployment and possible intervention into Haiti. See Sean M. Maloney, "Maple Leaf over the Caribbean: Gunboat Diplomacy Canadian Style?" in *Canadian Gunboat Diplomacy: The Canadian Navy and Foreign Policy*, ed. Ann L. Griffiths et al. (Halifax: Dalhousie University, 1998), 166–71. Commodore L. C. A. Westropp commanded a Canadian joint task force, based on TG 300.1, that consisted of *Preserver*, *Athabaskan*, and *Skeena* and deployed in Haitian waters in mid-January 1988.

12. Palmer, *On Course to Desert Storm*, 124.

13. Ibid., 133–34.

14. Commodore Duncan E. "Dusty" Miller and Sharon Hobson, *The Persian Excursion: The Canadian Navy in the Gulf War* (Clementsport, NS: Canadian Peacekeeping Press, 1995), 23–33. The TRUMP project was an expanded midlife refit of the four *Iroquois* destroyers—the Tribal class—"incorporating area air defence and command and control (C2) improvements, in order to give the fleet the ability to conduct truly independent task group operations in any threatened environment." Morin and Gimblett, *Operation Friction*, 32. For a comment on the Tribal (sometimes "280" or "*Iroquois*") Class name, see Ken Macpherson and John Burgess, *The Ships of Canada's Naval Forces, 1910–1993* (St. Catherines, ONT: Vanwell Publishing, 1994), 169.

15. Morin and Gimblett, *Operation Friction*, 182.

16. Ibid., 191.

17. Rear Admiral (ret.) Ken Summers, "The Canadian Navy in the 1990–1991 Gulf War" (Address to the 7th MARCOM Historical Seminar, Ottawa, 23 September 2005), 3. This work was published later; see Ken Summers, "The Canadian Navy in 1990–91 Gulf War: Some Personal Observations," in *People, Policy and Programmes: Proceedings of the 7th Maritime Command (MARCOM) Historical Conference (2005)*, eds. Richard H. Gimblett and Richard O. Mayne (Winnipeg: 17 Wing Publishing Office, 2008), 116.

18. Morin and Gimblett, *Operation Friction*, 262.

19. HMCS *Huron* Annual Historical Report (DHH 1991), 2/9–4/9 (hereafter *Huron* AHR 1991). *Huron*'s TRUMP upgrades were not completed, but a "decision was made to retrofit *Huron* with a similar upgrade of weapons, sensors and communications gear as had been installed in *Athabaskan*." *Huron* AHR 1991, 2/9.

20. *Huron* AHR 1991, 5.

21. The minutes of the meeting were attached to the *Huron* AHR at Annex C, "Minutes of Second MACOM Conference," 7 June 1991 (hereafter Second MACOM).

22. Second MACOM, 1–2.

23. Ibid., 2.

24. Ibid., 2–3.

25. Ibid.

26. Ibid., 5.

27. HMCS *Restigouche* Annual Historical Report (DHH 1992), 3–4.

28. Ibid., 4–5.

29. Maloney, "Maple Leaf Over the Caribbean," 171–77.

30. Laura J. Higgins, *Canadian Naval Operations in the 1990s: Selected Case Studies* (Halifax: Dalhousie University, 2002), 130.

31. Lois E. Fielding, *Maritime Interception and U.N. Sanctions: Resolving Issues in the Persian Gulf War, The Conflict in the Former Yugoslavia, and the Haiti Crisis* (San Francisco, CA: Austin and Winfield, 1996), 300–309; "United Nations Mission in Haiti (UNMIH), Background," at http://www.un.org/Depts/dpko/dpko/co_mission/unmihbackgr2.html, accessed 23 March 2004, 1–4.

32. Maloney, "Maple Leaf Over the Caribbean," 174.

33. Ibid., 175.

34. Ibid.

35. Ibid.

36. Higgins, *Canadian Naval Operations in the 1990s*, 129. Vice Admiral (ret.) Greg A. Maddison commanded the Standing Naval Force Atlantic from April 1993 to April 1994. For ten months during his command tour, he coordinated interdiction operations in the Adriatic conducted by three coalition task groups: his own SNFL, the Standing Naval Force Mediterranean, and the Western European Union Contingency Force. Maddison formed strong friendships during this tour with many senior NATO officers, including Admiral Jay L. Johnson, USN, who a few years later was the Chief of Naval Operations at the same time that Maddison was the Chief of Maritime Staff (CMS). Maddison remembered that during his CMS tour "it was a comfort . . . to know that I could just pick up the phone and talk to him . . . and the same for him." For Maddison's definitive account of the Adriatic experience, see Canadian War Museum Oral History Program Interview, 31D 6 Maddison, with Dr. Richard Gimblett, 28 September 2005. Maddison was CMS from 1997 to 2001, when he was appointed Deputy Chief of Defence Staff. The quote is from page 20 of the interview.

37. Maloney, "Maple Leaf Over the Caribbean," 177.

38. Ibid.

39. *1994 Defence White Paper* (Ottawa: Department of National Defence, 1994), 38.

40. Lehre and McLeod, "Canadian Naval Task Group in Op Apollo," *MWB*, 116.

41. James A. Boutilier, "The Canadian Navy and the New Naval Environment in Asia," *International Journal* (Winter 2002–3): 194.

42. Lieutenant (N) Colin McKeown, "Joint and Combined Operational Training: MARCOT '96," *Canadian Defence Quarterly* 26, no. 1 (Autumn 1996): 14, 17.

43. McKeown, "Joint and Combined Operational Training '96," 17.

44. HMCS *Fredericton* Annual Historical Report (DHH 1995), Annex B, 23.

45. HMCS *Calgary* Annual Historical Report (DHH 1995), Annex B, B-1–2/5 (hereafter *Calgary* AHR 1995).

46. Ibid., B-2–3/5.

47. Sean M. Maloney, *War with Iraq: Canada's Strategy in the Persian Gulf, 1990–2002* (Kingston: Queen's University, 2002), 35. Maloney had obtained message CTU 305.1.1 to MARCOM HQ Halifax, "Op TRANQUILITY, 27 September 1995."

48. *Calgary* AHR 1995, B-3–4/5.

49. HMCS *Regina* Annual Historical Report (DHH 1997), 3/16 (hereafter *Regina* AHR 1997).

50. Ibid., 6–7/16.

51. Ibid., 7/16.

52. Ibid., A-1–4; Martin Cohn, "Canadians on Patrol in Persian Gulf," *Toronto Star*, 4 May 1997.

53. *Regina* AHR 1997, 11–13/16.

54. Maloney, *War with Iraq*, 29–30.

55. HMCS *Toronto* Annual Historical Report (DHH 1998), "Chronological Narrative," A-1–2/12.

56. Ibid., A-2/12.

57. Ibid., A-3/12.

58. Maloney, *War with Iraq*, 30.

59. HMCS *Ottawa* Annual Historical Report (DHH 1998), n.p. The *Regina* briefing was found in the calendar sections of the AHR for November 1997.

60. Ibid., n.p.

61. Ibid.

62. HMCS *Regina* Annual Historical Report (DHH 1999), n.p.

63. Ibid.

64. HMCS *Calgary* Annual Historical Report (DHH 2000), B-12/19.

65. Declassified excerpt HMCS *Calgary* War Diary, 24 June 2000.

66. Ibid., 4 July 2000.

67. Ibid., 14 July 2000, 31 July–1 August 2000.

68. Ibid., 11–13, 21 August 2000.

69. Ibid., 28 August 2000.

70. HMCS *Charlottetown* Annual Historical Report (DHH 2000), Annex A, A-4/5.

71. Ibid., A-1/11.

72. Ibid., A-1–4/11.

73. Lieutenant Commander Ian Anderson, "Where the Willingness is Great . . . Leadership Lessons Aboard the HMCS *Charlottetown*—Operation Apollo," in *In Harm's Way: On the Front Lines of Leadership: Sub-Unit Command on Operations*, ed. Colonel Bernd Horn (Kingston: Canadian Defence Academy Press, 2006), 156.

74. Declassified excerpt HMCS *Winnipeg* War Diary, 21 March 2001.

75. Higgins, *Canadian Naval Operations in the 1990s*, 69. In 2002 Laura Higgins, at Dalhousie University in Halifax, published an unclassified case study of *Winnipeg's* tour in the Gulf region in 2001, which was an exceptional example of the single-CPF experiences in the region, and which included *Calgary* in 2000 and *Charlottetown* in 2001. Higgins conducted 52 interviews of U.S. and Canadian naval officials.

76. Declassified excerpt HMCS *Calgary* Post-Deployment Report, September 2001.

77. Declassified excerpt HMCS *Winnipeg* War Diary, 21 March 2001; Commander's Monthly Sitrep to MARPAC, 1 April 2001.

78. Declassified excerpt HMCS *Winnipeg* War Diary, 13–16 April 2001.

79. Higgins, *Canadian Naval Operations in the 1990s*, 69.

80. Ibid., 67–68.

81. Declassified excerpt HMCS *Winnipeg* War Diary, Commander's Entry, 16–27 April 2001.

82. Ibid.

83. Declassified excerpt HMCS *Winnipeg* War Diary, 18 April 2001.

84. Higgins, *Canadian Naval Operations in the 1990s*, 69–70.

85. HMCS *Charlottetown* Annual Historical Report (DHH 2001), A-4–5/11 (hereafter *Charlottetown* AHR 2001).

86. Declassified excerpt HMCS *Winnipeg* War Diary, 28 April 2001.

87. Ibid., 30 April 2001.

88. Ibid., 28 April–4 May 2001.

89. Anderson, "Where the Willingness is Great . . . ," 156; *Charlottetown* AHR 2001, A-5/11.

90. Declassified excerpt HMCS *Winnipeg* War Diary, 16 May 2001.

91. Ibid., 26 May 2001.

92. Ibid., 3 June 2001.

93. Ibid., 4 June 2001.

94. Ibid., 20 June 2001.

95. Ibid., 16 July 2001.

96. Ibid., 21 July 2001.

97. Ibid., 24 July 2001.

98. Higgins, *Canadian Naval Operations in the 1990s*, 75.

99. Declassified excerpt HMCS *Winnipeg* Post-Deployment Report, September 2001, A-3/15.

100. Higgins, *Canadian Naval Operations in the 1990s*, 77.

101. Richard Gimblett, *Operation Apollo: The Golden Age of the Canadian Navy in the War Against Terrorism* (Ottawa: Magic Light Publishing, 2004), 78.

102. *The Maple Leaf/La Feuille d'érable*, Ottawa, 7 April 2004, 12.

103. Ibid. Williams as a lieutenant commander had received the United States Meritorious Service Award in 1997.

104. Paul T. Mitchell, "Small Navies and Network-Centric Warfare: Is There a Role?" *Naval War College Review* 56, no. 2 (Spring 2003): 83–99. See also "The Canadian Navy's Communications Blueprint to 2010," n.d., and "The Canadian Navy's Information Management Blueprint to 2010," n.d. Mitchell cited the date as 2001 and this was probably correct.

105. Sharon Hobson, "Canada Aims for Defence Interoperability with U.S.," *International Defence Review* 1 (January 2001). No page number identified on the online version of this article.

106. Lehre and McLeod, "Canadian Naval Task Group in Op Apollo," *MWB*, 113.

107. Ibid.

108. Mitchell, "Small Navies and Network-Centric Warfare," 86.

109. Rear Admiral Ron Buck, "Canadian Perspectives on C4I Issues" in *Maritime War in the 21st Century: The Medium and Small Navy Perspective*, ed. David Wilson (Canberra: RAN Sea Power Centre, 2001), 130. The papers in the publication had been presented at the RAN's Maritime War in the 21st Century conference in Sydney in February 2000 (hereafter Buck, "Canadian Perspectives on C4I Issues").

110. *Naval Command, Control, Communications and Computers (C4)–Organization and Terms of Reference (Handbook 1)*, Revision 4 (Amend 4), May 2002, 10. This work stated that

the "vision" of the "AUSCANNZUKUS Naval C4 Organization" is "to be an organization at the forefront of battle winning maritime C4 interoperability," 8.

111. Dr. Paul T. Mitchell, "What Role for Small Navies in Network Centric Warfare?" *The Maritime Warfare Bulletin/Le Bulletin de Guerre Maritime* (2002): 81–82.

112. Lehre and McLeod, "Canadian Naval Task Group in Op Apollo," *MWB*, 113.

113. Mitchell, "Small Navies and Network-Centric Warfare," 90.

114. Ibid., 94–95; and Lehre and McLeod, "Canadian Naval Task Group in Op Apollo," *MWB*, 113.

115. Lehre and McLeod, "Canadian Naval Task Group in Op Apollo," *MWB*, 114. Lehre briefly described the Link systems in a footnote on the same page.

116. Ibid. For further background on Link 11 and Link 16, see *Understanding Link 16: A Guidebook for New Users* (Washington, DC: AEGIS Program Manager, 1998).

117. Lehre and McLeod, "Canadian Naval Task Group in Op Apollo," *MWB*, 113.

118. Buck, "Canadian Perspectives on C4I Issues," 128–29.

119. Ibid., 128.

120. Ibid., 130.

121. Ibid., 132.

122. Ibid., 130.

123. Lehre and McLeod, "Canadian Naval Task Group in Op Apollo," *MWB*, 114.

124. http://www.whitehouse.gov/mar11/coalition/coalitionupdate.html.

125. Commodore D. W. Robertson, "The Naval Task Group in Operation Apollo," *The Maritime Warfare Bulletin/Le Bulletin de Guerre Maritime* (2002): 60.

126. HMCS *Vancouver* Annual Historical Report (DHH 2001), A-11–13/16.

127. Lehre and McLeod, "Canadian Naval Task Group in Op Apollo," *MWB*, 109.

128. Vice Admiral (ret.) Greg R. Maddison, interview with Robert H. Caldwell, 25 January 2006.

129. Commander J. B. McCarthy, interview with Operational Documentation Detachment, Fifth Fleet, U.S. Navy, NHC, 12 March 2002, 2 (hereafter McCarthy interview, NHC, 2002).

130. HMCS *Preserver* Annual Historical Report (DHH 2001), 2–3/4.

131. *Charlottetown* AHR 2001, A-6/11; Anderson, "Where the Willingness is Great," 158–60.

132. Declassified excerpt *Canadian Task Group* (CATG) War Diary, 19–25 October 2001.

133. Degaussing is an operation—of Second World War vintage—which electrically neutralizes a ship's magnetic field, thereby allowing the ship a measure of immunity from detonating a magnetic antiship mine. Peter Kemp, ed. *The Oxford Companion to Ships and the Sea* (Oxford: 1992), 238.

134. HMCS *Halifax* Annual Historical Report (DHH 2001), 4–6/8 (hereafter *Halifax* AHR 2001).

135. Ibid., 6/8

136. "HMCS *Halifax* returns Home," "CBC Newsworld," 11 February 2002.

137. Declassified excerpts HMCS *Halifax* War Diary, 3 and 7 November 2001.

138. *Halifax* AHR 2001, 6–7/8.

139. Gimblett, *Operation Apollo*, 50. The nuclear war threat presented by India-Pakistan in the post-9/11 period is fully covered in Steve Coll, "The Stand-Off—How jihadi groups

helped provoke the twenty-first century's first nuclear crisis," *The New Yorker*, 13 and 20 February 2006, 126–39.

140. Declassified excerpt *Canadian Task Group* (CATG) War Diary, 21 November 2001.

141. Commodore D. W. Robertson, interview with Operational Documentation Detachment, Fifth Fleet, U.S. Navy, NHC, 11 March 2002, 6.

142. Ibid.

143. Steve Coll, "The Stand-Off," 126–29.

144. Gimblett, *Operation Apollo*, 47–48.

145. Robertson interview, 11 March 2002, 6.

146. Ibid.

147. Commodore Drew W. Robertson, "The Canadian Naval Task Group in *Operation Apollo*," in *Intervention and Engagement: A Maritime Perspective*, eds. Robert H. Edwards and Ann L. Griffiths (Halifax: Centre for Foreign Policy Studies, Dalhousie University, 2003), 364.

148. Captain Allan Du Toit, "The RAN in the Gulf 1990–2003," Maritime Interception Force Operations 2, and Operation SLIPPER Rotation One November 2001–April 2002 (Canberra: RAN Naval History Section, 2004), 1–3, 7 (hereafter Du Toit, "RAN in the Gulf ").

149. See, for example, the earlier reference to *AUSCANNZUKUS Naval Command, Control, Communications and Computers (C4)*, Revision 4 (Washington: 2002).

150. Du Toit, "RAN in the Gulf ," 2.

151. Ibid., 2–3.

152. Ibid., 3.

153. Ibid., 4.

154. Ibid., 5.

155. Ibid.

156. Declassified excerpt HMCS *Charlottetown* War Diary, 17 October–5 March 2002, 6.

157. Ibid., 14.

158. Declassified excerpt HMCS *Halifax* War Diary, 7 December 2001.

159. Gimblett, *Operation Apollo*, 51.

160. Ibid., 52.

161. Vice Admiral Ron Buck, interview with Steve Madely, 19 December 2001, Radio Station CFRA-AM.

162. Ibid.

163. Ibid.

164. Gimblett, *Operation Apollo*, 53.

165. Du Toit, "RAN in the Gulf," 4.

166. "Rob Gordon aboard HMCS *Iroquois* in the Arabian Sea," "CBC Newsworld," 22 January 2002.

167. Ibid.

168. Ibid.

169. Robertson, "Naval Task Group in Operation Apollo," *MWB*, 58.

170. Ibid., The countries abbreviated were, in order: Canada, France, Germany, Italy, the Netherlands, the United Kingdom, and the United States.

171. See Steve Coll, "The Stand-Off," for the potentially deadly conflict between India and Pakistan.

172. Declassified excerpt *Canadian Task Group* (CATG) War Diary, 7 February 2002.

173. In 2002 the U.S. Navy, the Royal Australian Navy, and Canada's Directorate of History and Heritage from NDHQ Ottawa all sent historians to serve with their ships at sea. This volume is a result of that early work.

174. McCarthy interview, 12 March 2002, 10.

175. Ibid., 10–11.

176. Ibid., 11.

177. Ibid.

178. Ibid., 12–13.

179. Robertson interview, 11 March 2002, 9.

180. Ibid., 9–10.

181. Robertson, "The Canadian Naval Task Group in *Operation Apollo*," 365.

182. Commodore James Goldrick, RAN, Memoir (Canberra: RAN Sea Power Centre, n.d.) 2–3.

183. Ibid., 3.

184. Ibid., 3–4.

185. Ibid., 4–5. See also *Effects Based Warfare*, ed. Christopher Finn (London: n.d.).

186. Declassified excerpt *Canadian Task Group* (CATG) War Diary, 6–7 July 2002.

187. Gimblett, *Operation Apollo*, 70.

188. Ibid., 66.

189. Lehre and McLeod, "Canadian Naval Task Group in Op Apollo," *MWB*, 109.

190. Gimblett, *Operation Apollo*, 70

191. Lehre and McLeod, "Canadian Naval Task Group in Op Apollo," *MWB*, 103–4.

192. Ibid., 107. The author can confirm this characteristic of wakes from personal experience on board HMCS *Algonquin* during June 2002.

193. Lehre and McLeod, "Canadian Naval Task Group in Op Apollo," *MWB*, 109–110.

194. Ibid., 108.

195. Ibid.

196. Ibid., 114.

197. Ibid.

198. Declassified excerpt *Canadian Task Group* (CATG) War Diary, 4 and 7 April 2001. At this time Lehre was commanding from HMCS *Ottawa*.

199. Ibid., 2–3 May 2001.

200. Ibid., 25 May 2001.

201. Vice Admiral Ron Buck, "Key Note Address—Intervention and Engagement: A View from the Bridge," in *Intervention and Engagement: A Maritime Perspective—Proceedings of a Conference hosted by the Centre for Foreign Policy Studies, Dalhousie University, and the*

Canadian Forces Maritime Warfare Centre, Halifax, 7–9 June 2002 (Halifax: Dalhousie University, 2003), 50–56.

202. Ibid.

203. Declassified excerpt *Canadian Task Group* (CATG) War Diary, 3 June 2002.

204. Ibid., 2 July 2002.

205. Ibid., 3 July 2002.

206. Ibid., 4 July 2002. For the MPA experience the previous fall and winter, see Major Neil Tabbenor, "CP 140 Joins the Fight: The Deployment of the Long Range Patrol Detachment: Operation Apollo, Rotation 0," in *In Harm's Way: On the Front Lines of Leadership: Sub-Unit Command on Operations* (Kingston: Canadian Defence Academy Press, 2006), 107–128.

207. Ibid., 3 July 2002.

208. Ibid.

209. Ibid., 6–7 July 2002.

210. Ibid., 8 July 2002. COWAN C was later known as CENTRIXS. See Jill L. Boardman and Donald L. Shuey, *Combined Enterprise Regional Information Exchange System (CENTRIXS); Supporting Coalition Warfare World-Wide* (USCENTCOM MacDill AFB: 2004).

211. Declassified excerpt *Canadian Task Group* (CATG) War Diary, 20 July 2002.

212. Ibid., n.d., August 2002.

213. Gimblett, *Operation Apollo*, 76.

214. Ibid., 74.

215. Commodore R. D. Murphy, interview with Robert H. Caldwell, 26 October 2005; Commodore R. D. Murphy, "Canadian Task Group ROTO 2 2003," *The Maritime Warfare Bulletin/Le Bulletin de Guerre Maritime* (2003): 56–59; and Gimblett, *Operation Apollo*, 74–77.

216. Captain Peter Jones, RAN Memoir (Canberra: RAN Sea Power Centre, n.d), 1 (hereafter Jones, RAN Memoir).

217. Murphy, "Canadian Task Group ROTO 2 2003," *MWB*, 56.

218. Ibid.

219. Ibid., 57; Lehre and McLeod, "Canadian Naval Task Group in Op Apollo," *MWB*, 104.

220. Murphy, "Canadian Task Group ROTO 2 2003," *MWB*, 57–58.

221. Ibid., 58.

222. Ibid.

223. Ibid.

224. Jones, RAN Memoir, 2.

225. Ibid.

226. Murphy, "Canadian Task Group ROTO 2 2003," *MWB*, 59.

227. Jones, RAN Memoir, 6.

228. Gimblett, *Operation Apollo*, 111.

229. Ibid., 116.

230. For the Helicopter Air Detachment experience, see Major Larry McCurdy, "Operational Readiness: Operation Apollo A, Helicopter Air Detachment Commander's Perspective," in *In Harm's Way: On the Front Lines of Leadership: Sub-Unit Command on Operations*, ed.

Colonel Bernd Horn (Kingston, ONT: Canadian Defence Academy Press, 2006), 167–82.

231. Ibid., 118. "Speech by U.S. Ambassador to Canada A. Paul Cellucci to the Economic Club of Toronto," 25 March 2003, at http://www.usembassycanada.gov/content/content.asp?section=embconsul&document=cellucci_030325.

232. Declassified excerpt HMCS *Iroquois* War Diary, Commander's Entry, 7 and 23 April, 24 May 2003.

233. Declassified excerpt HMCS *Fredericton* War Diary, Commander's Entry, 1–31 July 2003 (hereafter *Fredericton* excerpt 2003); and Gimblett, *Operation Apollo*, 122.

234. *Fredericton* excerpt 2003.

235. Declassified excerpt HMCS *Calgary* War Diary, Commander's Entry, 8 August 2003.

236. Ibid., 16 August 2003.

237. Ibid., 18 October 2003; Gimblett, *Operation Apollo*, 123.

238. Vice Admiral Ron Buck, "Speaking Notes for Return of HMCS *Calgary*," 14 December 2003, cited in Gimblett, *Operation Apollo*, 124.

239. Joy Gordon, "Scandals of Oil for Food," *Middle East Report Online*, 20 July 2004.

240. Joy Gordon, "The U.N. is US—Exposing Saddam Hussein's Silent partner," *Harper's Magazine*, December 2004. This point was also made by retired Canadian diplomat Paul Hennebaker, Waterloo University, a guest on the Television Ontario (TVO) program, "Diplomatic Immunity," 3 December 2004.

241. Robertson, "Naval Task Group in Operation Apollo," *MWB*, 60.

242. James Goldrick, review of Michael A. Palmer, *Command at Sea: Naval Command and Control since the Sixteenth Century* in *The Northern Mariner/Le marin du nord* 25, no. 2 (April 2005): 74.

243. Mitchell, "Small Navies and Network-Centric Warfare: Is There a Role?" 93.

244. I am indebted to Dr. Randy Papadopoulos for finding this quote at http://www.imdb.com/title/tt0200276/quotes.

245. Robertson interview, 11 March 2002, 9–10.

246. Jennifer Welsh, *At Home in the World—Canada's Global Vision for the 21st Century* (Toronto: Harper Collins, 2004), 192.

247. James Boutilier, "The Problematic World of the Navy's Second Century," in *The Naval Service of Canada 1910–2010: The Centennial Story*, ed. Richard H. Gimblett (Toronto: Dundurn Press, 2009), 215.

248. Michael Howard, "After the Peace," *Times Literary Supplement*, 23 September 2005, 10.

249. Geoffrey Till, "Navies and the New World Order," U.S. Naval Institute (USNI) *Proceedings* 131/3/1, 225 (March 2005): 60–62.

250. Colin S. Gray, *Another Bloody Century: Future Warfare* (London: Weidenfeld and Nicholson, 2005), 206.

251. Till, "Navies and the New World Order," 60–62.

252. See for example Dr. Allan English, Dr. Richard Gimblett, and Mr. Howard Coombs, "Beware of Putting the Cart Before the Horse: Network Enabled Operations as a Canadian Approach to Transformation," DRDC Toronto, 19 July 2005. As well there is Dr. Paul Mitchell's work, for example, see "Networked Power: Insurgents versus 'Big Army'," Hekmat Karzai and Paul T. Mitchell, a draft circulated on the internet by Howard G. Coombes, March

2006.

253. Roger W. Barnett, "Technology and Naval Blockade—Past Impact and Future Prospects," *Naval War College Review* 58, no. 3 (Summer 2005): 89. A. T. Mahan's article was in USNI *Proceedings* 12, no. 4 (1895): 856.

254. Captain (N) Peter Avis, "The Importance of Information Sharing to the Interdepartmental Security Approach," *Frontline*, no. 4 (July–August 2005): 32.

255. Vice Admiral Bruce MacLean, "Diversifying the Naval Portfolio," *Frontline*, no. 4 (July–August 2005): 11.

256. Vice Admiral Bruce MacLean, "Report on Canada's Navy," *Canadian Defence Review* 11, no. 4 (2005): 12. See also his "Diversifying the Naval Portfolio," 8.

257. http://www.pm.gc.ca/eng/media.asp?id=2095, 1–2.

258. Barnett, "Technology and Naval Blockade," 93–94. A 50-foot height of eye allows a horizon distance of about eight miles.

259. MacLean, "Diversifying the Naval Portfolio," 10.

260. The cyber war threat has been widely written about; indeed, the University of Calgary's Centre for Military and Strategic Studies conducted a conference in May 2012, *"Nobody Knows Anything: Canada's Cyber Insecurities."* The topics included Attackers and Targets, State of the Art in Defence, Deterrence, and "a blue sky assessment of the cyber environment in Canada five to ten years from now."

261. Till, "Navies and the New World Order," 62.

262. Brigadier Nigel Aylwin-Foster, "Changing the Army for Counterinsurgency Operations," *Military Review* (November–December 2005): 15.

263. Robertson, "Naval Task Group in Operation Apollo," *MWB*, 59; and Robertson "The Canadian Naval Task Group in Operation Apollo," 365.

Edward J. Marolda

T he key to the success of several post–Cold War multinational naval operations involving Australian, Canadian, British, and American navies was the trust, understanding, and mutual respect of leaders and commanders for one another in often challenging situations. Years of experience with combined (that is, multinational) operations, at-sea exercises, shore-based education and training, and professional and social interaction had created a corps of allied naval officers confident in the abilities of their foreign counterparts. The human element was and is the key factor that binds the operations of the Royal Navy, U.S. Navy, Canadian Navy, and Royal Australian Navy.

Despite the end of the 45-year-long Cold War in 1991, conflict continued to roil the international scene. Enforcing United Nations economic sanctions against Saddam Hussein's Iraq, managing the disintegration of Yugoslavia, separating combatants in East Timor, and responding to the terrorist menace after 11 September 2001 fully engaged the four navies of this study. The demise of the Soviet navy and the absence of a blue-water threat to control of the sea did not diminish the need for naval forces. Indeed, they became critical to resolving crises ashore whether that soil was an island adjoining Indonesia or the nation of Afghanistan located deep in the heart of Asia, hundreds of miles from the sea. Naval forces facilitated the operations ashore of air and ground components and prevented hostile actors from exploiting the sea for their own purposes. Littoral operations to deal with crises ashore were hardly uncommon for the navies of the world, and were indeed the norm throughout much of modern history, as persuasively argued by naval theorist Sir Julian Corbett. For instance, recognizing at the end of the Cold War that its mission had changed, the U.S. Navy promulgated a strategy appropriately titled . . . *From the Sea,* later refined as . . . *Forward From the Sea.*

Unlike the battles of Tsushima, Jutland, and Midway, which largely involved only the navies of the major antagonists, post–Cold War operations routinely demanded the cooperation of ground, air, and naval forces from many countries. The actions of the late 20th century and early 21st century more closely resembled the multinational and joint operations of the Korean and Vietnam wars.

The emphasis of post–Cold War operations, however, was peace support, not warfighting. The goal of these naval forces was to carry out UN Security Council Resolutions that required military forces to act either as deterrents or as enforcers. Because of the nature of the missions, naval commanders had to be sensitive to different even conflicting international and national imperatives and accommodate restrictive rules of engagement.

After many years of working together in NATO and other alliances during the Cold War, these four navies were familiar and comfortable with common doctrinal instructions and procedures. They employed common standardization agreements, multinational operational and tactical publications, and combined operations handbooks. Such written guidelines, however, did not guarantee the smooth functioning of combined operations. Every nation and every navy involved in a multinational operation brought to the situation different customs, traditions, procedures, tactics, and understandings. Each of the navies employed national rules of engagement as guides to the use of military force. Even with the most polished and precise set of instructions, there were misunderstandings and disagreements over the problems at hand and how to solve them. To work through these obstacles, naval leaders and commanders had to have confidence in their opposite numbers.

The four navies had at least a half-century history of practicing methods to work out multinational operational kinks. During the Cold War, the U.S. Navy, Royal Navy, and Royal Canadian Navy took part in literally hundreds of multi-ship, multi-aircraft exercises in the North Atlantic that honed their skills in command, control, and communications. All four nations were involved in similar activities in the Pacific, formalizing their interaction in a Combined Exercise Agreement. These activities were useful for ironing out dissimilar tactics and procedures but more importantly for putting officers of the different nations together to deepen personal relationships.

The allied navies also improved their technical ability to share information and enhance command, control, and communications through the five-nation AUSCANNZUKUS organization and the Tactical Information Data Exchange, or TIDE, Committee. By 1991 the Link-11 system embodied technical interoperability. Barriers to sharing information, however, whether due to technical incompatibilities, the high cost of requisite equipment, or national concerns over information security, frequently troubled inter-allied naval cooperation. Once again, the key to the conduct of successful operations was the trust shared by the multinational officers and commanders on the spot. Sailors have always had to work in the especially challenging maritime environment that has naturally fostered a "brotherhood of the sea." But after the Cold War, the leaders and commanders of the four navies under study functioned well together because they also shared many cultural, professional, and intellectual values and a belief in the value of collective security actions sanctioned by the international community.

Maritime Interception Operations

The first concerted post–Cold War effort in which the navies of the United States, United Kingdom, Australia, and Canada worked together was the Maritime Interception Operation (MIO) of 1990–1991 in the Arabian Gulf. The primary goal of the UN-authorized action was to compel through economic pressure the withdrawal of Saddam Hussein's Iraqi armed forces from the conquered nation of Kuwait. If war could not be avoided to accomplish that objective, the secondary goal was to prevent further imports into Iraq of tanks, guns, missiles, ammunition, and other war material. Washington hoped that the MIO, if conducted with minimum force and diplomatic sensitivity, would demonstrate allied solidarity in opposing Saddam's aggression. A successful MIO would also make it easier to put together an international military effort to oust the Iraqis from Kuwait.

As authorized by the UN Security Council, Australia, Canada, France, the Netherlands, United Kingdom, and United States (later joined by Argentina, Belgium, Denmark, Greece, Italy, Norway, and Spain) deployed naval forces to the region to enforce the embargo. Since he controlled the largest contingent of warships in the area, Vice Admiral Henry H. Mauz Jr., Commander, U.S. Naval Forces Central Command convened the first of a number of monthly meetings in Bahrain of the principal naval commanders. He and other leaders recognized early that close and frequent interaction among the international team members was imperative. A politically influenced disagreement between the U.S. and French representatives over potential patrol sectors might have fractured the naval coalition from the start, but the local officers readily worked out practical solutions.

The principal leaders from each navy decided that their forces would not be under the direction of any one commander but would work in "loose association." The conferees decided on patrol sectors, interception and boarding procedures, and other critical issues that took into account individual national capabilities and restrictions. Since the U.S., U.K., Canadian, and Australian navies had a long history of close cooperation, however, officers from these nations routinely served as task force commander exercising tactical control of the others.

One problem that surfaced in 1990 was the reluctance of the navies involved to freely share intelligence and planning information, and especially the details of each nation's politically determined rules of engagement. Several nations were initially reluctant to place their naval forces under U.S. operational control. These problems complicated but did not seriously impede the multinational operations.

In contrast, the on-scene commanders readily agreed to the employment of the ships, aircraft, and command systems best suited to particular missions. For instance, with relatively compatible command, control, and communications systems, the Royal Navy and the U.S. Navy took on the responsibilities for operations in the more dangerous Northern Arabian Gulf. Canadian warships, which lacked sufficiently robust anti-air defensive weapons, volunteered to manage the naval logistic effort in the Southern Arabian Gulf. This operational necessity, however, proved fortuitous, for it allowed the three-ship Canadian naval contingent to stand out as a discrete contribution to the allied cause.

After the war and into the late 1990s, the cost of maintaining naval forces on the Gulf maritime interdiction operations compelled many coalition nations to reduce or end their involvement. Moving some of the inspection regime ashore helped make up for the shortage of warships. The U.S. Navy also eased the operational needs of the multinational force by providing area-wide air defense, intelligence, and patrol plane support.

Allied ships and aircraft performed tens of thousands of intercepts, boardings, and diversions of suspect merchant ships that hamstrung the Iraqis. Throughout, and despite some problems, coalition navies successfully maintained the embargo on Saddam's overseas commerce mandated by United Nations resolutions.

Operation Sharp Guard in the Adriatic

The Royal Navy's Balkan-support operations in the Adriatic from 1991 to 1996 encountered similar difficulties but in general multinational naval cooperation overcame these challenges. In Operation Sharp Guard, NATO and Western European Union (WEU) naval forces imposed an economic embargo on the Federal Republic of Yugoslavia (FRY) overseas commerce and prevented arms from reaching the Serb, Croat, and Muslim combatants ashore. In their early cooperation, the navies of the two international groupings established individual but connected operational patrol areas in the Adriatic. Based on their positive experience with Standing Naval Force Atlantic (SNFL) during the Cold War, the maritime commanders involved were well prepared to carry out the contemporary mission. Their ability to employ the Link-11 data-sharing system also enhanced patrol operations. This sharing was facilitated by the U.S. Navy's employment of a guided missile cruiser or destroyer—called Red Crown—equipped with the Aegis battle management system to monitor the air space over the Balkans and the Adriatic. Red Crown shared this critical information for defending the naval armada against air attack and also helped coordinate the embargo patrol effort.

While each nation's rules of engagement differed in some respect from the others, all agreed that an attack by FRY forces on any nation's warship would be considered an attack on all, as provided for in NATO's Article 5. The officers involved also got a lot done through informal communication, for instance, using early mobile phones. Throughout Sharp Guard the navies involved practiced interception, boarding, air defense, and other measures that enhanced actual operations. Confidence in the other navies, especially the Dutch and French, was reinforced when the Royal Navy crews observed their international counterparts boarding and searching merchantmen in even the roughest weather.

The operation was a success. During the mid-1990s Sharp Guard forces challenged 74,000 ships, boarded and inspected almost 6,000, and diverted 1,500 to Italian ports for further inspection. As in the Gulf after 1991, naval commanders met monthly to coordinate operations and iron out difficulties. The allied navies came to appreciate the professionalism and dedication of their opposite numbers through direct observation and formal and informal interaction.

Naval operations are inherently flexible. Hence, the Royal Navy could take part in multinational naval operations while being ready to execute the vital national mission of providing air support to British forces in Bosnia if subjected to fire by the belligerents. In 1995 this flexibility enabled the Royal Navy and U.S. Navy to carry out air and missile operations from the sea when Italy restricted launching such missions from its land bases. The allied armada offshore was also prepared, if needed, to withdraw ground forces from the Balkans cockpit. Such flexibility was vital in the confrontation over Bosnia, the first time the NATO alliance engaged in combat, because not all member nations were politically comfortable participating in the hostilities.

While never tested by combat, the Bosnia embargo confirmed for the Royal Navy the wisdom of its previous efforts to improve interaction with other navies in combined training, compatible procedures and equipment, and actual operations. And familiar, informal interaction among the British and other naval leaders was the lubricant that kept the machine working smoothly.

Naval operations in the Adriatic benefited significantly from the existence of NATO's Standing Naval Force Atlantic, a mainstay of the Cold War experience. The NATO navies were long used to working together and commanding in this "fire brigade" formation and also the newer Standing Naval Force Mediterranean. For instance, on a rotating basis, a Belgian, Danish, or U.S. officer could direct the operations of the other nations. At the outset of embargo operations in the Adriatic, Canadian Commodore Greg Maddison served as the SNFL commander, and he quickly readied his multinational contingent for action in the Adriatic. This positive connection was forged through frequent exercises at sea—the U.S. Navy took part in 57 such multilateral exercises in 1992 for instance—and strengthened by allied tactical publications and similar guides. The entire Sharp Guard force operated under an Italian admiral, Commander, Naval Forces South, based in Naples, who was empowered to improve coordination among the navies.

While the U.S. Navy was not part of the Western European Union naval contingent, there were few differences in operating procedures between the NATO participants and the WEU formation. A problem of great potential, however, was the varying guidance among participating nations over the use of force on the embargo patrol. Force was never needed, but its use could have led to tactical confusion and misperception that always increases the risk of accidents. Another complication arose when the U.S. Congress prohibited the U.S. Navy from stopping the importation of arms to the Bosnian Muslims, under siege by their Serb antagonists. The navies on the patrol, however, quickly adjusted their operations to accommodate the American exclusion.

The U.S. Navy provided the Sharp Guard naval forces with critical support. P-3 Orion patrol planes armed with air-to-surface missiles flew overhead around-the-clock in case the Yugoslavian navy decided to contest the UN-sanctioned embargo with force. U.S. submarines under NATO control also kept watch on the Yugoslav navy. EP-3 electronic collection aircraft and U.S. intelligence facilities based in Spain and elsewhere also helped clarify the operational picture for the navies in the Adriatic. Yugoslav authorities tried on a number of occasions to breach the allied embargo— such as the oil tanker *Lido II*'s bold attempt to run the blockade—but almost all failed, adding significantly to the strain on the Serbian war economy.

Operation Stabilise in East Timor

For the first time in modern history, in Operation Stabilise during 1999 and 2000, the Royal Australian Navy (RAN) led the maritime component of a UN-sanctioned peacekeeping force. The occasion for this operation was the descent into chaos and bloodshed of East Timor, invaded and occupied by the Indonesian Army in 1976. Regime change in Jakarta raised the possibility of East Timor's independence, but significant elements of the Indonesia military and local Timorese militias violently opposed any such action. The Indonesian government agreed to UN supervision of the country's transition to independence. With a strong interest in the stability of its two closest neighbors to the north, the Australian government agreed to direct the complex and dangerous mission of the International Force East Timor (INTERFET).

Successfully transporting UN ground, air, and naval forces to East Timor; protecting them from air, surface, and subsurface threats; providing them with requisite logistical support; and maintaining the forward deployment for many months were vital responsibilities of INTERFET's naval component. Recognizing that its own resources were limited, the relatively small Royal Australian Navy quickly acted to assemble an international naval force. The Royal New Zealand Navy (RNZN) immediately joined the team. The RNZN and the RAN were already so used to operating together that one New Zealand naval officer observed that in essence his ship "became an Australian frigate."

Similarly, the Royal Australian Navy, in its direction of Operation Stabilise off East Timor in 1999, received the full cooperation and assistance of the U.S. Navy. The Australian and American navies were no strangers to one another, having fought side by side in Korea and Vietnam, and during the 1990–1991 Gulf War. Commodore J. R. Stapleton, RAN, the naval component commander, had spent his career working with the U.S., U.K., New Zealand, and other navies, so interoperability held no particular concerns for him. A 1999 U.S.-Australian command post exercise clarified the symbiotic relationship, easing the way for navies of ten nations to join Operation Stabilise.

As with other post–Cold War naval operations, differing national rules of engagement caused delay and some confusion. The assignment by contributing navies of liaison officers to the staffs and ships of INTERFET helped alleviate many such problems of communication. HMAS *Adelaide* controlled the tactical operations of the international warships present as the "composite warfare commander," a concept long used by the navies involved. The Australian commander was confident he could protect his contingent from air attack off volatile East Timor because USS *Mobile Bay* supported him with its advanced Aegis battle management system. The combat power, capability, and multinational character of the naval force deployed within sight of the East Timorese capital of Dili emphasized to those both ashore and afloat that the international community was serious about the UN commitment.

As with all major military operations in the late 20th century, more than 90 percent of the ammunition, fuel, food, heavy equipment and other materials needed by the INTERFET units ashore came by sea. HMAS *Tobruk* did yeoman service in that regard. Canadian replenishment ship *Protecteur* directed afloat logistic efforts off Dili, having gained invaluable experience during similar operations in the Caribbean and off Somalia. Differences in equipment, doctrine, tactics, and even customs and traditions among the naval coalition did not result in seamless operations. But, once again the ease with which Australian naval commanders could accommodate the political and operational needs of counterparts in the naval contingent proved vital to overall success. Within two months of its commitment to Operation Stabilise, INTERFET, including its naval component, had helped end violence in most of East Timor, allowing the start of the country's march to full independence.

The U.S. Navy in Operation Stabilise

Navies have throughout history used their power afloat in support of political objectives ashore, a function well documented by Julian Corbett and other naval theorists and strategists. That role was never more in evidence than during 1999 and the U.S. Navy's participation in Operation Stabilise. The unpleasant Somalia experience was fresh in everyone's mind. In contrast, the deployment of naval forces demonstrated American support for UN objectives while minimizing entanglement in the chaotic political and internecine conflict ashore that the deployment of ground troops risked.

Washington agreed to and encouraged Australia's lead in the UN-sanctioned Operation Stabilise. Its policies were guided by already heavy American commitments to conflicts in the Balkans and Middle East and conclusion that local nations with an interest in stability in their particular region should be in charge. The U.S. Navy and its commanders found themselves in the unfamiliar situation of taking theater operational direction from another country's military leader, an Australian army general.

This arrangement caused some initial complications and confusion, but the American and Australian militaries were no strangers to each other. The two navies had conducted hundreds of at-sea and command post exercises during and after the Cold War, the most recent being Exercise Crocodile 99 earlier that month.

The U.S. naval commitment was relatively small, but the Americans brought significant advantages with them to the operational table. USS *Mobile Bay* coordinated local air defense. Military Sealift Command ammunition ship USNS *Kilauea* was later joined by amphibious ships USS *Belleau Wood* and USS *Peleliu*. With minimal risk, the helicopter units from these ships helped deliver scarce food and water to the traumatized and hungry civilian population. The helicopters proved vital when the Australian IN-TERFET commander deployed his infantry units to remote positions on the border with Indonesia's West Timor and needed robust logistical support.

The Americans were pleased with the results of Operation Stabilise, which demonstrated their strong support for close ally Australia. The U.S. naval contingent was small but packed a punch, with the advanced command, control, communications, and air-defense capability of an Aegis guided missile cruiser; helicopter support for supplying the local population and INTERFET ground forces; and a Marine infantry battalion ready offshore for any contingency. Even though the military commitment to resolving the crisis in East Timor was limited, the naval presence offshore signaled to friend and foe alike that the United States stood behind the UN commitment to a free and independent East Timor.

Afghanistan and Iraq

The terrorist attacks on America of 11 September 2001 dramatically changed the nature and tempo of multinational naval operations. The terms peacekeeping and peacemaking no longer applied when stateless antagonists respected no political boundaries or norms of civilized behavior. Osama bin Laden and his al-Qaeda followers targeted not only the United States—"the Great Satan"—but the freedoms enjoyed or at least aspired to by much of the modern world. Killing or capturing terrorists, destroying their training camps, and denying them sanctuary in any recognized nation became operational objectives of the nations opposed to this assault on humanity. Understanding that the threat was universal, both the NATO and ANZUS (Australia, New Zealand, United States) powers quickly signed on to deal with it.

In Operation Enduring Freedom, the United States decided to overthrow the Taliban government of Afghanistan that had harbored Bin Laden and other al-Qaeda terrorists responsible for the 9/11 atrocities. In reference to Article 5 of the Washington Treaty and Article 4 of the treaty establishing ANZUS, these alliances had already announced that they stood with the United States in this confrontation. On 7 October Tomahawk cruise missiles fired from U.S. warships and British submarines, and attack aircraft from carrier USS *Enterprise* struck terrorist targets far inland in Afghanistan. Canada, Australia, Germany, France, and a host of other countries also pledged to support the effort.

Within days of the first attacks, NATO naval forces monitored merchant traffic using the Suez Canal, Royal Navy ships began intercepting suspicious merchant ships in the Arabian Gulf, Canada pledged a third of its naval vessels and its antiterrorist ground task force to the effort, and Australian naval forces prepared to expand their involvement in anti-Iraq maritime interdiction operations. During the last three months of 2001, naval forces from the United States, Canada, Australia, and the United Kingdom deployed to the Arabian Gulf to strengthen the MIO or to the North Arabian Sea from which coalition ships launched air strikes and conducted amphibious operations in connection with the war in Afghanistan. French and Italian carrier battle groups were heavily involved in these operations as were naval units from Germany, Greece, Japan, Bahrain, the Netherlands, Spain, and Poland. Managing more than 130 coalition naval vessels operating in the U.S. Central Command's area of responsibility could have been an enormous command problem; it did not prove to be.

Within a matter of weeks in the winter of 2001, U.S. and coalition military forces, in conjunction with the indigenous Northern Alliance, killed or captured the Taliban and al-Qaeda terrorists that stood and fought in Afghanistan and forced others to flee for safe havens in Pakistan or overseas. Coalition commanders concluded that escaping terrorists would try to reach like-minded Islamic radicals in Somalia, Sudan, Yemen, even Southeast Asia by air and sea. Beginning on 23 November, naval forces of the United States, United Kingdom, Canada, France, and Italy inaugurated leadership interdiction operations (LIO) in the Gulf of Oman and later the North Arabian Sea. Suspicious merchant vessels could be stopped, by disabling fire if authorized by higher command, and searched for terrorists. Forcible searches also required political permission.

To simplify command arrangements, in February 2002 the Canadian commander in the region took on responsibility for coordinating naval operations in the Gulf of Oman, Southern Arabian Gulf, and Strait of Hormuz. His charges included U.S., British, and French warships. Similarly, an Australian naval commander (rotating monthly with a U.S. naval officer) assumed responsibility for coalition MIO in the northern and central Arabian Gulf. During early 2002 coalition naval forces queried over 300 ships by signal or radio each month, boarded and searched over a third of them, and diverted a handful for a more thorough search. In the same vein, coalition warships by March 2002 had queried 7,244 ships in LIO and boarded 47 suspicious vessels.

As with other combined naval operations in the post–Cold War era, differing national rules of engagement made life complicated for naval officers. Moreover, U.S. security classification of intelligence and operational materials hindered the sharing of vital planning information with members of the coalition. But in general, the years of common operational experience and comfort with interoperable command and control procedures and communications systems enabled the allied naval officers to iron out differences and get on with the job.

Canadian-U.S. Naval Cooperation

The Canadian experience working in U.S.-led naval operations provides tactical insight on the challenges of relatively small navies serving in coalitions in which one member's resources in ships, aircraft, and sailors predominate.

In the 1990–1991 Gulf War, the Canadian contribution stood out. Ottawa deployed only three warships to the Arabian Gulf, in contrast to the 100 or more U.S. naval vessels in the region. The commander, however, succeeded in gaining American concurrence to his coordination of coalition ships operating at the underway replenishment area in the southern gulf. At one point in the Gulf War, he handled 10 warships and 20 logistic vessels at his station. Ottawa concluded that its forces could retain national autonomy and still make a solid contribution to the allied cause. The successful conclusion of the war and the positive experience of the Canadian Navy operating alongside the U.S. Navy engendered support for future operational cooperation.

In 1992 Canada deployed a single ship to the Gulf of Aqaba to conduct interdiction operations with the Americans. Concurrently, throughout the 1990s the Canadian government and people supported construction of 12 multipurpose *Halifax*-class patrol frigates that were ideal for these operations. During embargo patrol operations off Haiti in the Caribbean during 1993–1994, the Canadian Navy once again operated in a multinational force and on several occasions coordinated the actions of local U.S. and other surface and air forces.

In the mid-1990s the Canadian government continued to operate naval task groups on its east and west coasts but also readied a warship from each area for deployment on three-weeks' notice for global operations. In line with international realities, the Canadian Navy also put much greater emphasis in its training on serving in joint and combined ventures and the littoral operations related to peacekeeping operations. Staffs also grappled with how to make more user friendly NATO joint and combined rules of engagement and how to improve comprehension of international humanitarian law, use of force, and conflict resolution.

Canadian ships did not remain continuously on maritime interdiction operations in the Arabian Gulf during the 1990s but did support the oil embargo on Iraq with periodic deployments. During HMCS *Calgary*'s tour in 1995, the ship had no problem interacting with the U.S. Fifth Fleet forces. Indeed, the Americans were pleased that *Calgary*, because of her shallow draft, could patrol closer inshore in the northern gulf than their own ships. Two years later, HMCS *Regina* was the first to make predeployment preparations with the U.S. units of a Pacific surface action group specifically charged with maritime interception operations in the Arabian Gulf and then served with the Americans for the entire mission. On a subsequent deployment, *Regina* helped a U.S.-led group carry out a highly dangerous, nighttime mission only 20 miles off the Iraqi coast to seize three vessels planning to smuggle embargoed oil out of the country. Helped to one target by a U.S. Navy helicopter equipped with night vision gear, *Regina's* rigid hulled inflatable boat captured the smuggler and escorted it to a safer area for inspection.

Hardships strengthened the bond between Canadian and American sailors on maritime interdiction operations. The shared misery of serving in a region with summertime temperatures in excess of 110 degrees and high humidity, to say nothing of the potential there for sudden violent encounters with smugglers, reinforced mutual reliance and trust.

By summer 2001 it was a well-established practice for Canadian Navy vessels slated for Gulf interdiction service to work up for the deployment with an American task group. Such exercises by the two navies ensured all understood the tactics, techniques, and procedures; command, control, and communications guidelines; and rules of engagement to be employed on the actual operation. They took turns leading the task group, and with the help of legal officers from both navies they increased mutual understanding of rules of engagement.

So confident were the Americans in Canadian capabilities on the maritime interdiction operations that in 2001 the U.S. Fifth Fleet made HMCS *Winnipeg* the "mother ship" for MIO in the Northern Arabian Gulf and her commanding officer, the on-site commander. The Canadian unit was involved in the interception and inspection of 17 vessels that were carrying illegal Iraqi oil. One interpretive difference between the U.S. and Canadian navies was the method used by each to determine territorial waters. Americans measured from the low-water point while the Canadians used a "straight line" or "baseline" method. But these variances were accommodated and the team accomplished the mission.

In addition to training effectively with the Americans for combined Arabian Gulf task groups, the Canadian Navy enhanced interoperability with the U.S. Navy by equipping its ships with compatible gear. The ABCANZ-5 Information Exchange Project kept not only the Canadians and Americans abreast of developments in one another's information technology but that of the British, Australian, and New Zealand navies. The Canadians gained access (in U.S. controlled spaces) to the Internet-based, secret-level SIPRNET and were thus made privy to classified operational intelligence. The COWAN communications system enabled the allied navies to see the same detailed maritime picture of an operational area and contribute information to that composite understanding. The Canadian Navy was also able to exploit operational information and intelligence through technically interoperable satellite modems and the Link-14, Link-16, and Global Command and Control systems.

A Canadian Navy task group of five ships and a maritime patrol plane detachment were the first allied force to bolster U.S. Navy and Royal Navy elements in the aftermath of 9/11. Canadian leaders were especially pleased that their navy could quickly and dramatically demonstrate support to the Americans in an hour of need. The ships carried out fleet protection missions and leadership interdiction operations in the North Arabian Sea and the Arabian Gulf.

To coordinate the contribution to operations in Afghanistan and even broader regional missions, Ottawa established Commander, Canadian Joint Task Force–South-West Asia near the U.S Central Command headquarters in Tampa, Florida. Confident in their ability to do the job, Commander Fifth Fleet charged the Canadians with the mission of protecting a most important U.S. amphibious ready group. The Marines from that ARG off Pakistan went on to establish a forward operating base in the south of Afghanistan and then to seize Kandahar, heart of the Taliban terrorist movement.

In February and March 2002, a Canadian naval commander was tasked with coordinating naval activity in the Southern Arabian Gulf, Strait of Hormuz, and Gulf of Oman. He was responsible for the operations of 16 ships and aircraft from the United States and seven other countries.

There were two major events relating to Canadian-U.S. interoperability during the war against Iraq in early 2003. On the positive side, the Canadian Navy's LIO responsibilities expanded to include the Arabian Gulf from the Strait of Hormuz to the Kuwait/Saudi Arabia border. Exercising its sovereignty, because of political differences over the nature of the war,

Ottawa instructed its ships not to turn over any Iraqis captured at sea to the Americans. At the same time, the Americans provided less intelligence than they had before. But the march on Baghdad took only three weeks to conclude, so close U.S. Navy–Canadian Navy relations soon returned.

U.S.-Canadian naval interoperability markedly improved in the decade after the Gulf War. The latter sea service made a strategic decision to thoroughly integrate its operations with the Americans; join the U.S. MIO task groups covering the Arabian Gulf; enhance the professional development and operational experiences of Canadian naval personnel engaged in these operations; and equip Canadian ships with command, control, communications, and intelligence gear compatible with the American systems. This approach succeeded so well that after taking part in the oil embargo patrols and naval operations in support of the war in Afghanistan, the Canadians had earned the trust of the Americans for their operational competence and professionalism. Hence, Canadian commanders were placed in charge of vital operational areas and granted access to a broad range of U.S. intelligence, planning, and other information. At the same time, the Canadian Navy never lost sight of the fact that it reported to Ottawa and not Washington for political direction. The ability to integrate into the U.S.-led task forces while adhering to national political prerogatives truly empowered the medium-size Canadian Navy.

In short, the navies of the United States, United Kingdom, Australia, and Canada executed especially successful peace support operations between 1991 and 2003. That success was built on a foundation of close cooperation at sea during the previous half-century of the Cold War. The naval leaders and commanders of these nations had honed their operational skills after years of experience conducting multinational exercises, developing common tactics, techniques, and procedures, and adopting compatible command, control, and communications approaches. Even more important, these leaders had come to depend on and were confident of the reliability and professional competence of their fellow members of the seagoing fraternity. The operative word was and still is—trust.

CONCLUSION

Sarandis Papadopoulos

Our profession relies upon customs and traditions such as diplomacy, sovereignty, and assistance at sea, norms that are older than any nation here today. . . . This 1,000-ship Navy would integrate the capabilities of the maritime services to create a fully interoperable force—an international city at sea.[1]

—Admiral Mike Mullen, USN
Naval War College, 21 September 2005

Rather than opening a period of peace and reduced tensions, the last decade of the 20th century witnessed the release of local animosities from the restraints of the Cold War. Without the East-West confrontation curbing on fanaticism, virulent political or ethnic oppression, regional intimidation, or wide-ranging terrorism emerged and spread.[2] The record for confronting such challenges in Haiti, Chechnya, Somalia, and Rwanda was mixed. Given the test posed in aggressive, fragmenting, or "failed states," marked by "unconventional" combat, mustering the international consensus to intervene proved difficult. Such complexities prevailed in all of the cases presented in this volume, and made the period between 1991 and 2002 unstable and dangerous. In terms of global survival the stakes had become lower, but the frequency of local crises deserving attention had risen dramatically.

Other challenges of the 1990s made the period difficult for Australian, British, Canadian, and American military personnel. After the Cold War, their ranks dropped in number by between 25 percent and 37 percent, while they experienced a demanding operational tempo.[3] The remaining armed forces, strong by nation-state standards, were not tailored for "asymmetric" operations against diffuse opponents. Military operations in the television and Internet age also became more politically charged, fostering greater "informational complexity" than in previous conflicts.[4] Controversy followed many of these operations, even the successful ones. Nonetheless, naval forces offered still useful methods to deter state bullies, reinforce stability, minimize disasters, or suppress terrorism. Without combined naval interventions, limiting the crises outlined here would have proven more expensive to achieve and potentially more dangerous.

Most vital to the service members, these operations assumed a political charge. The 1991–1996 Balkan civil war stimulated only a fragile international political consensus to intervene. Informal favor by NATO members for both sides, and a confusing set of UN rules of engagement complicated the issue.[5] For these reasons, some U.S. politicians advocated defending the Bosnian Muslims, while others pressed for arms deliveries to let the ethnic group protect itself. The 1995 refusal of U.S. Army Specialist Michael New to serve with United Nations Preventive Deployment Force, resulting in his court-martial, stood as the most extreme individual rejection of the UN.[6] Less profound rejections played out in all of the nations studied to varying degrees.[7] Their response reflected an approach of accepting limited liability, appropriate given the ambivalence to UN commitments.[8] U.S. Senator John McCain, referring to the abortive Somalia commitment but eyeing the Balkans, proved emblematic of this view: "As the events of 1993 have demonstrated, it is in neither the U.S. interest nor the international community's to subject the U.S. decision-making on grave matters of state, and the lives of American soldiers, to the frequently vacillating, frequently contradictory, and frequently reckless collective impulses of the United Nations."[9]

Fortunately, Sharp Guard naval forces ameliorated the Balkan tragedy and prevented a wider war, while keeping intact national decisions.

Human Network

From the vantage point of the 21st century, that these four countries succeeding in pulling together and employing naval compatibility borders on the miraculous. Real strength lay in the relationships built over time as operators worked through these four crises together. Nothing else could have built a "human network" driven by trust to overcome the differences between such varied services. Four navies of widely differing sizes, located on three continents, culminated a 40-year drive to create a reliable and mutually dependent collaboration. Their commitment to interoperability came despite broad political, technical, and social changes at home. Harmonizing command and control systems, while all fleets confronted aging ships, absorbed much of the attention and proved most challenging.[10] However, the development and maintenance of trust among thousands of service members in ever-changing positions within their services fundamentally underpinned these operations and regularly enabled collaboration.[11] Virtually no other broad multinational effort has so consistently focused toward such a targeted end. Combined naval power demonstrates the human network in action.

For example, in 1999, General Hugh Shelton used the human network to offer his Australian colleagues American noncombat support for Operation Stabilise. This pledge, made below the level of formal agreement or treaty, enabled the planning of the humanitarian intervention to continue.[12] Subsequently, when the time came for Commodore J. R. Stapleton to marshal forces for East Timor, the recent joint exercise had already introduced him to many of its ship commanders. Those working relationships allowed the Maritime Component Commander to execute the naval side of Stabilise.[13]

While human connections enable effective coalitions, the former can also fade if not regularly renewed with multinational exercises, even at the expense of committing precious people, aircraft, and ships during hard political and economic times. Building the human element converts intangible allies into genuine friends, turning abstract multinational doctrine, varying tactics, and different equipment into the means for fulfilling military missions and political objectives. While current Indian Ocean and Arabian Gulf operations build trust, the exercises chiefly responsible for creating multinational capabilities must not be forgotten during the prolonged war on terrorism. Building combined competence requires sustained commitment and regular renewal in spite of other pressing obligations.

Constant Interaction

In response to the crises outlined here the navies of Australia, Great Britain, Canada, and the United States assembled an impressive range of capabilities for low-intensity conflicts. Such interoperability arose only after a great deal of sustained work, much taking place after 1990. Three of these case studies show the evolution of one element, maritime interception (interdiction) operations (MIO), through the decade. From a nascent and halting capability to enforce the Iraq embargo through the growing ability to restrain the Balkan conflict, allied navies ultimately created a method and organization for sea control, eventually denying al-Qaeda use of the global commons in the 21st century. Concurrently, the ambitious East Timor operation used sea control to buy important time for an oppressed Indonesian minority.

Building interoperability yielded important benefits. For example, after the 1991 Gulf War restored Kuwaiti sovereignty, the United Nations needed to limit Saddam Hussein's military power. A commitment in southern Iraq to enforce an arms and oil embargo risked introducing foreign soldiers, almost certainly from Australia, Britain, Canada, or the United States, into the part of the country neighboring Iran.[14] Such a ground force threatened to raise tensions in an already volatile segment of the Middle East and expose them to attack. Instead, the continued multinational naval embargo safely contained Iraq for 12 years and prompted much less opposition.

Specifically, in those operations the Royal Australian and Canadian navies committed ships to the Arabian Gulf for much of the 1990s. Beginning with HMCS *Calgary* in 1995, Canadian ships worked maritime interception duties roughly half of the time, some exercising with U.S. task groups en route to set in place a firm sense of allied practice.[15] These deployments took place as the similar commitment to Operation Sharp Guard wound down. When one recalls each such deployment represented 5 percent of total Canadian Navy surface strength, the implication is clear: operating together continuously reinforced confidence and expertise.

The cases show advantages beyond the addition of "more flags," as described by former U.S. Army General William C. Westmoreland during the Vietnam War.[16] Nor is this merely the creation, as one press account suggests, of a coalition solely to defend Middle East oil routes.[17] On the contrary, while one should see maintaining the energy trade as a key need of the global community, it and naval cooperation are important components of the globalization Admiral Mike Mullen described.[18]

Collaborative maritime interception operations have roots in the naval blockades practiced since 1700. Typically shipping control had been a form of warfare to pressure an opponent and cripple military strength. Since 1990, however, MIO represented a willingness to limit conflict, working under an international mandate. MIO has arisen before, only under different names. One British analyst in 1928 argued that the naval blockade seemed the best tool for applying international pressure without combat. In the words of Lieutenant Commander W. E. Arnold-Forster, its particular and valuable attribute lay in limiting small-scale wars while reconciling "the conflict between the interests of neutrals and belligerents."[19] Later, the League of Nations attempted to enforce such sanctions in the Spanish Civil War. While ineffective for stopping the conflict, naval power limited its consequences by evacuating foreign nationals and slowing the flow of weapons, two goals of the international community.[20] Discrete, and conducted on the open ocean, MIO serves the post-9/11 world by offering a key capability.

Greater naval collaboration enabled by trust and regular cooperation came to fruition just in time to confront late 20th- and early 21st-century crises.[21] Collaborating nations adapted Cold War military doctrine to tackle low-intensity conflicts. Given the intense tempo of the period, the multi-national naval option came not a moment too soon.[22] As evidence of this effort, one should consider the thousands of challenges directed at merchant vessels during the maritime interception operations described in this work.[23] Naval commitment gave provocative regimes and terrorists reason to avoid using the world's sea lanes. In addition, for governments reluctant to put "boots on the ground," navies became an attractive option. Better, naval multilateralism exceeded individual service capacities and outdid the cooperative capabilities of land and air services. Put succinctly, the working maritime coalition of Australia, Britain, Canada, and the United States, and others, is impressive in its own terms.

The preceding points suggest that multinational naval operations represent a strategic approach to influencing events ashore without infringing upon hostile or neutral territory. The analysis presented here offers neither self-justification nor an evasion of cases where maritime power failed. Rather, the present work offers insight into the capacity navies have to achieve political results.[24] The case studies here show how different sea services created the flexibility, built on a common purpose, to collaborate, shaping a positive result in four cases of local violence and war.[25] They also illustrate the long-term efforts needed to curtail aggressive governments and hunt for terrorists. Best of all, the services achieved results without bankrupting their own taxpayers or alienating the broader international community.

This last point leads to a tension inherent in multinational naval operations: fleets cost money and investing in interoperability seems a minimal payoff. Speaking politically, could these navies have achieved the same objectives with smaller, less capable forces? Paraphrasing one analyst, the response depends upon perspective; politicians will almost certainly always try to answer yes and lower their fiscal investment, while naval leaders will strongly object and ask for greater resources.[26] But the inverse was true strategically: could a single naval service accomplish the same political ends without foreign help? In answer, the political leader will gauge it riskier to operate alone, while the naval calculus will emphasize the less complex route of solely employing national forces, *if* available in adequate quality and quantity. Without such a blank check drawn from national resources, increasingly the norm in the 21st century, naval operators want to work with trusted foreign colleagues in a combined force.[27]

To illustrate that last point, the Canadian Navy gambled on purchasing interoperable systems, sacrificing other purchases by doing so. Only their Adriatic and Middle East operations showed the political and professional payoff on that investment when other nations placed their own ships and people under temporary control of their allies.[28] Such observations lead one to conclude that multinational operations will continue to satisfy the needs of both political and naval leaders in the future.

Combat exercises are the crucial adjunct to making these continuous operations happen. Only intensive exercises challenge officers and ratings to build combined forces possessing the capabilities required in a crisis. Exercises attune coalition naval personnel to the full range and limits of both allied naval credentials and the authority of the human network. Combat exercises make these continuous operations happen and constantly refresh the relationships upon which they depend.[29] Echoing Vice Admiral Horatio Nelson, Canadian Navy Admiral Greg Maddison made this point when outlining how the extensive workup of Standing Naval Force Atlantic built his group of ship commanders into "my band of brothers" for Operation Sharp Guard.[30] Without seeing full-spectrum competence in exercises, naval personnel cannot rely upon their partners' ability and commitment over time and in crises. Witnessing competence established and in action builds trust and sustains collaboration in both the short term and long term.

Liaison and Exchange

Unfortunately, interoperability can perish. In particular, the focus of military activity following 11 September 2001 is distant from NATO nations, and the number of exercises conducted between allied nations near Europe has dropped significantly since the 1990s. A complementary means for closing the seams between allies on an individual basis are exchange and liaison personnel, supportive of the human network in the same manner as combined exercises. During discussions in Australia and the United Kingdom, however, the historical team discovered that funds for exchange and liaison duty are often the first targets for cuts as operational demands rise.[31]

This study suggests the need for another perspective. Looking at Operation Stabilise, with liaison officers attached to the Naval Component Commander's staff and one fulfilling a crucial role as fuel logistician, the emphasis on understanding allies is vital.[32] Recall, too, that Major General Peter Cosgrove had served as an exchange student at the U.S. Marine Corps Command and Staff College 20 years before he commanded in East Timor.[33] In a converse example, Canadian ships and crews returned to the Arabian Gulf in 1995 after a three-year absence that rendered them a lesser known quantity to their allies. Only by building familiarity and trust could they step back into a leading role. Consequently, personnel assigned to an exchange billet or as a liaison to a foreign staff should be rewarded, in career terms, by their services. Combined duty must not be a professional poison pill, or it will never become widely accepted.[34]

Access and Trust

Technical capabilities and intelligence data offer important advantages, yet they also raise important questions of sharing sensitive information. In Operations Sharp Guard and Stabilise high-end American shipboard command and control systems lent battle management capabilities
not available to allied nations. Offering such data created the commonly
held maritime picture of the challenges and threats confronting forces,
enabling components to work together. It conversely raised challenges for
sailors forbidden to share national-level intelligence with allies. Only by
improvising solutions to work around that limitation could operational
sailors master risks to the force.

Why should coalition members share intelligence? In doing so they
should understand that the lower load offered by multilateral operations
does not merely reduce commitments by any single country, or lower
wear and tear on equipment and uniformed people. A combined naval
deterrent creates a symbolic example. As Major General Cosgrove noted of
East Timor, the warships' presence demonstrated a broad multilateral will,
"an important indicator of international resolve," as a discrete yet forceful
option when needed.[35] Key to maintaining the unity of that deterrent is
confidence in the shared understanding by all parts of the force.

These essays emphasize that multinational time *at sea* is vital in creating
the high-end dexterity needed for littoral and open-ocean combat. Crucial
as well, however, is sharing as much information as possible. Maintaining
intelligence under a "NOFORN" header—no foreign dissemination—on
systems such as the American SIPRNET and Canadian MCOIN serves the
needs of intelligence staffs better than it satisfies operational requirements.[36]
Only by avoiding constraints on information whenever possible will all participants believe the common maritime picture.

All ships, aircraft, and crews committed to a multilateral operation
ultimately remain under national control; committing them absolutely to a
multinational commander would effectively turn them into "a hired force."[37]
Multilateral naval operations are a tool, subordinate to national strategy and
policy, a constraint reflected in national rules of engagement, inconvenient
though they may be. National limits will always be in place, but offering
intelligence and receiving trust in return bridge the differences between

forces within a theater of operations.[38] In this manner sailors can believe their naval partners are providing them the full range of information, and not locking the best of it away in an allied admiral's safe.[39] While the patterns and practices of these four case studies do not answer all challenges posed by contemporary political crises, the cooperative basis offered by shared access will support and enable those other operations as well.

Brokering and Re-brokering

How do sailors master the operational complexities confronting them? Can their job become easier? Multinational operations in the 21st century confront the glare of media publicity, compelling national governments to respond to their respective publics; domestic opinion therefore reshapes the context of military operations. But because the politics of participating nations do not always coincide, combined military operations may move slowly and run the risk of becoming politicized.[40] The primary means of authorizing combined operations, through international organizations, also adds a consensus-based actor, by nature inclined to slow military responsiveness and complicate decisions. Rules of engagement will reflect these political limitations and can change over time. In parallel, practices will never be the same among all ships in a service. Even the slightest differences in how navies break down tasks, interpreting doctrine in different ways while still complying with it, complicate the integration of a coalition ship into two separate U.S. Navy strike groups. Such individuality creates the "tabula rasa" noted in one essay.[41] Only on-scene participants can solve these problems by clinching or re-brokering arrangements to suit particular operational needs.

For example, the initial 1990–1991 Arabian Gulf maritime interception operations lacked "plug and play" interoperability. Naval leaders settled for less-than-ideal discrete operating areas for different nations' vessels, with patrol sectors laid out to accommodate national needs, and only developed more comprehensive measures over a three-month period.[42] Interoperability refined through exercises, however, reduces the need for such complex arrangements.

The inevitability of political tension between coalition partners magnifies the need for trust between naval personnel from different countries if sea control operations are to work. The 2005 goal of Admiral Mullen, for globalizing sea traffic moderated by a "1,000-ship Navy . . . made up of the best capabilities of all freedom-loving navies of the world," suggests combined naval operations will become a more regular part of naval practice.[43] At the operational level the only proven means for making such operations work is ongoing negotiation and re-brokering of the human network to unify naval forces.

An added benefit of re-brokering arises in its role as the forum for innovation for operators. Rather than allowing doctrine or tactics to become static, the action of renegotiating arrangements, on each occasion, allows multinational navies to renew or "refresh" their procedures.[44] While on first blush re-brokering may seem a drain on resources and time, in actuality it represents an important contribution to building the human network, enabling successful naval operations by smoothing disputes and invigorating procedures.

If the vision of Admiral Mullen is to become reality, sailors around the world must continue to develop and reestablish trust in one another. The means for achieving that end will remain the human network, frequent interaction at sea in exercises, personnel exchanges, and increased freedom from high-level restrictions on offering information to allies, all enabled by on-scene brokering to handle the details. Absent these advantages, the only alternative will be to stretch operational personnel further, forcing them to create awkward workarounds to make coalition missions work. In essence, without high-level sponsorship for multinational operations the vision of Admiral Mullen becomes a chimera.

Only the shortsighted will view providing resources for further multinational naval collaboration as a waste. Recreating such skills without an existing foundation, as in the Arabian Gulf in 1990–1991, would require heavy initial investment until methods settle in place. Such improvised responses strain the liaison staff responsible and risk converting coalition advantages into liabilities. Counterfactually, such dangers would have prevailed if Australia had attempted the 1999 Stabilise mission on its own. Infantry strength alone in East Timor could not end the strife without support from allied air and seapower. If the mission had been attempted on the cheap, with minimal coalition support, a bolder Indonesian military and rebel militia would have endangered its more vulnerable intervening forces. Instead, a robust coalition force enhanced by prior investments in interoperable technology, combined doctrine, and rigorous exercises achieved its objectives quickly and with minimal loss of life. Whether the future judges these cases merely a fortunate convergence of practice, confidence, and technology, or something larger marked by a longstanding multinational doctrine—well exercised and managed through durably interoperable systems—will be decided today by national governments and service chiefs.[45] The historical analysis presented here demonstrates the advantages of making the professional down payments needed to build and reinforce the human network. Continuing them will unite navies, enhance trust, accelerate reaction time in crisis, and refine interoperability. These attributes will provide a framework for a peaceful and productive maritime common, a foundation for effective policy.

Notes

1. Admiral Mike Mullen (Remarks as delivered for the 17th International Seapower Symposium," Naval War College, Newport, RI, 21 September 2005), 7.

2. For a prescient work on the decentralization of conflict after the Cold War, see Martin van Creveld, *The Transformation of War* (New York: Free Press, 1991), especially 57–62. An update, emphasizing the international "multipolarity" of power, is S. Brown, "Multilateral Constraints on the Use of Force: A Reassessment" (Carlisle, PA: U.S. Army War College, March 2006), 15–21.

3. Richard Meinhart, "Strategic Planning by the Chairmen, Joint Chiefs of Staff, 1990–2005," U.S. Army War College, April 2006, 14, at http://www.strategicstudiesinstitute.army. mil/pdffiles/PUB703.pdf, accessed 5 June 2006. For military force reductions, compare International Institute of Strategic Studies, *The Military Balance 1990–1991* (London: Brassey's, 1990), 17–23, 60–61, 82–84, 156–57, with International Institute of Strategic Studies, *The Military Balance 2001–2002* (London: Oxford, 2001), 19–21, 49–50, 75–77, 185. In the same period, naval personnel reductions were RAN, 19.9%; RN, 31.5%; CN, 47%; USN, 38%, while numbers of warships fell: RAN, 7.2%; RN, 42%; CN, 24%; USN, 47.3%. Generally, Canadian force cuts proved highest, with Australia's the lowest. Budget numbers are complex, although in unadjusted U.S. dollars total Australian military spending rose 4.7%; British, by 9.3%; Canadian outlays fell by 19.9%; and American expenditures rose by 2.0% over the same period.

4. David Rudd, "Opening Remarks" in *Beyond the Three-Block War*, eds. David Rudd, Deborah

Bayley, and Ewa K. Petruczynik (Toronto: Canadian Institute of Strategic Studies, 2006), 2. This essay outlines the broader theme of post–Cold War media complexities quite clearly.

5. Steven R. Rader, "The U.S. Military Role in a Multilateral Framework," in *Peace Support Operations and the U.S. Military*, ed. Dennis J. Quinn (Washington: National Defense University, 1994), 55.

6. I am indebted to Mr. Frederick H. Codding for reminding me of the New case, where the soldier also refused to wear a UN shoulder patch and blue beret. See United States *ex rel.* Michael G. New, Appellant *v.* Donald H. Rumsfeld, Secretary of Defense and Les Brownlee, Acting Secretary of the Army, United States District Court for the District of Columbia, Civil Action No. 96-0033 (PLF), at http://www.dcd.uscourts.gov/96-0033-12-22-2004-1.pdf, accessed 31 May 2006.

7. Pierre Martin and Michel Fortmann, "Support for International Involvement in Canadian Public Opinion after the Cold War," *Canadian Military Journal* 2, no. 3 (Autumn 2001): 48–50.

8. David Jablonsky, "Army Transformation: A Tale of Two Doctrines" in *Transforming Defense*, ed. C. Craneed (Carlisle, PA: U.S. Army War College, December 2001), especially 56–59, at http://www.strategicstudiesinstitute.army.mil/pdffiles/PUB254.pdf, accessed 30 May 2006.

9. J. McCain, "The Proper United States Role in Peacekeeping," in *Peace Support Operations*, 91.

10. For the preeminence of technical interoperability, see the program of ComDef 2006, the 25th Conference on International Defense Cooperation, Washington, DC, at http://www. ideea.com/comdef06/program.htm, accessed 8 August 2006. Save the closing reception, no proposed session addressed human interoperability.

11. For a recent land reference to trust, see E. Elron, B. Shamir, and E. Ben-Ari, "Why Don't They Fight Each Other? Cultural Diversity and Operational Unity in Multinational Forces," *Armed Forces and Society* 26, no.1 (Fall 1999): 80–81.

12. David Stevens, "The Combined Naval Role in East Timor," chap. 4 herein, 109.

13. Ibid., 109, 126.

14. John Mackinlay, "Defining a Role Beyond Peacekeeping," in *Military Implications United Nations Peacekeeping Operations*, ed. W. Lewis (Washington, DC: National Defense University, June 1993), 31–32. In second-generation peacekeeping operations, the roles took place in the absence of a fully permissive environment. These operations are notionally positioned as UN Chapter "6 ½," meaning peacekeeping missions (addressed in the UN Charter's Chapter 6, for example, Cyprus from 1964, and Sinai since 1973) conducted in an environment more suited for peace enforcement (a Chapter 7 mission, as in Korea, 1950–1953, or Kuwait, 1991). See Roméo. Dallaire, *Shake Hands With the Devil: The Failure of Humanity in Rwanda* (Toronto: Random House, 2003), 40–41, 71–72.

15. Robert H. Caldwell, "The Canadian Navy, Interoperability, and USN-Led Operations in the Gulf Region from the First Gulf War to 2002," chap. 7 herein, 201–12.

16. William Westmoreland, *A Soldier Reports* (Garden City, NY: Doubleday, 1976), 114–15.

17. See Ted Koppel and Robert Siegel, "In the Gulf, a Coalition of the Floating," *National Public Radio: All Things Considered*, 6 July 2006, at http://www.npr.org/templates/story/story.php?storyId=5539126, accessed 7 July 2006.

18. Mullen remarks, 4.

19. W. Arnold-Forster, "Admiralty Staff History: The Economic Blockade 1914–1919," as reproduced in *Sea Power and the Control of Trade: Belligerent Rights From the Russian War to the Beira Patrol, 1854–1970*, ed. Nicholas Tracy (Aldershot and Burlington: Ashgate/Navy Records Society, 2005), 242.

20. Stephen Roskill, *Naval Policy Between the Wars*, Vol. 2, *The Period of Reluctant Rearmament, 1930–1939* (Annapolis, MD: Naval Institute Press, 1976), chap. 12.

21. The ideas in this paragraph stem from conversations between the authors of the Combined Operations project team members, especially Stephen Prince. See also H. H. Gaffney, *The American Way of War in the Emerging Strategic Environment: Remarks at the Army War College's Annual Strategy Conference, 9 April 2003* (Alexandria, VA: CNA, April 2003), 4–5.

22. On the issues surrounding military planning and operations in the post-1989 period, see Meinert, "Strategic Planning by the Chairman of the Joint Chiefs of Staff," 6.

23. Jeffrey G. Barlow, "The U.S. Navy's Role in Coalition Maritime Interception in Operation Enduring Freedom, 2001–2002," chap. 6 herein, 174.

24. This concern arose during discussions at Department of Defence Headquarters, Canberra, 20 July 2005.

25. Meinert, 14.

26. P. Haydon, "What Naval Capabilities Does Canada Need?" *Canadian Military Journal* 2, no. 1 (Spring 2001): 22.

27. This idea is not new. Captain Alfred T. Mahan suggested an Anglo-American naval consortium rooted in economics and common background, what 21st-century observers might label a shared culture, eliminating the need for a treaty. See Jon Sumida, *Inventing Grand Strategy and Teaching Command: The Classic Works of Alfred Thayer Mahan Reconsidered* (Washington, DC/Baltimore, MD: Woodrow Wilson Center/Johns Hopkins University Press, 1997), 82–92.

28. Caldwell, chap. 7 herein, 210–12; Barlow, chap. 6 herein, 179–81.

29. This concern also arose during discussions at Department of Defence Headquarters, Canberra, 20 July 2005.

30. Sarandis Papadopoulos, "The U.S. Navy's Contribution to Operation Sharp Guard," chap. 3 herein, 88.

31. Discussion with an audience of officers at HMAS *Watson*, 19 July 2005.

32. Stevens, chap. 4 herein, 118, 137.

33. Papadopoulos, "A Limited Commitment to Ending Civil Strife: The U.S. Navy in Operation Stabilise," chap. 5 herein, 155.

34. Discussion with U.S. Navy officer at the Naval Historical Branch, Portsmouth, England, February 2006.

35. As quoted in Stevens, chap. 4 herein, 102.

36. Caldwell, chap. 7 herein, 214–215.

37. C. von Clausewitz, *On War* (Princeton, NJ: Princeton University Press, 1984), 603.

38. For an older example of conflicting practices in multinational operations, see W. E. B. Du Bois, *The Suppression of the African Slave Trade to the United States of America* (New York: Longmans Green, 1896), 146, 178. See also http://www.gutenberg.org/etext/17700, accessed 24 August 2006. Flying an American flag immunized 1850s slavers from foreign

search, leading one Royal Navy captain to suggest "that at least one half of the successful part of the slave trade is carried on under the American flag," and this because "the number of American cruisers on the station is so small, in proportion to the immense extent of the slave-dealing coast."

39. An idea derived from Caldwell, chap. 7 herein, 238, especially his quotation from Commodore James Goldrick, RAN.

40. Brown, 12–14.

41. Caldwell, chap. 7 herein, 265.

42. Barlow, "The U.S. Navy's Role in Coalition Maritime Interception Operations in the Persian Gulf Region, 1991–1996," chap. 1 herein, 26–28.

43. Mullen remarks, 7.

44. We are indebted to the identification of this important advantage by Commodore G. D. Christian, RAN, in discussions at the Naval History & Heritage Command, 18 August 2006.

45. On the narrow, contingent windows of military methods and technology, see W. Murray and M. Knox, "The Future Behind Us," in *The Dynamics of Military Revolution 1300–2050*, eds. M. Knox and W. Murray (Cambridge: Cambridge University Press, 2001), 177. See also R. Gimblett, *Operation Apollo: The Golden Age of the Canadian Navy in the War Against Terrorism* (Ottawa: Magic Light, 2004), 22–36, 160.

AAW	Antiair Warfare
ABCA	American, British, Canadian, and Australian
ACC	Air Component Commander
ADF	Australian Defence Force
AG	Arabian Gulf
ANZAC	Australian and New Zealand Army Corps
ANZUS	Australia, New Zealand, United States
AO	Area of Operations
AOR	Area of Responsibility/Fleet Replenishment Ship
ASEAN	Association of Southeast Asian Nations
ASW	Antisubmarine Warfare
ATP	Allied Tactical Publication (NATO)
AUSCANNZUKUS	Australia, Canada, New Zealand, United Kingdom, United States
AUSCANUKUS	Australia, Canada, United Kingdom, United States
AUSCANUS	Australia, Canada, United States
AUTODIN	Automatic Digital Network
AWACS	Airborne Warning and Control System
BRITFOR	British Forces (in UNPROFOR)
C2	Command and Control
C4I	Command, Control, Communications, Computers, and Intelligence
CAS	Close Air Support
CBC	Canadian Broadcasting Corporation
CD	Classified Document
CEC	Cooperative Engagement Capability
CENTCOM	Central Command (U.S.)
CENTRIXS	Combined Enterprise Regional Information Exchange System

CF	Canadian Forces
CFMWC	Canadian Forces Maritime Warfare Centre
CINCSOUTH	Commander in Chief, South (NATO)
CJFACC	Combined/Joint Forces Air Component Commander
CJFSOCC	Combined/Joint Forces Special Operations Component Commander
CJTF	Combined Joint Task Force
CLF	Combat Logistics Force/Combined Logistics Force
CMS	Chief of Maritime Staff (Canadian)
CNA	Center for Naval Analyses
COMAST	Commander Australian Theatre
COMBEXAG	Combined Exercise Agreement
COMDESRON	Commander Destroyer Squadron
COMFLOT	Commodore Flotillas (Australian)
COMNAVSOUTH	Commander, Naval Forces South (NATO)
COMUSNAVCENT	Commander, U.S. Naval Forces Central Command
COWAN	Coalition Wide Area Network
CPF	Canadian Patrol Frigate
CPX	Command Post Exercise
CTF	Combined Task Force/Commander Task Force
CTG	Combined Task Group/Commander Task Group
CVBG	Carrier Battle Group
DCDS	Deputy Chief of Defence Staff (Canadian)
DDE	Destroyer Escort
DDG	Guided Missile Destroyer
DDH	Antisubmarine Destroyer (Canadian)
DESRON	Destroyer Squadron
DISN	Defense Information Systems Network
DJFHQ	Deployable Joint Force Headquarters
DJFHQ (M)	Deployable Joint Force Headquarters–Maritime

DMP	Director Maritime Policy (Canadian)
DSN	Defense Switched Network
ENFORCECOMS	Enforcement Coercive Measures
EOD	Explosive Ordnance Disposal
EXTAC	Experimental Tactics
FAC	Fast Attack Craft
FALINTIL	National Armed Forces for the Liberation of East Timor
FFG	Guided Missile Frigate
FFH	Halifax-Class Patrol Frigate (Canadian)
FOSIF	Fleet Ocean Surveillance Information Facility (U.S.)
FRY	Federal Republic of Yugoslavia
GCC	Gulf Cooperation Council
GCCS	Global Command and Control System
GCCS–M	Global Command and Control System–Maritime
GOO	Gulf of Oman
GPO	Government Printing Office (U.S.)
HOA	Horn of Africa
HODSU	Hydrographic Office Detached Survey Unit
IFF	Identification Friend or Foe
IFOR	Implementation Force (NATO)
INTERFET	International Force East Timor
IRST	Infrared Search and Track
JROE	Joint and Combined Rules of Engagement
JTF	Joint Task Force
KAA	Khawr Abd Allah
LFA	Land Forces Adriatic (U.K.)
LIO	Leadership Interdiction Operation
LPA	Landing Platform Amphibious (Australian)
LPH	Landing Platform Helicopter (U.K.)
LST	Landing Ship Tank

MACOM	Maritime Commanders (Canadian)
MARCOM	Maritime Command (Canadian)
MARCOT	Maritime Coordinated Operational Training (Canadian)
MARLANT	Maritime Forces Atlantic (Canadian)
MCC AST	Maritime Component Commander Australian Theater
MCOIN	Maritime Command Operational Information Network
MEAO	Middle East Area of Operations
MEU	Marine Expeditionary Unit (U.S.)
MIC	Maritime Interception Commander
MIF	Maritime Interception Force/Multinational Interception Force
MIO	Maritime Interdiction/Interception Operation
MPA	Maritime Patrol Aircraft
NAC	North Atlantic Council (NATO)
NAG	Northern Arabian Gulf
NATO	North Atlantic Treaty Organization
NAVCENT	Naval Forces Central Command (U.S.)
NCB	Noncompliant Boarding
NCC	Naval Component Commander
NCE	National Command Element
NGO	Nongovernmental Organization
NHC	Naval Historical Center
NHHC	Naval History & Heritage Command
NIPRNET	Non-Classified Internet Protocol Router Network
NSC	National Security Council (U.S.)
NTDS	Naval Tactical Data System
NVG	Night Vision Goggle
OA	Operational Archives (NHHC)
OAS	Organization of American States

OLOC	Operational Level of Capability
OTCIXS	Officer in Tactical Command Information Exchange Subsystem
PACMEF	Pacific Middle East Force (U.S.)
PASSEX	Passage Exercise
PERSTEMPO/OPTEMPO	Personnel Tempo/Operations Tempo
RAAF	Royal Australian Air Force
RAN	Royal Australian Navy
RASP	Recognized Air Surface Picture
RCN	Royal Canadian Navy
RFA	Royal Fleet Auxiliary (U.K.)
RIMPAC	Rim of the Pacific
RMP	Recognized Maritime Picture
RN	Royal Navy
RNZN	Royal New Zealand Navy
ROE	Rules of Engagement
ROTO	Rotation
RRF	Rapid Reaction Force
RRFOS	Rapid Reaction Force Operations Staff
RS	Red Sea
SAA	Shatt al-Arab
SAG	Southern Arabian Gulf
SCC	Sector Control Commander
SFOR	Stabilization Force (NATO)
SIPRNET	Secret Internet Protocol Router Network
SNFL	Standing Naval Force Atlantic (NATO), also STANAVFORLANT
SNMG	Standing NATO Maritime Group
SNFM	Standing Naval Force Mediterranean (NATO), also STANAVFORMED
SOC	Special Operations Capable

SOH	Strait of Hormuz
SPC–A	Sea Power Centre–Australia
SSK	Diesel Submarine
STANAG	Standardization Agreement (NATO)
TARPS	Tactical Air Reconnaissance Pod System
TLAM	Tomahawk Land Attack Missile
TNI	Tentara Nasional Indonesia (national armed forces)
TRUMP	Tribal [class] Update and Modernization Project (Canadian)
UAE	United Arab Emirates
UKTG	U.K. Task Group
UN	United Nations
UNAMET	United Nations Mission in East Timor
UNOSOM	United Nations Operation in Somalia
UNPROFOR	United Nations Protection Force
UNREP	Underway Replenishment
UNSC	United Nations Security Council
UNSCOM	United Nations Special Commission
UNSCR	United Nations Security Council Resolution
UNTAET	United Nations Transitional Administration in East Timor
USCG	U.S. Coast Guard
USCINCCENT	Commander in Chief, U.S. Central Command
USCINCPAC	Commander in Chief, U.S. Pacific Command
USN	U.S. Navy
WEU	Western European Union
WEUCONMARFOR	Western European Union Contingency Maritime Force